Compensation and Organizational Performance

Compensation and Organizational Performance

Theory, Research, and Practice

Luis R. Gomez-Mejia

Pascual Berrone

Monica Franco-Santos

M.E.Sharpe
Armonk, New York
London, England

To my wife Ana, my two sons Vince and Alex, and my daughter Dulce
—G.M.

To my wife Andrea, the love of my life, and my daughter Milena, the light of my eyes.
To my father George, my mother Grace, and my sister Lorena
—P.B.

To my husband Javi, my sons Ismael and Adrian, my parents Luis and Gloria,
and my sister Carolina
—M.F.S.

Library of Congress Cataloging-in-Publication Data

Gomez-Mejia, Luis R.
  Compensation and organizational performance : theory, research, and practice /
by Luis R. Gomez-Mejia, Pascual Berrone, and Monica Franco-Santos.
    p. cm.
Includes bibliographical references and index.
  ISBN 978-0-7656-2251-8 (pbk. : alk. paper)
  1. Compensation management. 2. Organizational effectiveness. 3. Executives—Salaries, etc.
  4. Performance standards. I. Berrone, Pascual, 1975– II. Franco-Santos, Monica. III. Title.

HF5549.5.C67G659 2010
658.3′2—dc22   2009031556

Printed in the United States of America

The paper used in this publication meets the minimum requirements of
American National Standard for Information Sciences
Permanence of Paper for Printed Library Materials,
ANSI Z 39.48-1984.

∞

EB (p)   10   9   8   7   6   5   4   3   2   1

CONTENTS

PREFACE

Compensation is the largest single cost in most organizations. Hence, the extent to which these resources are allocated effectively is likely to have a major beneficial impact on organizational performance. Conversely, when these pay resources are used poorly the results may be disastrous to the local firm and in some cases the negative repercussions may transcend organizational boundaries, harming society at large. This has been made evident since the collapse of Enron, Tyco, and WorldCom in the early 2000s, and the cataclysmic events in the financial markets and the mortgage industry at the end of that decade. Behind the scenes one usually finds that ill-conceived incentives (such as bonuses linked to revenues or rewards tied to data that could be easily manipulated) had much to do with these troubles.

This book addresses compensation and rewards from a strategic perspective. That is, it examines how the use of compensation dollars influence the behavior of employees and decision makers, and the implications this has for firm performance. The book has been written primarily for an academic audience, making extensive use of available research, but it should also be of value to sophisticated practitioners and consultants engaged in the design of compensation programs.

For classroom use, we envision this book as an excellent "stand-alone" text in advanced compensation seminars and a great adjunct to courses in human resources management, corporate governance, and even in strategic management.

Some chapters in this book had their origin in the now out-of-print book *Compensation, Organizational Strategy and Firm Performance* by Gomez-Mejia and Balkin (Southwestern Publishing Co., 1992). These chapters have been thoroughly updated and revised by the senior author (Luis R. Gomez-Mejia) along with Pascual Berrone and Monica Franco. Unlike this earlier work, this book has a distinct upper management orientation. This is because upper management is where most strategic decisions are made that will likely have direct influence on firm performance. Moreover, this book includes, unlike other compensation texts, full chapters dedicated to topics that spark heated debate both in academia and in the practitioners' arena, such as risk, social responsibility, and performance measurement.

We hope that you find this book useful and that you enjoy reading the book as much as we have enjoyed writing it.

Compensation and Organizational Performance

1 COMPENSATION AS AN EVOLVING FIELD

Past, Present, and Future

In their 1992 book entitled *Compensation, Organizational Strategy, and Firm Performance* Gomez-Mejia and Balkin lamented that "no other HRM [Human Resource Management] subfunction has been as guilty of a myopic focus as compensation, with its well-known predilection for tools and techniques" (p. 5). Almost 20 years later we find that there has been an enormous amount of theoretical and empirical work done on compensation issues, much of it appearing in mainstream academic journals. We believe that there are several reasons for the growth of this body of knowledge, which is critically reviewed in this book. These reasons are as follows:

1. Compensation's central variable of interest—money—represents the most generalized medium of exchange known to humankind. This means it is an integral part of practically all transactions occurring within and across organizational boundaries.

   why comp is important

2. Money is the quintessence of all business language, and top decision makers readily understand its significance. For example, designing staffing and training programs to select and develop employees to fit strategy may be appealing to personnel specialists but of little concern to upper management.

3. Compensation dollars have a direct impact (and in most firms the most important one) on the cost side of all financial statements. Not only does this make compensation a very crucial tangible resource to management, but the way in which it is allocated becomes a de facto component of the firm performance calculus. While procedures have been developed in HRM (e.g., human resource accounting, utility analysis) to estimate the cost-benefit sensitivity of intangible factors, such as improving employee attitudes, honing employee

3

skills through training programs, increasing the validity of selection methods and appraisal programs, and so on, most managers without an HRM background know little about and are less easily convinced by such data. Many practitioners and academics believe mathematical estimates of the value of HRM programs are abstruse and a bit confabulated. But when it comes to the expense side of the balance sheet, few doubt the importance of compensation in terms of its impact on the bottom line.

4. Of all the variables typically associated within the HRM field, compensation can be most easily manipulated and directly controlled by management. Thus, it has a great deal of inherent strategic flexibility. For example, it is much simpler (although by no means easy) to change the pay mix or pay system design than it is to replace employees and stay attuned to changing environmental conditions and strategic objectives. Variables such as employee characteristics, skills levels, and attitudes are difficult to mold in order to meet varying organizational contingencies—at least in the short term. The organization also faces significant ethical and legal constraints in trying to manipulate most other HRM subsystems to match its business strategies.

5. Unlike most HRM variables, compensation links directly to the conceptual frameworks of other mainline business fields (such as finance and accounting). In fact, most of this work has been done by scholars who do not identify themselves as part of the HRM field. Thus, one is able to draw upon a wealth of theoretical work and empirical research from various disciplines. Building on this literature, one can develop models and make predictions about the relationship between compensation strategies and firm performance.

6. The link between incentive systems and decision making has been well established in recent years. That is, an enormous amount of evidence in the academic press as well as the business press shows how CEOs, managers, and employees mold their decisions in an attempt to meet the implicit or explicit criteria of success as defined by the incentive system. Unfortunately, much of this evidence uncovers the ethical problems and gaming that improperly designed reward programs might trigger. From the now "classical" cases of Enron, WorldCom, and Arthur Andersen to the more recent cases involving Wall Street, one usually finds that so-called perverse incentives (for instance, managerial bonuses linked to revenue growth or billable hours for external auditors and consultants) have been a major force

in these debacles, not only for specific organizations but also for the global economy (some vivid examples may be found in Parloff, 2009; Loomis, 2009a,b; Burrows, 2009; and Goldstein, 2009). This means that incentive systems are a double-edged sword: they can help the organization achieve its strategic objectives or they can channel people's efforts in the wrong direction, perhaps into an abyss.

This chapter provides a context for the rest of the book. First, the traditional, conceptual roots of the compensation field and administrative procedures developed to operationalize them are briefly examined. This discussion provides a frame of reference for better understanding alternative approaches to the strategic study of compensation, which is the central focus of this volume.

Origins in Industrial/Organizational Psychology

The traditional underpinnings of compensation as an academic subfield are found in both social psychology (motivation theories) and labor economics (labor markets). Scientific management has also played a role in their development. Because the traditional foundations of the field are covered at length in most textbooks (e.g., Martocchio, 2009; Milkovich and Newman, 2009; see also Berger and Berger, 2008), we address only the most important points.

motivational theories

Equity Theory

The centrality of equity in compensation is reflected in the following statement by Wallace and Fay (1983, p. 69): "The critical theme that exists at the center of all compensation theory and practice is equity." Indeed, a great deal of academic and practitioner literature in compensation has focused on this construct under the general rubric of equity theory. Its underpinnings consist of exchange theory (Gouldner, 1960) and cognitive dissonance theory (Festinger, 1957), which originated in social psychology.

According to the equity paradigm, each employee in an organization exchanges a set of inputs or contributions (e.g., education, effort, long-term commitment) for a set of outcomes or inducements (e.g., pay, promotion, prestige). This exchange process takes place within a social setting, not in isolation. Individuals are constantly comparing their inputs relative to their outcomes vis-à-vis other employees (called referent others) inside and outside the firm. In what is perhaps the best-known version of equity theory, Adams (1965) argues that "distributive justice" is achieved when the proportionate relation between contributions and inducements is equal for all employees.

Thus, distributive justice as perceived by all parties defines equity according to the following ratio:

$$\frac{O_p}{I_p} = \frac{O_o}{I_o}$$

Where O_p = Employment outcomes of a given individual
I_p = Inputs of a given individual
O_o = Employment outcomes received by referent others
I_o = Inputs offered by "referent other"

The word *perceived* is crucial to most equity theorists. Employees do not assess the inducement contribution ratio in a rational, calculated manner but rather through a subjective determination of how the individual's ratio fares against those of other people chosen for comparison. In common parlance, equity theory holds that "truth is in the eyes of the beholder." If an imbalance is perceived, the employee will experience "cognitive dissonance" and try to correct this imbalance in a number of ways, such as reducing inputs (e.g., not taking work home), attempting to increase outcomes by voicing complaints to the supervisor, or joining in concerted action with other disgruntled employees to extract concessions from management. As an ultimate recourse, the individual is likely to leave the firm.

As argued by Milkovich and Newman (2009), money is one of the most visible components in employment exchange and, hence, it is an extremely important O_p and O_o to most people. Because individuals are likely to compare their pay/contribution ratio with other employees in the organization, as well as with employees in other firms, the key task of the compensation system from an equity perspective is to ensure that distributive justice is accomplished vis-à-vis the referent or relevant other. If wage rates for jobs within the company are set so that employees perceive a fair input/outcome balance relative to referents within the organization (internal equity) as well as a market referent (external equity), then equity is achieved. The importance of external equity is given added impetus in the work of Jaques (1961), who suggests the relevant standard in determining equity is intrinsic to the individual. This individual sense of equity depends on the employee's past wage experiences, which are used to judge appropriate levels of current pay. This means the compensation system must be perceived as equitable relative to pay standards of other firms (Jaques, 1979).

Achieving internal and external equity becomes paramount in the traditional compensation systems because it affects two critical employee behaviors: the individual's decisions to join and stay with the organization (Griffith, 2008; Schweyer, 2008). In addition, as noted by York and Brown (2008), companies have a fiduciary duty to spend money responsibly. This involves estimating the value or contribution of different jobs to the organization and the compensation made by similar companies for similar jobs.

In short, equity theory is concerned with notions of fairness and deservedness, which depend on a social comparison process inside and outside the firm. From a traditional perspective and to the extent that equity can be achieved by matching rewards to perceived contributions for each employee in relationship to referent others, the pay system accomplishes its primary mission. These notions are reinforced by the neoclassical labor market models.

Neoclassical Labor Market Theory

The second underpinning of traditional compensation theory and practice is found in neoclassical labor economics. The dependent variables in these models are the wage rate and employment level that are determined through the interaction of supply and demand for labor. As every undergraduate student taking an introductory economics course knows, ceteris paribus (e.g., perfect information and mobility), the wage rate of a given occupation is set at a point where the labor supply and labor demand curves cross. From this perspective, external equity is achieved if a firm pays the "going rate" in the marketplace for each job. These rates in turn reflect the relative strengths of supply and demand for different types of labor. With other things equal, the less employers are willing to pay (i.e., low demand) and the less pay workers are willing to accept (i.e., high supply) for a given job, the lower the wage rate will be.

Labor demand is derived from the market demand for a product or service, which slopes downward. The lower the price of a product is, the more units will be sold. To the extent that demand shifts to the right, consumers are willing to purchase more units at any given price. This causes a shift to the right of the labor demand curve. When this happens, employers are willing to pay more for any given number of employees hired. Labor demand is also a function of the marginal product of labor. Labor competes with other factors of production, such as capital, and will be utilized up to the point where labor can be substituted for other production factors (i.e., capital) more efficiently. The supply of labor, on the other hand, is said to depend on the availability of skills required to perform the job, training costs, and task desirability (Borjas, 2008).

Labor demand is aggregated across all employers, and labor supply is aggregated across millions of workers. Thus, the firm is depicted as a "price taker" that cannot influence market wages and must pay the prevailing rate in order to attract and retain employees (Borjas, 2008; Bronfenbrenner, 1956; Cartter, 1959; Ehrenberg and Smith, 1988). (However, this would not be true in the case of a monopsonistic company that is the sole employer in an area.)

The neoclassical economic model has two main implications for compensation practice and research. First, to attract and retain a qualified workforce, the firm must identify what the prevailing wage is for each of its jobs (Ingster, 2008; Rosen, 2008). Second, and related to the first point, the "going rate" in the labor market becomes the key factor for ascertaining job value or worth and, hence, external equity is defined as the extent to which the firm's pay rate for a given job matches the prevailing rate for that job in the external labor market (Fitzpatrick and McMullen, 2008).

Of course, compensation scholars have always realized the labor market is not perfect. Poor information, variations among workers in what they seek in a job (e.g., compatible coworkers versus a larger paycheck, willingness to accept risks versus more job security), transaction costs in changing jobs (e.g., loss of pension benefits, moving expenses), dual-career problems, discrimination and so on affect employment decisions. But even if one were to relax the stringent assumptions of perfect competition, a firm cannot stray too far from the competitive wage (Borjas, 2008). If it does, the firm soon finds itself unable to hire workers or compete effectively in the product market, because its labor costs are too high.

Practitioner Roots

The equity paradigm from social psychology and the labor market model from economics have had a profound effect on the field of compensation. In fact, all compensation textbooks rely on these models to justify in part the widespread use of job evaluation and salary surveys (to be discussed later). Whether these compensation practices, emerging through years of experimentation and in response to administrative demands, led academics to search for theories to justify them or whether the conceptual apparatus led to the development of operational systems to implement them is not clear. Most likely, it is an interaction of these two forces: Administrative procedures are developed to rationalize pay structures and the equity/labor market models offer a conceptual framework to support their use. Textbook writers, however, generally treat job evaluation and salary surveys as attempts to operationalize the constructs of equity and labor market rate. These procedures are briefly discussed in the next section. (Note: Given space limitations only a superficial treatment of these operational systems is possible here. For a more detailed description turn to Martocchio, 2009; Milkovich and Newman, 2009; and Gomez-Mejia, Balkin, and Cardy, 2010).

Job Evaluation and Internal Pay Structures

Job evaluation is perhaps the best-known and most commonly used procedure in compensation. In fact, the typical compensation text devotes over half of its chapters to the various steps involved in this process. *Job evaluation* is generally defined as a formalized system for ascertaining the relative value or contribution of different jobs (not individual employees) in an organization (e.g., Berger, 2008; Gross and Peterson, 2008; Wilson, 2008; Rosen, 2008; Ingster, 2008; Moody, 2008). It is intended to provide a rational, orderly, and systematic hierarchy of jobs based on their worth to the firm. Executives and managers are at the top of the hierarchy, while unskilled hourly workers are assigned to the bottom of the structure. In a large organization, hundreds or perhaps thousands of other jobs (e.g., administrative assistants, machinists, sales representatives, computer operators) fall somewhere in between.

To separate individuals' characteristics from the actual value of their contributions, the job is used as the unit of analysis. The job, independent of the incumbent, is evaluated as a group of positions that are similar in terms of skills, efforts, responsibilities, and working conditions. The higher the job is in the evaluation hierarchy, the more pay its incumbents receive, because the nature of their work is judged to be more valuable to the organization.

By design, most traditional job evaluation approaches draw a clear demarcation between the incumbent's performance and individual traits from the job itself. The upper and lower value limits of each job are established by assessing a job's worth relative to other jobs, and incumbents' earnings should not fall outside those perimeters, regardless of how well tasks are performed or how impressive personal traits are (Gomez-Mejia and Balkin, 1984b). So the question of interest from a job evaluation perspective is, "What is it that you do?" rather than, "How well do you do it?" The latter question is relegated to performance appraisal as a distinct and separate procedure. For example, the best assembler in a factory may have a PhD in electrical engineering, but because the job is ranked at the lowest level in the evaluation hierarchy, the worker's pay should fall somewhere between the minimum and maximum pay ranges established for assemblers, in spite of the impressive credentials.

While job evaluation systems preceded explicit formulations of equity theory (see earlier work by institutional economists such as Livernash, 1957 and industrial psychologists such as Viteles, 1941), the key objectives of job evaluation revolve around judgments of equity. The first judgment is to attain internal consistency in pay relationships. This can be accomplished through the development of a definite plan in which differences in pay are based on variations in job requirements and content, not people. This process focuses on the job rather than individuals, is easier to explain to employees, and enjoys wider acceptability. The second judgment, to provide the firm with a step-by-step procedure to document how pay decisions are made, is important from governance and legal perspectives. The third judgment is to achieve a common understanding as to the basis for pay allocation in large, complex organizations, which forces management to systematically identify factors that will be used to distribute rewards. Finally, as discussed in the next section, job evaluation allows the firm to link internal pay relationships to the labor market in order to achieve both internal and external equity.

Figure 1.1 outlines the steps that are followed in a typical job evaluation procedure. Most textbooks describe each of the components in painstaking detail (e.g., Milkovich and Newman, 2009; Gómez-Mejia, Balkin, and Cardy, 2010). The first step consists of job analysis, or gathering information about "what, how, why" of the various tasks involved in the job. Numerous procedures have been developed to conduct job analysis over the years (Ingster, 2008). The input from job analysis is used to identify similarities and differences in job content, either subjectively or through the use of computer-based algorithms (e.g., Gomez-Mejia, Page, and Tornow, 1979, 1982, 1985, 1987). This information is generally reduced to a written document that identifies, defines, and describes all jobs in terms of duties, responsibilities, working conditions, and requirements. This is commonly known as a *job description*.

Standard format job descriptions are then used to rate all jobs using a predetermined system. Several well-known job evaluation procedures have evolved over the years to do this. Some of these procedures are: ranking (ordering of job descriptions from highest to lowest based on relative assessed value); factor comparison (a variant of the ranking model); point plans (points are assigned to different aspects of the jobs being rated and added to create an evaluation composite); and policy capturing (use of regression equations to estimate the relative value of each job based on the firm's past practices). Almost all plans utilize a set of compensable factors or evaluative criteria to rate jobs. The Hay System, for example, uses three compensable factors: know-how, problem solving, and accountability. This system is perhaps the most widely used system today, even though it was invented almost 70 years ago by Ned Hay (Gomez-Mejia, Balkin, and Cardy, 2010).

The rating process then leads to a hierarchy of jobs based on assessed worth. For the sake of simplicity, most large organizations classify jobs into grades. In Control Data Corporation, for instance, thousands of jobs were

Figure 1.1 **Traditional Compensation Model**

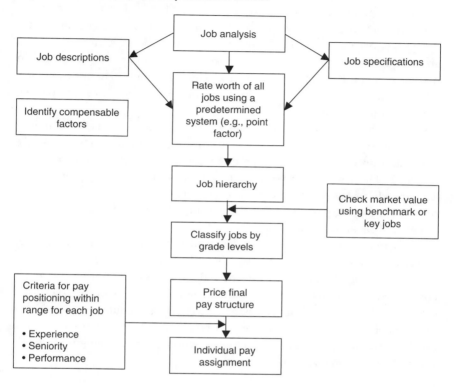

grouped into fewer than 20 grade levels (Gomez-Mejia, Page, and Tornow, 1982). Similarly, Gomez-Mejia, Balkin, and Cardy (2010) provide the example of a restaurant chain where 18 jobs and 87 positions are collapsed into six grade levels. All jobs in a given grade are judged to be essentially the same in terms of worth. The last step in the process consists of linking the job evaluation results (reflecting internal equity based on the employer's assessment of the job's worth) to the labor market.

Market Surveys

The second administrative mechanism most frequently used under the traditional models is the gathering of labor market data. This is done either by purchasing market information from consulting firms or, less often, by conducing in-house salary surveys (e.g., York and Brown, 2008). A quick Google search will reveal hundreds of commercially available Web sites (mostly run by consulting firms) offering salary survey data for most types of jobs at the local, national, and international levels. The ultimate objective is to learn the market values of different jobs and reconcile them with the results of internal job evaluation procedures. Because most positions are unique to a given employer, only key or benchmark jobs are used in market surveys. Key jobs are those for which accurate matches to similar jobs in other companies in a given labor market can be made (Fitzpatrick and McMullen, 2008).

The salary survey data for each job within a given grade level is then used to price all jobs previously classified into that grade. It is also possible to use regression procedures to link market data with job evaluation scores (e.g., Rosen, 2008). The organization has the choice to develop pay policies that lead, match, or lag behind the market rate. Presumably, to the extent that a firm can afford it, paying above-market rates should improve its ability to attract and retain high-caliber personnel.

Ultimately, market surveys are designed to ascertain whether external equity has been achieved. In the words of Fay (1989, p. 73): "External equity, as generally defined, refers to the range of wages and other monetary compensation paid by employing organizations in some labor market for a similar job. From an employee's perspective, external equity exists if his or her compensation package is equivalent to one offered employees with similar qualifications (e.g., education, experience) who hold the same job but work for a different organization."

Individual Pay Assignments

In traditional models, once the pay structure has been finalized by determining pay ranges for each job (following the procedures outlined earlier), the last step consists of assigning each individual a pay rate within the range established for his or her job. The position of a given employee's pay within the range depends on a number of factors, most commonly previous experience, company tenure, and assessed job performance. Some people refer to this as individual equity as opposed to internal equity (via job evaluation) or external equity (via market surveys) (Hellerman and Kochanski, 2008; Amuso and Knopping, 2008; Wilson and Malanowski, 2008; Grote, 2008; Niven, 2008; Graham-Brown, 2008).

Criticisms of Traditional Models

The equity paradigm and the neoclassical labor market models operationalized through the use of job evaluation and salary survey procedures have clearly dominated the field of compensation for the past 70 years. These perspectives have provided valuable insight in the past, and the administrative process to implement them has been of much practical use to employers. The fact that they are still widely used by practitioners and continue to be at the center stage of general HRM and specialized compensation texts attests to their remarkable endurance. This endurance is largely a result of the fact that, in the words of well-known compensation consultant Lance A. Berger, "to employees the most recognizable deliverable in a compensation program is their own pay package. It is essential to the organization that this deliverable be transparent. To the practitioner the challenge is to ensure transparency by rationalizing the employee's pay package as the end result of an unambiguous, disciplined, and explainable thought process . . ." (Berger, 2008a, p. 3).

Despite their popularity, the traditional models have provoked a fair amount of criticism over the years and, particularly among academics, has lead to the search for more complex compensation models that enable a strategic analysis of how pay resources may be used and that go beyond the "attraction, retention, and motivation" mantra often cited in the classical literature (Hills, 1987, 1989; Belcher and Atchison, 1987). These criticisms are discussed in the following section.

This section is meant to provide an antecedent to the new theoretical frameworks examined in this book, which treat compensation issues from a meso, integrated perspective that considers internal and external conditions facing the firm and that focuses on the entire organization (from the CEO down) as the unit of analysis.

The Deterministic Nature of Traditional Models

Both equity and labor market models and their operationalization (namely job evaluation and market surveys) have a largely deterministic view of the world. In essence, internal equity can be achieved if organizational rewards are distributed in proportion to job value (as per job evaluation), and external equity can be accomplished by pegging the organization's pay to that of the market (or at least within a narrow band around the going rate as determined through market surveys). This deterministic view has been questioned by practitioners and academics alike in a number of related ways.

First, most organizations have considerable discretion in terms of pay allocation, basis for pay decisions, and administrative procedures. In other words, organizations are confronted with a wide range of pay policy alternatives. Dramatic differences in the choices made are evident across firms (see Chapter 2). Second, compensation problems and challenges in each firm are typically unique and less structured than the traditional models would lead one to believe. Considerable creativity is required to synthesize large amounts of external and internal information and to develop a plan outlining the direction of a firm's future pay policy. Heavy reliance on "off-the-shelf" job evaluation procedures and surveys (typically conducted by consultants) emphasize a universal perspective that may not be relevant and may even be detrimental to the firm. Such prescriptive approaches ignore the environmental forces and business context that confront and impact the firm (Balkin and Gomez-Mejia, 1987b, 1990; Gross and Peterson, 2008; Makri, Lane, and Gomez-Mejia, 2006). Finally, due to the rapid increase in mergers and acquisitions as well as internal diversification, most organizations are complex, and varied compensation systems may be more appropriate for different parts of an organization. Traditional pay systems with their emphasis on consistency neglect the particular contingencies that confront diverse organizational units (Carroll, 1987, 1988; Martell, Carroll, and Gupta, 1992; Salscheider, 1981).

Inapplicability to Executive, Managerial, and Professional Ranks

Another problem with traditional pay systems is that their basic assumptions are largely inappropriate to higher occupational groups (such as upper management and knowledge workers). At these levels, it is nearly impossible to separate individual contributions from the job itself. In other words, the incumbent helps define and mold the job. Forcing managerial and professional employees into grade levels can be counterproductive because their contributions are the result of personal characteristics rather than of tasks performed. Given a more sophisticated workforce and the increase of professional and managerial ranks as the economy becomes more service-oriented, jobs are becoming more and more broadly defined. Job descriptions often become meaningless generalities. Therefore, to the extent that job analysis and job descriptions produce ambiguous data, the system on which they are based also has little validity.

Forcing a mechanistic pay system can backfire in some situations. For example, in the high-technology industry, scientists and engineers (S & Es) often contribute more to the organization than top executives do (Tremblay and Chenevert, 2008). Yet application of traditional evaluation procedures designed for a manufacturing environment are often used with disastrous consequences (Gomez-Mejia, Balkin, and Milkovich, 1990). By establishing an elaborate hierarchy of grade levels for scientists and engineers and making rewards contingent on fine distinctions in the nature of the task being accomplished, many high-tech firms foster competition, artificial barriers among people, fragmentation, and an individualistic climate in the workforce. The behaviors and culture fostered by traditional job evaluation procedures in this situation run counter to what it takes to succeed in a research and development (R & D) environment, namely, intense team effort, integration of activities among many individuals, fluid tasks, exchange of knowledge, and minimal status barriers to facilitate interaction among multidisciplinary S & Es working on common problems (Hamm, 2009; Welbourne and Gómez-Mejia, 2008; Tremblay and Chenevert, 2008).

Lack of Flexibility

The traditional lockstep compensation system based on job evaluation gives a high priority to pay relationships within a firm. These systems work reasonably well for firms faced with stable markets and high continuity in their socio-technical system. Such was the case, for example, of the automobile industry in the United States for several decades. However, these systems cannot be easily adapted to volatile economic environments or to rapid technological changes (Sydow, Schreyogg, and Koch, 2009). This has been evident in the recent crisis faced by the "big three" automobile companies, which necessitated an infusion of federal funds to cover so-called "legacy costs" (Welch, 2009). Once a job evaluation program is in place, it is difficult to change.

Because it relies on fixed salary and benefits associated with each level in the hierarchy (as set through job evaluation and market surveys), American industry's primary mechanism to cope with economic downturns is to lay off employees to reduce costs. For example, during the economic downturn at the end of the first decade of the twenty-first century (often cited as the worst since the Great Depression) few employers managed to cut costs without axing jobs (Jolly, 2009; Tuna, 2008). Globalization seems to have accentuated this trend (Das, 2009; Barboza, 2009), making the lack of flexibility in traditional compensation programs even more problematic (Gomez-Mejia, Balkin, and Cardy, 2010).

Questioning the Market

The traditional compensation models assume that pay norms exist among firms in a given market and that going rates for particular jobs can be identified. As noted earlier, wage surveys have been used for many years to operationalize the concepts of competitive pay or equitable market pay.

The use of wage surveys has also come under fire (Gerhart and Rynes, 2003). Early criticisms of the market rate can be traced to Dunlop (1957), who argued that it may be an illusionary concept. He found that workers performing almost identical work that required the same skills and was organized by the same union and in the same geographical area (Boston) were receiving a rate of pay that was markedly different among different employers, with 60 percent differences not uncommon. About 25 years later, Treiman and Hartmann (1981) reported a huge variance in the pay of identical jobs in the Newark, New Jersey, area with a ratio of almost 3 to 1 between highest- and lowest-paying employers. Foster (1985) found that after controlling for job content, company size, and company performance, differences between 35 and 54 percent in pay for identical jobs within the same industry were not uncommon. Foster (1985, p. 70) concluded that, "Clearly, the pay practices of firms in the same industry are often widely divergent. . . . No doubt, this means that employers, on the basis of carefully selected survey samples, can justify divergent pay practices (a point frequently ignored when competitive pay is analyzed and discussed)." Gómez-Mejia and Balkin (1992) showed that even within a relatively small and isolated county located far from any large metropolitan area (such as Alachua County in northern Florida), a large range in weekly pay for the identical occupation title was common. More recently, based on a computer search of salary surveys, Gómez-Mejia, Balkin, and Cardy (2010) note that 3-to-1 differences in pay level for identical job titles in the same labor market are not unusual.

In a review paper entitled, "Market Surveys: Dispelling Some Myths about the Market Wage," Rynes and Milkovich (1986) argue that both the construct and measurement of the market wage have not been sufficiently examined by either academics or the courts. Some of the problems with the market wage concept and its operationalization and salary surveys include (as per Rynes and Milkovich, 1986): widely divergent criteria as to how the "appropriate market" is defined, existence of multiple wage levels for the same job in a given market, differences in sampling methodologies and statistical analysis, mismatching of jobs among organizations with identical titles, and difficulties in estimating total pay (salary plus benefits and incentives).

This suggests that a fundamental assumption of the traditional compensation models—that the relevant market can be measured and used as a frame of comparison to adjust the internal job evaluation hierarchy—is overly simplistic and subject to wide interpretation. Clearly, firms have wide discretion in establishing wage levels and the manner in which the market rates are determined. Furthermore, it is likely that firms may subjectively choose multiple labor-market pay standings for various jobs and positions. These depend on the strategic value of particular employee groups and even specific individuals who are considered key contributors. (Note: For a more extensive discussion of these issues see York and Brown, 2008; and Rees, 2008.)

Obstacle to Professionalization

As noted earlier, human resource practitioners and academics alike realize that HRM needs to shed its old image of a low-level administrative function relegated to record keeping and paper shuffling, engaged in what seems like an endless creation of new forms and administrative procedures and responsible for the enforcement of petty rules despised by line managers. In part, the contemporary use of the term *human resource* rather than *personnel* is indicative of an attempt to dispel past stereotypes of a function pejoratively depicted as run by "glorified secretaries" and a depository of managers who had failed elsewhere in the corporation (Gomez-Mejia, Balkin, and Cardy, 2010).

Unfortunately, compensation specialists and consultants selling their wares (e.g., various point methods, universal "guide charts," and standardized market surveys) have been among the worst culprits in reinforcing a negative image of the HRM profession. Most compensation textbooks and many consultants' Web pages still contain page after page of instruments, techniques, surveys forms, and the like. However, many realize that a more professional image of the field can only be created if compensation becomes a business discipline rather than a personnel tool kit. This calls for a broader perspective on analyzing internal and external forces that impact the organization and the ability to devise pay systems to cope with them. In this context, the mechanics of the pay systems are a means to achieving business objectives rather than an end in itself.

Shouldn't Organizational Performance Be the Ultimate Goal?

The traditional compensation model reviewed earlier tends to be inward oriented, with the implied assumption that a system that enables a firm in an orderly fashion to "attract, retain, and motivate employees" will help it become "the employer of choice" and thus accumulate and utilize the best available human capital. While this may be true, it is only part of the story (e.g., Hausknecht, Rodda, and Howard, 2009). Firms can only outperform others when they have a successful business strategy and the compensation system helps support it from the highest-paid executive (whose decisions are very responsive to incentives) down to the lowest-paid employee. A strategic orientation involves developing a long-term vision and multifunctional programmatic steps to cope with the unique contingencies affecting the organization. The term strategy derives from the Greek word *strategia*, which is loosely translated as "art of the general." This refers to a concern for the big picture rather than tactical considerations.

While a strategic perspective on compensation has been advocated for almost 30 years (see for instance, Lawler, 1984; Milkovich, 1988), most recent progress in this direction has been made in the top executive ranks, perhaps coinciding with the rapid development of strategic management as a field in its own right. For this reason, this book draws heavily from this literature in contrast to the earlier book on this subject by Gomez-Mejia and Balkin (1992), which relied on the handful of empirical studies and conceptual pieces published by HRM researchers in the 1980s and early 1990s. We do, however, make a concerted attempt to show that incentive design at the top has repercussions for the entire organization and therefore should not be examined as a separate and isolated compartment.

Micro and Macro Processes

As a whole, the field of HRM (including compensation) has been most closely tied to organizational behavior and this is still true today (most members of the HRM division of the Academy of Management also belong to the Organizational Behavior Division). This means that despite the plea for more strategic thinking in compensation practice and research, compensation largely remains a functional area that most management scholars tend to classify as "micro." The inward focus of the traditional models reviewed earlier reinforces this view. In the meantime, it appears that most of the strategy-oriented research in compensation (by scholars such as Donald Hambrick, Sydney Finkelstein, Gerald Sanders, Robert Wiseman, and Bert Cannella, among others) now falls into what is loosely called corporate governance.This is unfortunate, as it tends to solidify a false barrier between compensation management and strategy as distinct fields even though they should be closely intertwined. While the dichotomy between macro strategic processes and micro human resource activities (including compensation) is still deeply grounded in the minds of many academics and practitioners, it is ultimately misleading. It discounts the necessity for strategic thinking at the behavioral level in general and the compensation function in particular.

Philosophy of This Book

Being mindful of the criticisms of traditional compensation systems, an alternative perspective guiding this book holds that the following are true:

1. The pay system must operate within the organizational context of strategic decisions and be an integral part of strategy formulation.
2. The compensation design for the CEO and the top management cadre is likely to have a cascading effect in an organization, shaping incentives and behavioral responses at all levels.
3. Compensation plays a major role, either explicitly or by default, in strategic decision-making processes, including formal systems for planning, implementation, and control.
4. Hybrid theoretical models are almost always needed to understand the causes and consequences of the adoption of particular pay systems.

Consistent with the four points made in the preceding paragraph, productive research and theory development in compensation may be enhanced in the future by greater cross-fertilization with other disciplines. This will allow compensation to transcend the traditional paradigms grounded in industrial/social psychology and labor economics to incorporate such notions as the development of systems for monitoring and incentive alignment, negotiating exchanges with internal and external coalitions, coping with environmental uncertainty, and balancing the needs and demands of multiple constituencies. It will also help bridge the fields of strategic management and HRM, as compensation is a key variable of interest to both domains even though with few exceptions these literatures run parallel to each other.

Throughout the book, several broad theoretical frameworks are examined that may be used to study a variety of compensation phenomena at a macro level of analysis. These are applied to analyze corporate governance issues at the top as well as broader compensation strategies affecting multiple organizational levels. A common thread throughout this book is the view of compensation as a pivotal organizational-wide control and incentive mechanism that should be analyzed in toto rather than in a compartmentalized piecemeal fashion. We are concerned with the interface between compensation systems, organizational strategies, and environmental forces and how their interaction affects firm performance. As such, we draw from many disciplines, most notably accounting, finance, economics, organizational theory, and strategic management.

Once again, this is not a book about compensation administration. There are no detailed discussions of the psychological and economic basis of pay as a tool to "attract, retain, and motivate" employees; the pros and cons of different techniques to achieve equity at the individual and organizational level; and the administrative operations of compensation as subfunctions within the general personnel umbrella. The reader who expects a traditional approach to the subject will be disappointed. As important as these issues may be, they are only incidental to this volume. Readers interested in pay administration concerns can turn to several recent books that focus primarily on compensation management issues (e.g., Milkovich and Newman, 2009 and Berger and Berger, 2008). Excellent sources of applied compensation research may also be found in the many publications of WorldatWork Association (for a listing, see www.worldatwork.org), previously known as the American Compensation Association.

We would like to remind the reader of the old adage, "There is nothing more practical than a good theory." Despite its scholarly trust, this book should help compensation professionals and consultants to do the following:

1. Prevent future problems (e.g., loss of key personnel) by neutralizing threatening forces beforehand (e.g., brain drain to competitors).
2. Advise top-level managers and work closely with other functional heads so that strategic pay decisions reflect the best available alternatives (e.g., group-based vs. individual-based incentives).
3. Reduce resistance to change by instilling a strategic pay mentality among line managers (e.g., willingness to give up merit pay prerogatives in lieu of team-based rewards).
4. Assist the organization to make adjustments in its pay system in response to anticipated environmental jolts (e.g., increase variable pay to provide a financial cushion to the firm if profits decline, instead of cutting costs by laying off employees) rather than be forced to make radical changes in a reactive fashion.
5. Design executive compensation programs that are conducive to the achievement of strategic goals.

More broadly, the research examined here should inform decision makers (including both senior executives and line managers) as follows:

1. Facilitate the negotiation and implementation of appropriate pay schemes with key internal groups or constituencies.

2. Search for sustainable, long-term competitive advantages and ways to support these by rewarding appropriate behaviors and decisions.

3. Respond in a flexible and customized manner to the specific needs of the total organization and its subunits on the basis of internal and external contingency factors that mediate the success of particular compensation strategies.

4. Be leery of generalized prescriptions for the pay system based on uniform mechanistic approaches that have deflected compensation's attention form the critical issue of using pay in a discretionary manner as a source of competitive advantage.

5. Place firm performance as the ultimate criterion of success for strategic pay decisions and operational compensation programs.

In conclusion, organizational members from the highest to the lowest levels in the pyramid respond to how they are rewarded, and hence, the design of the compensation system influences strategic choices made by top executives as well as how those choices are eventually implemented throughout the entire firm. Coupled with the fact that pay is the most important single expense in most organizations, in the long term firm performance depends on whether or not the compensation system is used effectively.

2 REPERTOIRE OF STRATEGIC PAY CHOICES

As noted in Chapter 1, the strategic perspective on compensation is based on two underlying assumptions. First, the pay system cannot be analyzed in isolation because its effectiveness depends upon how responsive it is to internal and external forces on the organization and the firm's structural configuration. If the pay system is not attuned to the macro organizational context within which it operates, then, at best, important policies are being missed and, at worst, pay policies are counterproductive or act as an impediment to the firm's overall strategic thrust.

The second assumption is that the organization has the discretion to choose from a large variety of pay policies and procedures, and each of these may have strategic implications. Even if the focus is on a narrow program such as gain sharing, there are "literally thousands of different ways to implement and structure a gainsharing plan" (Bullock and Lawler, 1984, p. 34). Each of these—e.g., participative versus nonparticipative plans—may be appropriate for a particular situation. Bullock and Lawler (1984), Welbourne and Gomez-Mejia (1988, 1991), and Gomez-Mejia, Welbourne, and Wiseman (2000) describe multiple contingencies affecting the relative success or failure of various gain-sharing plans. The same is true with most other pay-for-performance plans (Salimaki and Heneman, 2008).

A general definition of the term *compensation strategy*, which flows from the above two assumptions, can be advanced. Compensation strategy is the deliberate utilization of the pay system as an essential integrating mechanism through which the efforts of various subunits and individuals are directed toward the achievement of an organization's strategic objectives, subject to internal and external constraints. When properly designed, contingent upon the organization's strategic objectives and constraints, it can be an important contributor to the firm's performance.

Consistent with this definition, each firm faces a repertoire of pay choices. The degree of success associated with each of these depends on two factors. The first is how well the alternative(s) selected enable the organization to cope better with contingencies affecting it at a given point in time. The second is the extent to which the pay choices made are synchronized with the firm's overall strategic direction.

The purpose of this chapter is to map the domain of strategic compensation decisions. Eighteen *strategic pay choices* are distilled from the extant literature and discussed. These compensation strategy choices are not necessarily all-inclusive, but we believe they cover the most important alternatives facing organizations.

Two points need to be addressed before the actual compensation choices are discussed. First, much of this research is unfolding and remains at a relatively early and, in some cases, speculative stage of inquiry. A skeptic may ask the question, "How do we know that these 18 pay choices are really strategic?" In truth, there is no definite answer to that question because they are not empirically derived or drawn from a tight and well-developed theoretical framework. We are simply not there yet. Many of these choices have been identified by practitioners who must solve day-to-day problems that involve compensation issues, such as how to reduce fixed expenses while attracting and retaining top talent or how to set up diverse pay systems in multiple countries while maintaining some corporate-wide uniformity in pay policies (Gomez-Mejia and Werner, 2008; Newman and Floersch, 2008; Sanchez-Marin, 2008a, b; Montemayor, 2008; Makri, 2008; Wiseman, Gomez-Mejia and Cuevas, 2010). In that sense, we agree with Howard and Dougherty (2004, p. 41), who conclude that "the fact is that much of strategic compensation theory is untested theory in use." However, based on the literature reviewed here, there are sufficient grounds to believe that these dimensions are useful in understanding and analyzing compensation phenomena from a strategic perspective. So, while some healthy skepticism is in order, these 18 dimensions offer some basic analytical tools to conduct additional research on compensation strategies and to interpret much of the existing literature.

Second, each of the 18 strategic compensation choices discussed in this chapter represent two opposite poles on a continuum. In reality, as seen in Chapter 3, most firms fall somewhere between these two poles, and very few are designated as a pure type. For instance, a firm may rely on fixed pay much more than the typical firm, even though it offers some incentive compensation. None of these choices should be conceptualized and measured as mutually exclusive categories such as A versus B. They should, however, be viewed as relative gradings. Some organizations will be closer to A and some closer to B. Others will fall somewhere in the middle and a handful will be at the extremes. In other words, the labels should be seen as heuristic guideposts. An organization's choice for each dimension should be interpreted as a relative positioning on the scale or the extent to which it is more similar to one end than the other. In accordance with our definition of compensation strategy, an organization can decide deliberately where it wishes to be in terms of this continuum for each strategic compensation choice.

The 18 strategic pay choices are broken down into three broad categories reflecting the common themes underlying each set of choices: identifying criteria used to distribute rewards, assembling the compensation package, and administering the compensation system.

Criteria Used to Distribute Rewards

The strategic pay choices listed under this category are concerned with the most salient factors or criteria used to distribute rewards.

Job versus Skills

Job-based pay is the approach used in traditional compensation methods where the job, rather than individual characteristics, is the unit of analysis to ascertain value to the firm (Milkovich and Newman, 2009: Gomez-Mejia, Balkin, and Cardy, 2010). Because workers are paid depending on where their jobs fall in the structure, the wage rate generally changes only when the employee changes jobs. In skill-based pay (also known as knowledge-based pay), on the other hand, employees are paid based on the jobs they can do. That is, the abilities they have can be successfully applied to a variety of tasks and situations. The more "hats an individual can wear," the higher his or her pay. Thus, skill-based pay rewards the individual for versatility rather than for actual tasks performed. In the words of Klarsfeld, Balkin, and Roger (2003, p. 47):

> The application of skill-based pay challenges the traditional logic of pay determination, which assumes that the firm pays for the job and not the person. Job-based considers that the job itself is the source of value that a firm pays for, independent of the person holding the job. On the other hand, skill-based pay focuses on the individual employee as the source of value, and in particular, the specific bundle of skills that an individual brings to the employer becomes the basis for the rate of pay. In other words, the depth and breadth of each employee's skills determines the rate of pay. This is a very different philosophy from the conventional approach to worker compensation . . . the worker starts out at a flat hourly rate and then receives pay increases as he or she learns how to perform a certain job better or how to perform other jobs within the plant or department. The worker gets that hourly rate regardless of his or her job assignment.

Milkovich and Newman (2009), Giancola (2007), Ledford (1991), Tosi and Tosi (1986), Wallace (1991), and Gomez-Mejia, Balkin, and Cardy (2010) suggest that job-based pay works best in the following situations:

1. Technology is stable.
2. Jobs don't change often.
3. Employee exchanges are minimal.
4. The entire human resources philosophy stresses a hierarchical controlling orientation and longevity within the firm.
5. The organization believes that establishing clear distinctions among jobs provides an orderly approach to recognizing individuals who can take advantage of career paths and opportunities to move into new positions with fancier titles and greater responsibility.
6. Traditional jobs represent an important source of information for determining a person's role in the firm.

Skill-based pay, on the other hand, works best if the following conditions exist (Klarsfeld, Balkin, and Roger, 2003; Cabrales, Calvo-Amengol, and Pavoni, 2008; Lemieux, 2007; Guadalupe, 2007; Murray and Gerhart, 2000; Richards, 2006; Tosi and Tosi, 1986):

1. A supportive HRM philosophy is in operation that is characterized by mutual trust and a conviction that employees have both the ability and willingness to perform.
2. An entire array of HRM programs such as Scanlon plans, participative management, and job enrichment are in place to go along with skill-based pay. The latter has little chance to succeed as a freestanding compensation approach.
3. Technology and organizational structure experience frequent changes.
4. Employee exchanges are common.
5. Opportunities to learn new skills are present.
6. Employee turnover is relatively high.
7. Worker values are consistent with teamwork and participation.
8. It is important for employees to constantly upgrade their skills and knowledge to keep up with a complex technological environment.
9. Skills that are in high demand in the labor market tend to be bid up in what employers are willing to pay to secure them and, thus, the organization needs to monitor their market value closely on an ongoing basis.

10. The workforce has a positive attitude toward skill seeking, there are strong achievement norms, and individuals perceive that they can control the situation to acquire the skills valued and rewarded by the firm.

Performance versus Membership

When performance is used as a basis to distribute rewards, payment is provided for individual or group contributions to the firm. Strict *performance-contingent compensation* delivers payment for output or outcome and most closely resembles the operation of traditional piece-rate plans or sales commissions. Because strict performance-contingent compensation is feasible and desirable only in a very limited number of situations: when meaningful output measures are readily available, when these can be unambiguously attributed specific individuals or groups, and when interdependencies are low. Modified performance contingent plans are more practical in most cases (Gomez-Mejia, Balkin, and Cardy, 2010; Mahoney, 1989; Salimaki and Heneman, 2008). These plans include awards for cost-saving suggestions, bonuses based on behavioral performance measures (such as perfect attendance), and merit pay based on supervisory appraisals.

Membership-contingent compensation, on the other hand, provides the employee a paycheck and benefits for logging a prescribed number of hours of work (Fay, 2008; Gomez-Mejia, Balkin, and Cardy, 2010; Martocchio and Pandey, 2008). This assumes at least satisfactory performance is achieved to justify keeping the person on board. This operates as a qualifying step function, with unsatisfactory employees being terminated and those deemed satisfactory in a given job receiving the same or a similar wage. Typically, salary progression takes place by moving up through the grades based on length of time at the job, even when "there is either no association or a negative association between *experience* and relative rated performance" (Medoff and Abraham, 1980, p. 703). Furthermore, different performance appraisal systems appear to have little effect on this process (Gomez-Mejia, 1988a).

While most firms publicly embrace a pay-for-performance credo, sometimes with much fanfare, in practice a majority of companies primarily reward for seniority (Buchenroth, 2006; Gomez-Mejia, 1990b; Gomez-Mejia, Page, and Tornow, 1985). More than 20 years ago Hay Group Inc. found merit budgets for exempt employees hovered around the 6 percent mark, with the most typical spread between highest and lowest performers in the 5 percent to 7 percent range (Greeley and Ochsner, 1986). These consultants concluded that with only a 2 percentage point difference in treatment between highly rated performers and their lower-rated counterparts " it is very difficult to make a strong case for the pay-for-performance model in today's administration of pay programs" (p. 15). Two decades later, Buchenroth (2006) confirmed this point using perceptual data. Relying on employee surveys across several occupations and industries he concludes that, "Although performance-based pay isn't a new concept, it still is not widely used . . . 60 percent of employees stated those who had been at their company longest received the most pay, compared to just one-third (35 percent) who stated that their companies paid their higher performers more." Salimaki and Heneman (2008, p. 159) argue that this happens because "even though supervisors would want to differentiate between employees, they need to consider the broader effects of rewards on, for example, group harmony." In an empirical study conducted almost 25 years ago. Robert Cardy and Greg Dobbins (1986) demonstrated that affect plays a key role in performance appraisal despite organizational efforts to make this a rational and objective process. At the time of this writing (2010), firms continue to search for better ways to assess employee performance, but in our professional experience we still find widespread dissatisfaction with the appraisal process, and much of it is attributed to the fact that emotions influence both the supervisor's and the employee's perceptions of individual contributions.

In general, a focus on performance to distribute rewards is most appropriate when the organization's culture (Kerr, 1995; Kerr and Slocum, 2005) and national or regional cultures (Gerhart, 2008) emphasize a performance ethos, competition among individuals and groups is encouraged (Gomez-Mejia, Balkin, and Cardy, 2010; Pearce, 1987), the firm is experiencing rapid growth (Balkin and Gomez-Mejia, 1987a), relevant performance indicators are available (Franco-Santos, 2008), the firm competes through continuous innovation (Makri, 2008), and the available information technology facilitates the storage and use of performance data for compensation purposes (McGuire, 2008). Perhaps because these conditions are not easily met, performance-contingent compensation is not always feasible. As an alternative, firms rely on job-contingent and tenure-based pay, with compensation linked to the job held by the person and the length of time the person has been in that job (Milkovich and Newman, 2009). This offers three benefits to the firm: (1) it is administratively easy to handle, (2) length of time on the job may reflect mastery of that job, and (3) it might enjoy greater acceptability by employees since it is unambiguous and readily understood. Therefore, potential for interpersonal conflict is minimized. Performance-contingent compensation policies are examined in greater detail in in future chapters.

Individual versus Aggregate Performance

Individual contingent rewards (e.g., merit pay bonuses) are offered based on the notion that reinforcing desired employee behaviors are important for motivational reasons. The closer the link between desired behaviors and rewards, the more likely the employee is to engage in those behaviors in the future (McNatt, Glassman, and McAfee, 2007). Reinforcement theory (Cherrington, Reitz, and Scott, 1971) and expectancy theory (Graen, 1969) are most often used to justify the value of individual contingent rewards. These plans are also deeply rooted in the cultural myth that people who work harder and perform better should get more pay than those who are lazier and contribute less. They are intended to communicate clear performance expectations to each individual and give employees the opportunity to earn additional income through their own efforts. Merit pay, individual bonuses, special awards, and so on are commonly used programs designed to identify and recognize the unique contributions of each employee (Purcell and Huchinson, 2007; Salimaki and Heneman, 2008).

Aggregate pay-for-performance systems, on the other hand, use group contribution as a basis to distribute rewards. Thus, the payoff an individual receives depends on his or her performance as well as that of coworkers. Different levels of aggregation may be used to determine how performance is to be measured. These may include team performance (e.g., project bonuses), business-unit performance (e.g., gain sharing), and corporate-wide performance (e.g., profit sharing) (Howard and Dougherty, 2004; Gomez-Mejia, Balkin, and Cardy, 2010).

Reliance on individual contingent rewards has met considerable negative reactions from both management and employees (Campbell and Barron, 1982; Lazer and Wikstrom, 1977; Pearce, 1987; Rubenfeld and David, 2006). To a large extent, failures in individual-based pay-for-performance systems may be traced to the fact that these can work only in a limited number of situations. One or more insurmountable obstacles are often present. "Performance may prove too difficult to define or measure; desired performance may vary over time; and performance may depend on factors outside the worker's control" (Mahoney, 1989, p. 10). In general, individual-based plans are more likely to be effective when performance contributions can be attributed to specific employees, competition between employees is a desired outcome, there are few interdependencies, and the plan is framed in the context of a larger set of HRM programs (e.g., supervisory training, developmental activities, work planning, etc.) (Gomez-Mejia, Balkin, and Cardy, 2010).

Aggregate-based pay-for-performance plans are most effective under the following conditions (Gomez-Mejia, Balkin, and Cardy, 2010; Welbourne and Gomez-Mejia, 2008; Zingheim, 2007):

1. When the sociotechnical system within the firm fosters a cooperative structure: As noted by Pearce (1987, p. 187), "Aggregate incentive plans are based on the assumption that the greater the uncertainty, interdependence, and complexity organizational work, the greater the cooperation among employees required for successful performance and that individual performance-based pay can provide powerful disincentives for cooperation."
2. When the nature of the tasks per se does not allow clear identification of individual contributions: Aggregate incentive plans are easier to implement because individual contributions do not have to be singled out. They do not require unrealistic distinctions among employees.
3. When greater flexibility is desired: Typically, aggregate incentive systems offer greater flexibility in closely timing the reward to actual task accomplishment or in making pay contingent on specific targets or jobs. Unlike the most commonly used individual contingent reward (i.e., merit pay), aggregate incentives are not limited to a fixed fiscal budget and are given on a one-time-only basis to reward specific achievements.
4. When the task is difficult or unique and the employees are intrinsically motivated: Free riding is less likely to occur under these circumstances. Otherwise, group incentives may be vitiated by free riders or individuals who provide low work inputs and receive the same reward as other group members, because aggregate plans provide financial rewards to multiple contributors based on the achievement of common goals.

Perhaps a major reason why individual and aggregate pay-for-performance programs fail is that firms are increasingly using a combination of incentive plans under the assumption that this helps meet a dual need for recognizing individuals as well as reinforcing the team concept (Welbourne and Gomez-Mejia, 2008). While this may be true conceptually, multiple incentive options are problematic since these could send conflicting signals to employees. In the words of Rubenfeld and David (2006, p. 35):

> . . . the use of multiple incentive plans can introduce problems that are not always evident . . . . For example, employees working with multiple incentive programs may not have a clear understanding of the true priorities of the organization. With a clouded vision of firms' needs, employees may find themselves less motivated because they are uncertain of the relative importance of these needs. Additionally, by providing multiple incentive options, employees may perceive that only those behaviors that are rewarded deserve attention. Employees may begin acting only in the interest of achieving the payouts and neglect other behaviors that are not part of an incentive program but still are desirable in an organization . . . Although there is little research exploring interactions between multiple incentive plans, one can speculate that too many plans will distract em-

ployees no matter how appropriate and viable each of the plans might be when viewed individually.

Short-term versus Long-term Orientation

The short-term versus long-term orientation strategic pay choice has fueled much controversy (see Chapters 4 through 6 on executive compensation). The central issue is the time horizon used to measure performance and distribute rewards. Reinforcement theory and operant conditioning suggest that the closer to actual behavior the reward is provided, the greater its motivational impact (Hammer, 1975; Gerhart and Rynes, 2003; Rubenfeld and David, 2006). For most people, delayed rewards are less powerful than more immediate reinforcement. On the other hand, an organization's success depends more heavily on what happens in the long run than in the near term. This means that the reward system should be based on an extended time horizon.

The dilemma noted in the previous paragraph would not be problematic if the long-term success of the firm is the simple composite of short-term successes. Unfortunately what may improve the bottom line in the short run (e.g., laying off employees as a cost-cutting measure) may prove to be highly detrimental in the long run (e.g., reduced employee loyalty) (Cascio, 2006). So, organizations face an important strategic choice as to the length of time used to measure performance for pay purposes. This can range from daily (as in some piece-rate systems), to yearly (as in the case of merit pay and cash bonuses), to periods extending five years or more (as in some equity-based plans). The choice of which time period to use may have serious implications as to what employees, particularly executives in powerful positions, will try to achieve.

One of the major challenges related to strategic compensation choices is the development of effective means for leading the charge toward a long-term perspective. U.S. cultural forces emphasize a short-term orientation and interfirm mobility, so it has been difficult in the past to reorient employees and managers toward rewards contingent on long-term performance (Gerhart, 2008; Gomez-Mejia and Welbourne, 1991; Makri, 2008; Sanchez-Marin, 2008a,b). In addition, short-term performance is easier to quantify and executives are often reluctant to commit to long-term goals because they appear risky and rather nebulous (Gomez-Mejia and Welbourne, 1988). A stream of research suggests that, independent of national culture firms that compete through innovation tend to emphasize long-term incentives (Makri, Lane, and Gomez-Mejia, 2006; Makri, 2008; Yanadon and Marler, 2006).

Carroll (1987) and others argue that firms with business strategies designed to maintain existing market share are more likely to have objective data that can be used to reward short-term performance at different levels in the organizational hierarchy. Firms that are undergoing fast growth and are aggressively expanding their market share often do not have reliable objective performance data on hand. Thus, they emphasize long-term performance based on subjective assessments.

Risk Aversion versus Risk Taking

An important strategic pay choice is whether to reward or punish employees' risk-taking behavior. Most research on this topic relates to the top executive level (see Chapters 4–6). This is in part because executives have more control over decisions and are rewarded accordingly (Berrone and Otten, 2008). Stonich (1981) suggests that Japanese workers are more willing to make risky decisions and engage in innovative, entrepreneurial endeavors *within* their firms because they are less concerned with the potential negative effect of these activities on job security. Greater job security allows managers to take calculated risks without worrying about the consequences of their business decisions on continued employment and income. Some U.S. firms allow individuals to undertake risky projects without risking their jobs. For example, 3M is a "no-layoff" company that designates special funds to encourage new ventures and links rewards to the eventual outcome of such projects (Gomez-Mejia, Balkin, and Milkovich, 1990). This, however, is the exception.

In general, high-growth companies in the United States reward risk taking (while established firms with a stable market share encourage risk aversion (Gomez-Mejia and Welbourne, 1988). Younger, risk-taking employees gravitate toward high-growth companies with greater opportunities for career advancement and financial gains (Mayo, Pastor, Gomez-Mejia, and Cruz, 2010). This, in turn, supports the entrepreneurial climate desired by these firms. Mature firms, on the other hand, are content with their current technology and products and are likely to discourage behaviors that deviate from standard operating procedures. Unlike growing firms, however, they provide more job security. As discussed later in the book (Chapters 4 and 5), recent thinking and empirical research on this issue suggest that most people have the capacity to seek or avoid risk depending on the favorableness of the situation facing them (Wiseman and Gomez-Mejia, 1998; Devers et al. 2008).

Corporate versus Division Performance

One of the main concerns in the empirical research on compensation strategy is the level of aggregation used to measure firm performance. This is particularly important when designing pay packages for top-level executives, but it is also a crucial issue in such aggregate incentive systems as gain sharing and profit sharing.

The highest level of aggregation is *corporate performance,* which refers to the entire organization regardless of its size or the number of industries in which it competes. For instance, a conglomerate may be operating in such diverse areas as tourism, manufacturing, and retailing. Thus, corporate-level performance would correspond to the performance indicators for the firm as a single entity. *Business unit* or *division performance,* on the other hand, refers to "the level in the organization at which responsibility for the formulation of a multifunctional strategy for a single industry or product market area is established" (Hitt, Ireland, and Hoskisson, 2009). In a company with a single product line, the business and corporate levels would be the same.

The level of aggregation used to measure firm performance for pay purposes has strategic relevance in the following scenarios:

1. The larger and more diverse the company, the more difficult it is for top executives to evaluate the performance of various business units. This may prompt the firm to rely exclusively on objective performance indicators for each unit (e.g., return on assets). This may have some serious drawbacks (see Chapter 9).

2. The greater the distance between individual inputs and the level at which performance is assessed, the more tenuous is the perceived effect of employees' personal contributions to overall performance and rewards based upon it. Thus, the motivational effect of an incentive system tends to be diluted as the performance level becomes more aggregate.

3. The more interdependent the various units of the firm are, the more difficult it is to identify the contributions of a given unit. For instance, it is demoralizing to workers and managers if their unit's performance is low, thereby affecting their pay. However, this may be attributed to other units that "did not come through" (e.g., suppliers, sales).

4. When utilizing only division performance as a measuring rod to distribute rewards, the corporation loses synergy. It may have less influence over its business units than desired and loses control over how pay should be allocated. At the other extreme, relying strictly on corporate performance allows some divisional managers and employees to receive undeserved rewards.

5. It may be important for a corporation to use headquarter staff as

an integrative force involved in decisions affecting corporate performance. Costs can be reduced by centralizing functions under one umbrella. In these conditions, division performance is not totally under the control of divisional managers since it reflects the contributions of corporate involvement.

6. Because employee knowledge of products is unique at each location, the corporation may be unable to transfer employees between headquarters and the division.

Firms that have narrow and relatively stable product market domains and are vertically integrated base pay on corporate performance (Gomez-Mejia and Welbourne, 1988). Because corporate staff is involved in decisions that impact division performance, performance assessment among all divisions should reflect the effectiveness of the corporate role. In other words, financial indicators of performance for each unit partly reflect the contributions of headquarters. Because division performance is only partially the responsibility of divisional managers, it should not be used exclusively to distribute rewards among them.

According to Kerr (1995); Leontiades (1980); Gerhart (2000); Wright, Gardner, and Moynihan (2003); and others, division performance is the appropriate unit of analysis for pay purposes among firms that expand through acquisitions. Acquired firms remain relatively independent of the acquirer, and division performance is a more meaningful indicator of unique contributions to overall corporate wealth. Reliance on division performance also enhances an entrepreneurial climate within each unit and prevents managers accustomed to autonomy from moving into other firms when a takeover occurs. Another reason for using division performance for these firms is that the product knowledge of employees is unique at each location. Therefore, the corporation is not concerned with transferring employees between headquarters and the division.

External versus Internal Equity

This compensation strategy dimension concerns the extent to which the organization places more emphasis on meeting market prices for labor, *external equity,* than maintaining consistency in the pay structure, *internal equity.* Quite often these two objectives are at odds with each other. For example, internal equity dictates that assistant professors in business administration be paid less than associate or full professors who have a longer publication record and more seniority. However, because salaries of assistant professors have skyrocketed in recent years, many business schools have opted for matching or exceeding market rates when recruiting at this level. However, the pay of senior faculty already on board has increased at a modest pace. The end result of this policy is *pay compression* and, in many instances, *pay inversion.*

According to Newman and Floersch (2008, p. 171), "companies always wrestle with external and internal equity issues." The choice of external versus internal equity has strategic relevance for a number of reasons. First, employers must balance the desire to be fair to current employees with the need to cope with going rates in the labor market to recruit high-quality employees (Milkovich and Newman, 2009). Also, the employer may make a "triage" decision. That is, it must decide which employee group's pay will be adjusted upward to keep up with external rates and which one will be allowed to lag behind the market based on its relative importance to the firm (Claes, 2008). Ideally, of course, all jobs should be paid at or above market, but this is seldom feasible given cost constraints. Second, the traditional, lockstep compensation system based on job evaluation gives a high priority to pay relationships within the firm. Unfortunately, these systems often have difficulty adjusting to a rapidly changing economic environment (Weinberger, 2007).

Thus, firms often find themselves caught in a dilemma. They either emphasize consistency and predictability, using job evaluation at the expense of maneuverability, or utilize a flexible-adaptive approach that provides managers with the ability to respond to market jolts yet face the risk of an anarchical pay structure that leads to increased costs and lower employee loyalty. Part of the danger here is that greater pay flexibility may be associated with perceptions of unfairness. In the words of Howard and Dougherty (2004, p. 43):

> Some reward strategies may affect employee attitudes concerning pay satisfaction, pay fairness and organizational commitment in ways that run counter to strategic intentions. If people are either dissatisfied with their pay or feel unfairly paid, they are less likely to respond favorably to any attempt to motivate them.

In this regard, it is interesting to note the empirical findings of Weber and Rynes (1991). While firms that emphasize internal equity place less weight on market survey data than those that emphasize external equity,

> The former did not place more emphasis on job evaluation. Put another way, internally oriented respondents were distinguished more by their reluctance to act on market data . . . than by any tendency to place greater emphasis on job evaluation per se. The reluctance of internally oriented managers to cut

pay when market rates were lower than their firm's current rates resulted in their paying more on the average than externally oriented managers. This result suggests that having an internal orientation may be an expensive proposition if it prevents a firm from taking advantage of lower competitive rates in an external market (p. 107).

The extent to which divisions are autonomous or dependent may make a difference on the relative emphasis placed on external versus internal equity. If autonomous, external equity is the main concern. The opposite would be true for dependent divisions (Gomez-Mejia and Welbourne, 1988). The more linkages, interactions, and interdependencies that exist among various units, the more important it is to maintain internal pay consistency. Employees' frame of reference transcends the boundaries of any particular unit. If there is minimal interface among various units, then each is less restricted by a concern for consistency and freer to pursue its own market policy.

Another factor likely to influence the emphasis on internal versus external equity is the technological intensity of the firm (Saura-Diaz and Gomez-Mejia, 1997; Yuen, 1990; Tremblay and Chenevert, 2008). In the words of Tremblay and Chenevert:

> Designing a pay structure often requires both a detailed analysis of jobs and a job evaluation system. This traditional approach, described as bureaucratic and rigid, should be more appropriate and effective in organizations that operate in stable technological and general environments . . . a strategy heavily oriented toward internal equity hinders and constrains the decision-making process and creates multiple bureaucratic structures. In contrast, technology-intensive organizations must be sufficiently agile and flexible to rapidly respond to several factors such as personnel shortages, intense competition in recruiting technical specialists, and substantial wage fluctuations in the market. (2008, p. 4)

Hierarchical versus Egalitarian

The hierarchical versus egalitarian strategic pay dimension concerns whether the firm allows a wide cross section of the workforce to partake in the same reward system or a differential reward structure is established by organizational level and/or employee group. For example, the number of management levels eligible to receive bonuses or long-term income may range from only the CEO in some firms down to line supervisors in other companies. Some firms develop elaborate pay incentives for specific employee groups (such as R&D; Makri, 2008) while others make these accessible to all employees (Franco-Santos, 2008).

The strategic importance of this issue is attributed to a number of factors. First, if pay and perquisites are closely linked to upward mobility, this tends to produce a traditional organizational hierarchy based on a pecking order. Employees develop a corresponding expectation as to what it takes to succeed in the organization. While performance may play a role in this process, time on the job is frequently the main predictor of upward mobility (Buchenroth, 2006; Lawler, 1989; Medoff and Abraham, 1980; Ronan and Organt, 1973). If the firm instead deemphasizes the traditional differentials between job grades, allows individuals to increase earnings without moving into management, and minimizes status-related perquisites, an egalitarian atmosphere is more likely to emerge. This, in turn, can influence the organization's culture. According to Hambrick and Snow (1989) and Kerr and Slocum (1987, 2005), the hierarchical pay structure engenders a "clan" type of culture. This means that an organization is held together not so much by a system of labor contracts or "tit for tat" exchanges as by a set of common values, norms, and beliefs and intense socialization into the firm's culture. An *egalitarian pay system,* on the other hand, produces more of a "market" type of culture. The relationship between firm and individual is strictly contractual, and there is less expectation of a long-term commitment. A second strategic implication of this pay policy choice is that use of an egalitarian approach may allow companies to deploy the workforce into new areas, projects, or positions without changes in formal grade levels. However, this may be done at the expense of a stable workforce (Milkovich, 1988).

A *hierarchical pay structure* is more prevalent among mature firms that focus efforts on harvesting current market share and are satisfied with their existing profit levels (Gomez-Mejia and Welbourne, 1988). At the opposite end, companies that aggressively try to expand their market share, willingly take risks, and heavily invest in new ventures and product areas are more likely to follow a more egalitarian pay pattern.

Pay Dispersion versus Pay Homogeneity

More recent literature has focused on horizontal pay dispersion, that is, variance in pay within ranks or within jobs. Perhaps this is a reflection of a growing practice called broadbanding, whereby job grades are collapsed into fewer grades. This leads to greater differentials in pay for individuals holding the same job title (Gomez-Mejia and Sanchez-Marin, 2006). Most of the empirical work on this issue has been conducted in the top executive ranks, perhaps because the data is more easily available for this group (see Chapter 5).

As a whole, this literature suggests that horizontal pay dispersion is dysfunctional for the firm since it engenders feelings of inequity (Wade, O'Reilly, and Pollock, 2006; Cannella and Holcomb, 2005; Devers et al. 2007). This is more likely to be a serious problem when there is high interdependence across individuals under a particular job title who are presumed to have the same level of responsibility (Siegel and Hambrick, 2005). However, much research remains to be done on this issue. Less dispersion could also present a problem if, in fact, greater dispersion is justified. For instance, academic departments in research universities tend to have high pay dispersion among faculty of the same rank. Artificially reducing that dispersion may lead to the loss of star faculty to competing institutions. The crucial question is to what extent pay dispersion may be legitimized based on the demonstrable inputs of individual contributors. Otherwise, perceptions of pay unfairness may ensue, particularly among key contributors who are precisely the kinds of employees the firm cannot afford to lose.

Qualitative versus Quantitative Performance Measures

Next to the short-term versus long-term issue, the qualitative versus quantitative strategic pay choice receives the most attention in the literature (Franco-Santos, 2008). The central concern here is the extent to which criteria used to reward employees, particularly executives, are derived from an objective, outcome-oriented, formula-based numerical index or, alternatively, are based on subjective assessments, inferential judgments, or other qualitative strategic, political, and organizational factors (see Chapter 9). The literature suggests that, on the one hand, difficulty of monitoring tasks leads to greater use of quantitative performance measures, yet, on the other hand, a greater need to foster innovation leads to the greater use of qualitative performance measures (Makri, Lane, and Gomez-Mejia, 2006; Makri, 2008).

A relatively large body of research has evolved around the question of how much influence the degree of corporate diversification has on the use of quantitative versus qualitative measures of performance. This literature pertains mostly to managerial pay. (This literature is reviewed in greater detail in Chapters 4, 5, and 6.) The purported relationship is: As the corporate portfolio expands, the more dissimilar the business units become. Corporate executives are less able to control diverse business units because they cannot understand or accurately interpret idiosyncratic data unique to each unit. As a result, highly diversified companies rely on objective, formula-based, quantitative indicators of performance (such as market share and return on investment) for pay purposes. Requiring very little subjective judgment or interpretation on the part of corporate executives, pay is comparable among subunits. Low diversity is associated with superior knowledge of business units' operation. Corporate management is therefore more likely to make judgment decisions and formulate performance expectations based on many factors (e.g., changes in environmental conditions, product characteristics) as opposed to relying exclusively on quantitative formulas. In the words of Frederikson, Hambrick, and Baumrin (1988, p. 257), the performance judgment for each business unit of a less diversified firm may be shaped by "beliefs about what constitutes good performance, an awareness of other firms' performance levels, beliefs about the severity of particular organizational problems or symptoms, and attributions regarding top management's ability to alter the firm's performance."

As empirical evidence strongly suggests, more diversified firms generally rely on output controls, while less diversified companies rely on behavioral and process controls. Berg (1969, 1973) reported that in conglomerates, corporate control was carried out by linking rewards of division managers to quantitative financial measures of their units. Very little discretion was exercised by corporate executives in passing judgment on how well the individual was actually managing the division. Apart from whether corporate executives could make meaningful judgments about businesses of which they may know little, Berg reported another rationale for relying on quantitative results. By not making executives of acquired divisions dependent on corporate headquarters, independence and entrepreneurship are fostered. Berg also implied that this serves to retain managers, who are used to high autonomy, in the acquired businesses.

Lorsch and Allen (1973) examined compensation practices of two conglomerates and one vertically integrated firm. They noted several important differences. Conglomerates relied almost exclusively on financial results and formula-based approaches to distribute rewards among division managers. Vertically integrated firms, on the other hand, associated a division manager's compensation with the performance of the entire corporation and used the superiors' subjective evaluation process to arrive at bonus amounts. Bonuses involved inferential assessments and judgment calls not tied to predetermined indices.

Pitts (1974, 1976) found similar results to those of Lorsch and Allen. Firms that had grown through aggressive acquisition of unrelated businesses were more likely to rely on objective, formula-based approaches to reward division managers. Pitts contrasted these to firms that had diversified slowly through internal expansion. Among the latter group, the corporation's performance was also considered when calculating the division manager's bonus. The process was largely subjective and involved significant interaction between the division manager and corporate executives.

Using a sample of 22 firms, Kerr (1995) indicates that diversification also plays a major role in whether a firm uses objective or subjective procedures to determine pay. Firms that grow by increased penetration of existing markets or by diversifying into closely related markets rely on subjective evaluations. Top executives have had a chance to absorb changes slowly and learn the way different units operate. A benefit of this approach, according to Kerr (1995, p. 251), is that "the practice of cross-fertilization and the emphasis on corporate rather than individual performance promotes a systemic perspective in managers . . . requiring careful consideration of interdependencies and system-wide consequences of decisions." More recent research using agency theory suggests that diversification increases information asymmetries between corporate headquarters and business units. This makes it more difficult to monitor the business units subjectively; and, hence, there is greater reliance on objective performance indicators (Franco-Santos, 2008).

In short, these studies suggest that as diversification increases:

1. Quantitative indices are used to appraise managerial performance.
2. Objective formulas are used to determine pay allocation to various units.
3. Performance measures are more likely based on subunit performance rather than on corporate results. Furthermore, the process of diversification also has an effect on how much a firm relies on subjective versus objective formulas.

Napier and Smith (1987) reported on data that disagreed with those of other researchers. This data showed that less diversified firms use more objective pay criteria for payment of managers. According to Milkovich (1988), the discrepancy may be explained by the fact that earlier studies focused on business unit general managers only, whereas Napier and Smith (1987) focused on a more heterogeneous group of corporate-level managers. In any case, the preponderance of evidence to date suggests that diversification and the use of objective data go hand in hand. Apparently, this is not always true.

At the business unit level, firms that are aggressive in exploring new market opportunities and those at an early developmental stage should rely on subjective performance measures. Firms not sharing those characteristics should emphasize objective performance criteria to distribute rewards (Carroll, 1987; Kerr and Kren, 1982). Two reasons are given for this recommendation. First, a subjective assessment process of performance is more appropriate when managers are expected to act as entrepreneurs. Quantifiable performance measures are difficult to find for this group, are very crude, such as "meeting business plan on schedule," and generally not very meaningful. Therefore, subjective judgments are more appropriate. Second, for mature firms trying to maintain secure positions in relatively stable product or service areas, objective data is more readily available, particularly for publicly traded companies where stock price may be used as a barometer of market performance (Fama and Jensen, 1983a, b). In addition, the performance of these firms is less susceptible to dramatic fluctuations, and more predictable formula-based compensation packages may be implemented. While focused on the CEO rather than divisional managers, Caranikas-Walker and colleagues (2008) made a similar argument and found some empirical support for these assertions.

Assembling the Compensation Package

The next subset of compensation strategy dimensions concerns the design choices that face the firm when assembling a compensation package. Choices of market positioning, pay mix, reinforcement schedules, and the relative emphasis placed on monetary versus nonmonetary rewards are discussed.

Compensation Level versus Market

The extent to which the firm's total compensation package, including salary, incentives, and benefits, exceeds that of its competition is referred to as "compensation level versus market dimension." This is a critical strategic pay choice for many reasons.

First, compensation level is an important determinant of pay satisfaction, which is in turn one of the best predictors of employee attrition (Lawler, 1981; Gerhart and Rynes, 2003; Gomez-Mejia, 1985; Gomez-Mejia and Balkin, 1984a; Ronan and Organt, 1973; Rynes, Gerhart, and Parks, 2005; Weiner, 1980). Likewise, pay level is one of the most important factors potential recruits consider when selecting alternative employment opportunities (Rynes, 1987; Brown and York, 2008). Thus, the amount of total compensation received by employees relative to other opportunities they may have has a clear effect on attraction and retention.

Second, a firm may choose to lead the market either across the board or only for highly targeted employee groups. The former is likely to enhance a firm's ability to recruit new hires and to reduce attrition throughout the entire organization. It can also create a climate where employees feel that they are part of an elite group. "Blue chip" companies, such as 3M, IBM, and Procter & Gamble, are well known for following this strategy. On the other hand, an organization may deliberately decide to be clearly ahead of the competition in total pay for some employee groups while staying at or below market for others. This is an important strategic decision that explicitly recognizes the importance of certain groups, even if it discriminates against others.

For example, smaller, high-technology organizations heavily channel their pay dollars toward R&D employees and drain resources from other departments such as production and marketing (Coombs and Gomez-Mejia, 1991; Tremblay and Chenevert, 2008). Likewise, as noted earlier, some universities may decide to pay substantially above market for certain faculty groups, while barely meeting the minimum pay requirements to attract and retain mediocre faculty in other areas. This practice shows favoritism to employee groups that the organization feels can make a greater contribution to its "core technology" or mission.

Third, organizations entering periods of decline are obviously concerned with labor costs. In this situation, establishments usually slow down the rate of pay increases or may even seek pay concessions. This may work in the short run as a cost-saving device for "internal employees that are partially sheltered from the vagaries of the external market . . . [and] may be tolerated if for no other reason than ignorance of the market rate" (Newman, 1988, p. 199). According to Newman (1988), declining organizations must place an extreme value upon high-quality monitoring of the environment. "Consequently, reward systems designed for these groups must be particularly attuned to, competitive with, external market wages" (p. 205).

Fourth, pay level should be associated with the level of risk, although two contending forces may be at work here. The more aggressive firms, those which continually seek new product and market opportunities, require employees to take more risks. Therefore, high base pay relative to competitors should be offered to those employees to compensate the higher risks incurred (Carroll, 1987). On the other hand, growing firms making riskier business decisions (such as those in the high-technology sector) may offer a lower base salary relative to the market and (as will be discussed later) offer greater incentives in pay mix to minimize fixed costs (Balkin and Gomez-Mejia, 1987a, 1990; Saura-Diaz and Gomez-Mejia, 1997; Tremblay and Chenevert, 2008).

While economic theory predicts that "below-market salaries" is not a tenable long-term policy since employees would migrate to other firms, the evidence as to the real effect of this policy is unclear. This is in part because the market itself is a matter of subjective definition (as noted in Chapter 1). In the words of Weinberger (2007, p. 42):

Historically, compensation professionals have supposed the market price of a position to be the absolute standard for defining its value. The prevailing view holds that profound human resource consequences will ensue when the salary rate for a position varies from market average; that is, a rate deficit is presumed to occasion employee turnover and impede recruitment. However, the market rate sensitivity of individual employees is often uncertain. Despite the elevated staffing risk associated with a market lag in salary, it is far from inevitable that a company will fail to secure the desired quantity or quality of employees for a position. Owing to personal (e.g., unwillingness to relocate) and job-related circumstances (e.g., company culture), it is hard to predict the propensity of employees to pursue, let alone be aware of, higher paid positions outside the company. For any individual, the "market" is an abstraction that has little valence unless made tangible as a viable employment alternative.

Fixed Pay versus Incentives

Fixed pay versus incentives is another compensation strategy dimension that has received much attention in the literature. Organizations face a choice between paying employees the same amount on a predictable basis (e.g., monthly paycheck) or providing a substantial portion of an employee's income on a variable basis. The latter choice is pegged to ups and downs of preestablished performance criteria. Variable compensation comes in a wide variety of forms, such as individual bonuses, team bonuses, gain sharing, profit sharing, and literally hundreds of stock ownership programs. Based on a sample of 16,000 managers across 200 firms, Gerhart and Milkovich (1990, p. 664) report that "organizations distinguish themselves through decisions about pay contingency or variability rather than through decisions about the level of base pay." The proportion of pay that is variable has continued to increase during the past decade, both in the United States and elsewhere, perhaps as a reflection of global hypercompetition (Richards, 2006; Sanchez-Marin, 2008a,b).

As shown in Chapters 4 through 6, much of this concern is in the area of executive compensation. At the top executive rank, providing only half of the individual's compensation on a salary basis is not unusual. The remainder usually comes in the form of bonuses and long-term income intended to tie the executive's personal fortune to that of stockholders. Likewise, heavy reliance on variable pay is common in sales environments where commissions are used in lieu of behavioral monitoring or direct supervision. In recent years, however risk sharing has been extended to a broader set of employee groups, particularly when the payoff of their work to the firm is uncertain, direct supervision is ineffective, and work outcomes are long term. Reliance on variable compensation for R&D employees, for example, serves to key their attention toward the development of commercial applications, rather than pure research per se, and used to strengthen R&D team cooperation through the generous dispensation of team-based bonuses (Welbourne and Gomez-Mejia, 1991). Tenure long-term incentives are also heavily utilized in the high-technology industry to bond able scientists and engineers to the firm (Gomez-Mejia, Balkin, and Milkovich, 1990; Milkovich, Gerhart, and Hannon 1991; Saura-Diaz and Gomez-Mejia, 1997; Tremblay and Chenenert, 2008). (The major types of performance-contingent pay policies are reviewed and critiqued in Chapter 10.)

The risk-sharing concept in compensation has also been applied across organizations (see, for example, Gomez-Mejia, Welbourne and Wiseman, 2000; Werner, Tosi, and Gomez-Mejia, 2005). This is partly a function of a firm's life cycle and strategies. Firms facing financial constraints, such as companies supported by venture capital, try to improve their position in the relevant labor market by influencing employees' perception of *future* income stream. If they are successful in creating employees' *anticipatory* feelings, the company may recruit and retain high-talent employees without tying up the firm's scarce cash (Gomez-Mejia and Balkin, 1985). For instance, employees may be willing to work for a fledgling firm at very low wages because they have faith that if the business succeeds they could become millionaires. Business failures far outstrip successes, but such optimism may be enough, particularly among younger employees, to delay immediate gratification in hopes of high long-term returns.

In other words, firms that are hungry for cash while expanding their market share prefer to offer low salaries while adding to the incentive component of the pay mix (Saura-Diaz and Gomez-Mejia, 1997). This gives them more flexibility to shift resources into growth areas and keep the lid on fixed expenses. In turn, employees are willing to accept higher risks if these are perceived to be associated with opportunities for larger incomes. Stable firms that operate in a mature market offer employees more security and a higher salary plus benefits but lower probabilities of earning large incentives via bonuses or equity sharing (Balkin and Gomez-Mejia, 1984, 1986, 1990; Salscheider, 1981). Some recent literature suggests that treating all incentive pay as "variable" may obfuscate more than clarify the meaning of pay at risk (Devers et al. 2008; Cruz, Gomez-Mejia, and Becerra, 2010; Gomez-Mejia, Larraza-Kintana, and Makri, 2003; Wiseman and Gomez-Mejia, 1998). The reason for this is that incentive plans vary widely in the amount of risk involved depending on target difficulty, environmental uncertainty, criteria used to distribute the award, downside versus upside potential, and performance sensitivity.

Frequency of Rewards

This pay strategy dimension refers to the reinforcement schedule used by organizations to distribute rewards. Each firm faces a choice as to how often rewards should be distributed and how chronologically close they should be to desired behaviors (e.g., meeting agreed-upon deadlines). The choices derive from the traditional reinforcement perspective. To promote desired behaviors, rewards should be closely tied to actual accomplishments. Further, the schedule of reinforcement has a profound effect on how long a newly learned behavior persists before it regresses to former behavior patterns during periods when rewards are unavailable (such as when budgets are cut). As noted by Rubenfeld and David (2006, p. 36), "the frequency and timing of an incentive plan's payout should be logically sequenced with the completion of the criteria. Motivation theory suggests that rewarding employees soon after the completion of a task strengthens the link between the desired performance and the reward, making it more likely that employees will work toward achieving the desired performance now and in the future."

At an individual level, the frequency and magnitude of reinforcement and whether it is variable or continuous is less important from a motivational standpoint than rewards that are contingent on the achievement of specific goals (Frisch and Dickinson, 1990; Latham and Dossett, 1978; Gerhart and Rynes, 2003). This literature suggests that noncontingent rewards have little effect on an individual's behavior. The drawback inherent with contingent rewards, however, is that individuals may be tempted to maximize goals that will trigger the rewards but ignore other important aspects of the job (Mahoney, 1989).

At a more macro level, the use of continuous interval-reinforcement schedules such as Christmas bonuses and merit pay raises encourage a short-term perspective, while a variable interval-reinforcement schedule based on deferred compensation may foster long-term orientation (Carroll, 1987; Kerr and Kren, 1982). Whether this is good or bad may depend on the firm's strategy. There is disagreement as to whether continuous reinforcement schedules should be used by firms with a high need for cost efficiency and a number of unstable tasks (Gomez-Mejia and Welbourne, 1988). This confusion reflects different opinions about whether short- or long-term goals are most relevant for each type of firm (empirical research here is almost nil).

Monetary versus Nonmonetary Rewards

There is a large volume of research dating back to the 1800s that investigates whether monetary or nonmonetary rewards are more important to employees (see classic review by Opsahl and Dunnette, 1966). As the name implies, *monetary rewards* involve tangible cash or benefit payment to employees such as merit pay adjustments, annual bonuses, employee stock ownership plans, and so on. *Nonmonetary rewards* are of an intangible nature, such as employment security, recognition, employee involvement in decision making, increased responsibility, and gift exchanges (e.g., Adams, 1991; Booth, Park, and Glomb, 2009).

Typically, employees do not rate pay as one of the most important aspects of their jobs. For two primary reasons, there has never been a clear understanding as to what this means to organizations. First, because avarice is a social taboo, there is a social desirability bias in employee responses to pay issues. Therefore, according to Seidman and Skancke (1989, p. 10), "Many employee surveys seem to indicate that money alone is not the best motivator, but it may rank higher than people care to admit to others—or to themselves. In practice, it appears that good old-fashioned cash is as effective as any reward that has yet been invented."

Second, since biblical times, much debate has taken place about the role of money as a motivator. Most HRM practitioners and scholars agree that the way pay dollars are allocated sends a powerful message to all organizational members as to what the firm deems important and the types of activities it encourages. Furthermore, people do those things they perceive will lead to a valued reward. This is just as true for the top executive as it is for the lowest paid worker. Thus, the distinction between monetary and nonmonetary rewards, while obvious at face value, may not hold under close scrutiny. Pay has a deep psychological and symbolic meaning that goes well beyond its purely materialistic value. Furthermore, as noted by Jeffrey and Shaffer (2007, p. 46) nonmonetary incentives "should still be considered extrinsic motivators because they are generally contingent on performance and are provided by a source outside of the individual."

Yet even with these caveats in mind, most organizations do have some choices as to how much emphasis is placed on purely calculative, utilitarian rewards versus a work environment that is interesting, challenging, developmental, and conducive to a moral commitment to the firm. For example, Amway is well known for its heavy reliance on monetary incentives, while Xerox and Texas Instruments have a long-standing reputation for providing intrinsic rewards through employee participation programs and job enrichment (even though they also use performance-based pay incentives) (Gomez-Mejia, Balkin, and Cardy, 2010). Lawler (1984) argues that a firm can acquire a competitive edge if it can provide both financial and intrinsic (e.g., achievement, recognition) rewards to employees. Gomez-Mejia and Balkin (1985; Balkin and Gomez-Mejia, 1985) admit pride in one's work, career advancement, and self-actualization are important rewards. However, "the pot at the end of the rainbow" is a very powerful lure to attract quality employees and keep them highly committed to a particular company. This is particularly true in tight labor markets such as those faced by high-technology firms (Masters and colleagues, 1992; Milkovich, Gerhart, and Hannon, 1991; Saura-Diaz and Gomez-Mejia, 1997).

Hambrick and Snow (1989) argue that the relative emphasis on monetary versus nonmonetary rewards should depend on certain organizational characteristics. According to them, firms that seldom make major adjustments in their technology, structure, or methods of operation should make a concerted attempt to infuse intrinsic rewards whenever possible. The rationale given is that achievement-oriented employees demand excitement, recognition, and responsibility in their jobs. However, there is little glamour associated with this type of firm. Organizations undergoing frequent changes and expansion, researching product and market innovation, and utilizing multiple technologies generally provide those intrinsic rewards because of the very nature of the business. According to Hambrick and Snow, this means that those firms do not have to devote as much attention to work designs that offer intrinsic rewards to attract and retain achievement-oriented employees. Likewise, as noted by Makri (2008), one of the most important rewards for R&D employees is the autonomy and discretion to pursue their own interests. However, this greater freedom tends to be associated with greater earnings, so once again the boundary between monetary and nonmonetary rewards is not clear-cut.

In recent years, companies have instituted family-friendly policies that often involve nonmonetary rewards such as the ability to work from home (telecommuting) and flexible work hours (Mayo et al. 2010). In general, these nonmonetary rewards are most effective when they are congruent with the demographic characteristics of the workforce. For instance, Mayo and colleagues (2010) found that one of the main predictors of telecommuting is the proportion of international employees hired by the firm. But consistent with the point we made earlier, telecommuting is positively correlated with the use of variable compensation. Mayo and colleagues (2010) argue that this happens because of the difficulty of supervising employees at home. Thus, when telecommuting is offered, the incentive system serves as a partial substitute for monitoring. In short, the literature strongly suggests that for nonmonetary incentives to have the desired motivational impact they should be accompanied by financial incentives.

Administering the Compensation System

The last set of compensation strategy dimensions concerns the policies and procedures that govern the organization's pay system. The administrative apparatus is strategically important for two major reasons: First, it provides the context within which compensation decisions are made. If the mechanisms used to distribute rewards conflict with the criteria used for payment or the design of the compensation package, then the effectiveness of the pay system suffers. For example, egalitarian rewards may be more effective in a more decentralized, open, participative system than in a highly centralized, secretive, nonparticipative system.

Second, and building on the previous point, the administrative framework does not exist in isolation from the organization's strategy or environmental forces impacting the firm. The delivery mechanism for the reward system must be designed to facilitate the implementation of a firm's strategy. It must also assist the firm in coping with forces that exist in the external environment.

Third, how the pay system is administered plays a major role in the level of pay satisfaction. This in turn directly affects employee turnover. For example, Dyer and Theriault (1976) found that the inclusion of administration variables in a regression equation more than doubled the explained variance of pay satisfaction over the variance explained, by including a large number of factors such as salary level, job inputs, and perceived job difficulty. Similar results were reported by Weiner (1980). More recently, a great deal of literature dealing with procedural (fairness of the process used to make decisions concerning rewards) and distributive justice (fairness of the amount and allocation of rewards) has suggested that perceived justice in the administration of the pay system is critical in terms of its effect on employee motivation and morale (Meyer, Becker, and Vandenberghe, 2004; Gomez-Mejia, Balkin, and Cardy, 2010; Welbourne, Balkin, and Gomez-Mejia, 1995).

Relatedly, some recent work on ethics suggests that when it comes to compensation administration, integrity on the part of managers is seen as a nonnegotiable value by most employees. Consistency and fairness in how pay is administered reflects whether ethical decisions are truly implemented in practice or the firm just "walks the talk" (Montemayor, 2008). From the perspective of employees, unethical pay practices include arbitrary pay allocations, lack of clear procedures to distribute rewards, and favoritism. All of these may be indicators of poor compensation administration (Gomez-Mejia, Balkin, and Cardy, 2010).

Administrative variables most relevant to compensation strategy are discussed next.

Centralization versus Decentralization

Centralization versus decentralization refers to the degree to which pay decisions and approval procedures are tightly controlled by corporate headquarters or delegated to various plants, divisions, and other subunits within a firm. Lawler (1984) argues that when headquarters can provide expertise that is not available to subunits and when internal equity is an important organizational goal, centralized pay makes the most sense. Miles and Snow (1984) make a similar argument and suggest that centralized pay should be implemented under two conditions.

First, if substantial savings and economies of scale can be realized, pay decisions should be centralized. For example, corporate headquarters can hire a full-fledged compensation department with specialists in job evaluation, salary survey, and benefits. Duplicating these services in various subunits would be prohibitive and inefficient. Second, when the organization is in a sensitive position regarding legislative requirements, administration demands a highly centralized compensation function. This may happen, for example, if an increased number of suits are being brought against a company under Title VII.

Carroll (1987) and Balkin and Gomez-Mejia (1990) note some additional conditions under which centralized pay may be more appropriate. One such condition exists in firms that attempt to protect their market share and business units that try to retain their market position while minimizing costs. Companies following these objectives create a greater bureaucracy as part of their control function, particularly for compensation, which represents on average more than 50 percent of total costs.

On the other hand, decentralized pay works better under some conditions (Gomez-Mejia and Welbourne, 1988). First, decentralization would be more appropriate for large conglomerates in which strategic business units are very heterogeneous in terms of their mission, products, workforce, life cycle, and markets. Because of limited knowledge of local conditions, corporate headquarters cannot make good decisions about pay decisions. As an extreme example, California's state college system established a fixed pay scale for faculty by rank during the 1970s and 1980s. While this did not have much effect on the low-market areas (e.g., the liberal arts), it became a major problem for the high-market areas (e.g., business administration) characterized by high demand and a national shortage of qualified faculty. California colleges resorted to strange practices such as granting full professor status to freshly degreed PhDs in business in an attempt to recruit new faculty (Gomez-Mejia and Balkin, 1987a).

A second condition favoring decentralized pay consists of entrepreneurial, single-product firms that invest in risky ventures. These firms are characterized by informal pay policies, and many compensation contracts are one-of-a-kind deal with individual employees (Gomez-Mejia, Balkin, and Welbourne, 1990). A third condition is the extent to which the firm competes through innovation (Saura-Diaz and Gomez-Mejia, 1997). In the specific case of high-technology firms, Tremblay and Chenevert (2008, p. 8) argue that:

> ... compensation decisions must be considerably decentralized in technology-intensive firms to grant units and their managers the necessary leeway to react quickly and adequately to internal and external labor market pressures (e.g., increased capacity to recruit technical staff, retaining key resources who would otherwise go to competitors). In a turbulent environment such as the high-technology industry, decisions are best made by those most capable of rapidly accessing the necessary information rather than solely by top managers.

One model that has worked reasonably well in many organizations is a local operating compensation function. It assists unit managers in making pay decisions and program implementation. Members of the compensation staff at corporate headquarters act as consultants to the business units. The local unit compensation managers have access to headquarters' expertise, yet they retain the autonomy to make decisions suitable to local conditions.

In recent years, much of the theorizing and research concerning centralization versus decentralization of the pay system concerns international companies operating in multiple countries with different legal systems, cultures, traditions, and institutions (Shelton, 2008; Newman and Floersch, 2008; Balkin, 2008; Salimaki and Heneman, 2008). In a sense, the questions are similar to those posed under corporate diversification, but the answers become far more complex as now there is another layer of contingencies to deal with. Most experts agree that a central compensation staff in corporate headquarters is needed, while at the same time responsiveness to local conditions is paramount as the firm cuts across national boundaries, particularly to culturally distant regions (Giancola, 2007). Hence, a local operating compensation function is needed in most cases. Referring to a recent survey by WorldatWork and Wyatt Consulting of 228 global companies, Salimaki and Heneman (2008, p. 161) conclude that:

> In practice, the results of global compensation practices . . . demonstrate that there is not a single, dominant approach to managing global compensation; companies are evenly split between a centralized (globally integrated) and decentralized (locally responsive) approach to their global compensation

structure (49 percent centralized versus 51 percent decentralized). However, both groups expect to see a growing trend toward greater centralization in the near term. The primary objectives for having a centralized compensation structure are to have a consistent link between rewards and results, and to have a consistent position with regard to market and internal equity. The majority of survey respondents have a uniform approach to short- and long-term incentives and bonuses for executives and management (executives 82–83 percent, management 52–65 percent), while less than half have a uniform global approach for professional employees (35–44 percent).

Open versus Secret Pay

There is relatively extensive literature, most of it appearing in the late 1960s and early 1970s (e.g., Lawler, 1965, 1967), that revolves around the question of how much pay information should be divulged to employees. Interestingly enough, after a long hiatus, this issue has been "rediscovered" in a recent paper published in the *Academy of Management Review* by Collela and colleagues (2007).

Clearly, organizations vary significantly on how much employees know about their coworkers' pay. At one extreme, some firms require all employees to sign an oath, under penalty of termination, that they will not divulge their pay to other employees. At the other extreme, as in the case of most public universities, some organizations make pay information widely available and even publish individual pay data in employee newspapers. The best-known advocate of open pay systems is Edward Lawler (1965, 1967, 1984, 1990), who for years has argued for greater employee access to compensation information. His rationale is that, first and foremost, keeping pay a secret does the organization no good. Employees overestimate the pay of coworkers and superiors, and this leads to greater pay dissatisfaction. Second, he argues, pay secrecy engenders low trust and more dependent employees. According to Lawler, when pay is made public, greater pressure is on management to administer the compensation system more fairly and effectively because its flaws cannot be hidden under a shroud of secrecy.

Limited empirical evidence to date suggests that Lawler's assertions may be true in some situations. However, open pay is not for everyone. Balkin and Gomez-Mejia (1990) report that, based on a survey of a large sample of compensation managers, open pay systems function better in organizations in which the culture emphasizes employee participation and involvement, trust, strong employee commitment, and egalitarianism. The rationale for these findings is that open pay can only lead to constructive dialogue and mutual respect if the organizational context is supportive of and breeds a nurturing, caring employee-relations climate. Otherwise, open pay can actually exacerbate hostilities and conflicts and add fuel to an already volatile situation.

In their conceptual paper, Collela and colleagues (2007) argue that a pay secrecy policy is complex since it involves many choices such as divulging individual pay information, pay ranges or average pay raises, restrictions on how difficult it is to obtain pay data, knowledge about pay amounts versus pay mix and the like. It is seldom an all-or-nothing policy and as it is true of other compensation strategy dimensions, it is best understood along a continuum. According to Collela and colleagues (2007), there are both costs (e.g., conflict potential) and benefits (e.g., fostering transparency in culture) to pay openness; yet not all organizations will experience the costs and benefits to the same degree. In their words:

> This would appear to depend, in part, on the quality of employees, their individual needs and perceptions, and the history of those employees with the employer. Employers can therefore be "profiled" based on their employees in order to predict which of them should choose pay secrecy policies. For example, an organization that has many high-quality employees whom it would like to retain and also has high recruiting and training costs, all else being constant, should be more likely to use pay secrecy than an organization that does not . . . Other employees with different cost/benefit trade-offs should be expected not to employ pay secrecy. An organization with employees having a low need for privacy, but with a history of organizational unfairness and distrust, should not use a pay secrecy policy. For this organization, pay openness could help with perceptions of fairness and trust, as well as potentially improve work motivation and performance. In addition, this organization may prefer to enhance the mobility of its dissatisfied employees and, thus, should prefer pay openness as a way of making outside opportunities more appealing. (pp. 63–66)

Participation versus Nonparticipation

Much has been said about the value of employee participation in organizations, and compensation is no exception. Firms have a great deal of discretion as to how much participation employees are allowed in setting pay policies and distributing rewards.

Several compensation programs are based on the assumption that getting employees involved and rewarding employee suggestions that may improve current methods of operation ultimately enhances firm performance. Most gain-sharing programs, for example, are centered on employee participation and make extensive use of employee committees to generate ideas and suggestions (Welbourne and Gomez-Mejia, 1988; Gomez-Mejia, Welbourne, and Wiseman, 2000). Some team-based incentive systems and profit-sharing plans also rely heavily on inputs from employee committees to distribute rewards (Gomez-Mejia and Balkin, 1989; Gomez-Mejia, Welbourne, and Wiseman, 2000; Welbourne and Gomez-Mejia, 1991).

Despite much lip service paid to the value of employee participation among academics and practitioners alike, a "top-down" approach to pay administration is quite typical. This is particularly true among the vast majority of firms that rely on traditional job evaluation procedures. Management chooses the specific job evaluation system (usually with the help of an external consultant), the compensable factors, methods to link job evaluation results to market data, pay policies, and so on. Likewise, most compensation and pay grievance committees are normally appointed by management.

Gomez-Mejia (1992) found that (as reported by compensation managers) greater employee input is more common in the following types of organizations:

1. Entrepreneurial firms
2. Companies with a large proportion of highly educated professional employees
3. Companies that have faced sudden environmental jolts. For example, computer firms that have lost substantial market share in a short period of time
4. Firms that offer a large proportion of an employee's pay on a variable basis
5. Companies that are willing to implement innovative reward schemes

Low employee participation, on the other hand, fits the traditional bureaucratic compensation approach used by most mature firms.

While the concept is nothing new (e.g., Lawler, 1986), in recent years much attention in compensation circles has been paid to the so-called "high-involvement" organizations, or firms that actively foster employee participation. These firms are characterized by flat organizational structures with product- or customer-focused units rather than functional centers such as marketing, production, and research and development. According to Richards (2006, p. 39):

> Firms with high-involvement philosophies are most likely to introduce compensation strategies that reflect that philosophy. High-involvement

firms typically have team-based rewards, strategies that include variable pay program (skill-based pay, gain sharing, employee ownership), and flexible benefits. Rather than top-down control of information, these pay practices are established through open participative processes including broad input by stakeholders and open information sharing. It is necessary to encourage expertise by transmitting information to employees at the lowest levels of the firm. High-involvement compensation strategies require a culture of information sharing and consultation, enabling greater problem assessment, problem solving and self-directed work across the organization.

Bureaucratic versus Flexible Pay Policies

Bureaucratic versus flexible pay is a crucial strategic decision when designing the administrative apparatus of any pay system. It reflects how tolerant administration is of alternative approaches, the amount of discretion it allows to create exceptions, and the ability it has to make unique judgments depending on the idiosyncrasies of the situation.

Organizations vary widely on this dimension. For example, Gomez-Mejia, Balkin, and Welbourne (1990) found that in many start-up firms, the pay package of managers and other professionals is often decided by entrepreneurs and venture capitalists while they socialize at informal settings and react to their "instincts" or "gut feelings." At the other extreme, in many civil service jurisdictions, an employee's pay is based strictly on job grade, and promotional decisions through the grade hierarchy are made based on test scores and seniority (Gomez-Mejia, 1978). Similarly, some labor contracts are highly regimented, and time on the job is the main determinant of career progression within the firm.

In some cases, managers have a great deal of flexibility in making some pay decisions but very little in others. This creates an interesting dynamic. For example, college deans have a lot of freedom in deciding how much to offer outside applicants. However, deans are limited in allocation of pay among existing faculty. This generally contributes to a severe pay compression problem and attrition by superior faculty. The primary way for a faculty member to substantially improve his or her pay is to move on to other institutions. In fact, Gomez-Mejia and Balkin (1992) found that on average, over a 20-year period, the "future value" of each move to an individual faculty member exceeded $40,000. This is far superior to any merit pay adjustments received during this same period by a faculty member who stays at the same institution.

Bureaucratic pay systems have been criticized for a number of reasons. They prevent managers from making decisions that are most appropriate in a given situation, and they do not allow the organization to adapt the compensation system as the firm's strategic orientation changes (Lawler, 1986, 1990). Balkin and Gomez-Mejia (1990) and Tremblay and Chenevert (2008) found that this criticism is clearly justified for entrepreneurial and rapidly growing firms. However, the situation is not as clear-cut in more established organizations. As firms get larger, more mature and complex, and more entrenched in a given market niche, their natural tendency is to "rationalize" pay decisions by developing procedural mechanisms to systematize pay allocations. For these firms, too much flexibility, ad hoc decisions, and frequent modifications to the pay system can result in a lack of coherent policies. Also, because organizations have long memories, it is difficult to make those changes smoothly without the system losing continuity and credibility (Hambrick and Snow, 1989). The challenge for these firms is to develop systems that are formalized yet flexible enough to allow modifications when necessary (Milkovich and Newman, 2009).

A Holistic Approach to Linking Compensation Choices and Business Strategy

The most common approach represented in the compensation literature is to adopt one of the taxonomies from strategic management and then attempt to delineate a compensation strategy profile that seems to characterize firms within each of the organizational strategy categories. Authors generally provide a list of pay choices that represent an "ideal" compensation type for each strategic grouping (e.g., Broderick, 1986; Fay, 1987; Montemayor, 1996). There are several important assumptions implicit in most of this work that should be pointed out before moving on to Chapter 3, which describes several typologies relevant to strategic compensation choices.

First, it is generally assumed that organizational strategies are causal antecedents to compensation strategies. Thus, the latter, along with other functional strategies, should flow directly from the firm's overall strategy. In the words of Fay (1987, pp. 119–120), "Strategic compensation planning is a derived process, in that its starting point is based on overall organizational goals and objectives. . . . this is because compensation is a tool, and tools rarely are ends in themselves." A similar view is advanced by Milkovich and Newman (2009) and Milkovich and Broderick (1991). Second, as noted earlier, it is possible to find meaningful patterns in a stream of compensation decisions, even if these emerged over time through trial and error.

Third, the observed pay patterns that may have evolved historically are not necessarily the most appropriate ones given the organization's overall strategies.

Current ways of allocating pay and existing compensation policies may be well entrenched, yet these could still be separated from organizational strategies. For example, as noted by Gomez-Mejia, Balkin, and Milkovich (1990), many firms rely on job evaluation procedures for R&D workers, even though "this may foster competition, artificial barriers among people, fragmentation, and an individualistic climate in the work force. These behaviors and culture often run counter to successful R&D environments. A successful R&D operation often requires intense team effort, integration of activities across many individuals, fluid tasks, exchange of knowledge, and minimal status barriers to facilitate interaction among multidisciplinary scientists and engineers working on common problems."

A common reason for separation was alluded to earlier. Compensation professionals are seldom in the strategy-making tier of an organization and are not often regarded as fully participating members of the executive team. Compensation practices are often based on custom, imitation of other firms, administrative convenience, and ad hoc programs developed through narrow functional lenses (Coombs and Rosse, 1992). As a result, the firm may not fully adapt its compensation strategies to organizational strategies, and there may be a tendency to maintain the status quo in the pay system despite significant changes in business strategy and environmental conditions.

Fourth, a notion borrowed from organization theory and the strategy literature is that the effectiveness of the pay system and its contributions to firm performance depend on the cohesion between organizational and compensation strategies (see Chapter 3). Several normative terms are used interchangeably in the literature to denote the degree of alignment between the two. These terms include "congruency," "consistency," "match," and "fit" (e.g., Berger, 1991; Burack, 1988; Devanna, Fombrum, and Tichy, 1981; Rothwell and Kazanas, 1988; Schuler, 1987; Tichy, 1983). In the words of Milkovich (1988), "The degree of fit between compensation strategy and organization strategy contributes to firm performance by signaling and rewarding those behaviors that are consistent with the organization's objectives." This goodness-of-fit premise, derived from contingency approaches to the study of organizations, means that "there is no best way to organize" (Tosi, Rizzo, and Carroll, 1990, p. 15) and "effectiveness at realizing intended strategies depends significantly on the existence of a match between strategies and organization" (Gupta and Govindarajan, 1984, p. 27).

Summary

This chapter has examined the strategic pay choices that have received the most attention in the literature. The choices made for each of these should be attuned to the organization's overall strategic objectives and contingencies affecting the firm. Another central theme throughout this chapter is that each of these dimensions cannot be studied in isolation. They must be viewed in the context of a larger framework where different strategic pay choices interact with each other as well as with organizational and environment forces. While each of the strategic pay choices has been introduced individually in this chapter for the sake of clarity in presentation, these rarely occur as independent entities form strategic groupings or patterns. These composite pay patterns, in turn, are related organizational strategies that are themselves aggregates of many complex, interactive, individual strategic decisions. Chapter 3 examines the composite strategic pay terms emerging from the dimensions discussed here, the taxonomies of corporate and business unit strategies most frequently used to study an organization's strategic orientation, how the strategic pay patterns relate to the corporate and business unit strategic groupings, and the consequences of these linkages subsequent to firm performance.

3 PAY CHOICES AND ORGANIZATIONAL STRATEGIES AS AN INTERRELATED SET OF DECISIONS

The previous chapter examined the key strategic pay choices organizations can choose, as well as the contingency factors and policy implications of those choices. The central thesis of this chapter is that firms seldom make these choices one at a time. Pay choices are not formulated in a vacuum. They are affected by internal and external contextual factors that require distinctive pay mechanisms. Moreover, these pay choices are an interrelated set of decisions that evolve into common patterns or themes. Likewise, the organizational strategies driving these pay choices also form strategic groupings.

While compensation policies and practices differ widely across organizations, creating and using generic compensation and organizational strategies in both research and practice offer several benefits. First, generic strategies capture the essential commonalities of individual, situation-specific strategies and enhance our understanding of broader strategic patterns. Second, they provide a basis for making systemic decisions that are internally consistent yet comprehensive in nature. They may be used to allocate resources and formulate pay policies among diverse subsidiaries and divisions in complex organizations, as well as within a given business unit. Third, taxonomic efforts may be of value to practitioners by reducing a large number of variables to a manageable model of the situation, which reduces any unwarranted variability of strategic actions. Fourth, in addition to simplifying the vast array of variables a researcher must consider, a typology has the advantage of providing gestalt. That is, each type within a taxonomy reflects a holistic combination of interacting attributes.

Following this vein of thought, this chapter examines strategic pay choices and organizational strategies at a higher level of aggregation. First, the overall strategic compensation patterns resulting from the intercorrelation of the pay choices presented in Chapter 2 are discussed. Next, the major taxonomies used to classify firms into strategic groupings are described. We later discuss the relationship between pay choices that fit with the strategic patterns described here. This material provides a foundation for further examination of how pay schemes vary as a function of firms' strategic groupings and how their interaction, in turn, affects firm performance (this issue is discussed in Chapter 5).

Internally Consistent Pay Strategies

This chapter deals with the issue of the fit between organizational characteristics and pay practices. The ultimate dependent variable when making strategic pay choices is organizational performance and, despite the wealth of research that focuses on the link between pay and performance, results are often disappointing. This line of research is more popularly known as "pay-performance-sensitivity" research (Gomez-Mejia and Wiseman, 1997) and it has been based on neoclassical tradition in economics and agency formulations. A positive relationship between executive compensation and firm economic performance would be consistent with the predictions of agency theory. This is the dominant theoretical framework in this stream of research and will be discussed at length in Chapter 4. According to its arguments, pay-for-performance rewards to managers are meant to align the interest of the manager with those of the shareholder (Fama and Jensen 1983a,b; Jensen and Meckling, 1976) since these rewards provide incentives to managers to initiate strategies that boost future economic performance (Eisenhardt, 1989). The positive link between executive pay and firm results captures the notion that managers are compensated for their contribution to the firm.

However, the large body of empirical literature surrounding this relationship has only provided mixed results. For instance, studies by Larner (1970), Masson (1971), Hirschey and Pappas (1981), Murphy (1985), and Deckop (1988), among others, found positive and significant relationships between executive compensation and firm performance. More recently, some authors have reported correlations as high as 0.61 (Boyd, 1994) or 0.41 between CEO pay and Return on Equity (ROE) (Belliveau, O'Really, and Wade, 1996). Some others have reported positive correlation between ROE and specific components of executives' total compensation. For instance, Douglas and Santarre (1990) calculated a correlation of 0.36 between ROE and cash compensation, similar to the 0.365 of Winfrey (1990). Gerhart (2000) reviewed selected articles between 1990 and 1998 and found that most of the studies provided evidence that firm performance was higher when some sort of pay-for-performance plan was used. At the opposite extreme, Meeks and Whittington (1975), Kerr and Bettis (1987), and Garen (1994) found very little or no relationship at all between executive pay and profit. Low and even negative correlations between these two constructs were found, ranging from −0.03 (Finkelstein and Boyd, 1998) to −0.193 (Kroll, Theorathorn, and Wright, 1993). Jensen and Murphy, the authors of what is perhaps the biggest study in the field (1990a), which considered a total of 10,400 CEO years of compensation and performance data, indicated disappointment for the low pay-for-performance sensitivity found. Their finding indicated that for every thousand-dollar change in firm value, the CEO's salary changed by only 2 cents. In a more recent meta-analytic review, Tosi and colleagues (2000) tested the relationship between firm size, performance, and CEO compensations. Results of this study indicated that firm size accounted for more than 40 percent of the variance in total CEO pay, while firm performance explained less than 5 percent of the variance.

As a whole, firm economic performance has appeared to be weakly linked to executive compensation (Gomez-Mejia and Balkin, 1992; Tosi et al. 2000) (see Chapter 5). Final conclusions have been so elusive that the failure to identify a robust relationship between executive compensation and firm performance has led Gomez-Mejia (1994) to compare this relationship to the search for the Holy Grail, leading researchers into a "blind alley" (Barkema and Gomez-Mejia, 1998).

To unravel this situation, some scholars made a call for a contextual and contingency analysis of the links between organizational features and executive compensation in order to make relevant contributions to the field (Barkema and Gomez-Mejia, 1998; Gomez-Mejia, 1994; Gomez-Mejia and Wiseman, 1997). As a result, scholars have recently begun to examine more proximal and direct behavioral outcomes of compensation instead of just financial results (what Baysinger and Hoskisson [1990], refer to as strategic controls).

Unfortunately, research in this area is still limited and major questions about alignment and fit remain largely unanswered. Despite the almost nine decades of executive pay research, it was not until the late 1980s that the first comprehensive review of compensation strategy literature appeared. In their review, Milkovich, Gerhart, and Hannon (1991) indicated that research on this issue had not kept up with its importance. Milkovich highlighted that policies and practices differ significantly between firms and across employee cohorts within organizations, although evidence regarding these differences is mostly anecdotal and sporadic. These differences indicate that managers have the discretion to choose from an array of pay policies (see Berrone and Otten [2008] for a discussion on this issue). That is, the pay policies are affected not only by environmental factors such as industry, technology, size, and the like but also by the preferences of those who set up these policies.

To fully understand this issue it is important to realize that strategic pay choices seldom occur in isolation; rather, they tend to form meaningful clusters or patterns. This means firms choose multiple pay strategies that are internally consistent. In his original review, Milkovich concluded that "the effects of compensation strategy and the degree of its 'fit' with organization strategy on performance remains unplowed turf. Considering the elusiveness of the notion of the 'degree of fit,' it seems like risky research." However, Gomez-Mejia and colleges challenged this statement and conducted several studies regarding fit.

Two separate analyses, one heuristic (Gomez-Mejia and Welbourne, 1988) and one empirical (Gomez-Mejia and Balkin, 1992), strongly suggest that pay choices evolve into two distinct patterns. Furthermore, firms that adopt a particular compensation strategy within each of these patterns also make other related pay choices germane to that pattern.

The first study (Gomez-Mejia and Welbourne, 1988), reviewed 18 different papers on compensation strategy issues during a 15-year period (1973–1988). By subjectively recording and sorting compensation strategy dimensions postulated by various authors, they were able to extract two underlying patterns. The first one, labeled *mechanistic*, "reflects formalized rules and procedures that routinize pay decisions and are applied uniformly across the entire organization" (p. 181). The second pattern, labeled *organic*, consists of "pay practices that are more responsive to varying conditions, contingencies, and individual situations" (p. 183).

A more powerful statistical study by Gomez-Mejia (1992) used actual data from 243 firms on their pay choices, which were based on managerial responses to a battery of 48 items. A factor analysis of that data again suggested that two major strategic compensation patterns emerged in which most firms fall somewhere between the two poles, labeled *experiential* and *algorithmic*. In short, algorithmic strategies emphasize mechanistic, predetermined, standardized, repetitive procedures whereas the experiential pattern is flexible and adaptive. These two patterns are profiled in Table 3.1. The subscales defining each of the compensation strategy dimensions and the factors on which they correlate are shown in Table 3.2.

Algorithmic Pay Pattern

The first pattern in Table 3.1 is designated *algorithmic* because the main emphasis is on the use of predetermined, standardized, repetitive procedures

Table 3.1

Summary Profile of Experiential and Algorithmic Compensation Patterns

	Compensation Strategy	
	Algorithmic	Experiential
Basis for Pay		
Unit of analysis	Job	Skills
Criteria for pay increases	Tenure	Performance
Level of performance measurement	Individual	Individual and aggregate
Time orientation	Short-term	Long-term
Risk sharing	Low	High
Strategic focus	Corporate	Division and business unit
Equity concern	Internal consistency	Market driven
Reward distribution	Hierarchical	Egalitarian
Type of control	Monitor of behaviors	Monitor of outcomes
Design Issues		
Salary market policy	Above-market pay	Below-market pay
Benefits market policy	Above-market benefits	Below-market benefits
Incentives in pay mix	Low	High
Total compensation	Low future potential with higher immediate payoffs	High future potential with lower immediate payoff
Reinforcement schedule	Fewer rewards with low frequency	Multiple rewards with high frequency
Reward emphasis	Nonmonetary	Pecuniary
Administrative Framework		
Decision making	Centralized pay	Decentralized pay
Pay disclosure	Low	High
Governance structure	Authoritarian	Participative
Nature of pay policies	Bureaucratic	Flexible
Superior dependency	High	Low

Source: Based on the research of Gomez-Mejia (1992).

that can be used to process pay decisions with minimal attention to mitigating circumstances, exceptions to the rule, and external contingency factors. The key distinguishing features of the algorithmic pay pattern are as follows:

1. Heavy reliance on traditional job evaluation procedures
2. Seniority as an important criterion in pay adjustments
3. A short-term performance orientation with appraisals conducted at the individual, rather than group, level
4. Minimal risk sharing between employees and the firm

Table 3.2

Compensation Elements Associated with the Algorithmic and Experiential Pay Patterns

Basis for Pay	Strategic Compensation Pattern
Jobs vs. Skills	
Firm uses a job-based pay system. That is, factors within the job are key determinants of the amount of pay.	Algorithmic
Company relies on a skill-based pay system. That is, individuals are rewarded in part on their mastery of job skills.	Experiential
The job is a more important factor than an incumbent's ability or performance in the determination of pay rates. Heavy emphasis is placed on job evaluation procedures to determine pay levels.	Algorithmic
Performance Emphasis	
Firm has a strong commitment to distribute rewards based upon contributions to organization.	Experiential
There is a large pay spread between low performers and high performers in a given job.	Experiential
An employee's seniority plays an important role in pay decisions.	Algorithmic
Individual vs. Aggregate Performance	
Individual appraisals are used almost exclusively with little variance in performance ratings.	Algorithmic
Interdependencies are seldom taken into account when making decisions about an individual's pay.	Algorithmic
Short- vs. Long-term Orientation	
The pay system has a futuristic orientation. It focuses employee's attention on long-term (two or more years) goals.	Experiential
The pay system rewards employees for short-term accomplishments during a fixed time period.	Algorithmic
Risk Sharing	
A portion of an employee's earnings is contingent on achievement of group or organization performance goals.	Experiential
Compensation system is designed so that a significant proportion of total labor costs is variable in nature.	Experiential
Firm strongly believes that employees should be risk takers with some of their pay.	Experiential
Corporate vs. Business Unit Performance	
Corporate performance is used as criteria for pay decisions concerning top management and aggregate incentive programs (e.g., gain sharing, profit sharing) for employees.	Algorithmic
Division or business unit performance is used as criterion to reward executives and determine aggregate incentive dollars for employers.	Experiential
Internal Consistency in Pay Relationships vs. Market Forces	
Internal pay equity is an important goal of the pay system.	Algorithmic

Basis for Pay	Strategic Compensation Pattern
The firm tries hard to achieve comparable pay relationships across different parts of the organization.	Algorithmic
The firm gives a higher priority to internal pay equity than to external market factors.	Algorithmic
Emphasis on Hierarchy and Status Differentials	
The compensation system reflects a low degree of hierarchy. In other words, firm offers a minimum of perks (reserved parking spots, first-class air travel, etc.) to top executives.	Experiential
Firm offers special pay packages and privileges as status symbols to the higher echelons in the organization.	Algorithmic
Firm tries to make pay system as egalitarian as possible. There are very few special rewards available to any "elite" groups of employees.	Experiential
Quantitative vs. Qualitative Performance Resources	
Firm relies heavily on objective performance measures (e.g., earnings per share, return on investment) as a basis for top executive pay and aggregate incentive programs (e.g., gain sharing, profit sharing).	Experiential
Firm relies on subjective evaluations to monitor subordinates.	Experiential
Pay Policy Relative to Market	
Preferred position of organization's salary levels with respect to competitors is clearly above market.	Algorithmic
Preferred position of organization's benefits level with respect to competitors is clearly above market.	Algorithmic
Role of Salary and Benefits in Total Pay Mix	
Base salary is an important part of the total compensation package.	Algorithmic
Base salary is high relative to other forms of pay that an employee may receive in the organization.	Algorithmic
Benefits are an important part of total package.	Algorithmic
Employees' benefits package is very generous compared to what it could be.	Algorithmic
Role of Pay Incentives in Total Pay Mix	
Base salary is an important part of the total compensation package.	Algorithmic
Base salary is high relative to other forms of pay that an employee may receive in the organization.	Algorithmic
Benefits are an important part of total package.	Algorithmic
Employees' benefits package is very generous compared to what it could be.	Algorithmic
Role of Pay Incentives in Total Pay Mix	
Pay incentives such as a bonus or profit sharing are an important part of the compensation strategy in this organization.	Experiential
Pay incentives are designed to provide a significant amount of an employee's total earnings in this organization.	Experiential

(continued)

Table 3.2 *(continued)*

Basis for Pay	Strategic Compensation Pattern
Frequency of Rewards	
Bonuses are provided often; frequency of bonuses is viewed at least as important as their magnitude.	Experiential
Organization provides a variety of deferred compensation plans in addition to bonuses.	Experiential
Firm relies on annual pay raises, which may include both a merit and a cost-of-living component.	Algorithmic
Reliance on Pecuniary vs. Nonmonetary Rewards	
Firm tries, hard to meet the psychological needs of employees by offering intrinsic rewards through such means as job enrichment and quality of work life programs. Monetary rewards are underemphasized.	Algorithmic
While intrinsic aspects of the job are not ignored, firm clearly uses pecuniary rewards as a crucial part of its human rewards strategy.	Experiential
Administrative Framework	
Pay policy is applied uniformly across all organizational units.	Algorithmic
The personnel staff in each business unit has freedom to develop its own compensation programs.	Experiential
There is a minimum of interference from corporate headquarters with respect to pay decisions made by line managers.	Experiential
Pay Disclosure vs. Secrecy	
Firm keeps pay information secret from employees.	Algorithmic
Firm has formal policies that discourage employees from divulging their pay to coworkers.	Algorithmic
Firm does not openly disclose the administrative procedures on how pay levels and pay raises are established.	Algorithmic
Participative vs. Authoritarian Pay System Design	
Employees' feelings and preferences for various pay forms (e.g., bonus vs. profit sharing) are taken very seriously by top management.	Experiential
Many different kinds of employees (individual contributors, managers, personnel staff, executives) have a say in pay policies.	Experiential
Pay decisions are made on an autocratic basis. Firms tend to "follow the book" very closely. Very few employees have any input to pay decisions.	Algorithmic
Administrative Framework	
Pay system is highly regimented with procedures carefully defined.	Algorithmic
Compensation structure is very complex yet changes very slowly.	Algorithmic
While general rules exist, many pay decisions are one of a kind with considerable discretion on a case-by-case basis.	Experiential

Source: Based on the research of Gomez-Mejia (1992).

5. A corporate strategic focus with an emphasis on internal equity and hierarchical position as the basis to distribute rewards
6. Monitoring of behaviors rather than outcomes
7. Heavy reliance on base salary and benefits in the pay mix with minimal variable compensation
8. Above-market pay with high job security
9. More bureaucratic, formalized pay policies

Several corollaries revolve around the characteristics listed above. The *algorithmic pay pattern* is associated with low emphasis on deferred income with the pay of top executives linked to corporate performance indicators. Because of a "lead market" salary policy and tenure-related compensation, employees find it difficult to obtain a comparable pay package elsewhere and spend many years with the firm. Upward mobility through a narrowly defined grade structure is encouraged as a means for employees to increase their income within the "internal labor market." This creates an organizational climate that promotes commitment and discourages employee attrition. Relative position in the vertical structure is the best predictor of an employee's pay, and the immediate supervisor serves as a gatekeeper in promotion decisions through the annual appraisal reviews. Because behaviors, rather than outcomes, are measured in the appraisal process, superiors exercise much judgment and subjectivity in assessing the performance of subordinates. This means that the reward system encourages high dependence on superiors with a top-down, decision-making structure. Paradoxically, even though subordinates' performance is frequently measured by supervisors and the variance in performance ratings is quite low, tenure, along with its associated income and perquisites, is nonetheless the main factor explaining position in the hierarchy. The administrative framework is highly centralized, pay secrecy is enforced, employee participation is not encouraged, and compensation policies and procedures are carefully defined.

Experiential Pay Pattern

The second pattern empirically derived in the study by Gomez-Mejia and Balkin (1992), and profiled in Table 3.1, may be designated *experiential* because the firm's compensation strategies are flexible and adaptive. Thus, these strategies can be molded to respond to changing circumstances, factors mediating their effectiveness, sudden environmental shifts, and idiosyncratic situations.

The algorithmic and experiential compensation patterns have opposite orientations. The experiential pattern emphasizes:

1. Skills and personal attributes, rather than job evaluation procedures focusing on work tasks, as a basis for pay determination
2. Demonstrated performance, rather than tenure, as a basis for pay progression
3. Performance assessments at multiple levels, including individual, team, business unit, and corporate levels
4. Multiyear considerations in the distribution of rewards, particularly for top-level managers
5. Extensive risk sharing between employees and the firm
6. A greater emphasis on assessing division performance, rather than overall corporate performance, for firms with several business units
7. More sensitivity to the market, rather than internal equity concerns, in setting pay levels
8. De-emphasis of hierarchical structures in favor of more egalitarian pay schemes
9. Greater reliance on outcomes, rather than supervisory judgments, of performance for divisional managers, resulting in less dependence on corporate superiors
10. Lower pay relative to the market ("follow market" policy) yet offers an attractive pay package. The package incorporates substantial incentives and premiums on top of fixed salary and benefits and makes greater use of deferred income, in addition to cash incentives for a broad cross section of employees.
11. Multiple rewards given at frequent and sometimes unpredictable intervals. Money is used explicitly as a mechanism to influence employees' behavior and creates a calculative, utilitarian employment relationship.

The administrative framework of the *experiential pay pattern* is decentralized, and lower organizational levels and local units have much discretion in allocating compensation dollars. There is little trepidation about making pay open and sometimes using these public displays to motivate other individuals in the organization to work harder toward the achievement of strategic goals. There is greater solicitation of employee inputs, and pay policies are flexible and can change depending on situational factors rather than simply following rules of the book. Let's now review organizational strategy taxonomies that will later be linked to these pay choices.

Multilevel Organizational Strategies

Early theorists portrayed strategy as a situational art in which top executives would develop a comprehensive plan of action that is idiosyncratic to the organization. Much of the development was presumed to be done through "gut feeling." That is, consideration would be given to the types of activities appropriate to environmental opportunities and threats, internal strengths and weaknesses of the firm, and managerial values (Chandler, 1962; Andrews, 1971). The "old" field of business policy relied heavily on case studies. It assumed that each situation was different and that detailed scenario descriptions would help students arrive at a gestalt feel of the situation and lead them to develop their own unique approaches to the problem. Firm strategy was primarily viewed as an adaptation mechanism, cogently discussed only relative to competitors' strategies and myriad characteristics and nuances that were unique to the organization.

The modern view of strategy began to emerge in the 1970s as an attempt to develop normative models and theories that could generalize across broad classes of situations and, therefore, serve to guide future research. This new approach began to question the early assumptions that firm strategies were so unique to a given situation that no general models or propositions could be developed. As in the emergence of other scientific fields, strategic management (which by most accounts is less than 30 years old) has placed a great emphasis on the development of typologies or taxonomies to classify organizational strategies. Typologies are then used to examine how environmental factors, internal organizational features, and managerial values relate to these strategic classifications. Literally dozens of strategy typologies have been developed since the 1970s, although they tend to overlap (e.g., Hambrick, 1984; Segev, 1989). In this book, the focus is on firm strategy groupings that are most useful for analyzing compensation-related strategies.

Organizational strategy typologies have been developed at two different levels of analysis: corporate (in what business should the organization be?) and business unit (how does the firm compete in a given business?). The main strategy taxonomies and their underlying dimensions at each of these levels are reviewed next. We also examine how the strategic compensation patterns relate to the organizational strategies.

Corporate-Level Strategies

As noted earlier, corporate strategies refer to the top level of the entire organization, regardless of the number of different industries in which it competes or how many divisions or business units it has. The main strategic concern at this level is the mix of businesses the corporation should hold and the flow of resources between the businesses. Thus, top corporate executives handle this portfolio in a manner similar to how a mutual fund manager administers a portfolio of stocks. The corporate portfolio consists of an array of strategic business units (SBUs) that may be very similar to or completely different from each other. Some units have little in common. At the corporate level, the main strategic decisions concern acquisition, divestment, diversification, and flow of funds. A great number of "portfolio" models have been developed to study corporate level strategy (e.g., Boston Consulting Matrix, General Electric Grid, Shell Planning Grid), and their primary concern is on how resources should be moved across business units depending on their relative market share and rate of growth. However, the taxonomies most pertinent to compensation strategies are those concerned with extent and process of diversification.

A review of the literature reveals a great deal of variation in the way both extent and process of diversification are conceptualized, defined, and measured (see Ramanujam and Varadajaran [1989] for an extensive discussion of these issues). However, there are five key elements that underlie most of this work that have implications for compensation strategies and their contribution to firm performance.

1. *Heterogeneity of customers.* This refers to the number of markets, industries, and constituencies served by the corporation.
2. *Product/service similarity.* The degree to which the corporation's products or services are related or unrelated
3. *Unit interdependence.* Following earlier theoretical work by Thomson (1967), unit interdependence concerns the extent to which different business units are autonomous or share many resources in common.
4. *Diversification mode.* The degree to which a corporation relies on internal business development, vis-à-vis acquisitions as a means of entering new markets
5. *Diversification rate.* Rate at which the corporation grows by adding new businesses to its portfolio

At least 60 different taxonomies have been developed to classify corporations according to extent and process of diversification (Ramanujam and Varadajaran, 1989). In this book, attention is devoted to the taxonomies that have been most commonly used in previous research in the strategy field and that are useful in conceptualizing and studying compensation phenomena. Table 3.3 summarizes how selected taxonomies capture the five elements listed earlier.

Table 3.3

Key Dimensions Underlying Corporate Diversification Taxonomies

| | Type of Diversification | | | | | | | | | | |
| | Extent of Diversification | | | | Patterns of Linkage | | | | | Diversification Process | |
Dimensions	Single product	Dominant product	Related Product	Unrelated product	Vertical	Constrained	Linked	Multibusiness	Conglomerate	Evolutionary	Steady state
Heterogeneity of Customers	Minimal	Low	Medium	high	Minimal	Low	Medium	high	Very high	Very high	Low
Degree of Product Similarity	High	Medium	Low	Minimal	Very high	High	Medium	Low	Minimal	Minimal	High
Unit Interdependence	—	High	Medium	Low	High	High	Medium	Low	Minimal	Minimal	High
Diversification Mode	—	Internal	Mixed	Acquisitive	Internal	Internal	Mixed	Mixed	Acquisitive	Acquisitive	Internal
Diversification Rate	—	Slow	Medium	Fast	—	Slow	Medium	Medium	Fast	Very fast	Slow

Type of Diversification

The best-known typology, particularly in its compensation applications, is that developed by Rumelt (1974, 1977). In the Rumelt framework, extent of diversification is defined according to a fourfold taxonomy based on percent of revenue derived from various products.

Single-Product Firms. Single-product firms obtain 95 percent or more of their revenue from a single-product domain. These firms are characterized by homogeneous customers and a high degree of product similarity.

Dominant Product Firms. Dominant product firms derive between 70 and 94 percent of their revenues from a single-product domain. These firms are characterized by low customer heterogeneity, medium product similarity, high unit interdependence, an internal diversification mode, and a slow pace of diversification.

Related-product Firms. Related-product firms derive less than 70 percent of their revenues from a single-product domain, and the remainder from a related-product domain. These firms are characterized by medium heterogeneity of customers, some product similarity, medium unit interdependence, internal and acquisitive diversification modes, and a moderate rate of diversification growth.

Unrelated-Product Firms. Unrelated-product firms receive less than 70 percent of their revenues from a single-product domain, and the reminder from an unrelated-product domain. These companies are characterized by high heterogeneity of customers, little or no product similarities, low unit interdependence, an acquisitive diversification mode, and a fast rate of diversification growth.

Patterns of Linkage

Rumelt (1974) identifies several patterns of linkage between business units.

Vertical. Vertical linkage refers to a vertically integrated business, such as an automobile manufacturer owning an aluminum firm that produces inputs necessary in the production of cars. These firms are characterized by homogeneous customers, high degrees of product similarity and unit interdependence, and an internal diversification mode.

Constrained. With a constrained linkage, a single core strength or character-istic permeates all the businesses owned by the firm. For example, in the hospitality industry, a hotel chain may own a restaurant chain. These firms are characterized by low customer heterogeneity, medium product similarity, high unit interdependence, an internal diversification mode, and a slow rate of diversification growth.

Linked. If business units are linked, then each firm in the portfolio relates to one other firm but not necessarily to more than one. These firms are characterized by medium heterogeneity of customers, medium product similarity, medium unit interdependence, internal and acquisitive modes of diversification, and a medium rate of diversification growth.

Multibusiness. Multibusiness linkage refers to a corporation comprised of a relatively small number (two to four) of unrelated businesses. These firms are characterized by high customer heterogeneity, low product similarity, low unit interdependence, both internal and acquisitive modes of diversification, and a medium rate of diversification growth.

Conglomerate. In a conglomerate, many different businesses are owned by a single corporation, and little attempt is made to link them together. These firms are characterized by very high customer heterogeneity, minimal product similarity and unit interdependence, acquisitive diversification, and a fast rate of diversification growth.

Process of Diversification

The Rumelt framework portrays a static view of diversification in which firms are classified into a predetermined taxonomy. In an attempt to examine how firms diversify, Pitts (1974), and later extensions by Leontiades (1980) and Kerr (1995), developed a dichotomous taxonomy based on differences in the process of diversification.

Evolutionary Firms. Evolutionary firms grow by aggressively acquiring diverse firms into their portfolio. These firms are willing to change industries by pur-chasing or divesting businesses. Actively searching for opportunities in diverse markets and industries, these companies have a distinct external orientation and are eager to engage in acquisitions, mergers, and joint ventures. They are char-acterized by very high heterogeneity of customers, minimal product similarity and unit interdependence, and a very fast rate of diversification growth.

Steady State Firms. Steady state firms choose to compete within their respective industry or industries and to expand either by greater penetration of present markets (nondiversified growth) or by investment in internally generated diversification (internal growth). Because of their inward focus, these companies "are concerned with the internal development of new products and technologies and with coordination across business units" (Kerr, 1995, p.159). These firms are also characterized by low heterogeneity of customers, high degrees of product similarity and unit interdependence, and a slow pace of diversification growth.

Overarching Strategic Compensation Patterns and Corporate Strategy

The upper portion of Table 3.4 shows the most prevalent compensation patterns (algorithmic or experiential) associated with various corporate strategies. Figure 3.1 presents a model that summarizes much of the conceptual and empirical research on the underlying predictors of strategic compensation patterns at the corporate level. According to that model, an experiential compensation pattern (see Appendix 3.1 for a detailed listing of strategic pay choices associated with various corporate strategies) is inversely related to knowledge of organizational transformations on the part of corporate managers, the degree to which pooled interdependence is prevalent among SBUs, corporate growth that is internally generated, commitment to a narrow product line/market niche, organizational complexity, and the need for a unitary corporate-wide ethos. On the other hand, an experiential compensation pattern is a positive function of the rate of new business acquisitions under the same corporate umbrella, the need to encourage independent thinking and entrepreneurial activities on the part of divisional managers, cash flow constraints, and the heterogeneity of SBUs. A review of the supporting literature follows.

Berg (1969, 1973) noted that large diversified firms, roughly equivalent to the "unrelated products" or conglomerate group in Rumelt's taxonomy, attempt to maintain an entrepreneurial atmosphere. They accomplish this by providing variable bonuses, high risk sharing, rewards based on business unit performance, and low dependence on superiors. These pay characteristics are associated with the experiential compensation strategies.

Encouraging an entrepreneurial culture in conglomerates makes sense because each business unit is independent and shares few resources in common. Furthermore, corporate level managers are unlikely to have significant experience in more than a few of the firm's businesses. Each business unit

Table 3.4

A Summary of Strategic Compensation Patterns Associated with Various Corporate and Business Unit Strategies

	Strategic Compensation Pattern
Corporate Strategy	
Extent of diversification	
Single-product	Experiential
Dominant-product	Mixed
Related-product	Algorithmic
Unrelated-product	Experiential
Patterns of linkages	
Vertical	Algorithmic
Constrained	Algorithmic
Linked	Mixed
Multibusiness	Experiential
Conglomerate	Experiential
Process of diversification	
Evolutionary firms	Experiential
Steady state firms	Algorithmic
Business Unit Strategy	
Strategic patterns	
Defenders	Algorithmic
Prospectors	Experiential
Analyzers	Mixed
Dynamic growth	Experiential
Rationalization/maintenance	Algorithmic
Life cycle	
Start-up stage	Experiential
Growth stage	Experiential
Mature stage	Algorithmic
Decline stage	Algorithmic

enjoys substantial freedom, and the pay system encourages SBU managers to experiment by making the magnitude of potential rewards for top management proportionate to level of risk assumed. According to Berg, attempts to administer a compensation system centrally under such conditions and to base a SBU manager's pay on the judgment of "naïve" top executives in corporate headquarters is likely to demoralize divisional managers and dampen creativity and local initiatives.

Along a similar vein, Lorsch and Allen (1973) noted that vertically integrated firms, roughly corresponding to related- and dominant- product classifications in the Rumelt typology, have the opposite compensation strategies of conglomerates. That is, the evaluation of each division manager is based on the performance of the corporation as a whole, high dependence on superior's feedback, and relatively low "at risk" pay.

Figure 3.1   **Key Factors Underlying Observed Variations in Compensation Strategies at the Corporate Level**

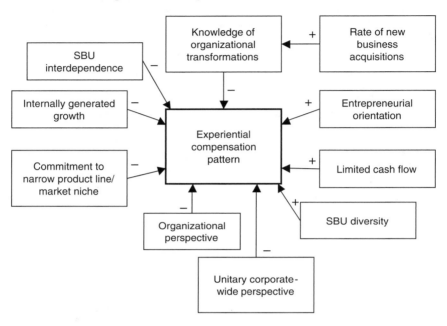

Two reasons were advanced by Lorsch and Allen for this observed pattern. First, top executives in vertically integrated firms know a great deal about each of the businesses. Second, all units in these corporations are highly interdependent and share many common resources. Therefore, it is difficult to make unambiguous performance attributions to any one unit. Likewise, Salter (1973) made a cogent argument that corporate-division and interdivision relations play a major role in reward system design for top management. As diversification increases, the interdependence between divisions and the corporation and among divisions declines. As each division or business unit becomes a unique entity, the reward system acquires more of the characteristics of the experiential reward pattern, with a tendency to define managerial rewards in terms of results of operating units, rather than the corporation as a whole.

This would be particularly true of conglomerates where interdivisional sharing of resources tends to be nil.

Relatedly, Balkin and Gomez-Mejia (1990) report that single-product firms (in which the corporation and business unit are one and the same) are associated with lower pay levels relative to the market, high emphasis on incentives in the compensation mix, reliance on long-term income, and flexible pay policies. All of these reflect an experiential pay pattern. Several related reasons may account for this.

First, single-product firms do not need a compensation system with elaborate rules to govern pay decisions. Less complexity in the organization demands fewer detailed policies and procedures to cover multiple contingencies. Second, top management in single-product firms is more likely to foster an entrepreneurial climate, with many decisions made on an ad hoc basis as unique situations arise. The HRM function is less formalized, with extensive prerogatives given to line managers in making personnel-related decisions. Third, a long-term orientation becomes important in single-product organizations that are interested in "nurturing" a particular product and market, particularly those that are at the initial stages of growth where they are preparing for rapid expansion along a narrow product line. A more flexible, organic compensation system with generous long-term pay offerings is more suitable to these conditions. Fourth, heavy reliance on incentive pay by single-product firms may be a useful strategy to attract and retain employees, while at the same time underemphasizing expensive fixed pay components (salary and benefits) relative to more established, mature firms. Such a compensation strategy would free scarce dollars in the short run and allow more investment to finance continued expansion. Although pay level may be below market for these firms, employees may choose to work there in exchange for greater potential returns in the future. Gomez-Mejia and Balkin (1985) found that to be the case among smaller, high technology firms in the New England area that provide up to 70 percent of an employee's pay on a variable basis. Similar results were reported several years later on a much larger sample of high technology firms by Milkovich and colleagues (1991).

Balkin and Gomez-Mejia (1990) also report that as corporate strategy shifts from a low to a higher level of diversification (but still remains in the related business category with substantial interdependence among units), the compensation system becomes more bureaucratic and inflexible, exhibiting many of the traits associated with the algorithmic compensation pattern. These more highly diversified firms are characterized by an above market or going rate pay level, greater emphasis on salary and benefits vis-à-vis incentives, less long-term pay, more pay secrecy, pay centralization, job-based pay, a weaker pay for performance linkage, and a less egalitarian, more autocratic administration of the compensation system. As additional business units are added to the corporate structure, pay comparisons across business units are made by corporate management. Pay policies that ensure fair, consistent treatment of employees in different business units are developed at the corporate level. Internal pay equity, operationalized through job evaluation procedures, becomes increasingly important as diversification increases.

Two primary reasons account for the algorithmic compensation strategies observed among related-product firms. First, diversified companies with interdependent business units do not wish to provide much autonomy to divisional managers or to design pay packages that encourage entrepreneurial behaviors among SBUs whose activities and goals are deeply intertwined. The main task of the pay system is viewed as one of control. Thus, compensation policies and procedures are designed to link SBUs to corporate headquarters, foster dependence on superiors, and reduce risk taking at the local level. Second, related business companies are keenly interested in creating a systemic, rather than a fractionalized, view of the total organization. Uniform, standardized pay policies and procedures across SBUs reinforce a unitary corporate perspective. This means that managing the potential conflict in the pay system between the desire for fairness and equity and the need for adaptiveness and differentiation becomes a major challenge for related-product corporations.

Balkin and Gomez-Mejia (1990), however, warn that the findings discussed here are only applicable to corporate diversifiers where corporate management possesses a core of management expertise that relates to the different businesses in the corporation. Their sample did not include conglomerates, where the business units are heterogeneous and highly independent.

In a separate study including a large sample of conglomerates, Gomez-Mejia (1992) found that as firms diversify by acquiring SBUs that share little in common, the overall compensation strategy shifts to a more experiential style, similar to that of single-product firms. As can be seen in Figure 3.2, he reports that the average scores on the algorithmic-experiential continuum (where higher scores indicate a more experiential orientation) were 0.74, 0.40, 0.45, and 0.51 for single-product, dominant-product, related-product, and unrelated-product firms, respectively. These findings are consistent with those reported earlier by Berg (1973) and Lorsch and Allen (1973). So it appears that the relationship between degree of diversification and the extent to which a firm relies on a more experiential compensation pattern is U-shaped rather than linear, with single- and unrelated-product firms relying on more experiential compensation strategies and dominant- and related-product firms utilizing a more algorithmic approach.

As noted earlier, Rumelt (1974) describes corporate strategy not only in terms of extent of diversification but also according to patterns of linkages across business units. The underlying concept behind his five types of linkages (vertical, constrained, linked, multibusiness, and unrelated business) is the

Figure 3.2 **Underlying Factors Affecting Compensation Strategies at the Business Level**

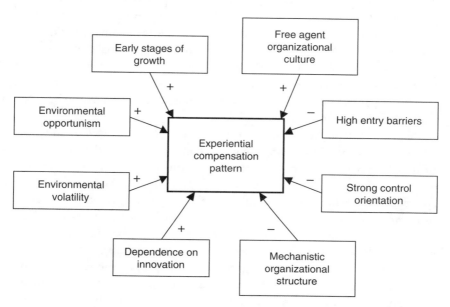

degree to which divisions share common resources and are subject to pooled interdependencies. No empirical research examining how reward systems vary according to each of these configurations exists. However, the same logic used for diversification extent should apply here. One would expect vertical (i.e., an integrated chain of businesses) and constrained (i.e., all business units related to a single core or characteristic) patterns of linkages to rely on more algorithmic pay strategies because of greater interdependencies across units. One would also expect that firms consisting of unrelated businesses would lean toward experiential pay strategies. Linked firms, where some of the business units are related, would more likely fall somewhere between the algorithmic and experiential pay patterns.

Process of Diversification and Strategic Pay Patterns

The research reviewed so far relies primarily on Rumelt's framework and takes a largely static view of diversification strategy. Outlining the compensation strategies associated with each category, this research provides important insights. However, a number of researchers argue that it is not enough to stop at the "extent" or patterns of linkages. There is also a need to examine how compensation strategies vary according to the process by which diversification takes place. Pitts (1976) reports that "acquisitive diversifiers," or firms that diversify by purchasing existing businesses, pay managers based on the performance of their unit, with little dependence on superiors to make a judgment of performance. Firms that diversify in this manner provide division managers with more autonomy, and a more experiential compensation strategy appears to be most appropriate. The opposite is true for firms that have grown through internal expansion (what Pitts calls internal diversifiers), where there is a greater degree of interdependence and interaction between managers of various divisions.

Reaching essentially the same conclusions, Leontiades (1980) and Kerr (1995) expand upon Pitts's earlier work. According to Leontiades, steady-state firms, which have a clear commitment to existing product/market areas and exhibit a strong reluctance to engage in mergers and acquisitions, are associated with a more intimate form of control by top management, inculcation of organizational values for junior managers, consistency in procedures, long careers with the company, and a system-wide perspective because of extensive interdependencies that exist across organizational subunits. Evolutionary-state firms, on the other hand, aggressively engage in mergers, acquisitions, joint ventures, and so on, even in unfamiliar areas. Among evolutionary firms, the management of change becomes crucial to survival. Entrepreneurship is encouraged, control is deemphasized to promote innovation, shorter tenure with the firm is the norm as the employment relationship is based on a calculative commitment, and a systemic perspective is discouraged because problems facing each business unit are unique.

Kerr (1995) found that compensation strategies vary according to these two diversification processes. Among steady-state firms, the reward system falls closer to the algorithmic pattern because superiors exercise a great deal of direct control over the rewards of lower level managers promoting greater dependence; nonmonetary rewards are important (e.g., job security); risk sharing is minimal; there is more emphasis on monitoring behaviors rather than outcomes; the strategic focus to distribute rewards lies in the corporation rather than the business unit; and achieving internal consistency in the pay structure is necessary to support a system-wide view. Kerr found that mechanistic job evaluation procedures such as the Hay Point factor system are commonly used among steady-state firms.

According to Kerr's (1995) findings, evolutionary-state firms have reward systems that share many characteristics with the experiential compensation pattern. Because corporate executives have limited knowledge of acquired business units that may be quite diverse, there is less dependence on superiors for feedback and performance evaluation. Monitoring occurs by linking rewards to outcomes, rather than through observation and judgment of subordinates' behaviors. The low level of interdependence among divisions lessens the need for centralized control and the establishment of mechanisms such as job evaluation to promote internal consistency in the pay structure across different business units. Evolutionary-state firms emphasize variable compensation in the pay mix (mostly through equity-based schemes) to promote a sense of ownership among division managers. At the same time, they circumvent the need to justify reward allocation decisions by corporate executives who may have little, if any, experience in each of the portfolio's businesses.

Kerr (1995) also found that the process of, rather than the extent of, diversification is the most important predictor of observed compensation patterns. He concludes that "the extent to which a firm derived revenue from a more or less narrow set of activities did not adequately explain the composition of the [compensation strategies] clusters . . . these results suggest that, in itself, a firm's level of diversification does not represent a primary influence on the design of its reward system" (p. 170).

Some caution should be used in interpreting Kerr's (1995) findings. They are based on interviews with a small sample of 20 firms, relying on a heuristic approach to make sense of his data. More recently and using the composite compensation strategy measure described earlier in this chapter, Gomez-Mejia (1992) found that in a sample of 243 firms, pay strategies do vary by diversification process in a manner similar to that proposed by Kerr (1995). Unlike Kerr, however, Gomez-Mejia (1992) found that both extent and process of diversification are important predictors of compensation strategy. Firms that are both highly diversified and evolutionary in nature are more experiential in their compensation strategies than firms that are less diversified and steady in nature.

In summary, these findings suggest that while extent of diversification and patterns of linkages among business units have a bearing on pay strategies, the process of corporate diversification can also affect where a corporation lies on the algorithmic-experiential compensation strategy continua. The algorithmic pay pattern is more prevalent among dominant- or related-product firms with vertical or constrained patterns of linkages that follow a steady-state diversification strategy. The experiential pay pattern, on the other hand, is more common among single-product or unrelated-product firms with multibusiness or conglomerate patterns of linkages following an evolutionary diversification strategy. The foregoing studies also suggest that the right fit between pay schemes and corporate strategy diversification is expected to have a significant impact on performance. In this regard, Henderson and Fredrickson (2001) argued that the effects of the long-term pay gap on firm performance are positively moderated by greater related diversification.

Business Unit Strategies

Strategic decisions at the business unit level primarily reside on the formulation of a multifunctional strategy for corporate subunits that operate in a single industry or product market area. While this definition appears simple at first glance, the business unit concept is not always clear-cut. If a company operates in diverse industries, business unit level would normally correspond to the division. In single-product firms, the business and corporate level would be identical. For related-product firms, however, the way a business unit is defined may be an arbitrary decision, depending on how much resource sharing and interdependencies exist across various segments of the corporation.

Corporations display much variability in how much autonomy is allowed in various divisions and how closely they are linked to each other (Kerr, 1995; Leontiades, 1980; Rumelt, 1974). Some corporations, particularly those practicing acquisitive growth, provide a great deal of autonomy to their divisions so that each may be considered a business unit in its own right with discretion to develop its own strategies. Corporations that grow slowly through internal resources, the steady-state firms, concentrate most strategic decisions at the corporate level and emphasize resource sharing and coordination. In this situation, business units are not treated as separate entities vis-à-vis corporate headquarters and each other.

At least 20 typologies appear in the literature, designed to classify business units responsible for their own strategy formulation into a parsimonious set of strategic groupings (see for example the reviews by Hambrick, 1983; Herbert and Deresky, 1987; and Segev, 1989). Over 80 classification labels with such exotic titles as explosion, domain offence, multiplication, slip, niche, climber, stuck in the middle, cash cows, dogs, and the like are used. Despite this bewildering diversity of proposed taxonomies and varying labels to denote each category, several recurrent themes are predominant in this literature.

Dimensions of Taxonomies

The key dimensions that underlie these typological schemes, most of which have compensation implications, are briefly described in the following discussion.

Environmental Dimensions. The first set of dimensions concerns the environment facing the business unit. The environment can be depicted in terms of four crucial factors:

1. Degree of uncertainty. The degree of uncertainty refers to how much accurate information is available to top management. Information is needed to predict environmental changes so that appropriate responses can be devised.
2. Volatility. Volatility is the rate of change in the firm's relevant environment (e.g., shifts in product demands, changes in technology, changes in legislation).
3. Magnitude of change. The magnitude of change refers to the amount of discontinuous change in the firm's relevant environment. For instance, in the medical field, appearance of ultrasonic imaging instruments in the early 1970s made electrodiagnostic instruments obsolete almost overnight. Many other similar examples of discontinuous change in that industry are provided by Mitchell (1989).
4. Complexity. This pertains to the number and heterogeneity of external elements that may impact the organization either singly or in an interactive fashion.

Production Process Dimensions. The second set of dimensions underlying most SBU taxonomies concerns the production process used by the firm. The four key factors under this are as follows:

1. Innovation requirements. Innovation requirements refer to the novelty of the production process used to transform inputs into services and products. For instance, a firm specializing in custom design of airplanes or a biotechnology company would rate high in this dimension.
2. Degree of standardization. The degree of standardization is the extent to which the production process is routine and relatively stable with few exceptions to established procedures; for example, the manufacturing process used to make pencils has not changed much over the past 100 years and is very routine in nature.
3. Fixed investments. Fixed investments are the amount of resources irrevocably sunk into the firm's core technology; for example, investments in production equipment and facilities are much greater on a per capita basis in a steel mill or an automobile assembly line than in an advertising firm or a management consulting company.

4. Technological diversity. Diversity is the extent to which the technology used in the production process is dissimilar or homogeneous; for example, the successful production of a lunar landing module by NASA involved the utilization of multiple technologies spanning several fields. The typical lumber company, on the other hand, utilizes a very homogenous technology to cut down trees, namely manual labor and chain saws.

Market Dimensions. The third set of dimensions interwoven across most SBU typologies concerns the firm's market interface and behaviors. Three factors play a major role here:

1. Rate of growth. As the term implies, rate of growth refers to sales expansion with respect to industry norms and previous sales volume
2. Product innovation. Product innovation relates to the number and novelty of new products/services launched by the firm. Volkswagen, for instance, did not change it basic car model for over 40 years, while General Motors has changed car designs every year since its inception.
3. Product market domain focus. Product market domain focus refers to whether a firm chooses a narrowly defined market niche (e.g., computer programs for medical applications) or cast a wider product net (e.g., software for statistical analysis, inventory, and home entertainment).

Managerial Dimensions. The fourth set of dimensions defining SBU taxonomies concerns the attributes of top management teams. Four factors frequently come into play here:

1. Risk taking. Risk taking is the degree to which top management teams are willing to make commitments that require substantial resources and to invest in projects with a low probability of success but high potential returns.
2. Degree of control Degree of control is the extent to which management develops elaborate procedures to standardize behavior and monitor employees' activities to ensure compliance.
3. Hierarchical emphasis. Hierarchical emphasis refers to how many levels in the organization are involved in making important decisions and the extent to which power, prestige, and influence are related to positioning in the "pecking order."

4. Environmental proactiveness. Proactiveness is the degree to which top management teams attempt to shape environmental forces and events, as opposed to taking a reactive posture to external threats and opportunities.

Organizational Structure Dimensions. The fifth set of dimensions underlying most SBU taxonomies refers to structural factors in the organization. The following three structural elements are commonly cited:

1. Centralization. Centralization is the extent to which decision-making authority is empowered at the top level, usually in a single location.
2. Modus operandi. When the internal organization is known for its formalized rules, procedures, and clearly defined roles, it is generally labeled "mechanistic." At the opposite end, an "organic" firm is characterized by flexible and adaptive rules and procedures, free-flowing and loose methods for accomplishing tasks, and wide discretion given to employees to define their jobs.
3. Focal unit. This refers to the unit of analysis used to organize the firm's operations. The two most common ones include the traditional functional breakdown (e.g., marketing, finance, production, personnel) and a product-based approach (i.e., by product line).

Cultural Dimensions. The sixth and last set of dimensions that distinguishes different SBU strategic groups is not as commonly mentioned as the first five, yet it implicitly or explicitly plays an important role in most SBU taxonomies. It is the organization's culture. The two most important cultural factors are:

1. Cultural climate. Cultural climate refers to whether a firm has an entrepreneurial climate (one that encourages individualism, risk taking, flexibility, creation of new ideas, willingness to experiment, and tolerance for mistakes) or a regimented climate (with tight controls, emphasis on compliance, risk avoidance, strict adherence to norms ["business as usual"], and low tolerance for mistakes).
2. Type of commitment. Commitment refers to the nature of employees' involvement in the firm. Two major concepts in this regard have a long tradition in the sociological literature (for a review, see Penley and Gould, 1988.) The first one has been coined *moral commitment,* to denote identification with organizational goals. This orientation emphasizes internalizing organizational norms, long-term attachment to the firm, loyalty, and a base of attitudes, habits, and values

that foster strong emotional allegiance to the employer. The second orientation, labeled *calculative,* represents an instrumental, utilitarian, hedonistic view in which employees are depicted as exchanging their contributions for the inducements provided by the organization. Employees and/or the organization are free to break this bond whenever the exchange is not of mutual benefit. Thus, calculative commitment is the opposite of moral commitment and involves little affective organizational attachment. Empirical evidence strongly supports the notion that these two types of employee involvement are distinct and independent and that firms vary on the extent to which they rely on one type versus the other.

In this book, the SBU taxonomies that have gained wide acceptance in the strategy field and that are useful for analyzing compensation strategy items are discussed. These taxonomies can be divided into those concerned with recurring viable strategic patterns and those focusing on structural features based on life cycle concepts. Table 3.5 summarizes how each of the dimensions discussed here relate to each of the SBU typologies used in this book.

Strategic Business Unit Patterns

Perhaps the best known and most widely used SBU typology was developed by Miles and Snow (1978). The Miles and Snow typology has proven to be very robust and adaptable as evidenced by its successful application to the study of a wide variety of strategic issues. It has been used to examine changes in R&D intensity (Hambrick, MacMillan, and Barbarosa, 1983); distinctive competence and performance (Snow and Hrebiniak, 1980); manufacturing and service strategies (Adam, 1983); strategic awareness (Hambrick, 1981); environmental scanning (Hambrick, 1982); strategic choice (Burgelman, 1983; Segev, 1989); and, most important to this book, compensation strategies (Broderick, 1986; Gomez-Mejia, 1992). Empirical results also provide strong support for its reliability and validity (Shortell and Zajac, 1990).

Based on three studies in four industries (college textbook publishers, electronics, food processors, and health care), Miles and Snow (1978) concluded that viable SBU strategies can be categorized into three basic types.

1. Defenders. Defenders are business units that prefer to maintain a secure position in a relatively stable product or service area. Rather than emphasizing new product development, they emphasize protecting the market share. Key features of defenders include (see Tables 3.5 and 3.6):

Table 3.5

Key Dimensions Underlying Strategic Business Unit Taxonomies

	Strategic Patterns					Structural Features	
	Miles and Snow			Gerstein and Reisman		Life Cycle	
Dimensions	Defenders	Prospectors	Analyzers	Dynamic Growth	Rationalization/ Maintenance	Growth Stage	Mature Stage
Environmental							
Uncertainty	Low	High	Middle	High	Low	High	Low
Volatility	Low	High	Middle	High	Low	High	Low
Magnitude of change	Low	High	Middle	High	Low	High	Low
Complexity	Low	High	Middle	High	Low	High	Low
Production Process							
Innovation requirements	Low	High	Middle	High	Low	High	Low
Degree of standardization	High	Low	Middle	Low	High	Low	High
Fixed investments	High	Low	Middle	Low	High	Low	High
Technological diversity	Low	High	Middle	High	Low	High	Low
Market							
Rate of growth	Low	High	Middle	High	Low	High	Low
Product innovation	Low	High	Middle	High	Low	High	Low
Product market domain	Narrow	Broad	Middle	Broad	Narrow	Broad	Narrow
Managerial							
Risk taking	Low	High	Middle	High	Low	High	Low
Degree of control	High	Low	Middle	Low	High	Low	High
Hierarchical emphasis	High	Low	Middle	Low	High	Low	High
Environmental proactiveness	Low	High	Middle	High	Low	High	Low
Organizational Structure							
Centralization	High	Low	Middle	Low	High	Low	High
Modus operandi	Mechanical	Organic	Mixed	Organic	Mechanistic	Organic	Mechanistic
Focal unit	Functional	Product	Mixed	Product	Functional	Product	Functional
Cultural							
Cultural climate	Regimented	Entrepreneurial	Mixed	Entrepreneurial	Regimented	Entrepreneurial	Regimented
Commitment	Moral	Calculative	Mixed	Calculative	Moral	Calculative	Moral

Table 3.6

Miles and Snow Scales for Measuring SBU Strategy Types

Defenders

A defender organization attempts to locate and maintain a secure niche in a relatively stable product or service area. The organization offers a more limited range of products or services than its competitors, and it tries to protect its domain by offering higher quality, superior service, lower prices, and so forth. Often, this type of organization is not at the forefront of developments in the industry. It ignores industry changes that have no direct influence on current areas of operation and concentrates instead on doing the best job possible in a limited area.

Prospectors

A prospector organization typically operates within a broad product-market domain that undergoes periodic redefinition. The organization values being "first in" in new product and market areas even if not all of these efforts prove to be highly profitable. The organization responds rapidly to early signals concerning areas of opportunity, and these responses often lead to a new round of competitive actions. However, this type of organization may not maintain market strength in all of the areas it enters.

Analyzers

An analyzer organization attempts to maintain a stable, limited line of products or services, while at the same time moves out quickly to follow a carefully selected set of the more promising new developments in the industry. The organization is seldom "first in" with new products or services. However, by carefully monitoring the actions of major competitors in areas compatible with its stable product-market base, the organization can frequently be "second in" with a more cost-efficient product or service.

Source: Charles C. Snow and Lawrence G. Hrebiniak, "Strategy, Distinctive Competence, and Organizational Performance," *Administrative Science Quarterly,* 25(2), (June 1980).

1. Stable forms of organization
2. A narrow and relatively immutable product domain with competition primarily on the basis of quality, price, delivery, or customer service
3. Infrequent adjustments in technology structure or methods of operation
4. A single, capital-intensive technology
5. Functional structure characterized by an emphasis on efficiency, extensive division of labor, hierarchical communication channels, and centralized control
6. A regimented organizational culture with an emphasis on moral commitment

2. Prospectors. The strategic patterns of prospectors oppose those of defenders. "Unlike the defender, whose success comes primarily from efficiently serving a stable domain, the prospector's prime capability is that of finding and exploiting new product and market opportunities" (Miles and Snow, 1978, p. 548). Even in the face of repeated failures, prospectors are willing to enter risky and unexplored product and market areas. Key characteristics of prospectors include (see Tables 3.5 and 3.6):

1. A strong concern for product and market innovation
2. A diverse product line
3. A product or divisionalized structure
4. A great deal of flexibility in its technology and administrative style
5. A management system that is decentralized, emphasizing loose planning, low degree of formalization, and lateral as well as vertical communication
6. An entrepreneurial organizational culture with a calculative commitment

3. Analyzers. Analyzers' strategies fall between those of prospectors and defenders. These SBUs are seldom first in new product or market areas, but they are often fast followers. They imitate the successful product or market innovations of prospectors. But, like defenders, analyzers try to retain a firm core of traditional products and customers. Key features of analyzers include (see Tables 3.5 and 3.6):

1. A balance between conflicting demands for technological and organizational flexibility on the one hand, and technological and organizational stability on the other.
2. A dual "technological core," one stable core that bears a strong resemblance to that of defenders (with high levels of standardization, routinization, and mechanization) and one flexible core that resembles that of prospectors (unstandardized, nonroutine, and organic).
3. An administrative structure and processes that try to accommodate both stable and flexible areas of operation, usually via a matrix organizational structure.

Organizational Life Cycle

The organizational life cycle is perhaps the most widely known structural variable used to describe a business unit strategy. Its central concept is that each business unit follows a cycle in the sale of its primary product. The stages of a business cycle are akin to those of the human biological cycle—infancy, adolescence, adulthood, and old age. These stages are purported to occur sequentially and in a hierarchical progression. They are triggered by both internal pressures (e.g., transition from entrepreneurial to administrative leadership; increasing age, size, and complexity) and external pressures (e.g., maturation of technology in industry; market saturation) (Adizes, 1979; Downs, 1967; Gray and Ariss, 1985; Greiner, 1972; Kazanjian, 1988; Kimberly, 1980; Lippitt, 1967; Mintzberg 1984; Quinn and Cameron, 1983; Walsh and Dewar, 1987). Its origin can be traced to the so-called production learning curve. Sales increase quickly at first as cost-per-unit drops because of "organizational learning," improvements in technology and production processes, and greater economies of scale. Then sales reach a point where volume flattens out and finally begin to decrease as the market is saturated (Day and Montgomery, 1983).

The beauty of the life cycle concept lies in its simplicity and the fact that "the most fundamental variable in determining an appropriate business strategy is the stage of the product life cycle" (Hofer, 1975, p. 788) and "empirical investigation has demonstrated that production processes normally move by a process life cycle that parallels the product life cycle" (Neidell, 1983, p. 32). Expanding on this theme, a number of authors have argued that HRM and compensation strategies vary according to the phase in which the firm's main product finds itself (Ellig, 1981).

However, life cycle models have been criticized in many fields, including marketing (Day and Montgomery, 1983), production (Dhalla and Yuspeh, 1976), entrepreneurship (Sexton, 1990), human resource management (Kerr and Kren, 1982), and strategy (Wiersema and Page, 1992). Major criticisms across these fields include:

1. Extending a biological analogy to organizations is questionable because they do not face stages with fixed chronological delimiters as living organisms do.
2. Different sets of policies may be appropriate for each stage. Therefore, it may be deceptive to offer universal prescriptions for any given organizational cycle.
3. The beginning and end of any given phase are difficult to measure reliably.
4. A business unit may have several products at different stages of the life cycle.
5. Many products enjoy a long maturity stage.

6. Life cycle curves do not always follow the traditional shape.
7. Life cycle theory does not account for radical innovations.
8. Authors often apply the term *life cycle* in a sloppy fashion to describe organization, corporate business unit, industry, or even functional strategies.

It would be beyond the scope of this book to delve into the controversy over the validity of life cycle models. Our position is that the life cycle concept, just like any simple model, can be criticized for being too naive. However, it is still a very useful heuristic device for understanding organizational processes and seems to be implicit in most business unit typologies, such as those of Miles and Snow (1978). For example, defender strategies refer to more "mature" business units and prospector strategies refer to "growing" business units. Similar overlaps may be found with other business unit typologies. In fact, Gomez-Mejia (1992) found that the way managers rate their business units in terms of life cycle vis-à-vis other typological strategies are highly correlated. This suggests that there is a common underlying dimension, at least perceptually. This is consistent with the earlier conclusions of Hofer (1975) and a comparative study of SBU generic strategies by Herbert and Deresky (1987). A sensible interpretation of life cycle research is advanced by Neidell (1983, p. 33), who suggested that "the [life cycle] concept, by itself and in concert with other empirical findings and theoretical constructs, can be a valuable tool for the analysis and development of competitive strategies."

While several phases have been identified by various authors, the following two categories are typical of life cycle stages used in previous compensation-related research (see Balkin and Gomez-Mejia, 1984, 1987a, 1990; Gomez-Mejia, 1992).

Growth Stage. In the growth stage, sales grow at 20 percent or more annually in real terms. Technology and competitive structure are still changing at this stage. Firms at this stage are characterized by a more entrepreneurial culture. (See Table 3.5 for other key features of firms at the growth stage.)

Mature Stage. In the mature stage, an organization's products or services are familiar to a vast majority of prospective users. Technology and competitive structure are reasonably stable. Firms at this stage are characterized by a more regimented culture. (See Table 3.5 for other key features of firms at the mature stage.)

Overarching Strategic Compensation Patterns and Business Unit Strategies

The lower portion of Table 3.4 shows the most prevalent compensation pattern (algorithmic or experiential) associated with various SBU strategies. Figure 3.2 presents a model that depicts the underlying predictors of strategic compensation patterns at the SBU level. This model indicates that an experiential compensation pattern at the SBU level is a positive function of an organizational culture that encourages utilitarian values and calculative commitment, an early growth stage in the SBU's product life cycle, a willingness to capitalize on environmental opportunities, a rapidly changing and unstable environment, and heavy reliance on innovation as a means to achieve competitive advantage. On the other hand, an experiential compensation pattern at the SBU level is negatively related to the presence of high entry barriers in the industry, a strong control orientation, and a mechanistic organizational structure.

The SBU typology developed by Miles and Snow (1978) has often been used in conceptualizing business unit strategies, particularly when examining compensation issues. In terms of structural characteristics at the business unit level, the life cycle concept has also played a pivotal role in the compensation strategy literature. The following discussion revolves around these typologies, focusing on the key elements responsible for a more experiential (or less algorithmic) strategic compensation pattern. (Appendix 3.2 shows a detailed chart of how different compensation strategy dimensions vary as a function of SBU strategies and life cycle stages.)

SBU Strategic Patterns: Miles and Snow Typology

Hambrick and Snow (1989), Miles and Snow (1984), Carroll (1987), and Wallace (1987) have all argued that the compensation strategy of a business unit depends on the extent to which it follows a prospector, defender, or analyzer strategy. Prospectors emphasize growth and capitalization of environmental opportunities through innovation, development of new products, and willingness to be first movers in new product or market areas, even if some of these efforts fail. This prospector strategy "is best implemented through an organic or loose, nonformalized organization that emphasizes decentralization of decision making and lateral communication" (Carroll, 1987, p. 345). Thus, a prospector strategy is associated with organic structures, fluid and complex tasks, and unstable environments with a rapid rate of change. This means that "there is less formalization and centralization managers are free to develop policies fitting their unique situations" (Wallace, 1987, p. 176). Furthermore, a free agent relationship between employee and firm is the norm. This means there is no expectation of a long-term commitment, and the employment contract is subject to change at any point in time, depending on the utility derived by both parties (Hambrick and Snow, 1989).

The compensation system of prospectors is likely to be closer to the experiential pay pattern, which is more suited to the prospector's organic orientation. According to Miles and Snow (1978), Wallace (1987), and Carroll (1987), the compensation strategy of prospectors should be characterized by a high performance orientation, external competitiveness, variable pay as a high proportion of total compensation, and an emphasis on aggregate incentives. Ironically, long-term incentives are generously given in an attempt to diminish a potentially high attrition rate of employees who show little attachment to their employer (Carroll, 1987).

Empirical evidence supports the notion that prospectors do indeed rely on more experiential compensation strategies. A field study by Broderick (1986) found that prospectors are characterized by a pay system with an external value orientation, high performance emphasis, extensive risk sharing, open communication, widespread employee participation, low standardization, and decentralized administration. Gomez-Mejia (1992) found that on the algorithmic-experiential continuum, prospectors scored the highest, indicating a very strong experiential orientation.

Among defenders, the compensation system assumes a more algorithmic orientation. These types of firms are characterized by highly formalized and centralized functional designs. They tend to define performance in terms of cost control, rather than market outcomes, and operate in a placid environment with stable tasks. High entry barriers in the industry allow many of these firms to develop an elaborate internal labor market that is relatively isolated from the vagaries of the external labor market. Employees are rewarded with job security and an expectation of upward mobility through the ranks in exchange for a long-term commitment to the firm. Furthermore, these firms discourage risk-taking behaviors because investments in existing technologies and processes are substantial and reliability is accorded a high priority. An experiential compensation pattern is less compatible with those conditions.

The algorithmic compensation strategies are more attuned to the defender's organizational structure. The pay system of defenders, according to Miles and Snow (1984, p. 49), should be characterized by "an orientation toward position in organizational hierarchy, internal consistency, and a total compensation heavily oriented toward cash (vis-à-vis long-term incentives) and driven by superior/subordinate differentials."

Empirical support for these assertions is relatively strong, although more research remains to be done. Broderick (1986) found that defenders share many of the characteristics associated with the algorithmic pattern. According to her findings, defenders emphasize internal rather than external equity, reward employees based on seniority, avoid risk sharing, keep pay communication and employee participation in the compensation system at a minimum, and develop a highly standardized and centralized administrative apparatus. Gomez-Mejia (1992) found that defenders score much lower than prospectors on the algorithmic-experiential continuum, corroborating Broderick's earlier findings (1986).

The analyzer category in the Miles and Snow taxonomy appears to follow a mixed compensation strategy somewhere in between the algorithmic and experiential extremes. Gomez-Mejia (1992) found that analyzers score 0.54 on the algorithmic-experiential continuum, as compared to 0.44 (high algorithmic) for defenders and 0.75 (high experiential) for prospectors. Similarly, Broderick (1986) found that the mean score across several compensation dimensions for analyzers falls somewhere between those of prospectors and analyzers.

In summary, it appears that the more mechanistic defenders rely on an algorithmic compensation strategy, while the more organic prospectors rely on a more experiential strategy. Analyzers fall somewhere in the middle of this continuum.

SBU Strategic Patterns: Gerstein and Reisman Typology

The Gerstein and Reisman (1983) typology has also been used to examine the relationship between SBU and compensation strategies. The main advantages are (1) that it is a hybrid of most existing SBU typologies and, therefore, has wide applicability across a broad cross section of firms, and (2) since it is easy to understand by practitioners, it is a valuable tool in survey research.

In a conceptual paper, Schuler (1987) argues that entrepreneurial and dynamic growth organizations require employees who are innovative, cooperative, long-term oriented, risk takers, flexible to change, and opportunity seekers. At the other end, firms that are more concerned with maintaining existing profit levels or cutting further losses (rationalization/maintenance and liquidation strategies, respectively) have a focus on short-term results "with a relatively low level of risk and minimal level of organization identification . . . employees need a short-term, narrow orientation . . . [there is] low organizational commitment, and a low need to remain" (Schuler, 1987, p. 13).

According to Schuler, compensation strategies for the two types of business units described have opposite orientations. The entrepreneurial and dynamic growth firms adopt compensation strategies that share many of the elements of the experiential compensation pattern. These firms place a greater emphasis on external equity, risk sharing, employee participation, and decentralized pay decisions. Business units falling in the rationalization/maintenance and liquidation strategy categories, on the other hand, have compensation strategies that share some commonalities with the algorithmic pattern. According to Schuler (1987), the compensation strategies of these firms are characterized by "short-term orientation, internal equity, low participation . . . few perks, fixed package, no incentives" (p. 9).

Based on a sample of 68 dynamic growth firms and 124 rationalization/maintenance firms, Balkin and Gomez-Mejia (1990) found empirical support for the notion that these two types of firms have different pay orientations. The rationalization/maintenance strategy is associated with a higher pay level relative to the market and more emphasis on salary and benefits vis-à-vis incentives. Pay policies in these types of firms are less egalitarian, involve less employee participation, and more job-based (suggesting a more algorithmic orientation). The dynamic growth strategy, on the other hand, is characterized by a more experiential pay orientation, namely a lower wage position relative to market, a greater reliance on pay incentives, egalitarianism, employee participation in pay decisions, and more use of skill-based pay.

SBU Structural Configuration: Life Cycle Models

With its roots in production and marketing, the life cycle concept has played an important role in strategic management. In the 1980s, life cycle models surfaced to the forefront of compensation strategy literature (Balkin and Gomez-Mejia, 1984, 1987a,b; Ellig, 1982; Milkovich, 1988).

Firms at the growth stage are associated with:

1. High dependence on new product innovation to get established in a particular industry (Tilles, 1966)
2. More variability in the firm's profits in response to market trends and shifts since fixed costs involving standardized technologies are relatively high as compared to more mature firms (Morrison, 1966)
3. A more unstable environment that calls for a greater willingness to take risks and a greater tolerance for ambiguity (Gupta and Govindarajan, 1984)

4. High rates of technological change (Hofer, 1975)
5. High rates of failure (Bell, 1982)
6. A sociotechnical system characterized by more risk-taking managerial and technical personnel (Ettlie, 1983)
7. Entrepreneurial managers who would rather work with employees who are willing to exchange job security and immediate rewards for the expected utility of anticipated growth (Balkin and Gomez-Mejia, 1987a,b)

For business units at the growth stage, the compensation system tends to be experiential in nature (Balkin and Gomez-Mejia, 1987a; Gomez-Mejia, 1992). These business units show a heavy reliance on incentives, rather than on salary and benefits, in the pay mix. This allows the firm at the growth stage to shift a substantial portion of its labor costs from a fixed to a variable expense. This provides the firm with a flexibility to push compensation costs into the future, when it is in a stronger financial position, and, therefore, to receive float from its workforce in the short run. Employees receive their incentives when the firm reaches its financial or other strategic goals. This compensation strategy allows the firm in the immediate present to make heavy expenditures needed to fuel future growth in R&D, technological improvements, product changes, and marketing efforts. By emphasizing incentives, employees working for these firms are more likely to be risk takers, which is a desired trait for these companies. The workforce may be willing to forego current income (relative to what may be obtained in comparable employment opportunities) in hopes of partaking in the anticipated profits if the firm succeeds. In this manner, incentive pay for these firms helps them not only to support future growth but also to attract a more "adventurous" workforce suitable to their needs and to motivate individual and group performance.

As firms mature, professional managers begin to replace entrepreneurs. One of the main tasks of these managers is to develop administrative mechanisms to formalize the organization, including the pay system. The firm's environment also changes, becoming more predictable with a stable market share. The rate of change in technology slows down, and greater economy of scale is achieved in the production process (Hofer, 1975). Employees hired into those firms are more security oriented and less willing to gamble their destiny with a fledgling company, even if it offers better future prospects.

The compensation system for mature firms is more algorithmic. That is, mature firms set up an administrative structure that deemphasizes incentives and rewards employees primarily through a regular paycheck. Job evaluation systems, such as the Hay Point factor method, are implemented. A formal pay hierarchy is established and is based on the job as the unit of analysis, rather than individual skills or contributions, with predetermined compensable factors used to make those decisions.

Although empirical research on the relationship between life cycles and compensation systems is limited, it supports the notion that firms at the growth stage rely on more experiential compensation strategies, while those at the mature stage use more algorithmic pay policies. Balkin and Gomez-Mejia (1987a) found that incentive pay as a proportion of the total compensation package is greater for firms at the growth stage of the product life cycle. Anderson and Zeithaml (1984) reported that pay level relative to competitors increases as a firm moves from a growth to a mature stage. Gomez-Mejia (1992), using the algorithmic-experiential continuum, found that growth firms score higher on the compensation strategy measure (0.72) than mature firms (0.42), indicating that the latter relies on algorithmic pay policies much more so than the former.

Stock options and other equity-based rewards are the vehicles most often used to drive the incentive programs for firms at the start-up and growth stages (Balkin and Gomez-Mejia, 1987b). Equity in the company may be offered generously to a broad cross section of employees. Since the stock is not publicly traded in most firms at early stages, the cost of stock to the firm is minimal. Stock ownership supports an egalitarian culture and a team approach that fosters risk taking and the entrepreneurial spirit. The use of stock options can also serve as powerful inducements to employees. They attract employees by promising the potential of large payoffs after the stock is publicly offered. They may induce employees to become more highly committed to the firm. Finally, stock options are designed to retain talent by placing restrictions on vesting rights to those who stay with the company for a certain period of time (usually three to five years).

Theoretical Propositions

The review conducted in this chapter offers the key factors that appear to underlie observed variations in compensation strategies at the corporate level, which can be summarized in the following propositions:

- Proposition 1. The greater the interdependence among business units, the more likely a corporation will rely on an algorithmic compensation pattern to facilitate the flow of human resources across permeable organizational boundaries.
- Proposition 2. An algorithmic pay pattern is more prevalent when there

is an extensive knowledge of organizational transformations in a central location; that is, when corporate managers know how business unit tasks should be accomplished to transform inputs into desired outcomes.

- Proposition 3. The greater the rate of new business acquisitions, the more likely a corporation will adopt an experiential compensation pattern to cope with multiple contingencies uniquely affecting different parts of the company.
- Proposition 4. Corporations are more likely to rely on an algorithmic pay pattern if growth is internally generated (e.g., as a technological or market spin-off) because resulting units tend to share a common pool of resources (e.g., R&D, facilities, personnel). This closely knit network calls for greater consistency and uniformity in compensation policies and procedures.
- Proposition 5. The more entrepreneurial a corporation is, the more likely it will utilize an experiential compensation pattern that deemphasizes control, encourages risk taking, and places a higher priority on long-term goals. Contrary to widely held beliefs, large organizations are not necessarily less entrepreneurial (see Balkin and Gomez-Mejia, 1988). Some of the largest and most successful corporations in the world frequently launch new business ventures in promising growth industries. These corporations attempt to gain a competitive edge by either creating their own entrepreneurial business units (such as IBM's personal computer business in the late 1970s) or by acquiring entrepreneurial businesses (such as Bristol-Myers acquiring genetic engineering firms in the 1980s). More entrepreneurial corporations adopt experiential compensation strategies because these offer greater flexibility and also reinforce an entrepreneurial spirit.
- Proposition 6. An experiential compensation pattern is more prevalent as business units become more heterogeneous in terms of markets, products, technology, and so on. This approach allows the corporation to be more adaptive to the idiosyncratic needs of each subsidiary.
- Proposition 7. An organization will rely on an algorithmic compensation pattern if its top managers desire to promote a unitary corporate-wide perspective. This may be the case, for example, in an owner-managed corporation or a closely held firm.
- Proposition 8. As organizations become more complex, an algorithmic compensation pattern becomes more prevalent in an effort to create a sense of order, rationality, and predictability.
- Proposition 9. Organizations that attempt to harvest an existing market niche by limiting themselves to a narrow product line are more likely

to implement algorithmic compensation strategies. These pay strategies engender greater consistency in procedures, more intimate forms of control by superiors, more stability in the workforce, more specialization in terms of assigned jobs, a focus of rules of the "game" to be followed by the entire organization, and tighter coupling of organizational subunits.

- Proposition 10. Organizations facing limited cash flows and a need to divert scarce funds to finance future expansion are more likely to follow an experiential compensation strategy with its emphasis on risk sharing, flexibility-variable pay, performance, long-term orientation, and outcomes as a trigger for rewards. These pay characteristics keep fixed and sunken costs to a minimum, while still allowing the firm to attract and retain a workforce that may be willing to exchange higher potential gains for lower immediate payoffs.

For companies that own two or more separate businesses under a corporate umbrella, several underlying factors are important determinants of the extent to which any given business unit (SBU) relies on an algorithmic or experiential compensation pattern. These relationships may be synthesized in the following propositions:

- Proposition 11. An experiential compensation pattern is more prevalent among SBUs that aggressively try to exploit environmental opportunities. This compensation pattern allows SBUs to develop tailored pay policies and procedures to deal with varied external threats and opportunities.
- Proposition 12. The greater the volatility and complexity of the external environment facing an SBU, the more likely it will rely on an experiential compensation pattern. These pay strategies are more easily molded to withstand environmental jolts. For instance, a rapid drop in sales may be cushioned by a corresponding decline in variable pay without a dramatic effect on profitability or employment level.
- Proposition 13. The greater the extent to which an SBU depends on innovation and technological breakthroughs for its survival, the more likely it will develop experiential compensation strategies. Because meaningful mechanisms are difficult to develop and flexibility is needed to nurture innovation, adaptable compensation policies and procedures are more appropriate for knowledge-intensive firms. For instance, variable incentive programs in a wide cross section of employees are instrumental in maintaining an egalitarian culture and team approach in order to foster

technological innovation. Variable pay gives management more freedom in distributing compensation dollars to employees and may be used as a powerful signaling device to emphasize meeting R&D deadlines, increasing market share, launching a new product, or any other objective that it makes a high priority.

- Proposition 14. An algorithmic compensation pattern will be more evident in business units with a mechanistic organizational structure. These SBUs are characterized by highly repetitive tasks, extreme division of labor, expendable workers, and activities that are relatively narrow and standardized. Historic data is available for control purposes; lines of authority and responsibility are clearly drawn; and monitoring activities are highly centralized in the top echelons of the organization. Employees spend long careers in the firm, moving through the ranks after "paying their dues" at each successive level. An algorithmic compensation pattern reinforces a mechanistic organizational structure by emphasizing uniformity, rules, and procedures, order and predictability, and centralized control in the pay system. The algorithmic compensation pattern is used by these firms because it is efficient, and efficiency, rather than adaptability, is perceived by top management to be more instrumental in accomplishing both personal and firm objectives. The use of formal compensation systems with job analysis, job descriptions, job evaluations, and salary structures are used to control costs. Managers are rewarded for reducing expenditures by operating more efficiently and maintaining a flow of steady, predictable profits and quarterly dividends.

- Proposition 15. An algorithmic compensation pattern is most likely to be found in business units where the start-up costs and entry barriers are substantial. In these organizations, investments in a core technology may be so prohibitively high that management will try to buffer this core from uncertainty. The compensation system may be used to discourage risk-taking behavior by penalizing (or at least not rewarding) employees for trying new methods or approaches outside established parameters. There is a general belief that deviation from the norm carries a greater downside risk than remaining loyal to the modus operandi. Furthermore, the internal labor market can be more easily protected from external jolts as industry entry barriers increase, facilitating the effective implementation of an algorithmic compensation pattern with its emphasis on hierarchy, rules and procedures, internal equity, centralized decision making, monitoring of behavior by superiors, and fixed pay.

- Proposition 16. An algorithmic compensation pattern is more common in firms that have a low tolerance for mistakes from managers or employees. The corporate control systems provide planned standards for performance and knowledge of results with the variances monitored between planned and actual performance. A mistake is viewed as undesirable because mistakes occur when planned outcomes are not attained. The managers and employees learn to meet or exceed planned standards in order to maintain their jobs and move up the career ladder over time. The organizational climate is such that employees understand superiors are not willing to support them when an assumed risk leads to a negative outcome.

- Proposition 17. An experiential compensation strategy is more likely to be followed by firms that are at the initial stages of growth and that are short on cash needed to finance future expansion. The distribution between fixed pay (salary and benefits) and variable pay (incentives) is skewed toward the latter in these organizations. This is particularly true if venture capital is being used either from the parent firm or from external sources. By maximizing the portion of total earnings that is variable in nature, the firm can disperse some of its risk across multiple employees. Because the proportion of labor costs to total revenues is higher at earlier stages of the life cycle, scarce resources are freed and may be directed to support expansion-related activities (e.g., open new market channels, invest in a larger facility, add office automation equipment). If the organization is successful, the variable pay is received by employees; if the firm fails to meet all its objectives, some variable pay is forfeited. This package design matches the high-risk/high-reward environment that faces employees.

- Proposition 18. An experiential compensation strategy is more likely to be present in organizational cultures whose value system rests on a calculative, utilitarian, free agent exchange between employees and the firm. The experiential compensation pattern is instrumental to this type of culture because it is not intended to reinforce loyalty or allegiance to an accepted way of doing and thinking. It does, however, generate a strong sense of ownership and responsibility for operations and decisions and an entrepreneurial climate, encouraging employees to pursue multiple leads with a minimum of organizational constraints.

Policy Implications and a Research Agenda for the Future

To our knowledge, only two recent studies followed the path forged by Gomez-Mejia and Balkin, supporting their earlier work. The first, by Rajagopalan and Datta (1996) argued that both managerial discretion and incentive alignment problems (agency issues) differ according to business unit strategy, using data on 50 investor-owned electric utility firms over a five-year period. In prospectors, not only do managers have more discretion, but also managerial behaviors cannot be specified a priori because of the greater uncertainty and focus on new products, markets, and creativity. Thus, incentives become especially important for promoting risk taking and a long-term orientation. According to their work, prospectors performed better on both accounting and market-based measures when long-term plans were used for senior managers. They also found that defenders did better on the accounting return measure when they used annual bonus plans and worse when they used long-term plans. Interestingly, their work shows the main effects of pay strategy to be essentially zero. Instead, effects depended on the business unit strategy, which is in line with the main premise of this chapter.

The second study (Boyd and Salamin, 2001) echoed the overall conclusion of previous studies. The authors used a unique sample of 917 employees from two large Swiss financial institutions along with some additional information. The authors found that pay systems are linked with divisional strategic orientation, but in a different form than was found in prior studies. Results indicated that strategic orientation affects the pay of all employees, not just top managers. Hierarchy had a significant effect on pay plan design and an interactive effect with strategic orientation. Additionally, orientation affects multiple aspects of the compensation plan. Findings of this study indicate that base salary can be viewed as more determined by individual characteristics (gender, age, hierarchical position) than by strategic orientation, while bonus is largely explained by strategic orientation rather than individual factors. As a consequence, the authors advocated relying on "base pay to preserve consistency, and on bonus to foster flexibility" (p. 790).

Besides the above studies, most recent studies have not addressed the categorization of strategies per se. Rather, the focus has been on the impact of pay on specific strategic decisions. Yet studies in this area are minimal. In a recent review, Werner and Ward (2004) lamented that outcomes of executive pay have been explored by a handful of studies while four times as many studies have looked at the determinants of executive pay.

Two recent studies focused on explicit strategic issues. Bigley and Wiersema (2002) analyzed the role of compensation in corporate strategic refocusing—measured as the percentage reduction in the firm's level of diversification. Carpenter (2000) found that CEO pay is reflected in strategic change—viewed as variation in firm strategy and deviation from industry strategic norms. He also found that changes in total CEO pay, long-term pay, and long-term pay structure were found to affect strategic change in a sample of large U.S. firms, but the effects of pay on change were positive when firm performance was low; the relationships were negative among the highest-performing firms.

Other studies analyzing the impact of pay on specific strategic actions include performance and fit (Carpenter and Sanders, 2002), shark repellents (Frankforter, Berman, and Jones, 2000), human capital and leadership (Miller and Wiseman, 2001), acquisition and divesture behaviors (Iskandar, Datta, and Raman, 2001; Sanders, 2001), stock repurchase programs (Westphal and Zajac, 2001), risk taking (Rajgopal and Shevlin, 2002), information disclosure (Nagar, Nanda, and Wysocki, 2003), internationalization (Carpenter and Sanders, 2004), and environmental performance (Berrone and Gomez-Mejia 2009). Collectively, results of these studies suggest that pay does influence executive action, but in a more complex manner than the one prescribed by the principal-agent framework (see Chapter 5). As a consequence, more research is needed to fulfill several important areas in which the amount of empirical research is almost nil. Fertile ground lies fallow for future work on the relationship between organizational and compensation strategies.

Gaps in the literature are abundant. One reason for this may lie in the overemphasis of agency theory as the general framework of analysis. But "fit" issues are especially important in developing a sustainable competitive advantage. Therefore, the resource-based view of the firm (RBV) may be a promising setting in which to build subsequent research. The RBV emphasizes that resources contribute to sustained competitive advantage not only by creating value but also by being rare, difficult to imitate, and lacking substitutes. If a resource adds value exclusively, it may help achieve competitive parity but not competitive advantage. If a firm follows the same best practices as other firms it can achieve parity at best. However, if the firm develops unique alignment between elements of its pay strategy and the business strategy, this can help to achieve an edge over rivals.

RBV has been obliquely used as a general framework for compensation. A notable exception is the work by Balkin, Markman, and Gomez-Mejia (2000), who extended the RBV to argue that innovation will influence both long- and short-term CEO compensation in high-technology firms. Specifically, they argued that in environments characterized by high uncertainty and high discretion, because innovation is more easily controlled by principals, CEOs will be rewarded more for innovation (e.g., R&D and patents) than for firm performance. Their results confirmed this proposition. Furthermore, Balkin and colleagues found no link between pay and ROA. But there is very little available research beyond this work. Additionally, other important taxonomies have been neglected. For instance, a major SBU taxonomy classifies firms as following a differentiation, cost leadership, or focus strategy (Porter, 1985). While some authors (e.g., Gerhart, 2000) have equated the cost leadership and differentiation strategies to the defender and prospector strategies respectively, it is not clear that this simplification holds (e.g., it could be the case of a prospector cost leadership firm). Most likely, future research on strategic pay schemes will require an interdisciplinary, systemic perspective that bridges HRM, organizational theory, and strategic management.

The following discussions outline a research agenda concerning the issues that the authors believe require immediate attention.

Mixing Compensation Strategies

In terms of both specific pay strategies (e.g., internal vs. external equity) and overall strategic pay patterns (i.e., algorithmic vs. experiential) organizations have substantial discretion as to where they wish to be on a continuum. That is, it is not a categorical decision of whether to adopt one set of pay choices (e.g., algorithmic) versus another (e.g., experiential) but to what extent to be one way or the other. However, little is known about whether this can be done effectively for the entire continuum, or whether mutually inconsistent demands constrain a further mixing of elements of the two strategic pay orientations and produce an entropic condition. This raises the possibility that while firms may alter their compensation strategies over time, it is quite conceivable that the chosen strategies may be mutually exclusive within a given range. Therefore, further pursuit of one strategy may preclude pursuit of the other.

Relationships Between Corporate Culture, SBU Culture, and Compensation Strategy

Despite the wealth of research on the role of corporate culture in HRM practices (e.g., Fombrun 1983, 1984a–c, 1993; Fombrun, Tichy, and Devanna, 1984; Fombrun and Tichy, 1984; Fryxrell, 1990; Hybels and Barley, 1990; Kerr and Slocum, 1988; Ulrich 1984; Von Glinow, 1985), most of the evidence on the purported relationship between organizational culture and compensation strategy is anecdotal in nature (e.g., Cooper, 1991; Kay, Gelfond, and Sherman, 1991; Gordon, 1991). Conceptual development is also relatively naive at this point and in need of more rigorous deductive models that examine how particular compensation strategies engender or follow from particular norms, myths, and beliefs in organizations (Gomez-Mejia, 1983, 1984, 1986). For instance, it is the authors' intuition that an algorithmic compensation strategy is more likely to be implemented effectively in an organizational culture known for its attachment to tradition and placing high value on continuity, regimentation, and security. On the other hand, an experiential compensation strategy is more likely to be implemented successfully in an organizational culture characterized by discontinuity, redefinition, and renegotiation of tasks and roles as new conditions emerge. Such firms also view uncertainty and insecurity as challenges that energize and stretch people so that they can thrive and grow.

Very little research exists beyond the work by Carpenter and Sanders (2004) on how multinational companies align their strategies and their pay choices. This area of research is particularly promising given the globalization process many firms have faced during the past three decades. Geographical and cultural distances are now important contingencies to be considered when designing pay strategies.

Strategic Employee Groups

Most research on compensation and strategy has focused on CEOs and top management teams as they generally are viewed as the most important employee group in organizations. However, an organization may have dozens or even hundreds of different employee groups performing diverse tasks, and their importance is likely to vary across companies. For instance, in high-tech firms, scientists and R&D employees are vital in securing the innovation pipeline. Similarly, in most research universities, faculty are viewed as more important than administrators and are treated accordingly. Some faculty members earn more money than department chairs, deans, or even the university president (Gomez-Mejia and Balkin, 1992). We need more conceptualizing and empirical research to help determine under what conditions an employee group becomes strategically important and how the reward system can be designed to take this into account. The empirical research and conceptualizing on compensation strategy to date, with the exception of top executive pay, is very global, treating all employee groups as a single entity. To the extent that algorithmic or experiential pay strategies may be more appropriate for different groups within the same organization this is clearly an area where additional research is needed.

Balancing Consistency and Contingency

Very little is known about how organizations buffer employee groups exposed to different pay strategies. However, buffering is likely to be an important problem when different pay systems and benefits are used for various SBUs, management layers, and employee populations (e.g., use of team incentives for R&D workers but not for production engineers). Carroll (1988) calls this balancing act one of the major challenges in the management of compensation. Yet minimal guidance is given to follow if pay is to be used differentially as a strategic tool.

Compensation as a Change Agent or a Follower

While some recent research has analyzed the role of compensation as a symbolic action to satisfy external and internal stakeholders and obtain societal acceptance (Westphal and Zajac, 1994, 1998, 2001), little is known about the extent to which the reward system can be consciously manipulated from the top to change the culture below. The relative effectiveness of such manipulation is not clear. Hearsay evidence suggests that pay allocation may be used as a powerful top-management tool to change organizational culture. For example, the deliberate linking of pay raises, promotion, and tenure decisions for faculty based on publication record seems to have had a major effect in changing the culture of many "teaching" schools to more research-oriented environments. Agency theory, as discussed in Chapter 1, argues that pay is an important signaling device. However, there is practically no empirical research on how this process works (or doesn't work) below the executive levels neither on the variables that mediate the effectiveness of deliberate signaling attempts via the reward structure.

Compensation Strategy as Derived from Organization Strategy

Related to the previous point, most of the literature assumes that compensation strategy follows from organization strategy (e.g., Milkovich et al. 1991). Pay strategy is often posited as just one more implementation element (along with marketing, production, etc.) of the overarching organizational strategy. Some authors go even further and discuss pay strategy as one of the specialized subfunctional strategies within HRM (e.g., Weber and Rynes, 1991). These views, however, are unnecessarily constraining and may not reflect organizational realities. There is plenty of evidence (as discussed here and in Chapter 6) to suggest that top corporate management and divisional managers formulate firm strategy largely in response to the characteristics of the compensation package (e.g., in terms of payoff criteria, variability, downside risk, long-term orientation) established by the board of directors. Quite often the compensation package for top management teams is not consciously designed to achieve strategic objectives, but may simply reflect the biases of the compensation committee of the board of directors, the consulting firm, and the executives' preferences. While recent research has focused more on the consequences of compensation schemes on organizational strategic actions, more research is needed to ascertain how compensation strategy is causally related in a prior manner to the strategies adopted by those individuals in a position of power at different levels in the organization.

Influence and Adaption to Environmental Changes

Most of the studies discussed in this chapter employ a cross-sectional research design and focus on explaining differences between firms' strategies in executive compensation. Studies examining changes in executive compensation over time as a response to environmental shifts are almost nonexistent. This issue is particularly important given that a change in environmental conditions may not only require a change in the organizational strategy but also an adaptive pay policy to follow such changes. In a recent research note, Cho and Shen (2007) used the context of deregulation in the airline industry to show that a dramatic environmental change that heightens managerial discretion leads to greater pay level and performance sensitivity of top management team compensation. They also found that the greater the magnitude of turnover among team members following the environmental shift, the greater the compensation change. Despite the good intention of these authors, knowledge about the relationship between environmental changes, redesign of compensation schemes, and organizational strategies is nil, inviting researchers to explore this line of enquiry.

Role of Dominant Coalitions

As noted in Chapter 1, dominant coalitions in organizations play a very important role in deciding how the reward system is to be structured. Research on this issue is practically nonexistent. The indirect evidence available suggests that this is a promising avenue to follow if an understanding of how compensation strategies come about increases. For example, the reward structure in many high-technology firms, with a very experiential orientation, reflects the value system of scientists and engineers who are part of the dominant coalition (Gomez-Mejia and Balkin, 1985). Likewise, the reward structure of firms that are funded by venture capital shows many of the characteristics of the experiential pay pattern (e.g., high variable pay and external market orientation), reflecting the wishes of the venture capitalists who are often actively involved in the management of the company (Gomez-Mejia et al. 1990).

A stream of research on the upper-echelons perspective (see Hambrick, Black, and Frederickson, 1992; Hambrick and Mason, 1984; O'Neill, Saunders, and McCarthy, 1989; Thomas and Ramaswamy, 1989) has proposed that the background characteristics of top managers and the board of directors can be used to predict the strategic choices of firms. A similar relationship may exist between the background of these individuals and the reward structure adopted by firms. The underlying argument here is that an individual's education and life experiences shape personal values and these, in turn, determine choices made. McCann and Gomez-Mejia (1989, 1990, 1992), for example, found that how managers conceptualize international issues affecting their firm reflect their professional experience. Similar arguments about the relationship between an individual's background (e.g., functional area of origin) and decision outcomes may be found in Hayes and Abernathy (1980), Lawrence and Lorsch (1977), and Miles and Snow (1978). It would be interesting in future research to ascertain how the background and individual characteristics of the dominant coalition affect a firm's compensation strategies. These issues are covered again in Chapter 5.

Flexibility Versus Calcification

Presumably, one of the key advantages of a strategic approach to compensation is that the reward system can be molded to fit varying situations, contingencies, and objectives (see Chapter 5). However, organizations are reluctant to change HRM systems once they are installed, and these systems quite often remain in place for years after they outlive their usefulness. This happens because employees develop expectations, and compensation practices become "psychological contracts," which are difficult to change. This is one of the problems plaguing gain-sharing and profit-sharing plans. Because employees expect monetary rewards from these programs, they react very negatively and voice widespread dissatisfaction with the company when they do not materialize (see CompFlash, 1991; Welbourne and Gomez-Mejia, 1988).

A related issue that is rarely discussed in the literature is that the coordination of pay strategies and the SBU or corporate strategy should reflect the intended (i.e., future) rather than the "de facto observed" (i.e., present) organizational strategy. For instance, pay strategies should not be designed to match the corporation's current level of diversification but should be guided by the direction in which the organization's diversification strategy is expected to move. If a dominant-product firm is trying to diversify into unrelated products and a conglomerate plans to trim down by selling unrelated SBUs, then perhaps an experiential pay strategy should be phased into the former and an algorithmic pay strategy slowly introduced into the latter.

Related to this issue is the importance of strategic change and how it interacts with compensation. Recent research has advanced some elements on these matters. For instance, Grossman and Cannella (2006) found that internal corporate directors, CEOs/chairs, and other officers who own a significant proportion of company stock favor stability and were rewarded with higher total compensation for strategic persistence. They also suggested that external participants (large block shareholders) tended to favor change and therefore penalized persistence, although this prediction was not corroborated by their results.

In summary, more must be learned about how compensation strategies respond to firm strategies and the extent to which built-in inertia prevents the pay system from being attuned to the strategic demands of both the corporation and SBUs.

Role of Individual Differences and Choices

Some scholars have suggested that shareholder value creation is related more to the individual choices of employees than to their strategic choices, yet there has been very limited research concerning how individual differences affect employee reactions to compensation strategies (see Rynes et al. 2005). More work is needed to understand the effect of pay on employees' effort levels and their decisions to, for instance, select firms and either remain with their firms or leave. This is also important because, as seen in Chapter 5, these differences are likely to moderate the effectiveness of pay strategies. Individual differences are not random. They follow a certain pattern (e.g., more risk-taking personnel joining entrepreneurial firms). It may be possible to take this into account when deciding the position of a firm along the algorithmic-experiential compensation continuum in different situations. For example, Gomez-Mejia and Balkin (1989) report that individuals with a high propensity for risk and a high tolerance for ambiguity thrive in firms where variable pay is a substantial portion of total compensation. This, they found, was clearly the case among smaller high-technology firms. Forcing an experiential compensation pattern with high variable pay in more mature companies where the typical employee has a low tolerance for risk and a greater desire for certainty is met with resistance and engenders attrition. This research has uncovered just the tip of the iceberg, and no one can assume that compensation strategies may be implemented uniformly in the workforce without factoring in individual differences.

Linkage Between Top Management Compensation Strategies and Overarching Compensation Strategies

As seen in Chapters 6 and 7, much has been written about compensation strategies for top executives, particularly CEOs. However, very little is known about how CEOs interact with, or perhaps even determine, the compensation strategies of an entire organization. Agency theory, as discussed in Chapter 1, proposes that the structure of the CEO compensation package influences the reward system throughout the organization. Top executives are likely to reward subordinates' behaviors that are conducive to the achievement of their own objectives. Recently, Werner et al. (2005) found that ownership dispersion is associated with a decoupling of pay increases from firm performance and a closer linkage between pay increases and firm growth for all employees. This suggests that the impact of ownership structure on pay-performance relations cascades to lower rungs of the organizational ladder. But there is a dearth of research examining how this process works. Nor is there much research on how the conditions under which the "filtering down" of the incentive system for top executives may influence the firm's relative positioning along the algorithmic-experiential continuum.

Internal Compensation Strategy Versus Imitation

Much of the literature on compensation strategy assumes that organizations have much freedom to choose their own pay strategies, which, in general, are designed to be compatible with the overall firm strategy. This is reflected in the fundamental tenets summarized by Milkovich (1988) as "first . . . that compensation policies and practices differ widely across organizations and second . . . that the decisions managers and employees make help shape these differences; that discretion exists to choose among options and the processes used to implement them" (p. 263). This way of thinking is derived from the strategic choice view (e.g., Child, 1972; Miles and Snow, 1978; Mintzberg, 1980), a dominant paradigm in organization theory and strategic management. According to this perspective, which is very inner-directed, strategic decisions are made by key managers who perceive and interpret environmental situations in order to design proactively organizational responses. Because perceptions, rather than actual reality, play a major role here, a wide variety of organizational responses may be made, depending on managers' cognitive orientation and values.

As seen in Chapter 5, the primary determinant of whether the choices made contribute to organizational performance is internal congruency (between, for example, pay strategies and the organizational strategies adopted by management). However, it is quite possible that compensation strategies are chosen to imitate those of other firms in the industry (as many industrial/organizational economists would suggest), rather than being internally generated. Ample evidence of intense imitation in the compensation system across firms was found by Balkin and Gomez-Mejia (1987a) among high-technology companies along Route 128 in Boston, Massachusetts. An important reason behind the impetus to adopt experiential pay strategies (e.g., various forms of variable pay plans) may simply be attributed to imitation. Most likely, both internal forces and imitation play a role in the design of compensation strategies, but little is known about their relative importance and how compensation strategies may be idiosyncratically designed to gain a competitive advantage. Integrating the two partial views—one that focuses on strategic choices as a predictor of resulting pay strategies and the other that relies on imitation—would enhance an understanding of the determinants and consequences of pay strategies.

Compensation Strategies in an International Context

A crucial question that arises as a result of increased globalization of business is whether reward systems should be customized to meet the needs of individuals within diverse cultures or compensation strategies that work in a domestic environment can be easily transferred from one country to another. So, it is not just a question of molding pay strategies to organizational strategies but also of ensuring that the compensation system is attuned to the cultural milieu (Gomez-Mejia, 1988b; Gomez-Mejia and McCann, 1989; Gomez-Mejia and Welbourne, 1991; McCann and Gomez-Mejia, 1986; Sanchez-Marin, 2008a,b). For instance, bonus pay in Japan averages 26 percent of the norm for the United States.

One clear trend is that multinational corporations (not just American but also European and Asian) are standardizing pay strategies on a global basis. The question that must be raised, then, is whether global compensation strategies are most appropriate for these organizations. Can some compensation strategies be used effectively on a universal basis while others are customized to meet the specific needs of diverse national cultures? Because practically all research on compensation strategy has been conducted in the United States, generalizations on the conclusions of these studies imply that the U.S. example is most often considered to be the worldwide standard. However, well-known variances between countries of pay levels and makeup indicate that the U.S. case seems to be more of an outlier than the worldwide standard (Berrone and Otten, 2008). Tosi and Greckhamer (2004) showed that national cultures systematically influence executive pay. The higher degrees to which differences in power and status are accepted in a culture seem to lead to higher pay. Apparently, in cultures where differences in social status and positions of power are more socially accepted it is also more acceptable for executives to have higher pay levels and possibly more discretion to influence their pay. However, to be able to generalize the implications of given pay practices for the level and structure of pay, more comparative studies are needed. More importantly, differences in pay levels and structures across and within countries seem to remain over time and still exist when controlling for firm and executive characteristics such as firm size and executive age (e.g., Abowd and Bognanno, 1995; Conyon and Murphy, 2000; Kaplan, 1994; Murphy, 1999; Zhou, 1999). Moreover, very little is known about how international forces affect pay strategies and their effectiveness.

Given the growing importance of international trade, overseas manufacturing operations, increased growth of multinationals, new countries entering international trade, and the rapid changes in technology needed to keep pace with the world economy, this area of research clearly merits more attention. While research on the effect of culture on managerial practices has grown enormously since the early 1980s, very little of it has focused explicitly on compensation issues.

Summary

The central notion behind the taxonomic models discussed here is that both pay and organizational strategies consist of multiple elements that can be clustered into meaningful subgroups, and these, in turn, may be used to study a firm's relative standing along a number of key strategic dimensions. The empirical research reviewed in this chapter strongly suggests that different corporate and business unit strategies are associated with varying pay strategy configurations. A more experiential pay pattern is evident in single- or unrelated-product firms, multibusiness or conglomerate-type companies, firms that grow rapidly through aggressive acquisitions, prospectors and dynamic-growth business units, and those firms at the growth stage of their life cycles. At the other extreme, a more algorithmic orientation in the pay system is associated with dominant- and related-product firms with a vertically integrated chain of businesses. This orientation is also evident where all businesses relate to a single core strength or characteristic, companies that expand through internally generated diversification, defender firms with a rationalization/maintenance strategy, and companies at a mature or decline stage.

Appendix 3.1. A Profile of Compensation Strategies Associated with Various Corporate Strategies

	Corporate Strategies		
	Diversification Extent	Patterns of Linkages	Diversification Process
BASIS FOR PAY			
Unit of Analysis			
Job	Related product	Vertical/ constrained	Steady
Skills	Single unrelated product	Multibusiness/ conglomerate	Evolutionary
Criteria for Pay Increases			
Performance	Single unrelated product	Multibusiness/ conglomerate	Evolutionary
Tenure	Related product	Vertical/ constrained	Steady
Level of Performance Measurement			
Individual	Related product	Vertical/ constrained	Steady
Individual and aggregate	Single unrelated product	Multibusiness/ conglomerate	Evolutionary
Time Orientation			
Long term	Single unrelated product	Multibusiness/ conglomerate	Evolutionary
Short term	Related product	Vertical/ constrained	Steady
Risk Sharing			
High	Single unrelated product	Multibusiness/ conglomerate	Evolutionary

Low	Related product	Vertical/ constrained	Steady
Strategic Focus			
Corporate	Related product	Vertical/ constrained	Steady
Division/business unit	Single unrelated product	Multibusiness/ conglomerate	Evolutionary
Equity Concern			
Internal consistency	Related product	Vertical/ constrained	Steady
Market driven	Single unrelated product	Multibusiness/ conglomerate	Evolutionary
Reward Distribution			
Egalitarian	Single unrelated product	Multibusiness/ conglomerate	Evolutionary
Hierarchical	Related product	Vertical/ constrained	Steady
Appraisal Basis			
Monitoring behaviors	Related product	Vertical/ constrained	
Monitoring outcomes	Single unrelated product	Multibusiness/ conglomerate	

DESIGN ISSUES

Salary Market Policy			
Above-market pay	Related product	Vertical/ constrained	Steady
Below-market pay	Single unrelated product	Multibusiness/ conglomerate	Evolutionary
Benefits Market Policy			
Above market	Related product	Vertical/ constrained	Steady
Below market	Single unrelated product	Multibusiness/ conglomerate	Evolutionary

Incentives in Pay Mix			
High	Single unrelated product	Multibusiness/ conglomerate	Evolutionary
Low	Related product	Vertical/ constrained	Steady
Total Compensation			
High potential/ low immediate payoffs	Single unrelated product	Multibusiness/ conglomerate	Evolutionary
Low future potential/higher immediate payoffs	Related product	Vertical/ constrained	Steady
Reinforcement Schedule			
Multiple rewards/ high frequency	Single unrelated product	Multibusiness/ conglomerate	Evolutionary
Fewer rewards/ low frequency	Related product	Vertical/ constrained	Steady
Reward Emphasis			
Nonmonetary	Related product	Vertical/ constrained	Steady
Pecuniary	Single unrelated product	Multibusiness/ conglomerate	Evolutionary

ADMINISTRATIVE FRAMEWORK

Decision Making			
Centralized	Related product	Vertical/ constrained	Steady
Decentralized	Single unrelated product	Multibusiness/ conglomerate	Evolutionary
Pay Disclosure			
High pay openness	Single unrelated product	Multibusiness/ conglomerate	Evolutionary
Low pay openness	Related product	Vertical/ constrained	Steady

Appendix 3.2. A Profile of Compensation Strategies Associated with Various Business Unit Strategies

	Business Unit Strategies		
	Miles and Snow Typology	Gerstein and Reisman Typology	Life Cycle
BASIS FOR PAY			
Unit of Analysis			
Job	Defenders	Rationalization/ maintenance	Mature/decline
Skills	Prospectors	Dynamic growth	Start-up/growth
Criteria for Pay Increases			
Performance	Prospectors	Dynamic growth	Start-up/growth
Tenure	Defenders	Rationalization/ maintenance	Mature/decline
Level of Performance Measure			
Individual	Defenders	Rationalization/ maintenance	Mature/decline
Individual and aggregate	Prospectors	Dynamic growth	Start-up/growth
Time Orientation			
Long-term	Prospectors	Dynamic growth	Start-up/growth
Short-term	Defenders	Rationalization/ maintenance	Mature/decline
Risk Sharing			
High	Prospectors	Dynamic growth	Start-up/growth
Low	Defenders	Rationalization/ maintenance	Mature/decline
Strategic Focus			
Corporate	Defenders	Rationalization/ maintenance	Mature/decline
Division/ business unit	Prospectors	Dynamic growth	Start-up/growth

Equity Concern			
Internal consistency	Defenders	Rationalization/ maintenance	Mature/decline
Market driven	Prospectors	Dynamic growth	Start-up/growth
Reward Distribution			
Egalitarian	Prospectors	Dynamic growth	Start-up/growth
Hierarchical	Defenders	Rationalization/ maintenance	Mature/decline
Appraisal Basis			
Monitoring behaviors	Defenders	Rationalization/ maintenance	Mature/decline
Monitoring outcomes	Prospectors	Dynamic growth	Start-up/growth
Salary Market Policy			
Above market policy	Defenders	Rationalization/ maintenance	Mature/decline
Below market policy	Prospectors	Dynamic growth	Start-up/growth
Benefits Market Policy			
Above market benefits	Defenders	Rationalization/ maintenance	Mature/decline
Below market benefits	Prospectors	Dynamic growth	Start-up/growth

DESIGN ISSUES

Incentives in Pay Mix			
High	Prospectors	Dynamic growth	Start-up/growth
Low	Defenders	Rationalization/ maintenance	Mature/decline
Total Compensation			
High potential/ low immediate payoffs	Prospectors	Dynamic growth	Start-up/growth

Low future potential/higher immediate payoffs	Defenders	Rationalization/ maintenance	Mature/decline
Reinforcement Schedule			
Multiple rewards/ high frequency	Prospectors	Dynamic growth	Start-up/growth
Fewer rewards/ low frequency	Defenders	Rationalization/ maintenance	Mature/decline
Reward Emphasis			
Nonmonetary	Defenders	Rationalization/ maintenance	Mature/decline
Pecuniary	Prospectors	Dynamic growth	Start-up/growth

ADMINISTRATIVE FRAMEWORK

Decision Making			
Centralized	Defenders	Rationalization/ maintenance	Mature/decline
Decentralized	Prospectors	Dynamic growth	Start-up/growth
Pay Disclosure			
High pay openness	Prospectors	Dynamic growth	Start-up/growth
Low pay openness	Defenders	Rationalization/ maintenance	Mature/decline
Governance Structure			
Participative	Prospectors	Dynamic growth	Start-up/growth
Nonparticipative	Defenders	Rationalization/ maintenance	Mature/decline
Nature of Pay Policies			
Bureaucratic	Defenders	Rationalization/ maintenance	Mature/decline
Flexible	Prospectors	Dynamic growth	Start-up/growth
Superior Dependency			
High	Defenders	Rationalization/ maintenance	Mature/decline
Low	Prospectors	Dynamic growth	Start-up/growth

4 EXECUTIVE COMPENSATION

Theoretical Foundations

This chapter and the following two chapters focus on pay for top executives. While Mintzberg (1990) and other strategy theorists (e.g., Wooldridge and Floyd, 1990) have warned us about the danger of becoming overly obsessed with senior executives, nowhere else in a firm is there a stronger need for close linkage between compensation and organizational strategies than at the top executive level. There are three main reasons for this.

First, and most obvious, strategic decisions affecting the entire firm are normally made by top executives. Policy choices concerning growth or cutbacks, expansion via mergers and acquisitions or internal resources, diversification into unrelated or similar product lines, "harvesting" existing products by using present technology or investing in capital equipment and R&D, among others, are the responsibility of top management. Evidence suggests that the reward system plays a major role in how those decisions are made because executives are very responsive to what they perceive will lead to a personal payoff (Baysinger and Hoskisson, 1990; Devers, Cannella, Reilly and Yoder, 2007; Devers, McNamara, Wiseman and Arrfelt, 2008; Fong, Misangyi, and Tosi, 2010; Pennings, 1991; Zajac, 1990). As a result, a pay package designed to reinforce the wrong strategic choices (e.g., rewarding short-term results at the expense of long-term performance) will be highly detrimental to the firm's future success. At a societal level, the aggregate result of poorly designed executive compensation programs coupled with weak government oversight of dubious corporate actions may lead to widespread economic malaise and a sense of deep unfairness when top ranks seem to benefit from gaming the system (Loomis, 2009a; Parloff, 2009). For this reason President Barack Obama has called executive compensation (particularly in the financial industry) "immoral."

Next, in the typical firm, senior management provides general guidelines as to the form of the compensation package and payment criteria for all employees. Executives will set priorities for subordinates and reward those activities they perceive as consistent with their own incentive system (Cronquist et al. 2009; Fong et al. 2010; Gomez-Mejia, 1988a; Werner, Tosi, and Gomez-Mejia, 2005; Wade et al. 2006). Likewise, members at the lower ranks in the organization are quick to discern what the top echelon considers important and is willing to reward and will tend to act accordingly. Consequently, goals and objectives built into the executive compensation plan are likely to have a multiplier effect on the entire workforce.

Third, as a corollary to the previous point, executive compensation is critical to the firm's HRM subsystem because its incentive properties eventually filter down in the organization and signal to all employees those behaviors that will be conducive to personal success. As noted in Chapter 2, while the question of whether pay is a motivator is as old as humankind itself and continues to stir controversy, most behavioral scientists agree that employees tend to do things that they believe are recognized by their bosses. The way compensation dollars are allocated sends a powerful symbolic message throughout the organization of what is and is not valued (Devers, Wiseman, and Holmes, 2007; Dow and Raposo, 2005).

Partly because of its strategic importance, but also because of its high visibility and the large sums of money involved, executive compensation is perhaps the most controversial subject in this book. Annual pay packages of some CEOs may reach eight-digit figures, and seven-digit figures are now normal among Fortune 500 firms (Lublin, 2008). For instance, in 2008, the median estimated pay of Fortune 500 CEOs reached $8,848,000 (Lublin, 2008). Many individuals surpassed this number by a huge amount and it was difficult for the public to understand how these figures could be justified, particularly under conditions of weak firm performance. For instance, John A. Thain, CEO of Merrill Lynch, made $78.52 million even when shareholder return had dropped by 41 percent since he took the helm of the company at the start of 2007; Lloyd C. Blankfein, CEO of Goldman Sachs, made $68.5 million in 2008 although total shareholder return had decreased 17 percent since 2006; Kenneth I. Chenault, CEO of American Express, made $46.23 million in 2008 even though shareholder return was minus 13 percent the prior year; and Richard S. Fuld, Jr., CEO of Lehman Brothers Holdings Inc., earned $40 million in 2008 while shareholders' return was minus 14 percent in 2007.

At the heart of the debate is whether executives deserve to earn these exorbitant amounts. Critics complain that in the United States, the ratio of CEO income to that of the lowest paid worker is 20 times greater than in other industrialized countries (Deyá-Tortella et al. 2005). And a huge literature has focused primarily on the issue of whether or not these pay amounts are rational. Prior to 1997, at least 300 empirical papers had addressed this issue (Gomez-Mejia and Wiseman, 1997). Since 1997, Devers and colleagues

(2007) counted several hundred papers on executive compensation, with 99 of them appearing in top academic journals.

Interdisciplinary Conceptual Roots

Executive pay has provided very fertile ground for theory development across several disciplines. Several factors influence decisions on strategic compensation choice at the executive level; these are derived from paradigms that have emerged in diverse fields (see Figure 4.1).

The first of these paradigms is *marginal productivity theory*, which has its roots in macro- and microeconomics. It is primarily concerned with pay level. The three paradigms that follow focus on the *governance* aspects of executive pay—managerialism, agency theory, and the behavioral agency model—all of which borrow from political science, sociology, finance, and economics. They deal with pay level, risk sharing and risk bearing, fixed pay versus incentives, short- versus long-term orientation, type of performance measures, performance targets, and external versus internal forces.

The next theoretical perspective to be examined consists of sociological theories that emphasize hierarchical relationships and number of organizational levels as predictors of executive pay level. *Human capital theory* has its roots in labor economics and focuses on individual characteristics of the executive. It is primarily interested in pay level. The view of *executive pay as symbolism* has its roots in organizational behavior and focuses on the myth-forming and political aspects of executive compensation. It is concerned with pay level and reliance on qualitative versus quantitative performance measures. This perspective encompasses *tournament theory* and the concept of the executive as figurehead and political strategist. Tournament theory justifies large pay differentials at the top as a motivating force to induce greater competition (and hence, effort) at lower organizational levels. *Pay dispersion theory*, focuses on pay differentials within top executive ranks and argues that greater pay dispersion is associated with dysfunctional conflict, leading to poor individual and firm performance. And *self-selection theory* argues that pay incentives not only influence effort but also determine the type of executive that is attracted to the firm and the likelihood of staying employed in that firm.

Marginal Productivity Theory

The oldest and perhaps most enduring theoretical explanations of executive pay have their origin in classical and neoclassical economics. As described below, these represent analytical extensions of the theory of the firm.

Figure 4.1   **Executive Pay: Theoretical Frameworks and Associated Compensation Dimensions**

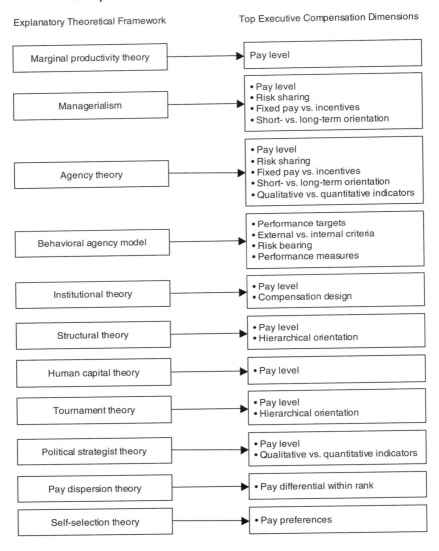

Explanatory Theoretical Framework   Top Executive Compensation Dimensions

| Marginal productivity theory | Pay level |

| Managerialism | • Pay level
• Risk sharing
• Fixed pay vs. incentives
• Short- vs. long-term orientation |

| Agency theory | • Pay level
• Risk sharing
• Fixed pay vs. incentives
• Short- vs. long-term orientation
• Qualitative vs. quantitative indicators |

| Behavioral agency model | • Performance targets
• External vs. internal criteria
• Risk bearing
• Performance measures |

| Institutional theory | • Pay level
• Compensation design |

| Structural theory | • Pay level
• Hierarchical orientation |

| Human capital theory | • Pay level |

| Tournament theory | • Pay level
• Hierarchical orientation |

| Political strategist theory | • Pay level
• Qualitative vs. quantitative indicators |

| Pay dispersion theory | • Pay differential within rank |

| Self-selection theory | • Pay preferences |

The Owner as Entrepreneur

In the classical theory of the firm, the CEO and the firm owner are one and the same. The entrepreneur comes up with an idea for a marketable product, starts the firm with his/her own resources, assumes all the risks for this investment, and is driven by a single-minded objective of minimizing cost per unit in order to maximize profits. In other words, there are no professional managers hired by external owners to perform administrative tasks. The entrepreneur is the executive and will either make all the gains or suffer the consequences of his/her actions.

If one assumes that there is perfect competition in the product and labor markets (i.e., perfect information, instant mobility of resources, large number of firms so that no single company can affect price, and rational behavior on the entrepreneur's part), one can make the following predictions:

1. The entrepreneur will manage the firm so that it uses the least cost combination of inputs (labor, materials, etc.) to produce the profit-maximizing level of output.
2. Profit maximization is achieved at the point where the marginal cost of production (the change in total costs with a change in the level of output) is just equal to the market price of the product.

Given this scenario, the compensation received by the entrepreneur is identical to the firm's net profits.

The Executive as Hired Labor

The neoclassical economic models relax the assumption that the entrepreneur and CEO are the same person. A professional executive may be hired to manage the firm, and this individual will be treated like any other input, receiving compensation in return for his/her services. Other things equal, the amount received will depend on the executive's marginal productivity, which, like any other factor of production, will be equal at equilibrium to that individual's marginal revenue product.

According to neoclassical economists (see Roberts, 1959), the marginal revenue product of a CEO is the total firm profit under his or her stewardship, minus the profit level that would be achieved if the firm was at the helm of the best alternative executive, plus the amount that would have to be paid to hire the latter. In other words, the marginal revenue product of an executive is not only a function of observed firm performance but also the opportunity costs of having him/her in command instead of someone else. If one assumes perfect information and mobility in the labor market and a wide range of alternative jobs open to executives and executives available to firms; then all executives will be paid at a rate equal to their marginal revenue products.

If the strict assumptions of perfect competition are relaxed, some neoclassical theoreticians maintain that executive pay will fall somewhere between a minimum and maximum level on a continuum, rather than on a precise equilibrium point (Roberts, 1959). The upper limit that the firm would be willing to pay the executive is his or her marginal revenue productivity; that is, the sum of "excess profits" under his or her command plus the cost of hiring a replacement. The lower limit is the minimum pay that the CEO would accept from the firm. This amount would equal the next best financial offer that he or she could command in the open market. The range of indeterminacy in executive pay can be quite large, and firm size then becomes an important determinant of where the range will ultimately lie. The size of the firm also has a role within this theoretical framework (Gomez-Mejia, Tosi, and Hinkin, 1987).

First, a smaller firm has a difficult time matching the profits of larger firms, even if it operates more efficiently. While profit per unit may be less in the larger firm, its greater volume of sales as compared to the smaller firm allows the larger firm to convert even a modest marginal gain in profit per unit into a larger amount of total profits. So, smaller margins may be associated with higher profits for larger firms, and executives will be rewarded accordingly up to the point where total profits begin to decline.

Second, the cost of paying for the CEO's services relative to the total revenue of the firm is a decreasing function of firm size. For example, in a firm with a total revenue of $20 billion, even a compensation package of $2 million for the CEO would be less proportionate in terms of total revenues than in a firm selling $5 million a year and paying its CEO $100,000 annually. In other words, the firm's ability to pay the CEO increases as the denominator in the ratio of CEO compensation to total revenue increases.

Third, the market for executives is likely to be segmented according to firm size. Thus, a large firm will fill vacancies by hiring replacement CEOs from other large firms. Given a more limited pool of potential applicants from which to recruit executives, a bigger company must pay a premium to attract and retain executives from other large firms. The actual pool of available applicants shrinks even more if one segments the executive market by industry. Firms prefer to hire CEOs from within the same or a highly related industry (McCann, Hinkin, and Gomez-Mejia, 1992; Hambrick, Finkelstein, and Mooney, 2005). This reduces the number of available alternatives and, thereby, bids up their market price.

Fourth, as discussed later under the human capital model, firm size, complexity of CEO tasks, and amount of responsibility entrusted to the CEO tend to go hand in hand. Therefore, as the firm becomes larger, one would expect a corresponding increase in CEO pay to compensate the executive for the skills necessary to carry out successfully the additional duties vested on the job.

In summary, this theoretical formulation suggests that executive pay level is a positive function of (a) firm performance under the executive's stewardship; (b) lower value of firm performance indicators if the next best alternative executive were to be hired as a substitute for the present CEO; (c) the compensation to be paid to the best alternative replacement; (d) best pay rate executive could obtain in the labor market; and (e) firm size.

Based on this discussion, the reader should not be left with the impression that firm size, rather than performance, should be the number-one determinant of executive pay level or that larger firm size leads to improved profitability. The implication that should be drawn is that in a continuum of executive pay levels with marginal revenue productivity setting the upper bound (or firm performance in more common parlance) and a lower bound set by "going rates" in the executive labor market, one can reasonably expect that firm size will make a difference. There is nothing in the arguments to suggest that increases in firm size, profit per unit, and total profit necessarily go together. That is true if one were to examine a broad cross section of firms, ranging from the smallest to the largest firms in the economy. But if one were to examine firms within a given size category (let's say small, medium, and large), there may be little, if any, relationship between scale of operations and total profits. Among the Fortune 1,000 group, for example, for any given firm, even tiny improvements in efficiency may produce greater company profits than would be obtained through further increases in size (Gomez-Mejia, Tosi, and Hinkin, 1987).

Governance Theories

Both the classical and neoclassical economic models treat the firm as a "black box." The executives are largely reactive and their pay level is determined by forces outside their control. Furthermore, these models portray a world where either the entrepreneur and executive are embodied in the same person or the owner hires the executive and sets his or her pay following a rational deductive process. While those simplifying assumptions are helpful for analytical purposes, the typical firm in most Western countries has a corporate structure with not one but hundreds, thousands, or even millions of owners, each having a small claim on the firm. The modern corporation is perhaps the greatest invention of the nineteenth century and offers many advantages over the single-owner firm:

1. It allows the accumulation of vast amounts of capital in a single organization by pooling the resources of many individuals so that the firm is not constrained by internal financing. Those superior resources can then be used for heavy investments in capital equipment, channels of distribution, R&D expenditures, and so on, that may not be possible otherwise. By the same token, larger economies of scale may lead to greater efficiency and lower cost per unit.

2. Risk can be spread across many stockholders so that large, expensive projects with uncertain payoffs may be undertaken, and limited liability protects the interests of any single stockholder.

3. Because the corporation has a "life of its own" and is independent of any one individual, its time horizon is much longer so that long-term investments can be made.

4. Authority can be delegated to managers who have specialized knowledge, thereby capitalizing on the unique skills of these individuals.

5. Because corporate stocks are openly traded, the security market can gauge the competitive performance of the firm, and its stock value will reflect that assessment.

While the corporate form of organization has some clear advantages, it also raises some disturbing questions concerning managerial behavior that were inconsequential in the traditional economic models. Because ownership is no longer identifiable in any real sense in the modern corporation, who determines executive pay? Since the executives themselves run the firm, is it possible for them to use their position of power to further their own interests, rather than those of stockholders? Both managerialism and agency theory deal with corporate governance issues arising from the fact that the decision-making process in those firms may be in the hands of professional managers whose interests do not necessarily coincide with those of atomistic owners.

Managerialism

The underlying premise of managerialism was succinctly stated by Berle and Means (1932, p. 25) many years ago: "The separation of ownership from control produces a condition where the interests of owner and of ultimate manager may, and often do, diverge, and where many of the checks which formerly operated to limit the use of power disappear."

Interestingly enough, the main ideologue of capitalism, Adam Smith, warned of problems stemming from the "separation of ownership and control" back in 1776 (Smith, 1937, p. 700):

The directors of such [joint stocks] companies, however, being the manager rather of other people's money than of their own, it cannot well be expected that they should watch over it with the same anxious vigilance with which the partners in a private company frequently watch over their own. Like the stewards of a rich man, they are apt to consider attention to small matters as not for their master's honor, and very easily give themselves a dispensation from having it. Negligence and profusion, therefore, must always prevail, more or less, in the *management* of the affairs of such a company.

The problem Adam Smith identified in the eighteenth century has a greater sense of urgency today, given the increasing dispersion of stockholdings in most American firms. Managerialists such as Berle (1931), Berle and Means (1932), Marris (1964), Williams (1985), Herman (1981), and Aoki (1984) argue that executives who run modern corporations are no longer motivated to maximize profits as the traditional economic models would lead us to believe. Rather, they are free to pursue their own interests, and often these do not coincide with those of stockholders. Managerialists make the following predictions about executive behavior that is unconstrained by external owners:

1. Executives are risk averse. Therefore, they will structure their compensation packages so that pay is flexible to move up as firm performance improves but will not suffer if performance declines. Therefore, variability, downside risk, and uncertainty are largely removed from their pay packages.
2. Firm performance will play a minor role in executive compensation decisions so that the economic well-being of the executive is largely decoupled from the firm's (and stockholder's) fortunes (Cennamo, 2008; Dyl, 1988; McEachern, 1975; Wright, Kroll and Elenkov, 2002). By the same token, executives are less likely to be fired, even as firm performance plummets (Salancik and Pfeffer, 1980).
3. Executives are driven to increase firm size, even if additional growth results in decreased profits. This may be accomplished via corporate diversification (Ahimud and Lev, 1981) or through mergers and acquisitions (Kroll, Simmons, and Wright, 1990; Wright et al. 2002). Managerialists impute two main motives to the CEO's "sales maximizing" behaviors. First, expanding scale of operations enhances the visibility of the firm. This promotes the CEO's prestige, appealing to his or her ego needs (Marris, 1964; Chatterjee and Hambrick, 2007). Second, firm size may be used by executives and hired consultants to justify higher pay at the top (Dyl, 1988; Tosi et al. 2000).

4. Executives are tempted to make decisions that have short-term pay-offs and to adopt accounting measures of performance that can be embellished to inflate annual reports (Aboody and Kasznik, 2000; Chauvin and Shenoy, 2001; Lie, 2005; Heron and Lie, 2007). Profit satisficing, rather than maximizing, becomes the norm (Galbraith, 1976). Long-term investments and incentive pay based on long-term results are discouraged because these are uncertain, and executives have little loyalty to any given firm (Marris, 1964). There is much interfirm mobility as executives jockey with each other for power, prestige, and additional income. Thus, there is little gain to be made by engaging in activities whose time horizon is several years down the pike and that may, in fact, show up as a cost in the annual balance sheet (Bergstresser and Philippon, 2006; Brouwer, 1984; Johnson and Kaplan, 1987; Heron and Lie, 2007; Meyer, 1983; Rappaport, 1978, 1981, 1986; Sears, 1984). Therefore, the executive compensation package tends to reward short-term performance.

How can executives get away with the self-serving behaviors described here? The first reason has already been discussed. It is difficult for isolated, dispersed stockholders to muster enough concerted power to discipline top management. Besides the logistic problems, no single stockholder may have enough at stake to launch a major campaign against company executives. Ultimately, the main restraint facing executives consists of changes in the price of marketable shares carrying limited liability so that stockholders may shift their investments from one firm to another. Managerialists, however, feel that this is not much of a constraint as long as the firm meets some minimum performance levels, which is not hard to accomplish for a well-established corporation operating in oligopolistic or quasi-oligopolistic markets.

Second, because of their privileged position, "information asymmetries" exist. The executives always know what is happening better than stockholders do, and may use this information imbalance to their own advantage (Holmstrom, 1979). It would be almost impossible for stockholders to have access to all the information involved in business planning, competitive strategies, R&D investments, choice of accounting methods, inventory methods, and depreciation procedures, to name a few. Thus, executives may use their superior knowledge to make decisions that are most beneficial to them. For example, R&D expenditures can be cut back over time and then kept at a very low level. This could have a very healthy impact on the annual reports for a few years, even if it could prove disastrous over, let's say, a 20-year period, at a time when present management would be long gone (Hill and Hansen, 1989).

Third, managerialists argue that the board of directors is generally ineffective in disciplining executives. This view is vividly exemplified in the following comments:

> The people who set the CEO's pay . . . they are the compensation committee . . . always conflicted, usually co-opted . . . they have the tricky task of setting salaries for their peers, who more often than not, are their friends. . . . The CEO, whose pay the committee sets, sits on both sides of the table. That's because 76 percent of board chairmen are also CEOs. Indeed, instead of laboring to serve the shareholders, a CEO looking to enrich himself could just do as well selecting a compensation committee whose members earn more than does . . . [because] committee members gauge the reasonableness of a CEO's salary again their own. . . . Management usually hires the consultant. And what consultant happy with his career choice would knowingly bite the hand that feeds him? (Fierman, 1990, pp. 5 and 66)

> Blowing it by the board of directors is usually pretty easy. Often enough, bosses who get big raises return the favor by handing out higher fees and benefits to the board. (Castro, 1991, p. 40)

> Wherever you find highly paid CEOs, you'll find highly paid directors. It's no accident. (Crystal, 1991, p. 40)

> Aggressive boards determined to rein in management's clout and rewards remain the exception rather than the rule. Pay committees too often take away with one hand and give back with the other. (Nell Minow, cited in *Wall Street Journal,* 2008a, p. R2)

> Compensation committee leaders feel torn between pleasing investors and pleasing the top brass. (Lublin, 2008)

Fourth, not only is the board accused of being ineffective, as illustrated in the above citations, but some argue that board members, just like executives, indulge in self-serving behaviors and often receive hefty fees and perks that cannot be justified on any rational basis (Boone et al. 2007; Herman, 1981; Fierman, 1990).

Fifth, the board may be used as an institutional mechanism to legitimize decisions beneficial to executives and give them a rational, objective image (Coles, Daniel, and Naveen, 2007). For example, equity-based pay on the surface may be used to tie the fortunes of the executive to those of stockholders. The more stock price appreciates (which is obviously good for stockholders), the more income executives receive. Following this logic, boards can grant executives multimillion-dollar contracts where the bulk of it is in the form of stocks. Managerialists, however, often see those plans as another plot to enrich top management, under a good faith pretense. According to Marris (1964, p. 25): "The stock option method, therefore, represents a way of paying gratuities to management *which* has the double advantage of ensuring that the whole cost falls on shareholders, while at the same time reducing the chance that the effect will be noticed."

In summary, managerialists portray a situation where managers can utilize their position of power in organizations to cater to their financial and non-pecuniary interests, perhaps at the expense of stockholders. The system of governance in major corporations is devoid of checks and balances because of a fractionalized distribution of ownership, and this works to management's advantage.

Agency Theory

Because of its overarching nature, agency theory has been referred to in several chapters of this book. However, most conceptual developments and empirical research on agency theory have taken place within the context of executive compensation. In the authors' opinion, agency theory is an extension of managerialism, although its roots can be found in diverse disciplines, such as accounting.

Agency theory recognizes that in most modern firms there is a separation between owners, called the principal, and hired managers, called the agent. Like managerialists, most agency theorists argue that this type of governance arrangement creates an intrinsic "moral hazard" for managers (Brick and Chidamibaran, 2008; Fogarty et al. 2008; Holmstrom, 1979; Jensen and Meckling, 1976). This moral hazard may be attributed to a number of reasons that greatly overlap with those advanced by managerialists. First, given that it is difficult for atomistic owners to convene or interact with each other, agents will enjoy much discretion to set policies and procedures for the organization, independent of the wishes of the principals. Second, because situations may arise where the interests of the principal and agent do not converge, the agent is likely to maximize its own utility, not that of the principal. Third, the agent's superior access to information gives it more power to extract concessions from principal.

In the parlance of agency theorists, the above conditions produce *agency costs* to be incurred by owners, where these are defined as the difference between net earnings when owners are the managers and observed net earnings under the agent's stewardship. At the very least, these costs include losses to the principal, because the agent does not act in the principal's interest, and the cost of monitoring the activities of the agent (Becerra, 2009).

Unlike managerialists, however, many agency theorists paint a more hopeful picture for stockholders. They view agency costs as a necessary evil that comes along with the advantages of the modern corporation (i.e., accumulation of needed capital risk spread, economies of scale, managerial specialization, etc.). Furthermore, many argue that it is possible to minimize the agency costs resulting from the separation of ownership and control. This can be accomplished through a system of monitoring the behavior of agents and the establishment of incentives that align the interests of owners with those of the executive.

Perhaps the best known theoretical exposition of the role of monitoring in reducing agency costs is that of Fama (1980) and Fama and Jensen (1983a). According to these authors, a firm can be viewed as a "nexus of contracts," written and unwritten, between its principals and its agents. These contracts, or "internal rules of the game," allow the organization to use the specialized knowledge of managers, while at the same time limiting their discretion. So, unlike managerialists, executives are not portrayed as having free rein to make decisions that may be detrimental to firm owners. Top management discretion is curtailed by "the rights of each agent in the organization and the performance criteria on which agents are evaluated" (Fama and Jensen, 1983b, p. 305). These contracts are enforced through an elaborate decision-making process. This process can be broken down into four stages (Fama, 1980).

The first stage is called *initiation* and is the responsibility of the agents. Top executives are expected to generate ideas and proposals for utilizing existing resources and scan the environment to identify available opportunities and potential threats. The second stage is called *ratification*. The action agenda developed by top management must be approved prior to implementation by an independent group of individuals, normally the board of directors. The third stage is called *implementation*. This consists of the execution of ratified decisions and is the responsibility of the agents. The fourth and final stage is called *performance measurement*. At this point, the principals or their representatives assess the contributions made by top management and will reward them accordingly. The initiation and implementation of decisions are designated as *decision management*. The approval and performance measurement functions are termed *decision control*.

According to Fama and colleagues, the use of decision hierarchies through which the higher level agents must ratify and monitor lower agents' initiatives and the existence of boards of directors who ratify and monitor the organization's most important decisions and who have the power to hire, fire, and reward top executives, " . . . offers an effective common approach to controlling the agency problems caused by separation of decision-making and risk-bearing functions" (Fama and Jensen, 1983b, p. 307). In fact, contrary to the tenets of managerialism, Fama joyfully proclaims that "in this nexus of contracts perspective ownership of the firm is an irrelevant concept" (Fama, 1980, p. 20).

In addition to the monitoring of agents, a second mechanism to reduce agency costs is the so-called incentive alignment. The focus here is not on supervising the behavior of managers or creating checks and balances in the decision-making system, but, rather, on rewarding agents for measurable results that are deemed to be in the best interest of owners. In order for incentive alignment to work as intended, it should complement, rather than be a substitute for, monitoring activities on the part of the principal. However, a number of factors affect the relative emphasis placed on each.

First, available information on agents' activities may be very limited, difficult to interpret, or too time-consuming and cumbersome to gather. Also, it may be nearly impossible for the principal to observe and evaluate directly the actions of management (Berrone and Gomez-Mejia, 2009; Grossman and Hart, 1983; Leland and Pyle, 1977). Therefore, the harder it is to obtain reliable information on the agent's behavior, the more likely the firm will rely on incentive systems that track outcomes, rather than the process leading up to them. Most incentive systems are tied to objectives, which are quantifiable indices of firm performance, such as return on equity, earnings per share, or changes in stock prices, that can be plugged into a predetermined formula to ascertain the executive's payoff. On the other hand, principals will seldom rely on incentive alignment alone, regardless of the difficulties encountered in monitoring the agent's activities (Makri, Lane, and Gomez-Mejia, 2006). Exclusive reliance on incentive payoffs tied to specific performance indicators can be dysfunctional. The agent may ignore other important dimensions of performance that are not directly captured in the compensation formula being used. For example, managers may cut back on capital expenditures to show higher year-end profits (and receive a larger bonus), negatively impacting the firm's competitive performance over time.

Second, if designed properly, the incentive structure of top managers will encourage mutual monitoring throughout the entire organization. The extent of monitoring can ensure that activities of lower level agents who are not perceived by those in higher ranks to contribute to valued outcomes are penalized or go unreinforced. Also, risk sharing between principals and agents will induce top executive ranks to closely supervise the behaviors of subordinates because their "neck is on the line" (Shavell, 1979).

While easy to distinguish conceptually, what constitutes monitoring and what represents incentive alignment are difficult for managers to separate in their minds (Tosi and Gomez-Mejia, 1989, 1994). Tosi and Gomez-Mejia developed two sets of scales to measure these two different constructs and had 175 managers rate them as they applied to their firms. The correlation between the two reached 0.81, suggesting that, perhaps because of the reasons discussed here, monitoring and incentive alignment are intrinsically dependent on each other.

Ultimately, according to Fama and colleagues, the marketplace is the final arbiter that decides which organizations survive and which ones will wither away. Management is not free to plunder the firm's resources in extravagant perks and compensation because concern for their personal reputation and the market disciplinary forces will keep them in check.

The permanence of the corporate form of firm governance is the best testament to its instrumental value and to its ability to control agency problems. Fama (1980, p. 292) summarizes what has become known as the *efficient market hypothesis* in agency theory as follows:

> The separation of security ownership and control can be explained as an efficient form of economic organization within the "sets of contracts" perspective. The firm is disciplined by competitors from other firms, which forces the evolution of devices for efficiently monitoring the performance of the entire team and its individual members. In addition, individual participants in the firm, and in particular its managers, face both the discipline and opportunities provided by the market for their services, both within and outside the firm.

The Behavioral Agency Model

The behavioral agency model developed by Wiseman and Gomez-Mejia (1998) integrates concepts from prospect theory (Kahneman and Tversky, 1979), behavioral theory of the firm (March and Shapira, 1987, 1992), and agency theory (Jensen and Meckling, 1976). Agency theory was discussed earlier. Prospect theory and the behavioral theory of the firm argue that risk preferences of decision makers and thus the amount of risk they take depends on how the situation is framed. Agency theorists, in contrast, continue to assume consistent risk aversion (Letza et al. 2008).

According to prospect and behavioral theory, decision makers are more inclined to take greater risks when they believe they are in a loss situation (situation is framed negatively). At the other end, decision makers will avoid risks when they believe they are in a gain situation (situation is framed positively). For example, a negatively framed situation would be one in which performance has declined over the years or is below the performance of similar firms in industry (Gomez-Mejia et al. 2007). Thus, decision makers are loss averse rather than risk averse, which affects how they respond to a bad (i.e., declining or below industry performance) or a good (rising or above industry performance) situation.

Wiseman and Gomez-Mejia (1998) argue that prospect and agency theories are complementary, so that combining them may improve the predictive and explanatory value of agency-based models of executive behavior. In their model, risk bearing mediates the relationship between how the situation facing an executive is framed (positive or negative) and the amount of risk the executive is willing to take. Risk bearing is defined as perceived risk to agent (executive) wealth that can result from employment risk or other threats to agent wealth. A self-interested individual is less concerned with maximizing future wealth by taking more risks than minimizing losses to present wealth. Reframing the problem of corporate governance in this way is important as executives may engage in more risk taking to reduce losses, not necessarily to increase personal wealth. By replacing an assumption of risk aversion with an assumption of loss aversion in models of corporate governance, Wiseman and Gomez-Mejia (1998) make several important predictions:

1. Positively framed problems (i.e., a gain context) increase risk bearing, and risk bearing, in turn, exhibits a negative influence on risk taking.
2. Rising firm performance over time elevates executive aspirations for future firm performance and thus decreases the probability of a gain context.
3. Risk bearing results from threats to future base pay (i.e., salary) and anticipated adjustments to that pay.
4. To the extent that future base pay (i.e., salary) is insulated from the threat of loss, executive risk bearing is reduced and executives may therefore be more willing to pursue contingent (i.e., performance-based) pay through riskier strategic choices.
5. Restructuring base pay (i.e., salary) into contingent pay (i.e., performance-based) creates a perceived loss for the agent.
6. Unexercised, positively valued stock options create risk bearing for the executive, which ultimately increases executive risk aversion.
7. Stock options do not create risk bearing for the executive when the down-side risk of stock options is set to zero.
8. A high, variable-pay target increases the probability that executives will face a loss decision context and ultimately leads to an increase in executive risk taking.

9. Variable-pay targets must adjust with performance to ensure that executives face loss decision contexts.

10. Reliance on market-based (external) outcome performance criteria increases the probability of a loss context (because executives have less control over them).

11. Reliance on accounting-based (internal) outcome performance criteria increases the probability of a gain context (because executives have more control over them).

12. Strong supervision of an executive by the board corresponds to more difficult performance targets.

13. Weak supervision of an executive by the board corresponds to easier performance targets.

14. The use of subjective performance criteria by the board creates uncertainty for the executive over how performance will be evaluated, increases agent risk bearing and ultimately reduces agent risk taking.

Sociological Theories

Institutional Theory

In recent years, perhaps due to increased globalization, greater attention has been paid to the influence of institutional and cultural factors on compensation practices around the world. With few exceptions (Berrone and Gomez-Mejia, 2009; Sanchez-Marin, 2008a,b; Gerhart, 2008; Newman and Floersch, 2008), most of this work is theoretical and focuses on top executives (Takacs-Haynes, 2008; Cennamo, 2008; Berrone and Otten, 2008). For instance, Balkin (2008) argues that it is impossible to explain the observed differences in CEO pay level and CEO compensation design around the world without examining the role of institutional forces such as mimetic isomorphism (practices of peer organizations), normative isomorphism (norms that develop in professions that receive similar training), and coercive isomorphism (corporate governance system, practices and regulations). Likewise, Wiseman, Gomez-Mejia, and Cuevas (2010) argue that institutional factors such as transparency, regulations, preferred leadership style, and networks affect executive compensation level and design of compensation package, not only across countries but also within industries. Gomez-Mejia and Wiseman (2007) and Gomez-Mejia, Wiseman, and Johnson (2005) add that institutional forces simply change the particular manifestations of agency problems but that the basic tenets of agency theory are not invalidated by institutional theory.

Structural Theory

The structural models of executive pay originated in the sociological tradition. This perspective holds that the compensation received by top ranks in a firm is a direct function of the number of organizational levels below them. Other things equal, the taller the organizational structure, the greater the earnings of top executives. The best known rationale for this relationship was provided by Simon (1957), who argued that organizations attempt to maintain appropriate salary differentials between management levels and establish these differentials not in absolute terms, but as ratios. The differentials between ranks are not determined by economic forces, but, rather, through cultural processes that create relevant norms of social stratification. The resulting pay scales are an attempt to maintain "internal consistency" of the managerial pay scale with the formal organization and to comply with cultural "norms of proportionality" between earnings of superiors and those of subordinates. The predicted earnings of a given executive would equal the pay of the immediate subordinate multiplied by a fraction representing a socially enacted norm of appropriate differentials. Simon implies that the norm hovers around a 30 percent differential between ranks and that it is fairly uniform across organizations. Based on the above logic, Simon (1957, p. 33) makes the following generalization:

> Businesses, like all large scale organizations, are roughly pyramidal in form, because of the hierarchical structure induced by the authority relation. Each executive has a certain number of subordinates at the level immediately below him and this number varies within only moderate limits in a given company and among a number of companies. . . . while we would expect to encounter instances of larger or smaller ratios [between earnings of managers and their subordinates], averages can be expected to be relatively stable.

In summary, in a manner somewhat akin to the traditional economic models, the structural perspective is very deterministic, with the earnings of executives being mechanically established as a function of number of levels below them and a fixed percent differential between their pay and those of subordinates. Unlike governance theories, structural models allow little room for contractual relationships, influence patterns, checks and balances, and other process variables as determinants of executive pay. Like the proponents of traditional job evaluation methods discussed in Chapter 1, this view treats observed pay levels as a natural outcome of a hierarchical pecking order in the organization.

Human Capital Theory

Unlike the theoretical formulations reviewed so far, human capital models focus on individual characteristics as predictors of executive pay (Gerhart and Milkovich, 1990; Buck, Liu, and Skovoroda, 2008; Finkelstein, Hambrick, and Cannella, 2009; Combs and Skill, 2003; Carpenter, Sanders, and Gregersen, 2001). This perspective holds that workers accumulate "human capital" over time based on learning. The total amount of learning at any given point in time determines how valuable the employee is to the firm and this, in turn, determines how much the employer is willing to pay for his or her services. The primary factors that contribute to learning are education, experience, and training (Becker, 1964). In fact, human capital theorists claim that it is possible to calculate a "rate of return" on investments made to increase learning along each of those dimensions (Mincer, 1975).

The human capital perspective has been specifically applied to executive compensation in a number of ways. The first, and most obvious, application is summarized by Agarwal (1981, p. 39): "The amount of human capital a worker possesses influences his productivity, which in turn influences his earnings. The same general reasoning should hold for executive workers as well. Other things being equal, an executive with a greater amount of human capital would be better able to perform his job and thus be paid more." As a corollary to this argument, executives are generally highly educated and possess many years of work experience in responsible jobs requiring much personal sacrifice. Few people have the ability, stamina, or willingness to pay the associated personal price in terms of stress, family life, loss of privacy, and minimal leisure time. So their higher pay may be seen as a return on this human capital investment (Gerhart and Milkovich, 1990; Buck et al. 2008).

Second, human capital may help explain the relationship between corporate size and executive pay (Hijazi and Bhatti, 2007). As firms get bigger, they also become more complex. Larger organizations are associated with (a) greater span of control for the executive; (b) taller hierarchy; (c) wider geographical dispersion; (d) larger budgets and resources to administer; (e) diversified strategic business units with unrelated products; and (f) exposure to many and sometimes conflicting environmental forces impacting different parts of the firm. Executives in larger firms should be compensated accordingly as a recompense for the additional human capital requirement needed to successfully carry out this job. And the additional dollars paid to the executive may be well justified because the potential cost of poor performance increases with organization size.

The third linkage between executive pay level and human capital is not as intuitively obvious as the previous two. Some theorists argue that one should not expect a close chronological relationship between executive pay and firm performance because of the delayed effects of human capital. Harris and Holmstrom (1982), for example, argue that learning is the most important force affecting executive pay and firms compensate executives for performance over their entire tenure with the firm, not necessarily on most recent observed performance. Likewise, Murphy (1986b, p. 62) concludes that:

> The rewards and penalties associated with measured current performance are spread over all remaining periods of contracted employment. Consequently, the relation between contemporaneous compensation and performance and the year-to-year variance of individual earnings vary systematically over the executive's career. Under the learning hypothesis, managerial ability is unknown and is revealed over time by observing performance . . . Since the rewards and penalties for unanticipated performance are spread over all remaining years of an employment contract, the effect of performance on compensation increases with tenure, as will the variance of compensation given any experience-earnings profile.

In other words, the performance of an executive depends on managerial ability, which is, in turn, a function of his or her human capital. Because ability is difficult to estimate at first, firms will track the executive's career and achievements over several years to allow for a more precise estimate of his or her performance. This approach reduces some of the uncertainty surrounding the measurement of an executive's relative success or failure (Murphy, 1986b, p. 62). Tracking allows the firm to distinguish between factors that affect observed firm performance and are totally beyond the executive's control (e.g., a market downturn) and those that can be attributed to the executive's actions. Therefore, " . . . an [executive's] compensation in one period depends on his performance in that period and his performance in the prior periods."

Executive Pay as Symbolism

Executive pay as symbolism holds that political factors, independent of firm size, performance, or an executive's productivity and market value, explicitly enter into executive compensation decisions. Its central thesis is that executive pay constitutes a powerful signaling force within the firm and sends symbolic messages that transcend immediate economic concerns to lower level managers and employees. Therefore, reductionist attempts to examine executive pay as a function of "objective" factors such as earnings per share and return on equity are likely to produce disappointing results. Two such models are reviewed here. The first, by Lazear and Rosen, originated in economics and the second, attributed to Steers and Ungson, came from organizational behavior.

Tournament Theory

This theory postulates that the chief executive officer in a firm is seen by other people in the organization as the winner of a lottery. His other compensation represents the proceeds received by being chosen in a game where the chances of winning are exceedingly small (Lazear and Shaw, 2008; Devaro, 2006; Scholtner, 2008). Such an analogy is used to provide a theoretical justification for the very large observed differences between CEO pay and that of lower-level executives. It also attempts to answer a question raised by many laymen as they read the annual executive compensation issue of *Business Week:* How can any human being be worth tens of millions of dollars in any single year? According to tournament theory, the enormous compensation received by CEOs has little to do with these individuals "deserving" it. Rather, it is used to send signals to other people in the firm that working harder and making the best use of their talents allows them to compete for the "trophy," perhaps leading to the number one spot. In other words, top executive pay is designed as the proverbial "pot of gold." This incentive system serves to energize the behavior of other managers by appealing to their greed. In this manner, what on the surface appears to be unfair and irrational compensation for the person chosen to be chief executive ultimately furthers the interests of stockholders. In their classical piece on tournament theory published almost 30 years ago, Lazear and Rosen (1981, p. 845) summarize the basic tenet of this theory:

> His [CEO's] wage is settled not necessarily because it reflects his current productivity as president, but rather because it induces that individual and all other individuals to perform appropriately when they are in more junior positions. This interpretation suggests that presidents of large corporations do not necessarily earn high wages because they are more productive as presidents but because this particular type of payment structure makes them more productive over their entire working lives. A contest provides the proper incentives for skill acquisition prior to coming into the position.

The Executive as Figurehead and Political Strategist

This behavioral perspective of executive compensation has been explicitly articulated by Ungson and Steers (1984) and Steers and Ungson (1987), with some subsequent extensions by Miller and Wiseman (2001). It relies heavily on earlier work by Pfeffer (1981), Mintzberg (1973), Weick (1979 a,b), Pondy (1978), and Cyert and March (1963). Unlike tournament theory, which focuses on outcomes (namely the incentive value of executive pay), these authors are more concerned with political and normative aspects of executive compensation. According to this view, the belief that executive pay should be closely linked with firm performance is based on the erroneous presumption of "functional rationality," namely, the idea that executive rewards such as bonuses or long-term income should be positively associated with the achievement of predefined goals, such as profitability. Rational approaches to the design of executive pay packages ignore the fact that organizations are pluralistic in nature with multiple constituencies (e.g., subunits, coalitions, and subcultures) and with diverse, and perhaps conflicting, interests. Executives are required to walk a thin line and cater to the needs of these different groups, much through personal charisma, bargaining, and consensus building. Therefore, executive pay can best be understood in terms of the role of political figureheads and strategists.

As figureheads, executives become symbols and are expected to act as boundary spanners to owners, government, employee groups, and the general public. As a result, effectiveness in the job and the executive's leadership qualities derive from this individual's ability to manage symbolic activity. Weick (1979 a,b) argues that the executive job is akin to that of an evangelist. As political strategists, executives are expected to manage multiple coalitions and transactions between these coalitions and external constituencies.

These political and symbolic functions are difficult to assess using a functional-rational perspective with its emphasis on "objective" and "bottom line" data. Yet, these are the most crucial components of the job. Criteria for evaluating relative success along these dimensions are often ambiguous and must rely on perceptual judgments. Trying to boil these down to an operational formula may lead to disappointing or even counterproductive results. Instead, assessment of the executive's performance should be conducted by ascertaining how this individual's behaviors help meet the needs of pluralistic groups inside and outside the firm. Steers and Ungson (1987, pp. 304–306) summarize this perspective as follows:

> . . . At times, it might be appropriate to decouple CEO rewards and performance . . . The role of the CEO encompasses other boundary transactions that relate principally to the enhancement of the company's image over time. In effect, attempts to couple CEO bonus, for example, to return on investment or other factors resembling those [used to reward] the divisional manager may prove to be illusory. At times, in fact, it might even be functional to loosely

couple or even decouple rewards from performance to accommodate political activities of the CEO that are in the best interest of the company but are
difficult to tie down to profitability measures in a given time period . . . The
formalization of the CEO compensation into a bonus formula may be unten-
able within a political context.

Pay Dispersion Theory

Structural and tournament theories emphasize vertical differentiation in pay
across organizational levels, with the general premise that increased pay differentials serve as motivators to those in a particular level to move up to the
next level. The competition gets harder toward the top, but rewards increase
accordingly for those who win the coveted price of a promotion. Pay dispersion theory, on the other hand, focuses on horizontal pay dispersion, or
the extent to which the amount of pay received differs substantially among
peers at the same organizational level. While most of this literature is fairly
recent (e.g., Wade, O'Reilly, and Pollock, 2006; Henderson and Fredrickson,
2001; Conyon, Peck and Sadler, 2001; Siegel and Hambrick, 2005; Cannella
and Holcomb, 2005; Shaw, Gupta and Delery, 2002; Wai-Lee et al. 2008),
its root can be traced back more than half a century to social comparison
(Festinger, 1954) and equity (Adams, 1965) theories. Essentially, researchers
considering horizontal pay variance tend to portray such dispersion in negative
terms, assuming that executives at a given level (such as the top management
team) share similar skills, knowledge, and human capital. Hence, greater pay
dispersion may be seen as a sign of inequity, which would lead to perceptions of unfairness, hard feelings, and lower satisfaction, all of which would
reduce cooperation. Interpersonal conflict would, in turn, threaten individual
and firm performance. This purported negative effect of pay dispersion on
firm performance is more likely to be observed in contexts where there is
high interdependence, requiring higher levels of coordination (Siegel and
Hambrick, 2005).

Self-selection Theory

While most of the theories discussed earlier focused on the effect of pay
on executive behavior (for instance, in agency theory incentive alignment
reduces the probability of opportunistic actions on the part of executives),
some scholars have recently shifted their attrition to the individual choices
of managers when deciding on the type of organization they wish to work
for. For example, Rynes, Gerhart, and Parks (2005) argue that the com-

pensation system exercises a sorting effect on managers, since individuals self-select themselves into firms that offer compensation packages that fit their preferences. Likewise, they will tend to leave firms where this is not the case. Other scholars, who believe the match of executive preferences with the structure of the compensation package (for instance, the proportion of incentives in pay mix) influences their decision to choose a particular firm or leave their current employer, include Fong et al. (2010), Dunford, Boudreau, and Boswell (2005), Carter and Lynch (2004), and Banker, Lee, Potter, and Srinivasan (2001).

Summary

In conclusion, executive pay has provided fertile ground for much conceptual work originating in different disciplines and academic traditions. The theories reviewed here are not necessarily contradictory, but represent different ways of examining executive compensation issues. One clear inference from these efforts is that executive pay is a very complex phenomenon that cannot be easily captured in any single model.

Executive pay can be studied at different levels of analysis. First, at the firm level, executive pay is said to be a function of microeconomic determinants (marginal revenue productivity and the firm's ability to pay), structural factors (hierarchical levels and firm size), and symbolic/political considerations (supporting role of figurehead and political strategist). Second, in the labor market, executive pay is expected to depend on the cost of hiring the best available replacement to the present executive and the going rate among firms of similar size. Third, at the stockholder level, executive pay is said to vary, depending on the distribution of ownership and the monitoring/incentive mechanisms established by the firm's owners to reduce agency costs. Finally, at the individual level, an executive's pay is said to increase as a function of personal ability and accumulated human capital.

To the extent that there is intense interaction and overlap among predictors of executive pay at different levels of analysis, it may be quite difficult, if not impossible, to reliably disentangle the unique effect of one variable from another. For example, firm size, distribution of ownership, and ability to pay are all likely to be correlated. This, however, has not discouraged investigators from attempting to discern empirically what factors determine executive compensation.

5 DETERMINANTS AND CONSEQUENCES OF EXECUTIVE PAY

Before the more narrowly focused empirical literature on the determinants and correlates of executive pay is discussed, the broader issue of how much potential influence top executives can exert on firm performance needs to be examined. In the context of this book, this question is important for two reasons. First, if the actual or latent impact is minimal, then linking executive pay to firm performance almost becomes a moot point. To hold management responsible for the firm's fate (by rewarding them when performance improves and penalizing them when performance decreases) would be demoralizing to executives if company performance depended on factors unrelated to how well the firm was being managed. In fact, Jensen and Murphy (1990a, p. 253) in their classical study suggested a similar hypothesis (which the authors believe is incorrect) that the "small observed pay-performance sensitivity seems inconsistent with the implications of formal principal agent model . . . [because] CEOs are not, in fact, important agents of shareholders . . . CEOs do not matter." Second, as implied in most of the theoretical models described earlier and consistent with the strategic pay perspective of this book, firm performance is the ultimate dependent variable in the question of whose interests are served by the hired top executives or the extent to which managerial behaviors and decisions are oriented to promote or deter the financial well-being of the firm's owners. If firm performance is unresponsive to managerial actions, then, by implication, compensation strategies for top management groups will be inert at best in terms of their effect on company performance.

Role of Executives in Influencing Firm Performance

Two separate streams of research have examined the role that top executives play in firm performance (see Gomez-Mejia and Wiseman, 1997; Makri and Gomez-Mejia, 2007; Devers, Cannella et al. 2007, for reviews). The first one comes from the fields of organization theory and administrative science. This group of investigators has expended much effort trying to ascertain the extent to which strategic choices (i.e., managerial decisions) or environmental forces (i.e., situational factors beyond managers' control) determine organizational performance. The typical question asked is: Do top executives make a difference, and if so, how much? At one extreme, scholars such as Chandler (1977) argue that managers have a great deal of influence on their firms' destinies, while others point to the primacy of environmental factors (e.g., Hannan and Freeman, 1977). Empirical evidence suggests that both sets of factors are important. The relative effect of managerial actions on firm performance becomes more potent as the time frame under investigation increases (e.g., Hambrick and Finkelstein, 1987; Hrebiniak and Joyce, 1985). For example, consistent with the findings of Lieberson and O'Connor (1972); Salancik and Pfeffer (1977); Weiner and Mahoney (1981); Smith, Carson, and Alexander (1984); Murray (1989) found that in the food and petroleum industries, management contributions to short-term performance are almost nil, but a large portion of variance in long-term firm performance may be explained by managerial (internal) effects. The underlying rationale for these findings is that management contributions to short-term performance are dominated by external circumstances, while a longer time span affords more room for maneuverability and strategic responses. Other studies that show the important effect of the length of time under consideration as a key moderator of managerial actions–performance relations include Hall and Liebman (1998); Leone, Wu, and Zimmerman (2006); Boschen and colleagues (2003); Core and Larcker (2002); and Hanlon, Rajgopal, and Shevlin (2003).

A second stream of research focuses on specific ways in which firm performance responds to managerial decisions (see Figure 5.1). Because of the extensive and complex nature of this research (which spans the fields of business policy, accounting, finance, and economics), only some of the key issues addressed by this literature are highlighted. The reader is also warned that the unprecedented macroeconomic turmoil at the time of this writing (2010, following two years of severe recession) is likely to spur much research in the future as to the effect of compensation design on top management decisions and the aggregate impact these decisions may have, not only on focal firms but also on the global economy. So far, most of this research has been anecdotal (based on the negative experiences of firms such as Countrywide Financial Corporation, Bear Stearns, Lehman Brothers, Merrill Lynch, and American International Group) and available in the business press (see, for instance, Loomis, 2009a; Parloff, 2009). It does strongly suggest that much of the economic upheaval at the end of the first decade of the twenty-first

Figure 5.1   **Impact of Top Management Positions on Firm Performance**

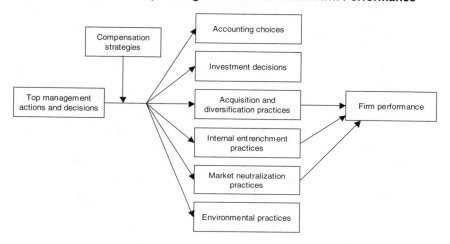

century may be attributed to ill-conceived incentive programs for the top corporate brass.

Accounting Choices

A large group of studies is concerned with the extent to which accounting choices may exert a negative or a positive impact on firm performance and whether these choices may lead to conflict between the interests of managers and stockholders. Five major policies of this type have been examined. The first one is the use of first in, first out (FIFO) versus last in, first out (LIFO) inventory cost-flow choices. Research suggests that although FIFO results in higher reporting earnings (which would benefit managers) than LIFO, FIFO causes lower cash flow because the firm pays higher taxes (Biddle, 1980; Dyl, 1989; Morse and Richardson, 1983). This, in turn, is associated with a correlative reduction in market value of the firm's shares (Biddle and Lindahl, 1982; Sven-Olof, 2007; Larcker, Richardson, and Tuna, 2007; Stevenson, 1984; Sunder, 1973, 1975).

The second accounting policy most likely to affect firm performance is the depreciation method chosen by management. (For a recent review of these issues as they relate to executive pay, see Jackson, 2008.) In general, straight-line depreciation will produce higher reported income (which benefits management) than accelerated depreciation, even when in many cases straight-line depreciation is contrary to the firm's interests (Groff and Wright,

1989; Holthausen and Leftwich, 1983). The investment tax credit choice is a third area in which accounting choices may affect firm performance. For instance, Hagerman and Zmijewski (1979) report that managers benefit at the expense of the firm's long-run performance by choosing the "flow-through" method. In this method, accounting income is increased by the amount of the tax credit during the purchase period (in contrast, the deferral method distributes tax credit over the life of the asset). A fourth accounting choice that may affect firm performance is the method used by management to capitalize interest associated with capital expenditures. Bowen, Noreen, and Lacey (1981), for example, found that by manipulating how interest is capitalized for reporting purposes, managers can increase the present value of their compensation stream at the expense of stockholders.

Finally, the choice of amortization periods may affect firm performance. The longer the amortization period, the higher the firm's reported income in the short run, and the higher the compensation received by managers is likely to be during their tenure with the firm (Groff and Wright, 1989). Hagerman and Zmijewski (1979) found that amortization periods under 30 years benefit stockholders, while those longer than 30 years benefit managers. Harris and Bromiley (2007) report that both incentives and bad performance foster financial misrepresentation; which, in turn, gets the firm into trouble in the long run. In a series of experiments, Jackson (2008) reports that managers tend to choose the depreciation methods that are more advantageous to them even if they represent nonmaximizing capital investment decisions.

Investment Decisions

How managers utilize organizational resources for future growth is another area in which managerial actions may have a substantial effect on firm performance (Hambrick, Werder, and Zajac, 2008). Similar to the under-accounting choices reviewed earlier, however, the self-interest of managers and those of the firm may not always coincide (Devers, Canella, et al. 2007). Investigators have examined three major investment dimensions that may affect firm performance. The first is the *level of risk*. Coffee (1988) and Morck, Shleifer, and Vishny (1988), for example, found that managers assume fewer investment risks than would be optimal for the firm. They tend to minimize their downside risk, which, in turn, reduces the downside risk of their compensation and possible replacement. This lowers the aggregate market value of the company. Other investigators documenting the effect of managerial risk orientation on firm performance include Bloom and Milkovich (1998); Gomez-Mejia and colleagues (2007); March and Shapira (1987); Gupta (1987);

Hill (1988); Loescher (1984); Norburn and Miller (1981); Ellsworth (1983); Dearden (1960, 1969); Hoskisson, Hitt, and Hill (1990); and Chatterjee and Lubatkin (1990).

The second investment dimension that has been extensively examined in both the practitioner and academic literature is the *time horizon* used by management (see review by Makri and Gomez-Mejia, 2007). The central concern here is that " . . . while the firm lives on, its managers do not. As such, they are only interested in firm performance for the time period in which they are employed, even if such time horizons lead to a present-value loss of firm value" (Walsh and Seward, 1990, p. 422). A number of studies suggest that executive compensation design influences the time horizon CEOs use in making investment decisions, such as investing in pollution control equipment (Berrone and Gomez-Mejia, 2009), capital investment decisions (Jackson, 2008), and firm leverage (Larraza-Kintana et al. 2007).

A third area pertaining to investment decisions made by managers that affect firm performance is R&D spending. This is related to the time horizon issue because R&D spending seldom pays off in the short run and, in fact, may have a negative effect on the compensation of managers whose tenure seldom outlives the return on R&D investments. Graves (1988), Hill, Hitt, and Hoskisson (1988), and Hill and Hansen (1989) all report that quite often the level of R&D expenditures among large U.S. firms is much lower than would be desirable and has long-term effects, including "declining innovation and productivity growth and loss of international competitiveness" (Hill and Hansen, 1989, p. 56).

Related to the prior point, a series of studies (Balkin, Markman, and Gomez-Mejia, 2000; Makri, Lane, and Gomez-Mejia, 2006; Washburn, Makri, and Gomez-Mejia, 2010) indicate that the nature of the executive incentive system not only influences how much R&D investments a firm undertakes but also attention to research quality as measured by patents, impact of the firm's research program on the patents of other firms, and use of basic or pure science.

Acquisition and Diversification Strategies

An extensive literature has examined the relationship between a firm's acquisition and diversification strategies, firm performance, and executive pay (see Santalo and Becerra, 2008, and Guest, 2009, for recent reviews). There is evidence to suggest that corporate diversification through mergers and acquisitions may be vigorously pursued by a firm in order to reduce management employment risks (Ahimud and Lev, 1981) and to justify higher executive pay (Guest, 2009; Kroll, Simmons, and Wright, 1990; Wright et al. 2002), even at the expense of profitability. The literature also suggests that performance differences between firms may be traced to type of diversification and process of diversification, both of which are largely controlled by management (e.g., Lubatkin, 1987; Montgomery and Singh, 1984; Salter and Weinhold, 1981). A separate group of event studies reports that the main beneficiaries in merger or acquisition announcements are the shareholders of acquired companies with an equivocal or negative effect on the acquiring company shareholders' wealth (see review by Duru and Reeb, 2002). Likewise, empirical evidence strongly suggests that acquiring firms typically suffer profitability declines, efficiency losses, and lower long-term capital market performance (Herman and Lowenstein, 1988; Magenheim and Mueller, 1988; Ravenscraft and Scherer, 1987).

In one of the largest empirical studies on the relationship between corporate diversification and CEO compensation, Duru and Reeb (2002) found that geographic diversification leads to a CEO compensation premium, while industrial diversification has the opposite effect. Contrary to much of the prior literature, Duru and Reeb suggest that CEO compensation policies are in line with shareholder interests when it comes to diversification. In their words "we document that while value-enhancing geographic diversification is rewarded, non-value-enhancing industrial diversification is penalized." As with much of the executive compensation literature, results are often incongruous even though most scholars utilize the same archival databases.

Internal Entrenchment Practices

Management may affect firm performance by blocking the firms' internal control systems that serve to provide checks and balances on managerial discretion (this effectively turns off the monitoring mechanisms suggested by agency theory). This may include:

1. The use of consultants and internal board members to avoid potential disciplinary actions by camouflaging and/or legitimizing questionable managerial decisions. (Conyon et al. 2009; Fierman, 1990; Meyer and Rowan, 1977; Perkins and Hendry, 2005; Williams, 1985; Tosi and Gomez-Mejia, 1989)
2. Withholding relevant information "from compensation committees when that information would attribute poor firm performance to bad management." (Coughlan and Schmidt, 1985, p. 45)
3. Controlling the board's agenda. (Coles, Daniel, and Naveen, 2007)

4. Embarking the firm on idiosyncratic strategies molded to the manager's unique skills, background, and personal interests. (Boone et al. 2007; Shleifer and Vishny, 1988)
5. Failing to step down in the face of continued poor firm performance that calls for the recruitment of new managers "who are neither associated with the past nor committed to inappropriate strategies and policies." (Salancik and Pfeffer, 1980, p. 654) (for related work on this point see research by Gomez-Mejia, Nunez-Nickel, and Gutierrez [2001] on Spanish newspapers)
6. Paying employees more in order to avoid internal conflict that may jeopardize the entrenched managers' position. (Werner et al. 2005; Cronquist et al. 2009)

Market Neutralization Practices

Managers of firms with substandard performance may attempt to prevent the market from exercising its disciplinary role (this removes another important constraint on managers as suggested by agency theory (see Yin-Hua, Tsun-Siou, and Pei-Gi, 2008; Zhao and Chen, 2008). Two mechanisms that may be used by executives to neutralize the market include so-called greenmail payments and poison pills. The former refers to the purchase of large blocks of stock from potential acquirers as a defensive measure without shareholder approval. Dann and DeAngelo (1983) and Bradley and Wakeman (1983) offer some evidence to suggest that greenmail antitakeover strategies produce negative abnormal stock returns for firms using it. Poison pills allow shareholders of the target firm to acquire additional shares or to sell stock to the bidding company at prices that are set arbitrarily. Malatesta and Walking (1988) and Ryngaert (1988) argue that management of the takeover target firm is the main beneficiary of poison pills, while its shareholders suffer decline in their wealth.

In summary, a broad spectrum of research indicates that firm performance is highly responsive to managerial behaviors and decisions. Furthermore, there are many situations where the policy choices confronting managers are such that what is better for a firm's shareholders and what may further management's interests are at odds with each other. The challenge from a compensation perspective is to develop pay strategies for top executives that evoke the types of behaviors and induce the kinds of decisions that are most conducive to improved firm performance.

The reader should not be led to believe, however, that compensation strategies designed to align the interests of executives with those of shareholders can produce miraculous results. Even under the best incentive programs, a large portion of firm performance variance is likely to reflect a myriad of unsystematic factors, which have little to do with management. Such factors include plain luck (e.g., formation of the Arab oil cartel in the 1970s producing "windfall" profits in U.S. oil firms; the AIDS epidemic in the 1990s fueling stock prices and profits of condom manufacturers); regulatory changes (as in the case of the airline industry); sudden changes in technology (introduction of the ultrasound machine in the early 1970s replacing electrodiagnostic imaging devices almost overnight); prolonged market upturns (as most of the 1980s) or market downturns (as in most of the 2000s to date); financial crisis (as the subprime meltdown at the beginning of the twenty-first century); government subsidies to foreign competitors, shifts in interest rates, and so on. Tosi and Gomez-Mejia (1992) estimate that approximately 18 percent of the total variance in firm performance may be accounted for by managerial decisions in response to the incentive structure, which means that more than five times as much variance can be attributed to other unsystematic factors.

Manipulation Practices

Recent literature has been concerned with how executives may engage in gaming or manipulation of data to "look good" in order to receive incentive awards (for recent reviews see Devers, Cannella et al. 2007; Deyá-Tortella et al. 2005; Anderson, Boylan, and Reeb, 2007; Harris and Bromiley, 2007; Zhang et al. 2008; Cennamo, Berrone, and Gomez-Majia, 2009). For example, some have noted that the timing of awarding and cashing of stock options takes advantage of stock returns that are normally low or abnormally high (Lie, 2005). Others have noted that executives routinely manipulate information to meet bonus performance targets or cash in their equity-based pay when stock prices are artificially inflated (e.g., Bergstresser and Philippon, 2006; Coles, Hertzel, and Swaminathan, 2006; Callaghan, Saly, Subramaniam, 2004; Fenn and Liang, 2001; Sanders and Carpenter, 2003). With few exceptions, these practices are not illegal, yet they are self-serving and may be considered unethical (Deyá-Tortella et al. 2005).

Environmental Practices

One of the most recent issues to be tackled in the executive compensation literature is the extent to which executives are rewarded or penalized for good environmental policies. Berrone and Gomez-Mejia (2009) argue that firms attempt to gain legitimacy by instituting policies that are friendly to the environment, and thus greater legitimacy has positive firm performance consequences in the long run. Integrating institutional theories, agency theory, and environmental management literature, these authors found support for several environment–CEO pay-related hypotheses using longitudinal data on 460 pollution-causing firms in the United States. They found that in these industries, good environmental performance increased CEO pay; pollution-prevention strategies affected executive compensation more than end-of-pipe pollution control; and that long-term pay increased the level of success with pollution-prevention strategies. Contrary to their expectations, Berrone and Gomez-Mejia (2009) found that firms with an explicit environmental pay policy and an environmental committee did not reward environmental strategies more than those without such structures, suggesting that these mechanisms only play a symbolic role.

Our attention is now turned to the empirical research on the determinants of executive pay.

Mixed Evidence on Executive Pay After Nine Decades of Research

As noted earlier, executive pay has been thoroughly researched using empirical methods. In the refereed academic journals alone, we estimate that over 1,200 such papers have been published during the period 1925 to 2010. The first such piece known to us was published by Taussig and Barker in 1925. This issue has been studied by scholars from such diverse fields as sociology, economics, accounting, finance, political science, management, and industrial relations (Gomez-Mejia and Wiseman, 1997; Devers, Cannella et al. 2007).

Despite this incredible amount of work, results are generally disappointing and mixed. Authors often reach diametrically opposed conclusions when testing the same hypothesis and even when using an identical set of data. For example, one group of investigators found little or no relationship between executive compensation and firm performance (e.g., Kerr and Bettis, 1987; Jensen and Murphy, 1990a; Tosi and Greckhamer, 2004), while others claim the exact opposite (e.g., Hall and Liebman, 1998; Masson, 1971; Morgan and Poulsen, 2001; Murphy, 1985). These extremes are exemplified by comments such as "there is no rational basis for the compensation paid to top management" (Kerr and Bettis, 1987, p. 667) and "the research evidence to date strongly supports the conclusion that executives use incentive compensation in ways that benefit themselves at the expense of shareholders"

(Devers, Cannella et al. 2007, p. 1028) vis-à-vis "top executives are worth every nickel they get" (Murphy, 1986a, p. 125). Several reasons may account for these diverse findings.

Reliance on Archival Data and False Sense of Objectivity

With very few exceptions (e.g., Cruz et al. 2010; Larraza-Kintana et al. 2007; Tosi and Gomez-Mejia, 1989, 1994; Zajac, 1990), investigators tend to rely on archival data available in databases such as Standard & Poor's Compustat Disclosure, and other similar sources when studying executive compensation. It is very tempting for academics to rely exclusively on this data because of its easy accessibility and low cost. (As everyone knows, gathering your own data may require years of hard work and substantial resources.) Besides, scholarly journals have an insatiable appetite for this type of research. Given the publishing pressures in many universities, many academics consider this data too good to pass up. Unfortunately, executive pay is a very treacherous research area. Pitfalls abound, most of which are generally ignored or treated very lightly (particularly in the field of management, where the level of sophistication in financial accounting is low).

One problem with the use of these databases is that researchers are constrained by the information included in them, and tenuous assumptions are frequently made. A second almost fatal problem is that it is not always clear how comparable the reported data may be across firms and over time. Despite an objective facade and a common metrics (dollars), there is enough ambiguity in the way some of the data are reported that one may well be comparing apples and oranges when using archival information on CEOs. In fact, it is doubtful that the data meet some of the most rudimentary quality requirements from a measurement perspective in terms of validity and reliability.

Interestingly enough, most investigators don't realize (or don't address the issue) that firms use widely different formulas when reporting executive compensation or even firm performance for that matter. To understand the meaning of a given pay figure, one would need to know the formulas used by the company. But finding this out is a tough task. Even though the Securities and Exchange Commission now calls for transparency in the actual formulas used (see Longnecker and Krueger, 2007), only a few companies give enough details to make the calculation. Thus, while hundreds of studies have correlated executive pay with just about every variable in sight (e.g., profitability, firm size, industry type, age of executive, executive tenure, etc.), a robust interpretation of the findings may be quite elusive.

Different Methodologies

Authors use widely diverse sampling strategies, time periods, and statistical methods. For example, the number of firms included in the samples ranges from 2,200 (Jensen and Murphy, 1990a) to 50 (Lewellen, 1971). Time periods range from 30 years (Antle and Smith, 1986) to one year (Crystal, 1988). Likewise, archival data has been subject to an endless array of statistical manipulation, including weighted regression techniques (Lewellen and Huntsman, 1970), pooled cross-section time series (Murphy, 1986a; Boschen et al. 2003), nonparametric tests (Antle and Smith, 1986), residual analysis (Ciscel and Carroll, 1980), logistic regression (Beatty and Zajac, 1994), and text analysis (Berrone and Gomez-Mejia, 2009). Given the diversity of approaches and also the nature of the methodology, inconsistent results are found. As noted by Devers, Cannella, and colleagues (2007, p. 1039):

> Our review revealed that compensation research broadly suffers from a number of conceptual and methodological issues. For example, we found little consistency in the operationalization of many important constructs of interest. Particularly troubling was the use of ambiguous or inconsistent measures of firm performance, compensation, and risk (both action risk and perceptual risk). We also found the selection criteria for sample frames, time lags, covariates, and statistical methodologies to be wide ranging. We believe that the broad, disconnected nature of the field, coupled with the conceptual and methodological heterogeneity noted above, continues to constrain the advancement of executive compensation research.

Dynamic Effects

It is difficult to capture the dynamic and lag effects of variables affecting executive compensation. An executive pay package in a given year or a given period may reflect not just what happened in the most recent past, but also the assessment of this individual's performance throughout his or her entire career with the company and what is expected for the future (Core and Larcker, 2002; Leone, Wu, and Zimmerman, 2006). Typically, executive compensation studies limit their time frame to no more than five years. This presents a problem, according to Lambert (1983, p. 443), because an "agent's compensation in one period depends on his performance in that period and his performance in previous periods. Principal uses an agent's performance over the entire history of his employment to diversify away some of the uncertainty surrounding the agent's action." In particular, gains on stock options can be very distorting when examining year-to-year changes in executive pay. For example, if a CEO decides to cash out his or her option one year, he or she is unlikely to have done so in several years before or to do so again in the near future.

Complexity of Equity-Based Pay

Executives may receive up to one-half of their income from long-term pay items such as deferred bonuses, stockholdings, stock options, dividend units, phantom shares, pension benefits, and so on. Much of this type of compensation remains shrouded in mystery (Makri and Gomez-Mejia, 2007). While these items may represent an integral part of the total executive compensation package, calculating their actual value, with no generally accepted formula for doing so, can be a nightmare. Different estimation procedures can yield widely different results. For example, Lewellen and Huntsman (1970) found that bonus and salary are highly correlated with long-term income. Antle and Smith (1986), on the other hand, found them to be totally independent. Masson (1971) argued that equity-based pay is the most important component of the executive pay package, while Kerr and Bettis (1987) and Jensen and Murphy (1990a) argued that it is almost insignificant.

The central problem is that, unlike salary and cash compensation, long-term gains do not constitute realized pay at a given point in time but a promissory note contingent on future events. Estimating the "present value" of such long-term income programs requires that numerous assumptions be made concerning interest rates, opportunity costs of holding stock options, future market value of stockholdings, and so on. While complex mathematical formulas have been devised (e.g., Black and Scholes, 1973; Antle and Smith, 1985), they all include several parameters that must be crudely estimated, bringing their validity into question. According to Kerr and Bettis (1987, p. 649):

> . . . The resulting estimated value of an option changes every day, often by a substantial amount, depending on the price of the stock. Options amplify changes in stock's prices. The dominant question in determining the value becomes the selection of the day on which the option is to be valued. Stock options are an important component of executive compensation that should be studied. However, there appears to be no theoretically and empirically appropriate method for evaluating them.

Likewise, Finkelstein and Hambrick (1988, p. 544) argue that "there are so many forms of financial compensation, and they are so complex, that calculation of a CEO's financial income is often intractable or misleading."

Crystal (1988) comments that it is rare to find an executive who understands the value of his or her long-term income. To circumvent these methodological problems, most researchers rely on the Black-Scholes formula to calculate equity-based pay or some variant of it; but what it means and its behavioral consequences are still poorly understood (Devers et al. 2008).

Operationalization of Firm Performance

The measurement of the performance variable, which is a crucial factor in most executive compensation studies, is in itself highly controversial. As noted by Devers, Cannella, and colleagues (2007, p. 1020), "the link between firm performance and executive compensation becomes more or less elusive, depending on the variables examined and the pay elements considered." Authors have operationalized firm performance in terms of stock market returns (Kerr and Bettis, 1987; Boschen et al. 2003; Gibbons and Murphy, 1990), accounting profits (Deckop, 1988; Adams, Almeida, and Ferreira, 2009; Leonard, 1990), or a combination of the two (Gomez-Mejia, Tosi, and Hinkin, 1987; Tosi and Gomez-Mejia, 1992). When researchers cannot agree on what performance is, then the results are often inconclusive or conflicting. As discussed later in this chapter, this also presents an interesting dilemma to practitioners who are trying to design executive compensation programs that align the interest of stockholders and managers.

Perhaps the oldest and most widely used indicator of firm performance is profitability. However, this measure has been severely criticized because it may not reflect a firm's underlying value or performance. It is argued that executives can manipulate these numbers to make themselves look good (Dyl, 1989; Groff and Wright, 1989; Hunt, 1986). Some perfectly legal "tricks" that may be used to improve the bottom line include depreciation policies (accelerated versus straight-line); inventory procedures (FIFO versus LIFO); use of short-term, noncapitalized leases to obtain productive equipment; and window-dressing techniques such as holding borrowed money as cash until the end of the year. For instance, following the large increases in oil prices in late 1990 as a result of Iraq's invasion of Kuwait, oil industry executives found ways to hold down reported profits by channeling the increased revenues into various "hidden" budget accounts. For example, money was held in reserve for future environmental expenses, R&D investments, maintenance programs, and so on (Hayes, 1990). This practice, which conformed with accounting standards, was used to reduce potential public and congressional outcry in response to a rapid price hike in oil-related products such as gasoline and heating oil.

As an alternative to profitability measures, other researchers have advanced the notion that stockholder's welfare—measured in the form of increases in stock price or dividends paid—should dictate executive's pay (Fong et al. 2010, Coughlan and Schmidt, 1985; Murphy, 1985; Rappaport, 1978). But these measures are not immune to criticism. Paying out cash dividends will raise a stock's price. But raising cash dividends decreases funds available for reinvestment and R&D. This lowers expected growth rate and depresses the price of a stock in the long run, with the effects perhaps occurring at a time when another executive will bear the brunt of the problem (Brigham, 1985). Stock prices are also very sensitive to external events that may have little to do with how efficiently a firm is being run and that are totally beyond management's control. The use of "abnormal return" methodology, which attempts to disentangle general market trends from firm-specific effects on a company's stock prices, can often "result in false inferences about the presence of abnormal performance" (Brown and Warner, 1980, p. 205). In order to identify "abnormal" price performance, the researcher must first evaluate what is "normal" or expected, given the usual influences on security prices. Performing this evaluation requires a number of important assumptions and arbitrary judgments regarding definition of relevant market, parameter estimations, and distribution properties of excess returns (see Brown and Warner, 1985; McNichols and Manegold, 1983).

Ultimately, one must deal with the philosophical question of whether outcome measures of firm performance, which are the only ones available in archival databases, are the most appropriate indicators to examine. It may be that, in fact, most boards make complex judgments about the performance of both the CEO and the firm that are, of necessity, highly subjective (see Puffer and Weintrop, 1991; and Perkins and Hendry, 2005). Furthermore, too much reliance on objective indicators of firm performance for compensation purposes encourages executives to maximize the value of coefficients that are part of the evaluation formula. Maximizing these coefficients is often at the expense of other, less quantifiable elements (e.g., innovation) that are crucial to the firm's interests in the long run.

Estimating Performance of an Incumbent's Best Replacement

It is extremely difficult, if not downright impossible, for researchers to estimate the various performance outcomes under alternative stewardships. If a replacement would not perform better than the incumbent, the latter's high pay may be justified—perhaps even as compensation for the high career risk of working for a company that is performing poorly. For example, the board of directors of American Express Co. provided the company's CEO, Kenneth I. Chenault, with a huge raise in 2008, one of the worst years in that firm's history. The raise was given in recognition for his perceived excellent work in dealing with a financial crisis in the industry due to the subprime debacle and the belief that another CEO was unlikely to produce better results (WSJ 2008a: A Survey of CEO Compensation, April 4, 2008).

Collinearity Among the Variables

Finally, as noted earlier, one of the most difficult methodological problems when trying to isolate the unique impact of a variable on executive pay is the fact that most relevant factors are highly correlated. For example, firm size, profits, number of levels in the organization, age and experience level of executives, and even distribution of ownership co-vary together. Therefore, in many instances the use of significance tests for individual variables proves to be unreliable because of the proverbial "chicken-and-egg" question. To eliminate multicollinearity, some transformation of the data is necessary. Unfortunately, "such transformed variables often bear only the faintest relationship to the hypothesis being tested" (Ciscel and Carroll, 1980, p. 615). As a result, making causal inferences about the effect of a particular variable on executive pay vis-à-vis some other variables can be tenuous, and often the conclusions reached simply reflect the ideological persuasion of the writer.

Inferential Leaps

As noted earlier, with only a handful of exceptions (e.g., Tosi and Gomez-Mejia, 1989, 1994; Cruz et al. 2010; Larraza-Kintana et al. 2007; Zajac, 1990), authors use archival data on executive pay to generate proxies for behavioral phenomena that are far removed from the underlying constructs purportedly being measured. Therefore, one is forced to make large "leaps of faith" to draw inferences from the obtained results. For instance, the efficacy of monitoring and incentive alignment mechanisms is frequently tested by correlating executive pay and firm performance. A positive correlation is interpreted as evidence that the executive compensation contract has aligned managerial and owner interests and that this alignment has caused managers to maximize profitability. On the other hand, lack of a relationship is generally interpreted to mean that "results are inconsistent with the implications of formal agency models of optimal contracting" (Jensen and Murphy, 1990a, p. 226). Quite often, the degree of monitoring exercised by the board is inferred from equity concentration of a firm, which is treated as a dichotomous variable. Firms can be assigned to an "owner-controlled" class when there is the presence of a single equity-holder owning a particular percentage or more of the outstanding stock and to a "management-controlled" class when there is not. Usually this percentage cut off is set at 5 percent ownership of the firm's outstanding stock. Or researchers continue to use the proportion of "insiders" on the board as a measure of firm-specific knowledge and "outsiders" as a measure of board independence (Coles, Daniel, and Naveen, 2008).

Larraza-Kintana and colleagues (2007) illustrate the danger of using archival proxies as representation of behavioral intentions. For instance, R&D expenditures have traditionally been used as indicators of risk taking (see Devers et al. 2008). Yet, when asked to rank the risk of a large number of strategic choices, Larraza and colleagues found that IPO executives actually rank R&D investments as very low, relative to investments in other strategic choices. They see this as a low-risk alternative in an industry where competitive advantage can only be attained through continuous innovation

Because of all the tenuous inferences involved, Tosi and Gomez-Mejia (1989, p. 185) have gone so far as to suggest a moratorium on this type of archival-based research:

> Despite the enormous amount of effort and expenditures in "*mining*" these public databases, results are disappointing and often conflicting . . . All things considered, overreliance on archival data that treats the executive compensation process as a black box has led into a blind alley. While easy to use, it is doubtful that continued "number crunching" of these databases will provide much additional insight on the determinants of executive pay . . . a more fruitful avenue to pursue in understanding executive pay issues is to focus more on the process and less on the observed "objective" measures.

In summary, empirical research on executive compensation is far from an exact science, and there is much room for personal interpretation, according to the researcher's biases. Therefore, readers should approach this literature with a healthy amount of skepticism. When all conceivable predictors are used in the equations, the total amount of explained variance ($R2$) in executive pay seldom exceeds 35 percent, and most often hovers in the 20 to 30 percent range. Even if one focuses attention on the components that reach statistical significance, the presumed causal factors often flip-flop from study to study. The manner in which findings are posited and interpreted generally comes as no surprise, depending on the writer's background and known prejudices.

What We Know So Far About Executive Pay

This section critically examines the voluminous literature on the determinants of executive pay, focusing on statistical findings.

Role of Company Size and Performance

As discussed earlier, traditional economic theory assumes that managers will operate a firm in the most efficient manner to maximize profits. Neoclassical economists conclude, based on deductive reasoning, that executive pay should reward performance that maximizes profit, although firm size may play a role when there are market imperfections. Nonorthodox economists taking a managerialist perspective argue that executive pay is primarily a function of firm size, with company performance relegated to a "satisficing" role. This controversy between so-called profit maximizers and sales maximizers has been going on for over half a century. The debate has sparked hundreds of empirical studies dealing with this seemingly simple question: Does executive pay reward top management's ability to expand corporate size or to increase profitability? The findings appear to support both sides of the issue.

The first researchers to test the *sales maximization hypothesis* were Roberts (1959) and McGuire, Chiu, and Elbing (1962). Both found that, after controlling for sales level, firm profits had little to do with executive compensation. Their findings supported Baumol's (1959) contention that executives pursued what they deemed to be a prestigious (and more financially rewarding) goal of increasing the size of the firm they manage. These findings were rebutted in several studies initiated by Lewellen (1968, 1969), Lewellen and Huntsman (1970), and Masson (1971), who criticized previous researchers for not including measures of long-term income in the form of stock options and other stock-related pay arrangements. By developing their own estimates of "total compensation," they reached diametrically opposing conclusions as exemplified in the following statement by Lewellen and Huntsman (1970, p. 718):

> The evidence provides strong support for the hypothesis that top management's remuneration is heavily dependent upon the generation of profit . . . indeed, sales seem to be quite irrelevant. The clear inference is that there is a greater incentive for management to shape its decision rules in a manner consonant with shareholder interests than to seek the alternative goal of revenue maximization.

Since the early 1970s, researchers have refined their multivariate methods, changed the operationalization of key variables, and used larger and more diverse samples, but they have failed to provide conclusive evidence on either side of the debate. Larner (1970) and Hirschey and Pappas (1981) found that executive pay is most directly linked to profit. Ciscel (1974) found that size, rather than profit, was the main predictor of executive compensation, particularly when the earnings of the entire executive group were considered. Smyth, Boyes, and Peseau reanalyzed Lewellen and Huntsman's model and made corrections for multicollinearity and heteroscedasticity. Unlike Lewellen and Huntsman, they concluded that executive pay "depends on a utility function of both sales and profits" (1972, p. 79).

Using sophisticated "residual analysis" to attenuate the collinearity problem between firm size and profits, Ciscel and Carroll (1980) reached the same conclusions as Smyth and colleagues (1975). Across the Atlantic, Meeks and Whittington (1975) found that profit had no relationship to executive pay; instead, size was the main predictor. Posner (1987) and Kostiuk (1990) found support for the position that executive compensation can best be predicted by firm size, while Deckop (1988) found evidence that executive compensation was related (albeit very weakly) to profits measured as percentage of sales. Dyl (1988) reported that both firm size and performance are significant determinants of executive pay. In a related vein of research, Schmidt and Fowler (1990) report that top executives who engaged in major tender-offer or acquisition activity received a significant increase in their compensation that "appears to be driven more by organization size than by performance" (p. 569). More recently, Hijazi and Bhatti (2007) justified the high percentage of variance in CEO pay attributed to firm size to the fact that "company size is closely related to job complexity and employer's ability to pay" (p. 58).

The debate has been fueled by those who view reported profit as a contaminated criterion of performance and who have developed sophisticated alternative measures based on the firm's stock value. Masson (1971) and Murphy (1985) found that executive compensation was more strongly related to stock performance than to accounting measures; Coughlan and Schmidt (1985) concluded that, although statistically significant, they only explained 5.4 percent of the variance in executive compensation based on stock market data alone. To make matters more confusing, Kerr and Bettis (1987) conclude from the results of their study that "in general, boards of directors do not consider performance of a firm's stock when changing CEO's salaries and bonuses. Neither overall market movements nor abnormal [stock] returns were associated with adjustments in compensation." Loomis (1982) and Crystal (1990) share the same pessimistic feelings about the low explanatory value of stodgy market data expressed by Kerr and Bettis.

In what is perhaps the most ambitious attempt to ascertain the pay-performance relation (including pay, stock options, stockholdings, and dismissal) for CEOs, Jensen and Murphy (1990a) studied 2,213 chief executive officers serving 1,295 corporations during the period from 1974 to 1986, for a total of 10,400 CEO years of data. Despite their earlier findings, which reported a strong relationship (e.g., see Jensen and Meckling, 1976; Murphy, 1986a,b), and when faced with the evidence at hand, these authors drew a bleak picture of the CEO pay-performance linkage:

> The empirical relation between the pay of top-level executives and firm performance, while positive and statistically significant, is small for an occupation in which incentive pay is expected to play an important role . . . our all-inclusive estimate of the pay-performance sensitivity-including compensation, dismissal, and stockholdings is about $3.25 per $1,000 change in shareholder wealth . . . In addition, our estimates suggest that dismissals are not an important source of managerial incentives since the increases in dismissal probability due to poor performance and the penalties associated with dismissal are both small. Executive inside stock ownership can provide incentives, but these holdings are not generally controlled by the corporate board and the majority of top executives have small personal stockholdings (p. 227).

In summary, the empirical evidence to date regarding the sales versus profit maximization hypothesis as a determinant of executive pay level is mixed at best. However, the weight of the evidence points toward a small, almost inconsequential, relationship between firm performance and CEO pay and a large correlation between company size and CEO pay (Tosi et al. 2000).

It's reasonable to expect that executives should be paid for firm size, which reflects the complexity of the job, as well as performance, which is an outcome measure. The problem remains, however, that relatively little variance in CEO pay is being explained and that performance typically lags behind size as a predictor of CEO compensation. While the observed level of statistical significance for the performance factor varies across studies and is interpreted according to the authors' preferences, most studies share something in common: The total amount of explained variance in executive pay attributed to firm performance is minimal, seldom exceeding 15 percent and often well under 10 percent.

Managerial Decisions, Financial Incentives, and Risk Sharing

While the linkage between executive pay level and firm performance is weak, there is strong evidence to suggest that executives do respond to what they perceive will lead to a financial reward (Berrone and Gomez-Mejia, 2009; Zajac,

1990, Hambrick et al. 2008) (i.e., the proverbial, "you get what you pay for"). The data suggests that the way the CEO compensation package is structured affects such key decisions as capital investments (Larcker, 1983; Bergman and Jenter, 2005), R&D investments and innovation efforts (Hoskisson, Hitt, and Hill, 1990; Makri, Lane, and Gomez-Mejia, 2006; Balkin, Markman, and Gomez-Mejia, 2000), mergers and acquisitions (Grinstein and Hribar, 2004; Wright et al. 2003), accounting choices (Dyl, 1989), dividend policies (Fenn and Liang, 2001), firm strategies (Dow and Raposo, 2005), and executives' job search behavior (Dunford et al. 2005). Unfortunately, few firms make CEO compensation contingent on strategic decisions that eventually impact performance. Pay contingencies involve risk sharing between the firm and the CEO. However, there is very little evidence that much risk sharing actually occurs. In fact, as noted by Devers and colleagues (2008), past research has shown little precision in how we measure and model the incentive alignment properties of CEO compensation in terms of strategic risk consequences for the firm.

Much of the research on risk taking has been done in the context of stock options. The classical rationale for stock options is that they offer upside potential but eliminate downside risk since the executive can only gain if the stock price increases. Hence, they encourage risk taking (assuming that higher risk leads to higher returns) while discouraging risk aversion. As a whole, research findings conflict on this issue (Sanders, 2001; Bettis, Bizjak, and Lemmon, 2005; Heath, Huddart, and Lang, 1999; Bergman and Jenter, 2005; Hall and Murphy, 2002; Becker 2006). Results tend to be more consistent with the predictions of the behavioral agency model: once the executive endows the stock gains he or she takes fewer risks in order to avoid potential losses (see reviews by Devers, Wiseman et al. 2007; Devers et al. 2008).

As noted earlier, the impact of CEO compensation design on risk taking is not well understood, in part because researchers often use crude measures of compensation, such as compensation level, stock options, and proportion of variable compensation in total compensation package. Hanlon, Rajgopal and Shevlin (2002) report that stock options increased the coefficient of variation in expected future cash flows (as a proxy for risk taking) from exploration in gas and oil firms. Datta, Iskandar-Datta, and Raman (2001) report that stock option pay encourages CEOs to undertake riskier investments. Similarly, Sanders (2001) reports that stock options are associated with greater risk taking because there have lower downside risk. However, others have found that the relationship between compensation elements and risk taking is either mixed or much more complex than meets the eye (Knopf, Nam, and Thornton, 2002; Schrand and Unal, 1998; Miller, Wiseman, and Gomez-Mejia, 2002; Dow and Rapaso, 2005; Carpenter, 2000).

Overall, the evidence supports many of the predictions of the behavioral agency model. Devers, Wiseman et al. (2007) found that the effect of endowment in stock option is to reduce risk taking. Devers and colleagues (2008) also report that the concepts of endowment, loss aversion, and diminishing sensitivity explain how CEOs respond to compensation design. For instance, they found that when exercisable options exhibit high spread value (greater endowment effect) CEOs invest in fewer strategic choices that involve uncertainty in order to mitigate downside compensation risk. Similarly, Larraza-Kintana and colleagues (2007), using survey data, found that a loss context (proxied by high employment risk and variability in cash-based pay) produces greater risk taking. On the contrary, a gain situation (low base-pay variability, positively valued stock options, and low employment risk) is associated with less risk taking. Consistent with the behavioral agency model or BAM, Zhang and colleagues (2008, p. 2), report that "CEOs were more likely to manipulate firm earnings when they had higher levels of out of the money options and when they had lower levels of stock ownership." While not focusing on compensation per se, a study by Gomez-Mejia and colleagues (2007) found that firms in a loss context (defined as family olive oil mills contemplating loss of family control of the business) are more willing to take business risks (defined as variability of earnings and acceptance of a higher probability of failure). Lastly, a study by Gomez-Mejia, Makri, and Larraza-Kintana (2010) on diversification reached similar conclusions. These authors found that family firms are less likely to engage in diversification, particularly international diversification, because it implies loss of family control, an important utility for these organizations. Accordingly, these family firms penalize executives with their pay for engaging in diversification activities, more so if this involves international diversification into culturally distant countries.

Firm Diversification and Executive Pay

Larger firms are more diversified than smaller firms (Rumelt, 1974). Another stream of research, some of which has been discussed at various points in this book, argues that it is not firm size per se that determines executive pay but the extent of firm diversification. However, these two variables are highly correlated.

Murthy and Salter (1975) examined the relationship between executive pay level and firm performance for companies whose sales come from a single business (dominant-product firms), firms that have expanded through the acquisition of businesses related to their original products (related-product firms), and large conglomerates that have grown by acquiring diverse businesses whose products are not related to each other (unrelated-product firms). They found that the relationship between executive pay level and performance is quite low for dominant-product firms, moderate for related-product firms, and high for unrelated-product firms. Expanding on this theme, Rajagopalan and Prescott (1990) report that extent of diversification is positively associated with executive pay in various industry groups. They interpret this to mean that " . . . at the topmost managerial levels, managers are rewarded for possessing diverse managerial skills that are useful in a variety of industry settings. Managers who possess transferable skills enjoy high mobility and are probably rewarded for their diverse business experiences and adaptability" (p. 537).

Murthy and Salter (1975) argue that as a firm grows by acquiring businesses that are unrelated to the original product, the executive's role begins to change from an operational "hands-on" management approach, emphasizing close supervision and centralized control, to a step-back mode, where the executive's primary role is to allocate resources to diverse business units and divisions. The board of directors has a difficult time evaluating the performance of unrelated business units on a subjective, qualitative basis because they do not understand the production process and market of diverse commodities. Likewise, it is harder for them to pass judgment on how well the executive's activities in unrelated-product firms contribute to organization performance. In this situation, the board relies on traditional, financial measures such as Return on Equity (ROE) or Earnings per Share (EPS) to evaluate the overall performance of the firm and the executive in charge. According to Murthy and Salter, this accounts for the observed stronger linkage between performance indicators and executive pay in unrelated-product firms, which also happen to be larger in size.

A similar stream of research has examined how autonomy level affects reward systems. Pitts (1974) found that external acquisitions and divisions whose products are unrelated to the major business have more autonomy than those divisions developing products linked to headquarters. Top executives in more autonomous business units are rewarded based on quantitative, formula-based criteria for the division. Those in less autonomous business units are evaluated based on both division and corporate performance, which makes objective division performance measures less crucial for pay decisions.

A number of recent studies show that diversification activities are often associated with CEO compensation design, although the cause and effect relationship may be unclear. That is, the design of the CEO compensation package affects diversification activities but diversification activities could also influence compensation level and pay mix (Gomez-Mejia, Makri, and

Larraza-Kintana, 2010). Bliss and Rosen (2001) examined merger activities and report that when stock ownership is low, CEOs devote more attention to profitability rather than growth and engage in fewer mergers. Grinstein and Hribar (2004) examined 327 mergers and acquisitions, reporting that CEO bonuses are positively tied to diversification activities. Wright, Kroll, and Elenkov (2002) classified firms into "vigilant" ($N = 77$) and "lax" ($N = 94$) monitoring, concluding that in the former category increases in CEO pay post acquisition are related to shareholder returns, while in the latter group CEO pay increases are tied to firm size. Similarly, Gomez-Mejia and colleagues (2010) found that when families own a significant portion of company shares, CEOs are penalized for aggressive diversification activities while in firms' with more dispersed ownership (weak family control) CEOs are rewarded for engaging in diversification.

Control Mechanisms and Executive Pay

While not addressing incentive mechanisms directly, Ouchi's work focused on the related issue of when "behavioral" or "output" controls are appropriate for divisional managers (Ouchi, 1977, 1978, 1979, 1980; Ouchi and Maguire, 1975). Use of output controls consists of gathering information about outcomes or consequences of managerial actions or decisions and would be most appropriate when knowledge of the transformation process is low. Behavioral controls, analogous to the "monitoring" mechanisms in agency theory, would be most appropriate when knowledge of the transformation process is high. These predictions are consistent with the transaction cost model discussed earlier (see Williamson, 1975; 1986a,b). That is, efficiency is achieved by reducing the transaction costs of negotiating, monitoring, and enforcing the agreement between the contracting parties (i.e., between top executives in corporate headquarters and division managers). In another empirical study on CEO compensation, Kerr and Kren (1992) found some support for the notion that "to the extent to which behavioral [vs. objective or outcome] information is considered in the evaluation process, performance should have a strong influence on pay where CEO decisions differ from typical industry decisions." More recently, Makri and colleagues (2006) and Washburn and colleagues (2010) report that behavioral information is more critical in assessing CEO performance for firms that are knowledge-intensive.

When neither behavioral controls nor output controls are feasible (because knowledge of the transformation process is weak and ability to measure outputs is low), Ouchi suggests that "clan control" is a better alternative.

By exercising this control, the organization can engender or instill a shared value system through socialization processes, selection procedures, and reliance on rituals and ceremony to create myths and a climate of cooperation. Such forms of control have long been used by religious orders throughout the centuries. Ouchi (1979, p. 845) goes on to suggest that "organizations in the public sector, in service industries, and in fast growing technologies perhaps should have cultural or clan forms of control."

Relatedly, Caranikas-Walker and colleagues (2008) made the argument that behavior-based contracts for CEOs offer the firm many advantages, although they are far more difficult to implement effectively because of the ambiguities involved. Behavior-based contracts allow the board to focus on CEO decision processes and behavior rather than outcomes. Thus, CEO decisions that support the organization's mission and goals would be positively rewarded even if there were negative organizational consequences in the short term. While employing behavioral-based monitoring strategies does not mandate subjective evaluation, human judgment offers the board a sophisticated method of evaluating CEO decisions and actions relative to shareholder interests. In particular, behavior-based evaluations can (a) incorporate judgments regarding the degree to which performance outcomes are due to the CEO's individual effort and ability rather than industry or other environmental forces and (b) provide a more comprehensive view of performance.

When the board is faced with firm performance that differs from what was expected (or if concerns for limiting investments in executive compensation or for decreasing CEO risk-bearing are priorities), the board will seek out more information to verify that the performance was the result of the CEO's unique ability and effort and not due to factors beyond the CEO's control. Board members may investigate industry norms and operational decision-making of the CEO, and make final performance judgments when they are satisfied with their explanations of performance. Thus, human judgment can potentially aid in purifying contaminated performance evaluations by factoring out situational or environmental factors that influence firm performance (Hambrick et al. 2008). Then boards of directors can reward CEOs in accordance with their unique contributions to organizational performance. Walsh and Seward (1990) suggest that board members are attempting to do this when they attribute CEO performance to either (a) CEO ability and effort or (b) constraints on CEO decision making.

Using a combination of surveys of board members, reputational rankings, and Compustat data, Caranikas-Walker and colleagues (2008) found equivocal support for the use of subjective performance assessments as determinants of CEO pay in a sample of 110 companies representing 21 industries.

Subjective performance measures together explained 2 to 3 percent of the variance in CEO pay beyond what is explained by objective performance measures. Moreover, the additional variance was not statistically significant. The objective performance measures explained a marginally significant portion of the variance in CEO pay only for the salary component. While these results appear consistent with the literature reviewed earlier, which has found little association between performance and CEO pay, further investigation has indicated that individual subjective performance measures significantly predicted some components of CEO compensation; that is, corporate reputation predicted salary and CEO performance rating predicted both bonus and long-term income. The utility of corporate reputation in explaining CEO salary supports the view that subjective performance evaluation may be useful to corporate boards in their monitoring role. By utilizing corporate reputation as an indicator of CEO performance, boards may be able to improve the accuracy of CEO performance evaluations. Corporate reputation has a long-term orientation and encompasses performance across financial as well as nonfinancial domains. Reputation may also reflect the unique contributions of the CEO more than other performance measures that may be affected by factors the CEO cannot control. The counterintuitive negative relationships between CEO performance rating and bonus, and between rating and long-term income, suggested the possibility of a moderator. Caranikas-Walker and colleagues (2008), report that the interactive effects of board composition and R&D intensity significantly influenced the relation between subjective performance evaluation and both components of CEO pay.

Market Factors

Surprisingly, very limited empirical research has been conducted on the relationship between demand/supply forces in the managerial labor market and executive pay, or how the going rate in the labor market affects decisions regarding executive compensation. Part of the reason may be that executive pay packages are highly individualized, similar to what you would find when a movie studio is trying to hire a star or when a baseball team attempts to pirate a pitcher from a competing team. The resulting pay package will depend on the idiosyncrasies of the situation and the negotiation skills of both parties. These subjective judgments play a major role when making competitive offers to executives. Even if one takes into account such factors as industry, company size, geographic area, and qualifications of the executive, the standard deviation of actual pay levels when using survey data may be huge (Gomez-Mejia et al. 2010).

Ciscel and Carroll (1980) found that the constant term in their regression equations, which included firm size and performance as independent variables and executive pay as dependent variables, showed a high explanatory power. They claim that the constant term reflects the minimum value of the dependent variable before the effects of the independent or explanatory variables are considered. Ciscel and Carroll (1980, pp. 10–11) speculate that the constant term reflects the " . . . equilibrium price of a Chief Executive Officer's time determined by the interaction of supply and demands for management skills . . . this [interpretation] indicates that attributing the value of the constant term to a market for managerial talent is not unreasonable." This interpretation, however, is questionable and requires a gigantic leap of faith. The constant term may reflect myriad factors (e.g., random events, decisions of compensation committees, distribution of ownership) other than the "true" market value of an executive.

There seems to be general agreement that industry is an important determinant of executive compensation practices. McCann, Hinkin, and Gomez-Mejia (1992) analyzed 812 executive transitions during the 1980s. They found that most executive replacements came from similar firms within the same industries as the hiring firms. This suggests that the executive labor market is rather segmented and that market rates for executives may be independently set within each segment. Peck (1987) found that total variance in executive compensation attributed to firm size varies from a low of 32 percent in the construction industry to a high of 66 percent in commercial banking. Ungson and Steers (1984) concluded that industry variables, represented by the intercept terms in the regression equations, were better predictors of CEO pay than either firm size or profits. More recently, a study by Sturman, Walsh, and Cheramie (2008) using longitudinal data of more than 9,000 executives found that "executives moving to more similar firms receive greater increases to pay than non-movers and those moving to less similar firms" (p. 290). Generally, the more competitive the industry, the more likely executive pay is linked to performance, although these relationships are rather weak.

In perhaps the most direct test of the labor market hypothesis, Perkins and Hendry (2005) interviewed members of compensation committees of several large British companies. They found that most of these committees determine "market pay" through a highly subjective process that involves comparisons with other executives in relevant industry labor markets. According to these authors " . . . the market as a determinant of reward is therefore a rather loose metaphor" (p. 145). For instance, one of the directors interviewed denied the existence of a recognizable market for executives "instead they are just key people in unique positions at a given moment in time, who are not readily interchangeable. Consequently, like for like comparisons are impractical" (cited in Perkins and Hendry, 2005, p. 1453). In another British study, Ezzamel and Watson (1998) concluded that market comparisons made by remuneration committees contribute to an upward pay bias since these judgments are highly subjective and tend to favor the executive.

Distribution of Ownership

As discussed earlier, the separation of ownership and control in the modern corporation is a central concern of managerialism and agency theory. The reader is reminded that both of these perspectives hold that owners of the firm (principals) hire managers (agents) to run the enterprise. Because it is difficult for atomistic stockholders to supervise the activities of top management, the latter may be tempted to engage in self-serving behaviors, perhaps at the expense of firm owners. Jensen and Meckling (1976), Fama (1980), Fama and Jensen (1983a), Demsetz (1983), and others argue that shareholders do, in fact, accomplish this rather efficiently, even in firms whose ownership is widely dispersed. However, most of the empirical evidence suggests that agency arrangements do not work as well as Fama and colleagues would lead us to believe. Even Jensen, one of Fama's closest collaborators and author of several classical agency papers, has publicly retreated from his earlier position (see Jensen and Murphy, 1990b).

While the precise functional relationship between the concentration of equity holdings and control of the firm is not known, research suggests that for very large firms, the percentage of stock required to exercise significant control may be quite small (McEachern, 1975; Salamon and Smith, 1979; Fong et al. 2010). As early as 1937, the Securities and Exchange Commission proposed that 10 percent stock ownership was a sufficient amount to control a firm. More recent research suggests that when a single equity holder controls as little as 5 percent of the voting stock, the equity holders can have a significant influence on the behavior of managers of a firm (Boudreaux, 1973; O'Reilly, Main, and Crystal, 1988; Palmer, 1973; Salancik and Pfeffer, 1980; Werner, Tosi, and Gomez-Mejia, 2005; Fong et al. 2010). Typically, although by no means universally accepted, researchers designate as owner-controlled those firms that have a single equity owner who controls as little as 5 percent of the voting stock. When there is no equity holder with at least 5 percent of the stock, the firm is called management-controlled.

With few exceptions (e.g., Finkelstein and Hambrick, 1988), studies have found evidence that when there is less stockholder (owner) control, the executive's personal income increases with very little relation to the performance of the firm. If a major stockholder exerts control over the executives, their pay is found to be more highly correlated with the performance variables. These findings have been consistently replicated using either a dichotomous indicator of ownership (most often the 5 percent convention discussed earlier) (e.g., Fong et al. 2010; Allen, 1981; Arnould, 1985; Gomez-Mejia, Tosi et al. 1987; Tosi et al. 1999; McEachern, 1975; Wallace, 1973) or a continuous measure (Dyl, 1988, 1989). Gomez-Mejia, Tosi et al. (1987, p. 67) argued that:

> An important portion of the compensation of managers in management-controlled firms may be decoupled from performance and, by inference, less in alignment with the owners' interests. These CEOs bear less compensation-related uncertainty and risk than those in owner-controlled firms. Executives in management-controlled firms can reduce their risk and force the owners to bear more because they have greater control over organizational decision processes.

A substantial amount of evidence in the area of mergers and acquisitions suggests that agency problems are common in corporations with widely dispersed ownership. Management-controlled firms are more likely to engage in mergers and acquisitions to justify higher executive pay, even if these activities result in lower overall corporate performance (Kroll, Simmons, and Wright, 1990; Wright, Kroll and Elenkov, 2002). Management-controlled firms engage in more conglomerate acquisition activities, often to the detriment of investors, than owner-controlled firms to diversify the employment risk of executives (e.g., risk of losing job, professional reputation) (Ahimud and Lev, 1981). Ahimud and Lev conclude: "The consequences of such mergers may be regarded as an agency cost" (p. 606). This conclusion is consistent with the earlier work of Palmer (1973) and the findings of Blair and Kaserman (1983) and Chevalier (1969) that management-controlled firms are involved in a greater number of antitrust activities.

Additional evidence provided by a number of studies suggests that agency problems defy easy solutions. Grossman and Hart (1983) argue that information asymmetries in management-controlled firms are used to the advantage of top executives at the expense of owners. Bhagat (1983, p. 310) found that executives in management-controlled firms may be successful in "passing amendments to corporate charters to maximize their own welfare, sometimes to the detriment of stockholders." Pfeffer and Salancik (1978) report that the probability of an executive being fired for poor performance is much greater in owner-controlled than management-controlled firms. Hunt (1986) argues that the choir of accounting and inventory methods in management-controlled firms is such that they artificially portray a more favorable image of the firm's financial picture. Finally, based on reports of 175 chief compensation officers in manufacturing, Tosi and Gomez-Mejia (1989, 1994) found that the actual level of monitoring and incentive alignment, the proportion of executive pay at risk, and long-term compensation were much greater in owner-controlled firms.

In short, it is difficult to ignore the large volume of research and circumstantial evidence suggesting that the distribution of ownership across firms is an important determinant of executive pay. The savings and loan crisis of the 1990s and the subprime crisis that followed offer an extreme example of what may happen when managerial authority goes unchecked. For example, the U.S. Government Accountability Office (GAO), which studied the reasons behind the insolvency of many of these financial concerns during the savings and loan crisis, concluded that the managers of bankrupt savings and loans "paid themselves like kings and treated themselves to extravagant expenditures" (*Boulder Daily Camera*, 1989, p. 78). Similar conclusions have recently been reached in the popular business press concerning the collapse of mortgage lenders at the start of the twenty-first century, which has ultimately rocked global financial markets (Bajaj and Creswell, 2008; Coy, 2009).

However, there is no conclusive evidence that owner-controlled firms perform more profitably than management-controlled firms. In an extensive review of the literature, Hunt (1986) cites several studies that show owner-controlled firms to be more profitable, several that show that management-controlled firms are more profitable, and others that show no performance differences. But, he suggests, methodological issues could account for the inconsistency in the results of these studies, particularly with respect to the dependent variable, *performance*. These studies, with few exceptions, use accounting-based performance measures and there is, for management-controlled firms, a "tendency for managers to report financial data in the best possible light" (Hunt, 1986, p. 114). If this is so, then real differences between the two types should be larger than reported. Thus, the magnitude of the differences in reported performance measures between management-controlled and owner-controlled firms would be masked by the reporting procedures.

There is other support for this interpretation. For example, Hunt (1986) discusses how the choice of accounting methods may improve the appearance of results. Other studies show that management-controlled firms are more likely to use inventory methods (Niehaus, 1985) and other accounting practices that will overstate earnings (Salamon and Smith, 1979). In addition, management-controlled firms will smooth income over several reporting periods. The "evidence with respect to ownership structure and income smoothing is a rather serious indictment of the performance studies which rely on unadjusted accounting methods of performance" (Hunt, 1986, p. 116).

Other agency costs are born by equity holders of management-controlled firms. The study by Salancik and Pfeffer (1980) cited earlier showed that there is longer executive tenure in management-controlled firms. Such a finding would only make sense if the performance of these firms was superior to that of owner-controlled firms. Yet the evidence does not support such an interpretation. A more logical position is that the managers, without pressure from the owners, are reluctant to replace themselves for poor performance. Further, Hayes and Abernathy (1980) argue that there is a greater propensity in manager-controlled firms to engage in activities to increase size, often through mergers and acquisitions that may not be economically efficient to the owners but are very beneficial to the managers (Hayes and Abernathy, 1980). The propensity of management-controlled firms to engage in growth-oriented strategies is consistent with the results of a study by Gomez-Mejia, Tosi, and Hinkin (1987), which reported that the basic salary of CEOs of management-controlled firms is correlated with firm scale (a size measure), while the strongest predictor of CEO pay in owner-controlled firms is performance.

Tosi and Gomez-Mejia (1992) developed a behavioral measure of monitoring and incentive alignment of top executives and correlated this measure with both subjective and archival measures of firm performance in two separate samples. Following the basic tenets of agency theory, the authors predicted that activities to increase the level of monitoring of CEOs and to induce a stronger alignment of CEO pay and performance would have positive effects on the performance of the organization. They found support for that hypothesis. They reported that monitoring mechanisms that align the interest of managers with those of the firm and that prevent managers from pursuing self-serving objectives are positively associated with both perceptual and archival firm performance measures.

Tosi and Gomez-Mejia (1992) also hypothesized that the effects of monitoring are expected to differ as a function of the ownership structure. They proposed that increased monitoring results in improved firm performance, and their data supported this proposal. (This was predicted in the theoretical work of researchers such as Shavell, 1979, and Holmstrom, 1979.) However, the effects are greater in management-controlled firms. There are two reasons for this. The level of monitoring is already much higher in owner-controlled firms than in management-controlled firms (e.g., see Dyl, 1988, 1989; Tosi and Gomez-Mejia, 1989), so one would expect that the marginal contribution of additional monitoring to firm performance should be greater among the latter. Given the lower observed threshold values on the monitoring dimension among management-controlled firms, firm performance should then be highly responsive to increased monitoring in this situation, as agency theorists predict. On the other hand, it is not unreasonable to expect that a truncated range on the monitoring dimension among owner-controlled firms would tend to attenuate its observed relationship with firm performance. Consistent with earlier findings of Lieberson and O'Connor (1972) Salancik and Pfeffer (1977), Weiner and Mahoney (1981), and Smith, Carson, and Alexander (1984), one would expect that monitoring can only exert a limited influence on firm performance, because the latter also depends on many factors beyond management's control. Thus, one could argue that among owner-controlled firms, monitoring is already close to reaching its maximum theoretical impact on firm performance, becoming relatively inert, and performance variance past that point can best be attributed to random and/or uncontrollable events.

A second, albeit more speculative, reason advanced by Tosi and Gomez-Mejia (1992), which may account for differences on the impact of monitoring on firm performance between the two types of firms, pertains to variations in the holistic organizational context. Support for this assertion is found in earlier work by Hansen and Wernerfelt (1989). These authors attempted to divide the interfirm variance in profit rates into economic and organizational components. They reported that organizational factors accounted for about twice as much variance in firm performance ($R^2 = 0.38$) as economic factors ($R^2 = 0.19$). Hansen and Wernerfelt (1989) attribute these results to the following:

> Managers can influence the behavior of their employees (and thus the performance of the organization) by taking into account factors such as the formal and informal structure, the planning, reward, control, and information systems, their skills and personalities, and the relation of these to the environment. That is, managers influence organizational outcomes by establishing context, and that context is the result of a complex set of psychological, sociological, and physical interactions. (p. 401)

Along the same vein, Tosi and Gomez-Mejia (1992) argued that when owners exert substantial influence over the firm, the organization culture and climate, strategic orientation, policies and practices governing various employee groups (divisional managers, midlevel executives, lower management levels, and workers), as well as the overall structure of the reward system, strongly reinforces a performance ethos. Therefore, monitoring of top management is one of the many factors that drive behavior, and, as such, its unique effects on firm performance would be more difficult to detect. On the other hand, in management-controlled firms, there is less incentive to operate in the owners' interests because the culture, strategy, policies, and reward structure reinforce behaviors catering to managers' interests. In this context, according to Tosi and Gomez-Mejia (1992), there would be little monitoring of top management teams and, if this is increased, there should be larger effects on observed performance.

The research leads to this conclusion: While it remains to be clearly demonstrated that there are performance differences between management-controlled and owner-controlled firms (and this may be partially accounted for by methodological matters), it is very clear that executives of management-controlled firms act in ways to suggest that they intend to pass on higher agency costs to the owners than executives of owner-controlled firms. However, these agency costs may be reduced in management-controlled firms through monitoring and incentive alignment mechanisms.

Role of Institutional Investors

An issue closely related to the debate on ownership concentration is the role played by large institutional investors (such as pension funds, investment funds, mortgage companies) in the management of firms in their portfolio, including executive compensation. The main point of contention is the extent to which these "passive investors," who may hold large blocks of shares, do not exercise control of any kind. Some argue that these external owners are quick to follow the "Wall Street" rule, selling their stock when dissatisfied with management instead of attempting to influence management or exercise control over the firms in their portfolio. While empirical research on this question is very limited, and indeed most of this debate has taken place in the mass media and in practitioner journals, the evidence available to date suggests that so-called "passive investors" actually do play an active watchdog role with firms in their portfolio.

According to Graves and Waddock (1990), " . . . institutional investors derive their power over top managers from the mere size of their equity holdings: heavy institutional selling can cause drastic declines in a firm's market value" (p. 78). There is also increasing empirical evidence that points toward a positive relationship between equity ownership by passive investors and managerial decisions that are in the long-term interest of the firm. This is at odds with the notion that institutional investors are driven by shortsightedness and do not really care about what happens within a given firm (because if a stock in an institutional portfolio shows signs of poor performance, presumably the fund manager will sell out and purchase a more favorable stock.) What firm executives do, according to this view, is of little import to these fund managers. Tests of this "hands-off" hypothesis concerning institutional investors have been conducted by examining long-term R&D investments as a function of institutional holdings. Several studies have shown a positive impact of institutional ownership on long-term R&D investments, suggesting that institutional investors are willing and able to exercise their influence on managerial decisions and that this influence is indicative of an enduring, rather than transient or short-term, relationship (see Jarrel, Lehn, and Marr, 1985; Hill and Hansen, 1989; Baysinger, Kosnik, and Turk, 1991; Hansen and Hill, 1991). Furthermore, Baysinger and colleagues (1991) and Hansen and Hill (1991) found that the influence on management (as measured by R&D investment decisions) is not any less from large institutional investors than from large individual stockholders.

Third, the large level of assets controlled by institutions makes efficient movement in and out of stock positions increasingly difficult (Nussbaum and Dobrzynski, 1987). "As a result, they have a tendency to become involved in corporate control when results do not live up to expectations" (Graves and Waddock, 1990, p. 77). Aoki (1984) and others (e.g., Herman, 1981) have argued that "passive" institutional investors have little choice but to become active owners in those firms where they hold a large amount of stock (which they define as 5 percent or more) because they cannot easily migrate to other firms when displeased with a given company. Reflecting this view, Hansen and Hill (1991, p. 12) note that:

> . . . many institutions are effectively "locked in" to their stockholdings. Unlike most individuals, institutions may take fairly substantial positions in a firm's stock . . . Given this, and the tendency of institutions to act in unison, many institutions cannot exit from a firm's stock without depressing the stock price and taking a substantial capital loss on the transaction. Due to the high costs of exit, institutions find themselves locked into a long-term relationship with the firm. Recognizing this, they may use their voting power and influence [over] managers . . .

Similarly, Baysinger and colleagues (1991, pp. 212–213) comment:

> . . . institutional investors who own large stakes in a company's stock are less able to move efficiently in and out of stock positions . . . Hence, they try to influence the return of their investment by becoming actively involved in a company's management.

More recent research is supportive of the important role played by institutional investors. Ke, Petroni, and Safieddine (1999) found that compensation in closely held firms tends to be more tied to strategic (subjective) than accounting (objective) indicators. Similar findings are reported by Caranikas-Walker and colleagues (2008) who found that institutional investors tend to emphasize strategic (subjective) performance indicators, which are more difficult to implement. Kraft and Niederprum (1999) report that ownership in the hands of institutional investors tends to have a negative impact on executive pay level. Likewise, Almazan, Hartzell, and Starks (2005) found that institutional ownership is negatively related to CEO total compensation and is positively related to the strength of pay–performance relations.

In short, the proposition that so-called passive institutional investors do not exercise ownership control of any kind or that their behavior relative to managers is markedly different from that of individual investors has received little support. This remains a fertile area for serious scholarly research on executive compensation.

Role of Families

A recent literature has focused on another ownership-related factor, namely, the active role of families in many organizations (which some estimate represent 85 percent of all firms around the world; La Porta, Lopez-de-Silanes, and Shleifer, 1999) in setting executive compensation policies. One of the concerns in the finance and organizational literatures dealing with family firms is the extent to which the family can use its power and privileged position to pursue its own objectives at the expense of other shareholders (Faccio, Lang, and Young, 2001; Shleifer and Vishny, 1997; Villalonga and Amit, 2006). Anderson and Reeb (2003, p. 654) summarize this "horizontal" agency problem as follows; "... families have the incentives and power to systematically expropriate wealth from the firm's other claimants, which suggests severe moral hazard conflicts between the founding family and minority shareholders."

In the specific case of diversification, Anderson and Reeb (2003) hypothesized that risk aversion or risk avoidance on the part of the family may induce the family firm to engage in greater diversification. And since diversification is associated with lower shareholder values (cf., Berger and Ofek, 1996), Graham, Lemmon, and Wolf (2002) and Anderson and Reeb (2003) reasoned that the purported family desire for greater diversification (to mitigate firm risk) would impose a cost of nonfamily owners interested in maximizing residual cash flows. Anderson and Reeb's empirical findings found no support for a positive relation between family ownership and diversification (it was actually negative); neither did they find that minority shareholders were penalized. Faced with these surprising findings, Anderson and Reeb suggested a rational economic explanation, namely that family firms avoid diversification in order to focus on the firm's core competence, and that this policy was beneficial to minority shareholders as well.

In an empirical study of 360 firms, 160 of them being family controlled and the rest (200) not family controlled, Gomez-Mejia, Makri, and Larraza (2010) show that family firms tie CEO incentives to diversification decisions to a lesser extent than nonfamily firms. They also found that family firms are more willing to diversify as business risk increases, and that family firms derive greater returns from diversification than nonfamily firms. An earlier paper by the same authors found that family executives are paid less, but their pay is more insulated from business risk (Gomez-Mejia et al. 2003). For additional related research on the role of families, see review by Gomez-Mejia, Firfiray, and Cruz (2011, in press).

Organizational Structure

As discussed in Chapter 4, Simon (1957) proposed an alternative sociological view of executive compensation by arguing that it was not firm size per se that determined top executive pay but, rather, the organization's internal hierarchy. Firms attempt to establish pay differentials between levels as rations, and not in absolute terms. This theory predicts that top executive compensation should be greater in firms with taller organizational structures.

Mahoney (1979) found that the pay ratios between management levels are remarkably consistent across firms with an approximate 33 percent pay differential between levels in the hierarchy. Peck (1987) confirms this proposition by showing that the pay relationships among the five highest paid executives differ little by type of business. For example, on average, the second highest paid executive typically receives 67 to 87 percent of the highest paid executive's income, and the third highest receives approximately 55 percent of the top executive's pay. Thus, the empirical evidence supports the proposition that many organizational levels imply high pay at the top. However, these findings may simply be replicating what others have already found, namely, that firm size is an important predictor of executive pay. This interpretation is consistent both with span of control theory and with the findings of Blau (1970) and Child (1972), which suggest that firm size and number of levels are highly correlated.

Individual Determinants of Executive Pay

Most of the research examining the role of personal characteristics of executives on their pay is based on the human capital paradigm reviewed in Chapter

4. Results of earlier human capital research were quite straightforward (see Becker, 1975; Mincer, 1975.) On average, earnings increase with work experience. Human capital theory explains this increase as a return on investment in productivity-enhancing skills accumulated while working.

Other empirical evidence suggests, however, that additional factors come into play. It has been shown by Pascal and Rapping (1972), Medoff and Abraham (1980), and Harris and Holmstrom (1982) that more experienced managers earn more, even after controlling for performance. One explanation for this is that institutional norms help push up earnings of executives as they accumulate more experience. Years of experience may be used to "rationalize" pay decisions (Balkin and Gomez-Mejia, 1987b). Another explanation is advanced by Harris and Holmstrom (1982) who argue that senior executives earn more on average because they have had more time for their compensation to be bid up by the market. Harris and Holmstrom also argue that more senior executives pay a lower "insurance premium," as they are perceived by employers to be less risky. Therefore, they will be provided higher pay, even when one controls for observed performance. In the same vein, Murphy (1986b, p. 62) presents some empirical findings suggesting that "observing performance over several periods allows the firm to form a more precise estimate of executive ability." Because less is known about executives earlier in their careers, formula-based approaches linking pay to firm performance are frequently adopted in their initial years, but these programs are less necessary over time as the executive's "true" ability becomes better known.

In any case, there is much evidence supporting a correlation between amount of relevant experience and executive pay level. But whether increased earnings are attributed to improved performance as a result of accumulated human capital or some other factors is subject to interpretation.

Most of the empirical research on human capital theory originated in economics. However, investigators in other disciplines, such as management and industrial relations, have also examined personal characteristics of executives as potential determinants of their pay. Reviews of four such studies follow.

Roche (1975) studied age and executive mobility in relationship to pay. He found that through their mid-40s, compensation for less mobile executives was higher than that of the more mobile executives. The return to high mobility, however, became evident in the subjects' mid-50s, when highly mobile executives received much higher pay packages. This group was willing to take risks and felt very comfortable in the midst of rapid change.

Agarwal (1981) noted that internal work experience was a better predictor of executive pay than external work experience. Compensation of internal candidates is lower than pay packages for outsiders because a premium is not required to induce the latter to change jobs. Deckop (1988) also found that external recruits made more money than executives hired from within, and both earned more than the original founders. This suggests that individuals who are groomed within the company will eventually be less expensive than executives hired from other firms.

Gerhart and Milkovich (1990) studied a sample of 20,000 top- and middle-level executives. They report that human capital (as measured by years of education, years of labor market experience, firm tenure, and job tenure) and job responsibility level (as measured by the number of reporting levels from the board of directors to the position of the incumbent and number of management levels supervised) explain 69 percent of base pay level received and 24 percent of the variance in bonus as a proportion of base pay.

Hill and Phan (1991) report that while executive pay level rises with tenure, the relationship between executive pay and firm performance *decreases* as a function of tenure. Consistent with a managerialist interpretation and at odds with a human capital perspective, these authors concluded that "the longer the tenure of a CEO, the greater his or her influence over the board of directors, and the more likely it is that his or her compensation package will reflect his or her preferences. Consistent with this, an empirical test suggests that the relationship between CEO pay and stock returns weakens with tenure."

Aggarwal and Samwick (2003) found that greater responsibility and pay-performance sensitivity tend to go hand in hand. They demonstrated a linear relationship between hierarchical level and pay-performance sensitivity. This suggests that greater job complexity and greater decision-making authority are associated with greater accountability (through pay for performance).

More recently, Sturman, Walsh, and Cheramie (2008) found that firm-specific human capital is highly rewarded for executives to the extent that it is seen as a resource that contributes to a firm's competitive advantage. Lastly, a meta-analysis of 196 studies by Ng et al. (2005) found that proxies for human capital, such as job tenure, organizational tenure, work experience, and education, are significant predictors of amount of pay received. As a whole, then, the evidence is supportive of a positive human capital effect on executive pay.

Tournament Theory

As discussed in Chapter 4, Lazear and Rosen (1981) and others have portrayed top executive pay as a prize used to induce lower-level managers to work harder to win the prize, rather than as a reward commensurate with the executive's performance. According to O'Reilly and colleagues (1988, p. 259), "in this scheme the compensation of the CEO represents the prize in the lottery; hence those below this level will be willing to give up some of their earnings to be put into the prize for which they all compete." Presumably, this accounts for the very large observed differences between CEO salaries and those of executives at the immediate lower level.

Empirical research to test tournament theory has increased in recent years, and the findings are somewhat mixed. One study by O'Reilly and colleagues (1988) produced negative results. The logic of this study is as follows: The greater the number of competitors and, hence, the lower the chance of winning, the larger should be the prize, other things being equal. By finding in their sample that the CEO's pay was negatively related to the number of vice presidents, O'Reilly and colleagues (1988, p. 236) conclude "this was exactly the opposite of the result predicted by tournament theory." While their way of testing tournament theory is very creative and makes a contribution, given the paucity of research in this area, other interpretations for their findings are not hard to make. For example, some organizations are known for their generous use of vice presidential titles in lieu of higher pay to reward managers. Other firms use this title rather sparingly. Also, the span of control for the CEO varies significantly from one type of organization to another. One could also argue that the tournament "game" is not designed exclusively for vice presidents but for several managerial levels.

In the same study, O'Reilly and colleagues found that political factors unrelated to firm performance affect the level of executive pay. They report that one of the main correlates of executive earnings was the average pay level of the compensation committee of the board of directors. This committee is typically composed of CEOs from other firms. O'Reilly and colleagues (1988, p. 240) offer a behavioral explanation for these findings. A social comparison process "takes place whereby the compensation committee members perceive the appropriate pay level of the executive to be similar to their own." They go on to suggest that the CEOs are aware of this perceptual bias and will use their political clout to hire board members that are highly paid: "Since the CEO exerts considerable informal influence in selecting new members of the board, it may also be that the selection process itself can raise CEO pay if new members are selected whose pay exceeds that of the focal CEO" (p. 240).

Although concerned with distribution of ownership issues, rather than social comparisons, Tosi and Gomez-Mejia (1989) confirm the importance of influence patterns in executive compensation decisions. These authors found that in management-controlled firms, the influence exercised on CEO pay by the CEO and outside consultants is greater than in owner-controlled firms. Tosi and Gomez-Mejia also report that in management-controlled firms the influence exercised on CEO pay by major stockholders, the board of directors, and the compensation committee was less than in owner-controlled firms. The logic behind their findings is as follows: In owner-controlled firms the board represents the owners' interest because the owners, not management, are more influential in the selection of board members. This reduces the possibility of conflicts of interest arising between the executives and the firm. The board will ensure that there are "checks and balances" in the decision system so that executives will have little say in their own pay level. In management-controlled firms, on the other hand, board appointments are more likely to be controlled by management, and members serve at its pleasure. Consultants may be hired to legitimize the pay determination process. Likewise, management will play a stronger role in handpicking the compensation committee, and its members will feel obligated to represent the interests of the constituency that chose them. These governance issues are revisited in a later chapter.

Two other studies on tournament theory reached a different conclusion from O'Reilly and colleagues (1988). Based on a sample of 439 large U.S. corporations between 1981 and 1985, Leonard (1990) reports that pay differentials between ranks increase higher up in the hierarchy and are also greater when promotion rates are low. He reports that managers in flat organizations are paid less than those in tall firms. Executives in more hierarchically ranked firms earn up to 60 percent pay premium over those in flat organizations. These findings are not surprising and can be interpreted in many different ways, including a structural interpretation (Simon, 1959), a human capital interpretation (Agarwal, 1981), or a power interpretation (Tosi and Gomez-Mejia, 1992; Gomez-Mejia, Tosi, and Hinkin, 1987). However, Leonard (1990, p. 14) interprets these findings as providing support to tournament theory in that "high pay in top executive positions is used to motivate lower-level executives to compete for promotions. The expected value to executives of such a scheme can be maintained if the pay differential across levels narrows while promotion probabilities increase." Like much of the empirical research on executive compensation, how one interprets these findings depends on personal preferences because of intercorrelated measures and the difficulty of attributing causality to any given variable. For example, greater salary dispersion as a function of tallness may perhaps be attributed to a "tournament effect," but we can think of several alternative, equally plausible explanations.

A third study, by Ehrenberg and Bognanno (1990), used a creative method to test tournament theory and concluded that the fundamental tenets of the theory were supported. However, one can question whether their findings can be generalized in regard to "real life" executives managing complex business organizations. They analyzed data from the 1987 European Men's Professional Golf Association (PGA) tour. By assuming that the difficulty of the course and the adversity of weather conditions affect all players in a tournament equally and that players choose their effort/concentration levels, Ehrenberg and Bognanno (1990, p. 74) believe that their data is consistent with tournament theory predictions in that "the level and structure of prizes in PGA tournaments influence players' performance. Specifically, players' performance appears to vary positively with both the total money prizes awarded in a tournament and the marginal return to effort in the final round of play (a value that varies among players largely depending on how the prize money is allocated among finishers of different ranks)."

A study by Henderson and Fredrickson (2001) tested the tournament view that larger pay gaps create a motivational force that serves as a substitute for monitoring. They conclude that, consistent with a tournament explanation, competition for a larger reward reduces the need for monitoring. In a more recent paper, Gomez-Mejia, Trevino, and Mixon (2009) argue that for a tournament to have the desired motivational impact indicated by proponents of tournament theory, it is necessary to ensure procedural justice and agreement among tournament players as to the criteria required to win the competition.

In short, evidence in support of tournament theory is somewhat mixed. This may be attributed to the formidable difficulties involved in trying to operationalize tournament effects and the leaps of faith required when drawing motivational inferences from archival data. This seems like an area of inquiry where a laboratory experiment may be particularly appropriate for testing specific tournament hypotheses in a controlled environment. Field data and archival information are simply too contaminated to yield robust results when testing alleged tournament effects.

Executives as Figureheads

As discussed earlier, Ungson and Steers (1984) describe the duties of CEOs in terms of their role as political figureheads and strategists. While little empirical work has been conducted that directly examines these roles, available evidence suggests that interpersonal skills of the executives vary, and greater organizational savvy may lead to a better financial deal for the incumbent. Luthans (1988) reports that executives who moved rapidly to the top echelons in the firm were not necessarily the best managers (i.e., those who have satisfied, committed subordinates and high performing units). Many upwardly mobile executives were very good at creating a favorable image with their superiors and peers, irrespective of actual performance. This may be part of the reason behind the decoupling of executive pay and firm performance in some companies. It could be that shrewd executives, who have refined the art of "impression management," are able to negotiate large compensation packages in spite of their poor track record (Geneen, 1984). In particular, the relationship of the CEO with the board of directors might be an important determinant of how generously the board rewards the executive (Tosi and Gomez-Mejia, 1989). The nature of this relationship might well provide insights as to the level of CEO pay and the design of the CEO pay package in terms of salary, bonus, and long-term income. This aspect of executive compensation warrants more attention.

In a more recent study, Miller and Wiseman (2001) used a policy-capturing approach to examine the "figurehead" assertion that executive pay level is positively associated with followers' perceptions of a leader's ability. Their findings tend to be more consistent with a human capital explanation than a figurehead explanation. The main predictors of CEO pay were promotion history, degree earned, and university prestige. These authors conclude that:

> Results of this study undermine symbolic explanations of executive pay. In the absence of performance information, subjects did not view compensation data as a signal of performance or ability. This evidence challenges figurehead arguments as well as other theoretical perspectives regarding the role and symbolic nature of compensation. As argued previously, in the absence of performance information, employers may use compensation data regarding an applicant to judge the value of the applicant to the firm. Our results challenge this finding with regard to executives, and indicate that in the presence of other information (e.g., education and experience), compensation plays almost no role in influencing perceptions of executive competence. (p. 707)

Pay Dispersion

Research on horizontal pay dispersion has increased in the past 10 years or so. However, findings are mixed. For example, Bloom (1999) found that pay dispersion among professional athletes tends to be negatively associated with team performance. On the other hand, Conyon, Peck, and Sadler (2001) found no relationship between pay dispersion and performance. Siegel and Hambrick (2005) found that pay dispersion in the top management team is negatively associated with performance, but only when high coordination is needed, as in technology-intensive firms. Shaw, Gupta, and Delery (2002) found that high pay dispersion, individual incentives, and independent work contexts are associated with higher levels of workforce performance. On the other hand, Henderson and Fredrickson (2001) found the opposite; that is, greater pay dispersion under conditions of high coordination.

One thing missing in this line of research are measures of equitable performance criteria as perceived by the individuals involved. It seems reasonable that a top management team would accept greater pay dispersion if they believe that the criteria are fair, accurate, and consistent (Gomez-Mejia et al. 2010). In fact, lower pay dispersion may be seen as inequitable if there are large differences in the performance of individual contributors and this differential is not being adequately recognized.

Self-Selection

Research on self-selection, most of it conducted during 2000–2010, suggests that executives tend to accept positions and remain in those positions when the firm offers a compensation package that appeals to their preference. Dunford, Boudreau, and Boswell (2005) found that when executives believe pay is not adequate or when they incur high compensation risk, they are more likely to look for a job elsewhere. Carter and Lynch (2004) report that repricing of stocks that are "below water" is associated with lower executive turnover. Banker, Lee, Potter, and Srinivasan (2001) provided some results showing that more capable executives are attracted to organizations that offer greater levels of incentive pay. An older study by Gomez-Mejia and Balkin (1987e) based on expatriate managers reports that a match between incentives and personal expectations made a major difference in who completes the foreign assignment, and how long the employee stayed in the company upon return (even though other HRM policies such as selection and training were also important to success as an expatriate). Overall, these results are consistent with the commonsense explanation that executives are attracted to organizations with compensation packages that are more desirable to them.

The Role of the Tax System

There is a whole literature in finance and accounting concerned with the question of whether the compensation package of executives is deliberately designed to improve the alignment of management and shareholder interests or if it simply is reactive to tax legislation. Because of its volume and complexity, only some of this research is highlighted within the scope of this chapter.

Authors such as Lewellen (1968), Smith and Walts (1982), Larcker (1983), Eaton and Rosen (1983), and Murphy (1986b) seem to imply that equity-based managerial compensation schemes, such as stock option plans, are rationally adopted with the ultimate goal of maximizing the incentive effect on managerial behavior. Larcker (1983), for example, argued that "performance plans" are implemented because these promote a long-term orientation in managerial investment decisions. Brickley, Bhagat, and Lease (1985) and Tehranian and Waegelein (1984) report that the market reacts positively to the announcement of such plans.

On the other hand, it has been found that tax implications loom very large in the design of executive pay packages and that accountants, rather than specialists in human behavior and motivation, provide most of the input into those decisions. For example, Hite and Long (1982) and Miller and Scholes (1982) showed that tax advantages explain most adoptions of equity-based executive compensation schemes. Following 100 industrial firms over a 20-year period, Hite and Long (1982) discovered that even minute changes on marginal tax rates would have been sufficient to produce modification in CEO compensation contracts. Posner (1987) found that a surprisingly large number of firms wasted little time in making changes to their executive pay packages after passage of the Tax Reform Act in November 1986. This may be attributed to the fact that capital gains are treated as ordinary income, making equity-based compensation less attractive to executives.

Although mixed, the literature suggests that at least some firms may be adopting executive pay packages purely to offer a tax advantage to the CEO, rather than for incentive reasons. Tosi and Gomez-Mejia (1989) found that tax concerns seem to play a larger role in management-controlled firms, suggesting that opportunistic reasons may be part of this. Heron and Lie (2007) report that backdating of stock options (when some of the awards are timed retroactively to benefit executives) is often done as a response to changes in Securities and Exchange Commission reporting rules. Cho and Hambrick (2006) report that in the airline industry the incentive system shifted executive attention to strategic issues that were most relevant to changes in the regulatory framework. In short, to the extent that an executive pay package dictated by tax considerations may not be the best choice for a given firm, this would represent an agency cost in the terminology of agency theory.

Summary

In conclusion, executive pay is a function of many interrelated factors and cannot be meaningfully understood in a reductionist fashion. Both theoretical and empirical findings suggest that simplistic notions of performance–reward linkages do not seem to fare well when applied to top management. Because of the intrinsically ambiguous and customized criteria used to establish many executive compensation packages, this area is likely to continue as a focus of controversy among academics, practitioners, and the public at large. The next chapter examines the major policy choices that should be considered when designing such packages.

6 POLICY CHOICES, STRATEGIC DESIGN OF EXECUTIVE COMPENSATION PROGRAMS, AND IMPLEMENTATION

This chapter examines the major policy choices and dilemmas confronting the designers of executive pay packages. While the following discussion is based on many of the theoretical principles and empirical findings reviewed in previous chapters of this book, it is primarily concerned with implementation issues.

Dilemmas Confronting Designers of Executive Pay Packages

There are at least ten key policy choices that should be considered when designing compensation programs for top management teams. These choices are:

1. degree of exclusivity
2. opportunity costs
3. level of analysis
4. performance measurement
5. control mechanisms
6. type of governance
7. time horizon
8. degree of risk
9. degree of consistency, and
10. tax rules

Degree of Exclusivity

An egalitarianism versus elitism policy choice mirrors the hierarchical versus egalitarian strategic compensation dimension discussed in Chapter 2. Hierarchy refers to the "legitimacy of an unequal distribution of power, roles and resources," while egalitarianism is "the transcendence of selfish interests in favor of voluntary commitment to promoting the welfare of others" (Smith and Schwartz, 2002, p. 193). The number of management levels to be included in executive compensation programs is an important decision because it affects the firm's decision to develop a hierarchical or more egalitarian culture. The number of levels also affects the extent to which the interests of lower-level managers are aligned with those of top management and how much inducement there is for executives at one level to closely monitor the performance of the lower-level executives reporting to them.

If the CEO pay package is clearly separate from that of the rest of the staff, it can be personalized more easily. However, two separate packages will reinforce a more authoritarian, centralized, elitist type of reward system. This approach would be consonant with the postulates of tournament theory, whereby CEO pay and perquisites are deliberately set at a much higher level than those of subordinates. Presumably, this "prize" will serve to mobilize subordinates to better utilize their potential, perhaps allowing them to win the trophy at some point in their career. Tournament theory may also explain why the gap between lower- and upper-level employees has increased so rapidly in recent years. The restructuring of American business, beginning in the late 1980s, resulted in the downsizing of many levels of middle managers. Tournament theory predicts that reducing the number of levels of potential promotions will lower the incentives that workers have to strive for advancement unless there are offsetting increases in the pay associated with higher-level jobs. Raising CEO pay increases the ultimate prize that a manager can win through promotions, and thus offsets the disincentives of having fewer intermediate advancement steps.

In other words, the extent to which the incentive system covers different management groups, and not just the CEO or those immediately reporting to him or her, sends powerful signals to the rest of the organization as to what is valued and important. It can also promote a more participative, rather than a monarchical, image of the authority structure.

A greater number of firms are now moving incentive pay programs to lower levels of their companies (Carter, Ittner, and Zechman, 2009; Core and Guay 1991; Zattoni and Minichilli, 2009). Indeed, gain-sharing programs that reward employees for group outcomes are a common method of inciting the workforce (see Welbourne and Gomez-Mejia, 1988, for a review on this topic). The rationale provided by most firms is that expanding the coverage base enhances commitment and loyalty to the organization on the part of midlevel managers and junior executives. In an attempt to minimize status differentials, an increasing number of firms have also removed many of the perquisites that were once reserved for top management. For example, executive cafeterias and preferential parking have been eliminated in many companies to engender a spirit of teamwork and equality (Gomez-Mejia and Balkin, 1989). Many firms are realizing substantial benefits in involving more layers of management in strategic formulation, implementation, and decision making, which directly impacts the corporation's future. For this to work, the reward system must also become more egalitarian. Yet, inequality in pay is on the rise (for recent reviews see Devers et al. 2007; Werner and Ward, 2004). In the last decade, the share of total labor costs allocated to the upper echelons increased dramatically, while the opposite has been true at lower organizational levels. According to existing estimations, CEOs are paid between 250 and 500 times that of the average worker, and this differential has continually risen since the early 1970s (e.g., Hall and Murphy, 2003; Hymowitz, 2003; Reingold, 1997). Not surprisingly the CEO of Whole Foods market, John Mackey, received positive press in 2007 for his pay policy, which caps the chief executive's salary and bonus at 14 times the average worker's pay. *The Wall Street Journal,* Slate.com, *Harvard Business Review,* and *BusinessWeek* all mentioned the pay cap in favorable terms.

Moreover, by international standards elitism remains firmly entrenched in the United States. Strong pay gaps exist between American and foreign CEOs: U.S. CEOs made 23 times as much as CEOs in mainland China, ten times as much as CEOs in India, nine times as much as CEOs in Taiwan, five times as much as CEOs in Japan, and two to four times as much as their counterparts in Spain, the United Kingdom, France, Italy, the Netherlands, Germany, and Switzerland (Towers Perrin, 2002). Also the ratio of CEO pay to that of rank-and-file employees is much greater than it is abroad. According to a survey conducted by the consulting firm Towers Perrin, CEOs at 365 of the largest publicly traded U.S. companies earned $13.1 million in 2008 or 531 times what the typical hourly employee took home, while the ratio of CEO pay to the average employee's pay for the same sized British, German, or French companies is less than 5 percent what it is in the United States. Around the rest of the world, Latin America is the leader in pay disparity; but it does not come close to the United States. At the other end of the spectrum, Japan has the smallest gap between CEO and average-worker pay (see Table 6.1).

The causes for these disparities, which have remained fairly stable over time, are unclear. Certainly they cannot be attributed to performance differences. There is also no evidence that the market for executive talent is consistently tighter in the United States vis-à-vis other industrialized countries.

Table 6.1

Gap Between Salaries for CEOs and Rank-and-File Employees

Country	CEO compensation as a multiple of average employee compensation
Brazil	57
Venezuela	54
South Africa	51
Argentina	48
Malaysia	47
Mexico	45
Hong Kong	38
Singapore	37
Britain	25
Thailand	23
Australia	22
Netherlands	22
Canada	21
China	21
Belgium	19
Italy	19
Spain	18
New Zealand	16
France	16
Taiwan	15
Sweden	14
Germany	11
South Korea	11
Switzerland	11
Japan	10

Source: Based on Towers Perrin survey as reported in *Business Week* (April 2001).

The disparities reflect a complex web of economic, historical, cultural, and political factors that are very difficult to untangle, which makes it unlikely for any dramatic changes in the CEO pay structure to occur in the near future (see Haynes, 2008 for a related discussion on this topic).

Opportunity Costs

The policy choice between increasing versus decreasing opportunity costs is a specific case of the performance-versus-seniority strategic compensation dimension discussed in Chapter 2. Because of high attrition in the executive ranks and the difficulty of finding suitable replacements, the incentive system may be designed to penalize the executive for leaving the firm prior to a stipulated period of time. By increasing the opportunity cost of turnover, the firm may prevent the executive from being pirated by other organizations. For example, stock options worth several million dollars may not be exercised until the executive has been with the firm for, let's say, five years. Incentives that reward executive retention are commonly referred to as golden handcuffs.

The extent to which the compensation package deliberately includes a tenure factor in the payout formula should depend on the firm's strategic objectives. The organization may believe that minimizing turnover at the top will provide a climate of stability and promote commitment and loyalty among its employees. Fewer executive transitions may send a signal to all organizational members that long tenure is valued and rewarded.

On the other hand, a firm may feel that a fair amount of attrition at the top allows the company to bring in "fresh blood" and new ideas on a regular basis (see Hambrick and Fukutomi, 1991). The firm may be operating in such a turbulent environment that executives may have to be replaced frequently to tackle changing conditions. In those situations, rewarding for long-term tenure may actually be deleterious. The board of directors may find, for example, that in highly volatile environments, maximum productive tenure might be five years (Gomez-Mejia and Welbourne, 1989), whereas the Standard and Poor (S&P) 500 average CEO tenure is about eight years. The high-technology industry provides a case in point (see Coombs and Rosse, 1992). Short tenure for executives is an accepted norm in technology-intensive firms. Executive attrition is viewed by many as a positive force in this industry because product life cycles are quite short. Therefore, it becomes instrumental to hire new managers who are less committed to existing technology (Balkin and Gomez-Mejia, 1987b). Of course, many other issues related to top executives' tenure, such as age, educational background, and work experience, play a role in innovation-related decisions (Tyler and Steensma, 1998) and ultimately in firm performance (Shen and Canella, 2002).

Rather than being forced to terminate an executive for poor performance or keeping the individual on board past his or her prime, the reward system may encourage incumbents to seek employment elsewhere by minimizing the opportunity costs of moving. Obviously, a thin line exists between dysfunctional attrition (where there is no continuity in the organization, resulting in decreased performance) and positive turnover that allows leadership to be renewed on a periodic basis.

Level of Analysis

An organizational versus individual level of analysis policy choice is a special case of the individual-versus-group performance strategic compensation dimension discussed in Chapter 2. The evaluation criteria used for most top executives are generally based on the entire organization's performance (e.g., earnings per share, return on investment). If the firm does well, the executive's income is supposed to rise accordingly. The rationale for using organization-wide performance indicators is that the executive is ultimately responsible for what happens in the firm. This philosophy is consistent with the traditional "parity of authority and responsibility" principle espoused by early management theorists such as Fayol (1949). Because the "buck stops" at the chief executive's desk, this individual should incur the gains and losses resulting from the ups and downs of the firm's fortunes.

Reliance on organization-wide performance measures is also predicated on the fact that this information is readily accessible and can be objectively quantified (an assumption that is not always valid as suggested later in Chapter 9). Thus, this data may be convincingly defended to outside groups as criteria to allocate executive pay, and it is easier to communicate to multiple audiences (e.g., stockholders, board of directors, employees, media).

Compelling as the reasons may be for the use of these aggregate performance indicators, it may also be important from a strategic perspective to consider behavioral performance measures when dispensing executive pay. First, a substantial amount of research suggests that use of individual performance indicators, when perceived as accurate and reliable, are the best motivators in pay-for-performance systems (Carroll, 1987). Second, ignoring individual contribution measures and exclusively relying on organization-wide criteria may lead to an inordinate amount of attention being paid by the executive to "beat the numbers game." The executive may do everything possible to make aggregate indicators look good, even if this may prove to be detrimental in the long run (e.g., reducing R&D expenditures to improve profitability ratios), even participating in fraudulent accounting practices (O'Connor et al. 2006). Third, the effect of top executives on organizational performance may not be as great as generally assumed, because firm performance depends on many variables beyond the executive's control (see Chapter 5). For example, it may be quite possible for an executive to be doing an outstanding job during bad times, even though financial indicators would make him or her look like a dismal failure. Thus, one way to reward top management for desirable behaviors is through a compensation policy that considers the value of strategic actions, not just financial results. Yet, these assessments are often difficult to justify as they are subjective and depend largely on the "eye of the beholder," that is, the board and their compensation committees (Baysinger and Hoskisson, 1990), which are often scrutinized for their accountability. Moreover, as Wiseman and Gomez-Mejia (1998, p. 145) argue, under subjective monitoring, given the inherent ambiguity of the appraisal criteria used in the evaluation of senior executives: "because of the necessity of reaching consensus over those [subjective] criteria among a diverse and varying set of monitors, the use of judgmental criteria is likely to increase agent risk bearing, resulting in greater preferences for lower risk strategic options."

Performance Measurement

A profitability versus market-based indicators policy choice is generally unique to the compensation of upper echelons. As discussed in Chapter 5 and later in Chapter 9, one of the most controversial issues in executive compensation revolves around how firm performance should be measured. This debate raises a number of important strategic concerns regarding the criteria used to distribute executive pay.

The most commonly used organization-wide performance criteria in the United States consist of accounting measures of performance, such as earnings per share and return on equity. To the extent that certain milestones are met, the executive will receive an agreed-upon sum of money, either in the form of a bonus or stocks (Gomez-Mejia and Welbourne, 1989). However, some would argue that profitability figures are easily manipulated through creative accounting procedures. Obviously, this could have dysfunctional effects on the organization. Research in this regard is limited. A notable exception is the work by O'Connor and colleagues (2006) who show that large CEO stock option grants are associated with greater incidence of fraudulent financial reporting when (1) the CEO also served as the chair of the board of directors and the directors did not hold stock options and (2) the CEO was not the chair of the board but directors had stock options.

The importance that management attaches to showing good profitability figures could lead to a deliberate bypass of excellent investment opportunities or to economically inefficient decisions from the viewpoint of both the company and the economy (Brenner and Schwalbach, 2009). According to Rappaport (1978, p. 82), the use of measures such as earnings per share as a basis for executive pay may create a situation where "what is economically rational from the corporate or social viewpoint may, however, be an irrational course of action for the executives charged with decision making." A great case in point is given by high-tech firms. Based on a study of 184 large multiproduct firms, Hoskisson and colleagues (1990) report that incentives for division managers affect their risk orientation and, thus, their decisions to invest in R&D expenditures. More specifically, "incentives based on division financial performance are negatively related to total firm R&D intensity after controlling for industry R&D intensity, firm diversification, size, and group structure" (Hoskisson et al. 1990, p. 1). As Balkin and colleagues (2000, 1119) note, "emphasis on innovation implies a greater variability of outcomes and a greater probability of failure . . . because the relationship between senior managers' actions and firm performance is very uncertain in high-technology firms, executive compensation packages should be loosely linked to observed performance results." Yet, others suggest (e.g., Milkovich et al. 1991) that due to the complexity surrounding the R&D process, executives often hold information about the firms' technical abilities that is not available to shareholders. This exacerbates principal-agent information asymmetries (therefore R&D–intensive firms should increase the ratios of bonuses to base pay to focus managers' decisions on outcomes). Makri and colleagues (2006) recently attempted to reconcile these two views by suggesting that technology-intensive firms can simultaneously foster incentive alignment and manage risk aversion by rewarding executives using multiple performance criteria, which include both financial results and behavioral indicators.

As an alternative to profitability measures, some strongly believe that stockholders' welfare (measured in the form of stock appreciation, dividends paid, or abnormal rate of return) represent the purest form of performance criteria (Coughlan and Schmidt, 1985; Jensen and Murphy, 1990b; Murphy, 1986a). Unlike profitability indices, market-based performance indicators are more difficult for executives to manipulate. On the other hand, these measures are not trouble-free. Gomez-Mejia and colleagues (1987, p. 60) note that:

> Paying out cash dividends will tend to raise a stock's price. However, raising cash dividends decreases funds available for reinvestment and R&D, which lowers expected growth rate and depresses the price of a stock in the long run—with effects perhaps occurring at a time when another executive will bear the brunt of the problem. Stock prices are also very sensitive to external events that may have little to do with how efficiently a firm is being run and that are totally beyond management's control.

Also, and on philosophical grounds, many firmly believe that executives' pay should not be set on the basis of events that are, for the most part, out of their control—such as up-and-down movements in the stock market—and may lead to windfalls or minimal gains (Bickford, 1981; Ellig, 1984; Rich and Larson, 1984). These individuals recommend accounting measures as proxies for performance or a combination of stock price and profitability data.

More recently, some authors have suggested that broader measures of organizational performance should be used to assess executives' contribu-

POLICY CHOICES, STRATEGIC DESIGN, AND IMPLEMENTATION 193

tions. Coombs and Gilley (2005), for instance, suggest that CEOs ought to be compensated for effective management of both shareholders' and nonshareholders' needs. Using data from the KLD Research and Analytics, Inc. in a longitudinal analysis that covered 406 firms over seven years, the authors found that CEOs who simultaneously maximized social indicators and financial performances were rewarded with greater salaries, whereas CEOs who maximized diversity and financial performances obtained higher bonuses. In a similar vein, Berrone and Gomez-Mejia (2009) found that CEOs in highly polluting industries were rewarded for good environmental performance.

In designing executive compensation programs, it may be wise to base rewards on all measures (profitability, market-based, and social measures). The use of multiple indicators may provide a more accurate and reliable estimate of "true" firm performance, as elusive as that concept may seem (see Chapters 9 and 10). A composite criterion may also be easier to defend. Reaching agreement on the appropriateness of any single measure is difficult, and attempts to do so are likely to arouse suspicion (Weiner and Mahoney, 1981). Also important is relying on contingencies and contextual factors in the successful design of pay schemes (Barkema and Gomez-Mejia, 1998; Berrone et al. 2010; Gomez-Mejia and Wiseman, 1997). In this sense, different dimensions of performance will have different weight and importance based on the context in which the firm operates. For instance, environmental performance may be relevant in highly polluting industries (Berrone and Gomez-Mejia, 2009) and seat occupancy may be relevant in the airline industry (Davila and Venkatachalam, 2004).

Finally, the use of a composite criterion may be justified on methodological grounds because diverse firm performance measures are correlated. Gomez-Mejia and colleagues (1987) found that the most frequently used indicators of firm performance tend to load on a single factor when these are factor-analyzed. This means that they all measure an overall performance construct. Gomez-Mejia and colleagues (1997, pp. 59–60) offer the following explanation for this:

> Changes in levels of sales affect net income, the common denominator of the ROE [return on equity] and EPS [earnings per share] ratios. A firm's ability to pay dividends depends on its earnings. In financial markets, investors and credit analysts use the information contained in annual reports to form expectations about future earnings, thereby affecting stock prices. Changes in stock prices tend to follow the announcement of EPS, ROE, and dividend actions, indicating that the reports have important signaling effects. If the profitability ratios are all good, a stock price will probably be as high as is possible.

Given the importance of performance measures, we include a full chapter in this book to discuss the issue (see Chapter 9).

Control Mechanisms

Reliance on monitoring versus incentive alignment falls under the aegis of the qualitative versus quantitative performance strategic compensation dimension discussed in Chapter 2. The corporate governance literature has long stressed boards of directors as a primary mechanisms for monitoring managerial actions (Fama and Jensen, 1983a,b; Jensen and Meckling, 1976). If board vigilance is weak, managers are given more discretion to potentially pursue self-serving priorities (Daily and Dalton, 1994). Thus, the alternative is to tie the executive's income to that of the firm. In other words, when it is difficult to observe the behavior of the managers or when the manager knows more about the task at hand than the principal, monitoring becomes less relevant, greater emphasis is placed on measuring outcomes, rather than process, and rewards are based on observed results. That is, monitoring and incentive alignment act as substitutes for each other (Zajac and Westphal, 1994).

Outcome measures, such as the financial and accounting indicators reviewed in the previous section, are readily available. Thus, there is a temptation, in the parlance of agency theory, to rely on incentive alignment to control executives' behavior by explicitly linking rewards to measured results. In fact, most executive pay programs use formula-based approaches in lieu of monitoring. Boards find such formulas rather convenient for justifying executive pay packages to external and internal constituents such as unions, stockholders, and the general public. Yet research has not provided definitive evidence that monitoring and incentive alignment are pure substitutes. Tosi and colleagues (1997) created a laboratory design to compare the effectiveness of inventive alignment and monitoring. Results supported the idea that incentive alignment is positively related to economic performance, but authors did not find support for the positive expected relationship between monitoring and performance.

Moreover, from a strategic perspective, these mechanistic approaches should be used very cautiously. As noted earlier, many factors external to the firm such as changes in tax legislation and accounting standards affect financial performance, as well as stock price fluctuations. But the main pitfall here is that such barometers of relative success may not increase shareholder value or improve the long-term performance of the corporation (Verespej, 1987). In fact, the emphasis on quantitative, objective measures of performance has contributed to the problem of maximizing short-term gains (Carroll, 1987; Hambrick and Snow, 1989).

Some authors (e.g., Salter, 1973) recommend that both formula-based approaches and "softer" process-based measures of performance should be used to focus the executive's attention on the strategic goals of the firm. This, however, requires much concerted action as well as political compromises by multiple stakeholders (such as compensation committees, boards of directors, major stockholders, and top executives themselves) who would be required to make difficult judgment calls based on incomplete data and even conflicting sources of information.

Type of Governance

The type of governance chosen is generally applicable to the compensation of top executives who are in a position to use their power base to influence their pay. It concerns the process to be used in designing executive pay packages and the selection of individuals to participate in these decisions. The formality of the pay-setting process for executives increases with firm size. For example, Gomez-Mejia and colleagues (1990) found that venture capitalists often negotiate salary terms of executives in start-up firms while at dinner or having a drink. They negotiate compensation mix and level "by the seat of their pants." Most publicly traded firms in the United States, however, utilize compensation committees to make those decisions. Research in this area has shown that the presence of a compensation committee is an important tool to evaluate CEO performance and design appropriate rewards for top executives (Conyon and Peck, 1998). Baysinger and Hoskisson (1990) made similar arguments with regard to board composition as an important concern when assessing the strategic value of executive decisions.

Indeed, the ultimate responsibility for approving executive pay lies with the board of directors, which will vote on a final recommendation usually submitted by the compensation committee. Members of the committee typically include members of the board, consultants, and high-level officers of the personnel department. In addition to establishing executive pay policies in consultation with the board, this committee's responsibilities include "reviewing officer performance in order to allocate financial rewards, reviewing management succession plans, reviewing business performance and setting long-term strategic goals (such as those required for executive long-term incentive plans), selecting and removing senior officers, and maintaining oversight and control over executive perquisites" (Cook, 1981, 15).

In a sense, this recommendation and approval procedure comes closest to a pure operationalization of the monitoring concept advanced by agency theorists. Ironically, this also happens to be one of the main targets of criticism by those who believe there is minimal independent overseeing of the pay-setting process for top executives. That is, executives themselves "call most of the shots" when it comes right down to it (e.g., Conyon, Peck, and Saddler, 2009; Crystal, 1991; Fahlenbrach, 2009; Fierman, 1990). Even the chairs of the compensation committees at major corporations (outside directors who generally run other companies) report widespread dissatisfaction with the process. A survey by Hay and Associates found that only one-third of chairpeople feel their companies are doing a good job in linking shareholders' interests to executive compensation (see Kay, 1990).

According to skeptics, the reporting structure of those involved in making the pay recommendations ensure that executives do well financially, while at the same time provide a legitimate facade for the process. The senior personnel officer reports to the CEO and has a vested interest in maintaining an ongoing, positive relationship with that individual. The consultant, usually hired by the personnel officer, also wishes to maintain a relationship with the firm that is conducive to future business. For instance, according to fiscal year 2006 proxy filings, the boards of directors at 89.6 percent of Fortune 1000 companies retained the services of at least one compensation consulting firm (Equilar, 2007). The directors who serve on the compensation committee are often CEOs of other firms and have a strong identification with the CEO position and its associated rewards (see O'Reilly et al. 1988).

The CEO is usually an active member of the board of directors and, in some cases, might even be part of the compensation committee. In 1990, Fuchsberg (1990) noted that 214 CEOs of Fortune 1000 companies sit on four or more company boards outside their own. He calls it "the ideal second job," because receiving six figures for a few hours of work per year is not unusual. Across the S&P 1500 index, compensation committees held a median of five meetings in 2006, while the median value of total fees (including retainers and meeting fees) received by compensation committee chairs at S&P 1500 companies increased by 5.8 percent from 2005 to 2006 (Equilar, 2007). Median total board-level compensation for nonexecutive chairs at Fortune 500 companies increased from $258,500 in 2006 to $264,000 in 2007. For lead directors, median total compensation increased from $174,843 to $189,413 over the same period (Equilar, 2008).

Breakdowns in corporate governance structures leading to the problems discussed here were summarized by Williams more than 25 years ago as follows:

In practice, contrary to the basic tenets of the [compensation] model procedure, the chief executive often has his hand in the pay-setting process almost from the first step. He generally approves, or at least knows about, the recommendation of his personnel executive before it goes to the compensation committee, and may take a pregame pass at the consultant's recommendation too. Both [personnel executives and consultants] rely upon the good graces of the chief executive for their livelihood. The consultant in particular—who is typically hired by management—would like to be invited for a return engagement. The board's compensation committee doesn't operate independently of the chief executive either. (1985, pp. 66–67)

To reduce these monitoring problems, it is imperative to develop mechanisms that prevent conflicts of interest from arising. This requires a governance system that is riddled with checks and balances so that executive pay decisions are independently made and beyond reproach. Some suggestions are in order. First, it may be wise to establish multiple committees chartered with different responsibilities in setting executive pay (e.g., information gathering, review of the data, generation of proposals, examination of motivational impacts, and analysis of tax implications). The recommendation made by each committee should be completely confidential. Second, the compensation committee that integrates this information and presents its recommendations to the board should be exclusively composed of outside members, some of whom are not CEOs in other firms (e.g., academics, retired businesspeople). Third, a majority of the board should consist of independent directors. Lastly, the executive must be expressly forbidden from getting involved in any deliberations affecting his or her pay at any stage in the process.

In this regard, the notorious corporate scandals at the beginning of the twenty-first century, such as those at Enron, WorldCom, and Arthur Andersen in the United States and Parmalat, Elf Aquitaine, and ABB in Europe, brought sweeping reforms in corporate governance regulation such as the Sarbanes-Oxley Act. This act covered issues such as auditor independence, board independence, internal control assessment, and enhanced financial disclosure, but executive compensation largely eluded regulatory reform. Perhaps an exception refers to the so-called clawbacks, which are clauses in compensation packages that allow a company to recoup salary and bonuses from executives accused of misconduct or fraudulent accounting. Yet the effectiveness of this legislation remains dubious at best. According to an Equilar report, 64 percent of the 95 largest companies in the United States introduced clawbacks in 2008. However, these are "rarely enforced" (Weiss and Vedran, 2008). To date, research has neglected the role of these clauses.

Several principles of best practice and good corporate governance have been developed during the last decade by international organizations, private sector associations, and notorious consulting firms in the area. These include the 1999 Organization of Economic Cooperation and Development (OECD) Principles of Corporate Governance and the United Nations Guidance on Good Practices in Corporate Governance Disclosure. According to these "good" standards, a well-governed company is one that has mostly outside directors with no management ties who undertake formal evaluation of its directors, keep the CEO and the chairman roles separated, and are responsive to investors' requests for information on governance issues (transparency).

Because management control of firms through boards of directors is too strong in some organizations, the suggestions made above may be more easily said than done. The situation is exacerbated by the generally restrictive nature of corporate rules on terms of office, the nomination of candidates, and voting procedures. These make it difficult for owners of companies with widely distributed equity holdings to exert much influence on boards and managements. Furthermore, legislation on interlocking directorates is still quite lax. Tosi and Gomez-Mejia (1989) argue that since it is difficult for owners, but easy for management, to place members on boards, then it follows that the boards of management-controlled firms will act in ways consistent with the interests of the managers. As noted graphically in Figures 6.1 and 6.2, influence patterns do favor the CEO in management-controlled firms, and the structure of the CEO compensation package reflects this. This suggests that one way to strengthen the board is to weaken the influence of managers over it.

Tosi and Gomez-Mejia (1989) propose a solution that will give the owners more leverage over board selection and reduce managerial control. In this case, boards would be more responsible to owners' interests. These authors disagree with the position taken by some that investors prefer to be passive and spread their risk in such a way that it is not necessary for them to spend a great deal of time to influence the policies and strategies of the firms in which they hold equity. This may be true for some owners, but not for those who wish to exercise ownership rights. At present, such investors have limited choices. If they are unhappy with the management but unable to form a coalition with others, their alternatives are (1) to wait until management improves profitability, (2) to hope for a takeover attempt, or (3) to dispose of their stocks. These may be perfectly acceptable alternatives for some investors, but those who may wish to exercise ownership rights should not be forced into this passive mode because they have been disenfranchised by an entrenched management by virtue of ownership diffusion and corporate by

Figure 6.1   **Influence Patterns in Management- and Owner-Controlled Firms**

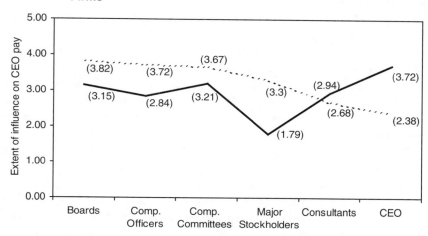

Solid line refers to owner-controlled firms

Broken line refers to management-controlled firms

Source: Based on the research of Tosi and Gomez-Mejia (1989, 1992, 1994).

Figure 6.2   **Characteristics of CEO Long-Term Income (LTI) and Bonus in Management-Controlled and Owner-Controlled Firms**

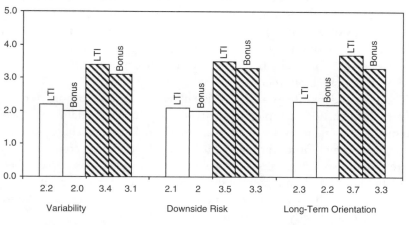

Source: Based on the research of Tosi and Gomez-Mejia (1989, 1992, 1994).

laws. Tosi and Gomez-Mejia (1989) advance a number of potential remedies for this problem.

A starting point for accomplishing this would be to remove management from the process of selecting board members. This could be achieved by the creation of independent offices, free from the hand of management, to manage the election of directors for publicly traded firms. They could make relevant performance information available to equity holders. They could facilitate coalitions of different stockholders and generally enhance owner involvement. Equity-holding managers would have rights similar to other stockholders for advocating candidates and positions.

This would require a federal law mandating that publicly traded firms use independent offices or agents to conduct director elections. These offices could be established outside the firm. They could be, for example, public accounting firms, law firms, or other organizations that may be created for that purpose. The board of directors for each firm could choose an outside agent, subject to the constraint that the agent does not have other business or professional relationships with the subject firm. The independent office would solicit slates for board election from stockholders. To minimize the number of slates but still provide opportunities for choice, the office could require that some minimum percentage of stock, say 1 percent, be held by individuals or coalitions who nominate candidates for the board.

To ensure that the competence and knowledge of the current management is represented in the election, the current board could nominate a single slate of candidates. The management of the firm would be permitted to nominate a slate to the extent that the candidates should meet the same holdings requirements as other equity holders. Information about proposals and programs of each nominated candidate or slate could be distributed in much the same fashion as is done under current practice, perhaps even in a simpler form. The equity holders could then select board members who hold positions similar to their own.

The independent office could also disseminate other information to equity holders through, for example, newsletters. These could contain proposals that might be useful to the larger population of stockholders. These could be a type of informal forum through which equity holders may communicate. There should also be provisions for arbitration or mediation processes when equity holders who do not control the legal minimum for slate nomination have grievances. This would limit the need for expensive legal action as equity holders seek to take advantage of ownership rights.

Tosi and Gomez-Mejia (1989) recognize that the proposal described here represents a departure from the current, general practice of board selection in the United States. Some of the issues that must be addressed in the development of legislation and its implementation include the following:

1. The effects of further intrusion of nonmarket forces into capital markets
2. The specific form of regulation (e.g., Should the requirement for independent election processes be applied to presently regulated firms such as public utilities? What percentage of equity should be required to be eligible to nominate a slate of candidates?)
3. The level of resistance of current management
4. The costs of independent elections and who must pay for them
5. The determination of suitable independent agents
6. How neutrality will be maintained

Finally, an often-neglected issue related to the type of governance is the degree to which companies manage their governance responsibilities, that is, the fiduciary duties of board members. During the financial crisis of 2008–2010, the public outcry about excessive compensation packages for top executives at failing financial institutions such as Lehman Brothers, AIG, Bear Stearns, Countrywide Financial, Wachovia, Washington Mutual, Fannie Mae, and Freddie Mac also extended the responsibility to boards of directors. In a *Wall Street Journal* article, under the subheading "Where were the boards?" (WSJ, 2008b), John Schnatter, the founder and chairman of the board of Papa John's International, Inc., commented:

> Accountability shouldn't end with the CEO . . . Boards of directors set the guidelines and compensation levels, and in the end are ultimately responsible for the performance of their CEOs and companies. They have a clear-cut fiduciary responsibility to provide oversight. We should not ignore their roles in contributing to this financial meltdown. Behind the CEO of every Freddie Mac, Bear Stearns or Lehman Brothers who led their company down a path toward financial ruin, there was a board of directors that sat by silently and let it happen.

But a strong legal precedent was set on August 9, 2005, when the Delaware Court of Chancery ruled in favor of The Walt Disney Company's board of directors in the shareholder derivative action that challenged the controversial hiring in 1995 and subsequent termination in 1996 of Michael Ovitz as Disney's president. Disney's stockholders claimed that the members of Disney's board at the time those decisions were made did not properly evaluate Ovitz's employment contract and the subsequent no-fault termination, which resulted in a severance package to Ovitz valued at approximately $140 million after only 14 months of employment. According to the court conclusions, despite the "spectacular failure" of the union between Disney and Ovitz and the "breathtaking amounts of severance pay," Disney's directors did not breach their fiduciary duties or waste Disney's assets (Kuckreja, 2005). This ruling fuels the ongoing debate regarding the extent to which board members should be held accountable for a firm's failures.

At the time of this writing, passionate debates about how to control and govern excessive executive compensation packages are taking place (e.g., Fong et al. 2010). Emphasis is placed on institutions that succumbed during the financial crisis in the first decade of the twenty-first century and that benefited from the government's bailout plans under both Republican and Democratic administrations. According to Smith and colleagues (2008), since the start of 2002, failing companies including Goldman Sachs Group, Inc., Morgan Stanley, Merrill Lynch & Co., Lehman Brothers Holdings, Inc. and Bear Stearns Companies, Inc. have paid a total of $312 billion in compensation and benefits, leading to public outcry. In Europe, explicit caps were established after the financial collapse. Germany for instance set up a cap of 500,000 euros for executives' salaries within institutions that received financial aid from the government. Others adopted voluntary pay cuts, such as Josef Ackermann, head of Germany's biggest bank Deutsche Bank, who announced he would not accept bonuses, forgoing the potential for millions in personal income to show "solidarity" with staff in a time of financial crisis.

While defendants of free compensation practices argue that pay contracts are freely established between parties and must be to attract talent, it is not clear whether executives at firms that participate in the bailout plan with taxpayers' money should continue receiving outsized compensation packages. Alan Johnson, a New York compensation consultant, noted in a *Wall Street Journal* article: "To the guy in Kansas making 60 grand a year and losing his house, it seems like madness to bail out firms at a favorable interest rate and see them have thousands of people making millions of dollars a year—and it is madness."

Time Horizon

Choosing a time horizon for reward distribution reflects the short- versus long-term strategic compensation dimension discussed in Chapter 2. Perhaps the most persistent criticism one hears about executive pay plans in the United States is that they promote a short-term orientation, often at the expense of long-term performance (see Loomis, 2009a, b; Parloff, 2009; Hyman, 1991).

Despite much lip service paid to the need for long-term thinking, very few firms actually design executive pay plans that are based on a balance of both short- and long-term goals (Stata and Maidique, 1980; Gomez-Mejia and Welbourne, 1989; Makri et al. 2006). Decisions regarding investments in capital equipment and R&D are often made with short-term financial statements in mind but with future and uncertain outcomes. As commented before, Makri and colleagues (2006) set up the basis for a combination of short- and long-term incentives using both behavioral and financial performance measures to overcome such controversies.

Because of the greater uncertainty associated with long-term income plans, executives generally prefer a shorter time frame in their incentive schemes (Tosi and Gomez-Mejia, 1989). Perhaps because executives are more influential in the decision-making process in management-controlled firms, their pay programs are more short-term oriented in those companies (Tosi and Gomez-Mejia, 1989, 1992). Ideally, however, executive pay should be based on a combination of short- and long-term performance. Many companies have changed their executive compensation plans in recent years to move away from a heavy emphasis on short-term results. Many companies incorporate long-term (e.g., five years) performance goals, as well as annual performance objectives, and executive pay is linked to both of these yardsticks. In addition, companies more often introduce qualitative measures in the evaluation and reward system of executives to avoid the pitfalls of formula-based approaches reviewed earlier, or at least so they say (see Chapter 10). For instance, 3M proclaims in its proxy statement: "Executive compensation is linked to company performance compared to specific financial and non-financial objectives. These objectives range from achieving earnings and sales growth targets to upholding the company's statement of corporate values (which include customer satisfaction through superior quality and value, attractive investor return, ethical business conduct, respect for the environment, and employee pride in the Company)." On the other hand, not all changes in an executive pay program have proved to be successful. A case in point was General Motors in the 1980s (Gomez-Mejia and Welbourne, 1989). Stock grants were generously provided to top executives in an effort to encourage a long-term orientation, but the plan allowed a large number of the stocks to become vested after one month—thus diluting the long-term motivational effect of the reward.

Unfortunately, perhaps because of the research problems in the area of executive compensation discussed in previous chapters, evidence regarding the beneficial effect of CEO long-term income plans on firm performance is not very encouraging.

Degree of Risk

Deciding the degree of risk in the CEO pay package design is a specific case of the risk aversion versus risk-taking strategic compensation dimension discussed in Chapter 2. Rappaport (1978, 1981, 1986) argues that executives, acting as agents of shareholders, are more risk averse than firm owners. If the company fails to meet some minimum profit level or if its stock price is depressed over a considerable period of time, the penalty for the executive is termination of employment. An executive's job security and pay are not protected by diversification in the same way as are most stockholders' portfolios. To maintain their standard of living, executives cannot usually absorb the loss of earnings to the extent that stockholders can afford fluctuations in income. Management's only method of spreading their own personal risk is through diversifying various projects or business units within the firm or through acquisition. As a result, executive pay packages should be designed to induce executives to pursue riskier objectives that may prove to be in the firm's best interest.

Common sense dictates that greater probability of failure should be associated with greater potential payoff. If risks and returns are closely coupled, executives may be motivated to make riskier but sensible decisions that are likely to improve their income and that of stockholders. The relative risk to the CEO of the firm's compensation policies can be analyzed in terms of three dimensions (Ellig, 1984; Tosi and Gomez-Mejia, 1989, 1992, 1994).

1. *Variability.* The degree of risk is lower when the executive pay package is designed so that a substantial portion of income is received on a stable, relatively fixed, predictable basis over time with minimum uncertainty.
2. *Downside risk.* The amount of risk is lower when the executive's pay package has a downside hedge against poor firm performance. For example, there may be a minor or no-penalty contingent on lower values of the performance indicators (e.g., Return on Equity). This means that while the executive's pay may go up considerably when performance improves, it is unlikely to go down if performance declines.
3. *Long-term orientation.* The longer the time horizon involved, the greater the amount of uncertainty (and, therefore, risk) in the pay schedule faced by the executive, because the number of unforeseen and uncontrollable events increases accordingly.

These three dimensions, while conceptually different, are highly correlated in practice (Tosi and Gomez-Mejia, 1989).

The relative risk of the executive compensation package should be unique to each type of firm, depending upon such factors as strategic goals, stage in life cycle, and environmental conditions. For example, entrepreneurial firms prefer to hire executives who are willing to sacrifice income in the early stages of the organization when capital is limited in exchange for large potential payoffs if the company succeeds (Balkin and Gomez-Mejia, 1987a). Mature firms, on the other hand, hire executives who are better at "harvesting" the current product and follow existing methods of operation. These firms are less interested in experimenting and risking money and capital with new ventures or projects. As noted in Chapter 5, these mature companies rely more heavily on fixed pay in the executive compensation package. The percent of executive pay at risk in mature firms is often less than half of what is found in entrepreneurial companies. Executives who are good administrators, rather than prospectors, are desired by those firms.

The downside risk for CEOs among mature Fortune 500 firms has tended to be nonexistent (see Jensen and Murphy, 1990a). This is particularly evidenced by the large so-called golden parachute contracts that have been negotiated in many of these companies. A golden parachute is a large sum of money—or a combination of cash, stock options, consulting contracts, and other benefits—that is paid to one or more executives in the event of a takeover or change in ownership of a company. The practice became popular in the 1980s, and now golden parachute arrangements are in place for almost 80 percent of companies in the S&P 500. The original motivation for golden parachutes was to provide managers the incentive to maximize shareholder wealth without the concern of job loss from change of control. But they may also create the incentive to run down a firm and make it an attractive takeover candidate, especially in the case of poorly performing firms that require substantial turnaround effort.

The Corporate Library examined 2001 and 2002 severance packages at S&P 500 companies in a study called "Golden Parachutes and Cushion Landings" and found that chief executives leaving S&P 500 companies pocketed $16.5 million on average. Concerns about golden parachutes were raised by outrageous cases. Take for instance the former CEO of Hewlett-Packard, Carly Fiorina, who received $21 million in severance pay when she was fired as CEO in 2005. She received an additional $21 million when Hewlett-Packard's board bought out her company stock options and pension benefits. Another example is former Gillette CEO James Kilts, who received a $165 million pay package after orchestrating the sale of Gillette to Procter & Gamble in

2005. He was particularly criticized by members of the Boston media, where Gillette was based; critics claimed he benefited financially at the expense of shareholders and the 6,000 jobs that were cut from the combined company. Renewed concern about golden parachutes came after the financial collapse in 2008, when CEOs of failing companies received their golden kiss-off. Some have suggested applying mitigation to severance benefits and shortening employment contracts. But according to figures from Board Analyst, only 2 percent of companies in the S&P 500 would reduce any part of a CEO's severance package if he or she gained alternative employment while still being paid.

Given the importance of risk issues, we have dedicated a full chapter to the discussion on key related elements (see Chapter 7).

Degree of Consistency

The degree of consistency in the CEO pay package reflects some of the basic issues covered under the corporate versus division strategic compensation dimension in Chapter 3. A challenge faced by large, complex firms with diverse business units or divisions is how to compensate executives with any degree of consistency across these units (see Chapters 3 and 4). Should the same formula be used for all executives, or should a separate deal be made with each executive responsible for a business unit or division? Use of the same formula for different parts of the organization can be easier to control administratively. More importantly, it promotes a greater sense of equity across units.

On the other hand, since each unit is generally confronted by its own unique contingency factors and operates autonomously, a custom-made executive pay package on a case-by-case basis makes the most sense. For example, a diversified conglomerate may have a manufacturing unit using traditional, large-batch technology to produce a well-established commodity with a relatively stable market. It may also own a fast-growing, high-technology unit with heavy R&D expenditures. The overall company strategy may involve using some of the profits from the mature subunit to finance the R&D activities and a future expansion of the high-technology subunit. To support this company strategy, each subunit may need to implement its own form of executive compensation package. Based on the findings of Balkin and Gomez-Mejia (1987a), one would argue that a low-risk compensation package (where salary is a high proportion of the total pay mix) makes more sense in the manufacturing unit, while a high-risk pay package (where variable pay such as bonuses and long-term income is a substantial portion of total earnings) would be more appropriate for the high-technology unit. Yet, as argued by Makri and colleagues (2006), these relationships may be more complex than expected.

As a general principle, the more independent and dissimilar the business units, the more appropriate custom-made executive packages would be. As noted earlier, Pitts (1974) found that the criteria used to evaluate executive performance and pay varies according to the autonomy of business units. Executives in semiautonomous business units are evaluated on both division and corporate performance with a combination of objective and subjective criteria. Thus, the design of their pay package and appraisal criteria levels overlap somewhat with those of corporate executives and other semiautonomous executives. The consistency across executives in terms of pay-package designs and payoff criteria is greater for related-product business units because they are interdependent, so it is difficult to isolate the unique performance contribution of each division.

While greater division autonomy and tailor-made CEO pay packages should go hand in hand from a contingency perspective, this also raises an interesting dilemma for evolutionary type corporations. In an attempt to reduce information processing for "naive" corporate executives, evolutionary type corporations may be inclined to displace more subjective strategic controls for tight financial outcome controls as the number of unrelated divisions increases (see Baysinger and Hoskisson, 1989; Bettis and Hall, 1983; Haspeslagh, 1982; Hill and Hoskisson, 1987).

As a final note, the reader is cautioned that executive compensation levels can be dramatically different across divisions, regardless of autonomy status (depending on such factors as number of employees, total budget, etc.). However, the design of the pay package (e.g., bonuses, stock options, degree of risk, etc.) and evaluation criteria (e.g., EPS, ROE) can be more or less uniform across these units as a function of their interdependence. In other words, executive pay level may be orthogonal to pay composition and performance appraisal criteria. For example, an executive in Unit X may receive five times the income of his or her counterpart in Unit Y. However, the relative proportion of salary, bonuses, stock options, and so on in the total pay package and the evaluation criteria may be identical for both. Issues pertaining to pay mix and pay level are covered later in this chapter.

Tax Rules

The consideration of firm-specific strategic factors versus tax and legal concerns plays a large role in executive compensation. Unquestionably, tax rates can make a major difference in an individual's take-home pay, particularly at higher income levels. Thus, tax rates must be taken into account when designing executive pay packages. Tax reduction, however, should not become an overwhelming goal. Tax regulations and accounting standards are constantly changing. Therefore, a corporation that immediately reacts to changes in tax codes might find itself in a quandary when additional changes are enacted shortly thereafter. Unfortunately, most boards rely heavily on consultants and tax accountants, and these individuals are often obsessed with "getting the most for the executive buck" with the Internal Revenue Service. The empirical research by Hite and Long (1982), Posner (1987), Desai and Dharnapala (2006), and others suggests that tax concerns indeed loom large in executive pay decisions. Desai and Dharnapala (2006) investigated whether incentive levels and governance affected tax sheltering. Tax sheltering strategies are generally pro-shareholder; however, the authors demonstrated that stock option grants negatively influenced tax sheltering, except in well-governed firms. They concluded that executives consider both firm and personal risks when making strategic decisions and therefore, unless firms are well governed, stock option pay does not align risk preferences.

Our position is that rather than making radical revisions to the executive compensation plan in reaction to every piece of IRS ruling, the firm's strategic objectives should come first. Tax legislation should be a secondary concern. It is probable that a firm's executive compensation plan will be completely out of line with its strategic business needs if it is too responsive to tax changes. Each executive pay component has strategic implications to the firm, regardless of its tax properties. For example, stock options with holding restrictions may be provided in an effort to make the executive feel as though he or she has a personal vested interest in the organization's long-term success. This same level of commitment may not be elicited by giving the executive a higher salary in lieu of stock options, even if this may be justified given a lowering of marginal tax rates and higher capital gains taxes in the 1986 Tax Reform Act. The limited evidence to date suggests that the composition of executive pay makes a difference in terms of managerial decisions, which gives more weight to these arguments (see review in Chapter 5)

In short, sensitivity to accounting and tax rulings is important, but the motivational effect of changes in pay mix in response to those regulations should weigh heavily when amending the CEO compensation package.

Elements of the Executive Compensation Package and Strategic Implications

A crucial issue raised at several points in this book is the pay mix of the compensation package, or the relative importance of different items in total pay received by the incumbent. In the broadest sense, pay mix can be analyzed in terms of a fixed component (salary and benefits) and a variable dimension (bonuses and long-term income), as discussed under the fixed pay versus incentives strategic compensation dimension in Chapter 2. Each of these will be discussed separately as they apply to top executives.

Base Pay

Base pay for executives is estimated to range between 20 and 80 percent of the total compensation package, although this figure is now a subject of controversy (Crystal, 1990; Kerr and Bettis, 1987; Makri, 2008). According to the data presented in Figure 6.3, base pay plus bonus accounted for more than 50 percent in 1989. But this participation showed a declining importance, reaching less than 25 percent in 2008. *The Wall Street Journal*'s executive career guide estimated that for the highest-paid executives (companies in the S&P 500), the average base pay stood at $1,275,908 in 2006. Salary and compensation surveys are normally used to identify the going market rate in the industry for firms of similar size. These surveys show that salaries vary dramatically by industry. For example, in 2007, the average total compensation for chief executive officers of utility companies was $6,750,000 compared to $11,500,000 for CEOs in the health care sector (Associated Press, 2008). Moreover, at the top executive level the "within industry" range in market rates can be huge. For example, among high-technology firms, a *New York Times* survey (April 5, 2008) showed that Lawrence Ellison, CEO of Oracle Corporation (sales of about $20 billion) earned almost eight times as much as Samuel Palmisano, CEO of giant IBM (sales of $99 billion, almost five times larger than Oracle). Similarly, Ivan G. Seidenberg from Verizon Communications (sales of $16,806 million) earned twice as much as Randall Stephenson, CEO of AT&T even though the former firm obtained lower shareholder return than AT&T. In many cases, these pay disparities cannot be explained by differences in shareholder returns, profitability measures, or even firm size.

In general, base pay remains fairly stable over time, although recently some companies have started to replace base pay for alternative components, showing a decline in short-term pay. Some firms have even induced executives to accept salary reductions in return for restricted stock or stock options (Murphy, 1999). In many firms, options have replaced base pay as a key component of executive compensation. *Forbes* magazine looked at compensation of top executives at the 500 largest companies in America for 2008 and found that 120 of the 500 chief executives had received pay cuts in terms of base pay and bonus. The average reduction in salary plus bonus for

Figure 6.3 **Historic CEO Compensation**

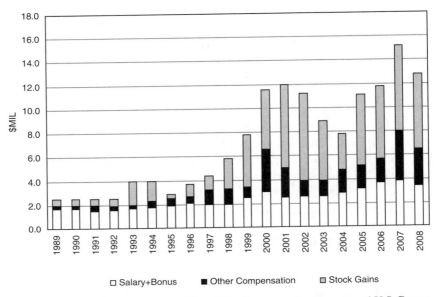

☐ Salary+Bonus   ■ Other Compensation   ☐ Stock Gains

Sources: Based on Forbes Annual Executive Compensation Reports and U.S. Bureau of Labor Statistics (www.bls.gov).

Note: Market value of stock owned and compensation figures are in 2007 dollars. The dates above represent the issue years for the Forbes Executive Compensation reports. For years 1989–99, our universe was the 800 biggest companies in the United States. For years 2000 through the present, the universe was the 500 biggest companies in the United States.

those 120 executives was 29 percent. It is worth noting that some of these executives still managed to deliver handsome returns to shareholders. Take for instance David Weidman, chief executive of Celanese. In fiscal 2007, the value of Weidman's salary plus bonus slipped 11 percent to $2.9 million. Yet Celanese shareholders have enjoyed a 64 percent total return in 2007 and 36 percent over the latest 12 months. During those stretches, the S&P 500 returned 4 percent and a loss of 7 percent, respectively.

A key characteristic of base pay is that it has minimal downside risk to the executive. All things considered, a heavy reliance on base pay in the pay mix may be dysfunctional because it is not easily adaptable to contingencies such as changes in organizational objectives and market conditions. Since salary adjustments are made each year and an annuity is received for all remaining years of employment, executives may be tempted to engage in activities that improve the short-run performance of the firm at the expense of long-term objectives. Furthermore, because base pay is generally taken for granted by the executive, it has less motivational value.

Benefits

In recent years, the amount of dollars spent on benefits and perquisites for executives is staggering for many firms. According to The Associated Press, the median 2006 total perks for the CEOs at 386 of Standard & Poor's 500 companies analyzed was $438,342 (an employee earning the minimum wage would need to work for more than 35 years to earn that amount). These include a variety of items such as membership in health clubs, luncheon and dinner clubs, use of private jets, vacation packages, cell phone expenses, financial planners, entertainment perks, free company goods, deferred compensation paid out when executives end their careers with the firm, and other items. The rationale for these types of rewards is that perks are great motivators that help retain irreplaceable employees. Yet, from a strategic perspective, many of these benefits may be difficult to justify. They are provided to the executive as a condition of employment, but they are seldom contingent on the achievement of strategic objectives. They are also an easy target of criticism by those who feel that executives earn more than they deserve. Critics contend these executives are receiving perks tax-free when they clearly have enough money to pay for their own travel costs and other luxuries. Indeed, it may be quite difficult for a person on the street to understand why almost one-half of larger firms pay for spouse travel when an executive earns more than seven figures a year. Some extreme cases such as a million-dollar birthday party (former Tyco International Ltd. CEO L. Dennis Kozlowski), a private NASA runway (Google), and free airfare for the whole family forever (Continental Airlines) are some of the most recent cases of exorbitant perks (see Table 6.2 for descriptions of the top ten CEOs perks).

In December 2006 the Securities and Exchange Commission (SEC) established new rules that required companies to disclose perks that cost more than $10,000, a much lower threshold than the previous requirement of $50,000, or 10 percent of total annual compensation. This new policy was the result of outraged public concerns about executive pay and perks including that of Jack Welch, General Electric's retired CEO, who was forced to disclose perks as part of a divorce proceeding. Welch's perks included country club fees, use of a Manhattan apartment and private jet, season tickets for Red Sox, Yankees, and Knicks games, as well as courtside seats at Wimbledon and the U.S. Open.

SEC officials believe that this new rule will begin to rein in perk excess.

Table 6.2

CEO Perks, 2006

Position	Executive	Company name	Industry	Perks, Other*	Total Compensation**	Description of Perks
Chairman, CEO	Weldon, William	Johnson & Johnson	Health/Drugs	$2,665,725	$28.56 million	"Other" category includes "CEC" dividends, plus tax reimbursements, contributions to defined benefit plans and perks. Perks comprised personal use of company aircraft ($156,013); car and driver for personal transportation ($35,304); and executive dining-room meals, home-security system monitoring fees, medical exams, and financial-planning services.
CEO, Chairman	Ulrich, Robert	Target	Retail	$2,536,479	$36.43 million	"Other" compensation of $2,536,479 included a big jump in supplemental pension plan values of $1.95 million and perquisites of $161,129, which included, among other things, personal use of company aircraft valued at $67,606, financial management expenses of $40,000, and commuting services of $30,588.
Chairman, President, CEO	Irani, Ray	Occidental Petroleum	Energy	$2,479,243	$55.63 million	"Other" compensation of $2,479,243 included, among other things, $45,306 in tax gross-ups related to the amounts paid by Occidental for spousal travel; and $1,240,865 for personal benefits. The personal benefits included security services valued at $562,589; tax preparation and financial planning services valued at $556,470; administrative assistance, club dues, automobile usage, airplane usage, and excess liability insurance. Nonqualified deferred compensation balance stood at $124,046,355.

CEO and Chairman	McNerney, W. James	Boeing	Aerospace	$2,063,539	$19.4 million	"Other" compensation of $2.06 million included perquisites of $1.6 million. Those perks comprised $63,053 for personal use of company aircraft associated with relocation, $268,396 for other personal use of aircraft—including $9,160 for use for attendance of outside board meetings. Boeing mandates use of company aircraft for security reasons. Perks also included $1,059,706 for relocation expenses. The amount for relocation includes $131,694 for expenses incurred in 2006
CEO	Wexner, Leslie	Limited Brands	Retail	$1,657,366	$9.38 million	"Other" compensation included, among other things, company contributions of $222,710 to retirement accounts, a non-recurring cash payment of $120,900, and $1.3 million paid in security services for Mr. Wexner and his family. The security program requires Mr. Wexner to use corporate-provided aircraft, whether his travel is business or personal.
CEO	Jeffries, Michael	Abercrombie & Fitch	Retailer	$1,593,518	$26.20 million	"Other" compensation included $776,723 for personal use of company aircraft and related tax gross-up of $184,790, among other things.
Chairman, CEO, President	Stevens, Robert	Lockheed Martin	Aerospace	$1,370,553	$18.60 million	"Other" category includes a $1 million company contribution in Mr. Stevens's name to a charitable organization. It also includes: use of company aircraft valued at $27,479; $64,483 for home security; $82,659 for tax gross-ups; $57,160 in matching contributions to a 401(k) plan and unused vacation days valued at $79,668. The filing put the present value of Mr. Stevens's pension benefits at $7.8 million. At the end of the company's last fiscal year his nonqualified deferred compensation stood at $2,933,666.

(continued)

Table 6.2 (continued)

Position	Executive	Company name	Industry	Perks, Other*	Total Compensation**	Description of Perks
Chairman and CEO	Peltz, Nelson	Triarc	Restaurants	$1,313,054	$16.50 million	Other compensation includes, among other things, $214,619 for unreimbursed personal use of corporate aircraft, $675,000 for security measures, $312,474 for dividends (and interest thereon) related to 2005 restricted stock award, and undisclosed amount for automobile and other transportation services, financial advisory services, and personal use of sports tickets.
Chairman and CEO	Bezos, Jeff	Amazon.com	Internet/Retail	$1,200,000	$1.28 million	Pay included salary of $81,840 and all other compensation of $1.2 million, which approximates the incremental cost of security arrangements for Mr. Bezos in addition to security arrangements provided at business facilities and for business travel.
Chairman, CEO	Chenault, Kenneth	American Express	Finance	$1,133,265	$29.14 million	The "other" category includes tax reimbursements, dividends, company contributions to defined benefit plans, executive life insurance, and perks such as $132,019 for personal use of company automobiles and $405,375 for personal use of company aircraft. Other perks: home security system costs worth $60,716; $69,187 for security during personal trips, and $35,000 in "cash flex dollars."

*Perks/Other reflects the category in SEC filings designated as "all other compensation," which typically includes perquisites. Under filing rules, the "total compensation" number comprises salary, bonus, stock awards, option awards, nonequity incentive plan compensation, change in pension value and nonqualified deferred compensation earnings as well as "all other compensation." For companies not required to file under the new rules, the Perks/Other figure reflects the category designated as "other annual compensation."

**Total Compensation is the value given to stock and option awards. This value is their compensation cost to the company, not the value of what the executive actually received.

Sources: Based on SEC filings and Wall Street Journal reporting.

Table 6.3

Ranking of Perks by Industry

Rank	Industry
1	Petroleum refining
2	Communications
3	Oil and gas extraction
4	Transportation equipment
5	Chemicals
6	Food
7	Paper
8	Electronic equipment
9	Instrumentation
10	Business services

Source: Based on Rajan and Wulf (2006) using data on company plane, chauffeured car, and country club membership.

At the time of this writing few companies are moving away from perks, but some are scaling back. Ford Motor Company's Executive Vice President Mark Fields will no longer use company aircraft for his personal trips home on weekends. In its proxy, Ford said that compensation for such trips totaled $517,560 in 2006.

Very little research has explored the benefits and drawbacks of perks in executive compensation. One reason for this is that perks represent only about 2 percent of total compensation in top publicly traded firms. Another reason is that these expenses are not written off as company perks but obtained through misappropriation. A notable exception is the work by Rajan and Wulf (2006) that analyzes confidential information from compensation consultants Hewitt Associates Inc. The data covered 300 large U.S. corporations from 1986 to 1999. According to the authors, those that offer more perks than others don't always fit the classic profile (companies with much free cash flow and few prospects). For example, of the 14 industries ranked by the authors, the second on the list is communications (Table 6.3), a highly competitive sector with ample room to grow. They also found that companies offer perks for reasons other than the private benefit of the recipient. Those include the lift that perks can supply to managerial productivity, which also benefits the company. For example, Rajan and Wulf show that larger outfits offer their CEOs company planes when it can save time. Company jets are less common at corporations headquartered in highly populated areas and close to major airports. Similarly, CEOs located in more densely populated regions with long commute times are the ones most likely to have chauffeur service provided. While researchers argue that if CEOs value their standing in the company then perks can motivate them more cost-effectively than the cash equivalent, the extent to which efficiency and managerial effectiveness are generated through these perks is not yet clear. What it is clear, however, is that extensive benefit discrimination is still practiced by many firms, which can have deleterious motivational effects on lower-rank employees. According to Hewitt Associates, the proportion of employees eligible for executive perks is almost infinitesimal, and only one perk covers more than 5 percent of employees (for instance, physical exams, with 6.5 percent of employees eligible on average).

Bonuses

Bonuses are short-term incentives linked to specific annual goals. At least in theory and since it is variable in nature, the bonus carries more risk to the executive than base pay. The actual degree of risk depends on the criteria that must be met to receive the bonus, and these vary widely. Performance indicators that are often used as a base for bonus payoff include earnings per share, dividends, sales, return on equity, and net profit. In addition, bonuses can be made contingent upon achieving concrete, qualitative goals such as obtaining a large government contract. Yet, Murphy (1999, 2000) finds that most executive bonus plans use a single-criterion performance standard that is based on an accounting earnings measure; net income being the most commonly used performance measure. Further, the target levels that are set for these accounting earnings measures usually are based on either the current year's budget or the previous year's actual performance.

Clearly, executive bonuses are widely used in industry. Equilar (2008) estimated that approximately 96 percent of S&P 500 firms use year-end bonuses to reward executives in 2006. According to this study, CEOs receive an average of 20 percent of base pay in the form of annual bonuses.

While executive bonuses are extremely popular, they should be used with caution. As the bonus component approaches up to two-thirds of a typical executive's annual salary, one can safely assume that it will have a powerful effect on this individual's behavior. Its strategic implications are obvious because executives are likely to maximize whatever criteria are used to trigger the bonuses. To the extent that meeting the set criteria may involve neglect of other crucial performance dimensions (e.g., customer relations, investment in plant and equipment) or focus the executive's attention on short-term results, the firm may be getting negative returns on its bonus dollars. Thirty-plus years ago, Rappaport (1978) blamed the executive annual bonus system, which emphasizes immediate gratification, for many of America's economic ills, so it is interesting to note that its use has continued to increase at an accelerated rate although its relative importance has plunged in favor of stock options and other long-term benefits (Equilar, 2008).

Furthermore, many bonus programs may constitute salary supplements that the CEO expects to receive regardless of firm performance changes. For 2004, a year in which AT&T's revenue dropped almost 12 percent and its net loss more than tripled to $6.1 billion, CEO David Dorman received a nearly $2 million bonus. Dorman's bonus was based half on AT&T's revenue and half on its net income, but the board's compensation committee could also modify the bonus 25 percent in either direction based on "competitive performance." Some recent data from Equilar (2007) suggests that this is not uncommon. Their study on CEO compensation shows that while most CEO bonus plans attempt to connect company performance to compensation, the value and prevalence of "discretionary bonuses" (those not linked to performance) remains high.

Long-Term Incentive Plans

Long-term incentive plans are extremely complex. Companies have developed more than 40 different plans (Ellig, 2006). In the most general sense, long-term incentive plans can be divided into two major groups: those that make the executive part owner in the firm and those that combine cash with equity-based compensation. Table 6.4 outlines the major types of long-term income programs under each of these categories. For additional details on each of those plans, the reader may refer to Ellig (2007) and Tauber and Levy (2002).

Because strategy is innately oriented to the long term rather than focused on tactical short-term considerations, there is perhaps no other compensation program where organizational and pay strategies come closer together than the so-called long-term income plans. No one can blame executives for maximizing personal gains under the plan, but experience shows that well-intentioned formulas often have disastrous long-term effects. A few examples help to illustrate this point.

If growth in market share is used as a criterion for providing stocks to the executive in a performance share plan, then the incumbent may be tempted to pursue an aggressive merger and acquisition program, even if this may not be in the best interests of shareholders. If stock options are granted based on profitability ratios, executives may be tempted to cut back on long-term investments. If no restrictions are imposed on when stock can be exercised, the executive may experience windfall gains by unloading the stock when the

Table 6.4

Most Commonly Used Long-Term Incentive Plans

Stock-Based Programs

- *Stock Options.* These programs allow the executive to acquire a predetermined amount of company stock within a stipulated time period (which may be as long as 10 years) at a favorable set price.
- *Stock Purchase Plans.* These plans provide a very narrow time window (usually a month or two) during which the executive can elect to purchase the stocks. The cost to the executive can be either less than or equal to fair market value. These stock purchase plans are commonly available to all employees within the firm.
- *Restricted Stock.* These plans provide the executive with a stock grant requiring little, if any, personal investment. In return, however, the executive is required to remain with the firm for a minimum length of time (e.g., four years); otherwise any rights to the stock are forfeited.
- *Stock Awards.* These plans provide the executive with "free" company stock, normally with no strings attached. They are often used as a one-time-only "sign on" bonus for recruitment purposes.
- *Formula-Based Stock.* This stock is provided to the executive either as a grant or at a stipulated price. Unlike other stock-based programs, however, the value of the stock to the executive when he or she wishes to redeem it is not its market price, but one calculated on a predetermined formula that normally uses book value (i.e., assets minus liabilities divided by the number of outstanding shares) as a criterion for payment. These plans are used when the board believes that the market price of an organization's stock is affected by many variables outside the control of the top management team.
- *Junior Stock.* The value of junior stock is set at a lower price than common stock, so that the executive is required to spend less cash upfront to acquire it. Unlike common stock, the owners of junior stock have limited voting and dividend rights. However, junior stocks can be converted to common stock upon achievement of specific performance goals.

Combination of Cash Awards and Stocks

- *Stock Appreciation Rights* (SARs). These plans provide the executive with the right to cash or stocks equal to the difference between the value of the share of the stock at the time of the grant and the value of that same stock when it is exercised. The executive is rewarded for the increased value of the stock, although no stock was actually granted by the firm. No investment on the executive's part is required. SARs maybe offered alone or mixed with stock options.
- *Performance Plan Units.* Under this plan, the value of each share is tied to a measure of financial performance such as earnings per share (EPS). For example, for every 5 percent increase in EPS, the firm may provide $1,000 per unit share owned by the executive. Therefore, if EPS increases by 15 percent, the executive will receive $3,000 for each share owned. The payment may be made in the form of cash or common stocks.
- *Performance Share Plans.* These programs offer the executive a number of stocks based on profitability figures using a predetermined formula. The actual compensation per share depends on the market price per share at the end of the performance or award period.

(continued)

Table 6.4 *(continued)*

- *Phantom Stock.* These plans pay executives a bonus proportional to the change in prices of company stocks, rather than changes in profitability measures. A phantom stock is only a bookkeeping entry because the executive does not receive any stock per se. The executive is awarded a number of shares of phantom stock in order to track the cash reward that will be received upon attaining the performance objectives. Award may be equal to the appreciation or the value of the share of phantom stock.

---

general equity market is up. Provision of restricted stock purchases at a significant discount (which has become quite popular lately) may lead to "the nearest thing in the executive suite to union featherbedding" (Crystal, 1990, p. 96).

A number of strategic concerns should be addressed when designing long-term income plans. The key strategic questions that should be asked are summarized in Table 6.5. First, the time frame for payoffs must be carefully thought out and based on the firm's idiosyncratic needs, rather than on trying to "keep up with the Joneses." For instance, in a high-technology, fast-growth firm, three years may be considered long term. In a mature service company, long-term may mean 10 to 15 years. A second important issue is whether executive tenure should be included as criterion for payment. If longer tenure is desired, length of service should be explicitly built in the formulas for dispensing and/or exercising stock options. This may be the case, for example, in a firm that is trying to establish stable leadership after a period of rapid succession in the top management ranks.

A third important policy choice is whether the plan is contributory. For recruitment purposes, outright stock grants make sense as a "sign on" bonus, but sharing the cost of the stock with the firm may be more appropriate for present incumbents. A fourth policy choice is whether benefits under the plan are pegged to profitability measures or are purely a function of market prices. If the company stock is highly volatile and its ups and downs may have little to do with the executive's performance, it may be appropriate to use profitability (which is more under the executive's control) as a partial criterion for payment.

A fifth, important issue in designing long-term income plans is whether mechanisms are established to prevent windfalls. This could be quite relevant, for example, when there is a "bull" stock market, as was the case throughout most of 2008 vis-à-vis the 1970s when stock prices remained very flat. Thus, a firm may wish to place a limitation on when stock options can be redeemed. The company may also develop indices that filter from the executive's earnings general movements in the stock market. Several financial formulas are available to compute "abnormal returns on stocks,"

Table 6.5

Key Strategic Pay Policy Questions in the Design of Executive Long-Term Income Programs

1. How long should the time horizon be for dispensing rewards?
2. Should length of service be considered in determining the amount of the award?
3. Should the executive be asked to share part of the costs and, therefore, increase his/her personal risk?
4. What criteria should be used to trigger the award?
5. Should there be a limit on how much executives can earn or a formula to prevent large unexpected gains?
6. How often should the awards be provided?
7. How easy should it be for the executive to convert the award into actual cash?

which are designed to accomplish precisely that. Sixth, the frequency of awards can vary. Stock purchase plans, for example, allow the executive to acquire stock at any time, but stock awards are normally provided on a lump-sum basis. If continuous reinforcement is desired, the stock purchase plans make more sense. Finally, an important consideration is the extent to which the plan offers the executive high liquidity. The value of common stock is determined by the marketplace, and it can be traded in the open market. In a sense, its value is similar to that of cash in that the executive can negotiate with the stocks outside of the organization. On the other hand, plans such as formula-based stock or phantom stock consist of "paper money" that can only be redeemed within the organization. Items that are more liquid give the executive a greater sense of financial freedom, but stocks whose value is determined within the organization give the firm more leverage in retaining the executive and pegging the award to desired objectives.

Research has called into question the traditional views of compensation design, which tend to hold that stock options promote alignment between the interests of managers and those of shareholders. For instance, Lambert and colleagues (1991) empirically demonstrated that the adoption of stock option plans reduced corporate dividends. Others (Healy, 1985a,b; Holthausen et al. 1995) have observed similar responses to other types of contingent compensation (e.g., annual bonuses). More recently, Larraza-Kintana and colleagues (2007) found that the value of CEO stock options is negatively associated with risk taking. Interestingly, this study suggests that pay devoted to essential expenses (specifically stable forms of pay) play a more important role in determining how much risk an executive should bear than the less stable forms of pay, which are largely allocated to nonessential use. This is exactly the opposite of what most compensation scholars have predicted about the role of compensation design and the bearing of risk (see more on this in Chapter 7). As noted earlier, long-term incentives are extremely complex and their effectiveness remains to be proven.

The pay mix communicates what the organization values, and it signals to the executive the type of performance that is desired and rewarded. From a strategic perspective, it is essential that designers of executive compensation programs ask themselves what type of behavior is most likely to be expected based on the set of rewards being proposed.

Summary

Executive pay is perhaps the most crucial strategic factor at the organization's disposal. It can be used to direct managerial decisions and indirectly channel the behavior of subordinates. Because most organizations follow a pyramidal structure, whatever is rewarded at the top is likely to have a multiplier effect throughout all segments of the business. Also, because of top management's control of organizational resources and their largely unencumbered decision-making power in terms of strategic choices for the firm, mechanisms used to reward executives are likely to have an enormous effect on the company's future.

Unfortunately, there is no simple model for understanding executive pay, and research results can be bewildering even to those who specialize in this area. Practitioners also face a wide menu of choices when designing executive pay packages. What this all comes down to is that many judgment calls must be made, and prescriptive statements are of little value (or perhaps counterproductive) when executive pay is being set. However, decisions made are more likely to produce desired results if they are based on an informed consensus of all the key stakeholders involved in the process, for example, compensation committee, board of directors, or major stockholders. This chapter has fleshed out several of the important issues that should be attended to in such deliberations.

7 RISK AND EXECUTIVE PAY

The concept of risk is perhaps one of the most central constructs in executive compensation research. While risk bearing and risk taking by managers have been increasingly discussed by compensation committees, HR experts, and scholars in the field, uniform metrics of risks and how to apply such metrics in determining executive compensation remains unclear. This is a contentious issue that has become paramount during the recent economic debacle and that has become an integral part of the conversation in the government's attempt to deal with what many people see as widespread "imprudent" or "reckless" risks taking by senior executives (Parloff, 2009; Loomis, 2009a). This chapter deals with major issues regarding the link between different forms of risk and the structure of pay.

The Concepts of Risk

The concepts of risks are crucial elements in compensation design. Defining risk is not an easy task. Unfortunately, definitions of key elements, such as "risk bearing," "risk taking," and "risk preferences" are surprisingly few in the current literature. Take for instance the work by Beatty and Zajac (1994), whose central theme for their study on executive compensation was risk bearing, although no formal definition was provided.

Indeed, the literature lacks explicit definition of risk concepts beyond those related to agency writings. Under this perspective, two roles for risk in compensation can be found. First, agents and principals bear some risk in the agency relationship. On the one hand, principals bear the so-called investment risk (the risk associated with their capital investment and often measured as the variation of economics returns). This investment risk is incurred by principals from the possibility that their investment will be lost or when returns fail to meet performance goals. Principals can reduce this risk by diversifying their portfolio of investments (Sharpe, 1964). This is why under agency theory, principals are assumed to be risk-neutral.

On the other hand, agents also bear risk. This risk may adopt the form of threats to employment status and personal wealth, often referred to as employment and compensation risks. Employment risk represents the possibility that the manager's employment is terminated either due to poor performance or insolvency of the business. Compensation risk refers to the potential variability of future compensation and it is generally measured as the proportion of variable pay or performance-contingent pay within the total compensation scheme (see for example Finkelstein and Boyd, 1998; Sanders and Carpenter, 1998). As explained earlier, an agent's employment and compensation risks are not diversifiable, because all (human) capital is invested in one firm. Unlike principals, agents are generally assumed to be risk-averse in their decisions on behalf of the firm under the basic model of agency theory.

Differences in risk preferences resulting in risk bearing have led to the placement of considerable importance on the sharing of risk between agents and principals. Specifically in question is the amount of risk principals should transfer to agents (through compensation design) in order to influence agent behavior so that they are in line with the risk preferences of the principal. Clearly, the concept of risk is a crucial element in compensation design.

The basic concept of risk can be traced back to Blaise Pascal, who developed the notion of probability to solve problems involving gambles. This was later expanded on by Bernoulli (Bernstein, 1996). Probability theory was the result of this work and contributed to risk knowledge by allowing for ex ante estimates of the degree of reliability in potential outcomes of these gambles. Risk was therefore distinguished from ambiguity, in which probabilities are unknown (Tversky and Fox, 1995). Our modern view of risk is largely rooted in the concept of probability, where we face a knowable but "risky" future vis-à-vis an unknowable ambiguous future.

As seen in Chapter 6, Tosi and Gomez-Mejia (1989) offered some key elements related to risk and compensation as they identified three dimensions of pay risk:

- Variability. The degree of risk is lower when the pay package is designed for a downside so that a substantial portion of income is received on a stable, relatively fixed, predictable basis over time with minimum variance.
- Downside risk. The amount of risk is lower when the pay package has a downside hedge against poor performance. For example there may be a minor or no penalty contingent on lower values of the performance indicators (e.g., return on equity). This means that although an

individual's pay may go up considerably when performance improves, it is unlikely to go down if performance declines.

- Uncertainty. Uncertainty in pay increases (and therefore risk) as the number of unforeseen and uncontrollable events affecting the payoff criteria increase.

A common element among the above dimensions is the role of loss, yet measures traditionally have been concerned with overall uncertainty (i.e., variance). For example, finance scholars (Sharpe, 1964; Lintner, 1965) continue to decompose the total variance in firm returns into two types of risk known as "systematic" (market) and "unsystematic" (business or idiosyncratic) risk, which is perhaps the measure of risk used most often in compensation research. This categorization of risk can be extended to four measures of firm risk: systematic market risk (beta), unsystematic market risk (sigma), systematic income risk, and unsystematic income risk (the latter two risk measures use return on assets [ROA] as the measure of firm income). Both market-based measures of risk (beta and sigma) are usually taken from the Capital Asset Pricing Model (CAPM), which is normally estimated using stock price and treasury bill data. Thus, parameter estimates and error terms in regressions become the measures of systematic and unsystematic income risk. Indeed, scholars have tended to gauge the efficacy of interest alignment by examining the relationships between pay and performance. However, implicit in the interest alignment argument mentioned earlier is the assumption that pay influences risk taking, which in turn affects performance. Thus, much prior compensation research has focused on the direct (but admittedly coarse and distal) pay-to-performance relationship.

Viewing agent risk bearing as the potential for loss of wealth also leads us to argue for a distinction between risk bearing as downside loss and uncertainty regarding future pay (see Miller and Leiblein, 1996). More recently the view of risk has been shifted toward the concept of potential for loss. This has important implications for how compensation plans are conceived and designed. For example, viewing risk as variability in outcomes leads us to measure agent risk bearing through the degree of volatility in the overall compensation design (a common practice in the field). Thus adding variable pay awards with no downside loss potential is assumed to increase agent risk bearing since it increases the variability of compensation over time. Yet it is not clear whether uncertainty in positive payoffs is truly relevant to agent perceptions risk. In the work of Sitkin and Pablo (1992), risk perceptions are a combination of the labeling of risky situations, estimation of probability and controllability of the inherent risks, and confidence in those estimates.

This definition is a synthesis of earlier work and reflects the implied nature of risk bearing found in some compensation models. That is, risk bearing reflects the degree of uncertainty regarding agent wealth.

Another important related concept refers to risk preference. Risk preferences deal with the individual inclination for or against risk. As will be discussed in greater depth in the next section, agency-based compensation research has built on neoclassical assumptions that individuals are inherently risk averse. In contrast, developments in behavioral economics (Asch and Quandt, 1988; Lattimore et al. 1992; Smidts, 1997) have challenged this simplistic view of risk preferences by finding that, in practice, decision makers exhibit a variety of risk preferences. Findings from this line of research suggest that models of compensation that assume agents are universally risk averse may lack descriptive validity and prescriptive power. More important, including variation in risk appetites in the utility function of the agents can significantly alter the conclusions obtained through decades of research (see Wiseman and Gomez-Mejia, 1998).

Theoretical Perspectives of Risk

Traditional Economic Perspective

Economists views on risk indicate that individual choices reflect the shape of their utility function. The shape of this function invokes specific preference labels of "risk averse" (concave), "risk neutral" (linear), and "risk seeking" (convex). The curve itself is measured by means of lotteries that do not refer to the satisfaction associated with the choice (Fishburn, 1989). Thus, changes in risk choices are modeled as changes in the utility function that is hypothesized to underlie the choices.

In this tradition, risk preferences are seen as an attitude toward risk that is both endogenously determined by one's utility function and exogenously influenced by risk consideration. In the context of compensation, these considerations are generally embedded in the principal–agent contract. Indeed, the impetus for the risk concept probably lies in the widely held assumption that the risk attitudes of shareholders and executives inherently diverge. As reviewed in Chapter 4, the principal is assumed to be risk neutral because the principal can diversify its capital (investment) in a bundle of firms, whereas the agent allocates all investment (human capital) in just one firm and, therefore, is assumed to be risk averse. The different appetites for risk between agent (averse) and principal (neutral) bring about the so-called risk-sharing problems (Eisenhardt, 1989). The various strategies suggested to solve these problems have generated two ideological streams within agency research: the positivist and the normative agency-principal (Beatty and Zajac, 1994; Eisenhardt, 1989; Jensen, 1983). The positivist stream is empirically based and has been more concerned with the proper mechanisms to solve the agency problems. In particular, this stream of research has highlighted the value of imposing a greater amount of executive compensation and wealth by coupling it with firm performance (Beatty and Zajac, 1994; Eisenhardt, 1989). This arrangement, designed to create a common fate between executives and shareholders through risk sharing, is formally referred to as *incentive alignment* in agency theory.

On the other hand, the normative agency literature is more mathematically based and therefore more abstract. It involves carefully specified assumptions, logical deductions, and mathematical proofs. The normative approach is concerned with the determination of the optimal contract under varying levels of outcome uncertainty, information asymmetries, and risk aversion (Eisenhardt, 1989). Eisenhardt (1989) noted the organizational research has tended to draw more from the positive rather than the normative agency arguments (for more on these two positions, see Beatty and Zajac, 1994; Eisenhardt, 1989; and Jensen, 1983). From an agency perspective, the challenge is how to align the agent's acts with the principal's goal of maximizing the performance of the firm (Bloom and Milkovich, 1998; Eisenhardt, 1989) (see Chapter 4).

The paradox here (and the one that has spawned contradictory predictions on agency theory) is that the principal cannot transfer too much risk to the agent (who is assumed to be risk averse). If they do so, the agent would then make excessively conservative decisions that might hurt the principal. That is, given that the use of incentive pay penalizes or rewards agents for outcomes partially outside their control, it may become dysfunctional as executives may be overly cautious when making decisions that affect the principal's interests (Bloom and Milkovich, 1998; Gray and Cannella, 1997; Miller et al. 2002). Of course, for this to happen, another important assumption is often made: large returns accrue large risks (Sharpe, 1964).

Behavioral Perspective

Challenging the inflexible assumption from agency theory that decision makers hold consistent risk preferences, Wiseman and Gomez-Mejia (1998) developed the behavioral agency model (BAM), which is based on a long stream of research that has flowed from Kahneman and Tversky's (1979) prospect theory (Bowman 1982, 1984; Fiegenbaum and Thomas 1986, 1988) and Cyert and March's (1963) behavioral theory of the firm (e.g., Bromiley, 1991; Singh, 1986; Miller and Chen, 2004). The theoretical approach proposes that decision makers utilize a contingency-based view to allow for the possibility of varied risk preferences depending on the context being faced. Indeed, the importance of this model of risk preference can be seen when there is uncertainty about modeling choice behavior. Specifically, several studies have found that decision makers appear to accept greater uncertainty in order to avoid loss, which contradicts traditional assumptions of risk aversion whereby decision makers are assumed to accept lower returns in order to avoid uncertainty (Highhouse and Paese, 1996; Kahneman and Tversky, 1979; Mowen and Mowen, 1986).

According to BAM (for more on this see Chapter 4), a decision maker's risk preferences, and in turn risk-seeking behaviors, change with the framing of problems. Problems are framed as either positive or negative using a reference point to compare anticipated outcomes from available options. BAM predicts that decision makers exhibit risk-averse preferences when selecting among positively framed prospects and exhibit risk-seeking preferences when selecting among negatively framed prospects. Underlying this shift in risk preferences between positively (gain) and negatively (loss) framed problems is the concept of loss aversion. Loss aversion concerns the avoidance of loss even if this means accepting a higher risk. Hence, "loss aversion explains a preference of riskier actions to avoid an anticipated loss altogether . . . risk preferences of loss-averse decision makers will vary with the framing of problems in order to prevent losses to accumulated endowment" (Wiseman and Gomez-Mejia, 1998, p. 135). From this vantage point, risk bearing is subjective in representing perceived threats to a decision maker's endowment (what the person believes is important to his or her welfare that is already accrued and can be counted on).

The BAM model extends reference-dependent framing to compensation and results in several predictions about the effects of stock options on executive behavior that challenge current beliefs about the nature and role of this form of compensation. The key argument is that executives count relatively certain forms of future income, such as base pay, in their calculations of personal wealth. Thus base pay may be analogous to an annuity that pays a fixed amount (which may grow with inflation) into retirement. Anything that threatens this future income stream is considered a threat of loss. By contrast, forms of future income that are highly uncertain, such as stock options, and highly variable, such as cash bonuses, are probably not counted. Therefore, actions that result in receiving this type of compensation are not viewed as "risky."

Interestingly, this approach allows for a negative relationship between risk bearing and an individual's willingness to accept additional risk (Bromiley, 1991; Miller and Leiblein, 1996; Palmer and Wiseman, 1999; Villena, Gomez-Mejia, and Revilla, in press; Wiseman, Gomez-Mejia, and Fugate, 2000), that is, a distinction between risk bearing and subsequent risk taking. Yet, the question of whether the increase in risk taking corresponds to improved performance, as assumed by some scholars, or results in deteriorating performance as suggested by Wiseman and Bromiley (1996) is still unanswered. This is so partly because of the poor definition of the risk concepts and their coarse operationalization, which are reviewed in the next section.

Of course, the perspective proposed by the BAM has important consequences for compensation research as a field. If the concept of compensation is to motivate executives to risk on behalf of shareholders, the payoffs from successful investments must compensate the risk perceived to the executive's personal wealth. That is, payoffs must be large enough to induce an executive to risk losing all future income that the executive has already counted as a personal wealth. An interesting element of this view concerns the effect of annual stock option awards. Executives probably count the current value if stock options are held as a part of wealth. Actions that threaten this value by lowering stock prices in the future when the executive wishes to exercise those options will be avoided in order to protect this portion of perceived wealth. Thus, it is likely that as the current value of held stock options rises, executives will increasingly prefer strategies that minimize stock price fluctuations over strategies that may promise higher stock prices but also increase stock price volatility.

Other Perspectives

Although it has received less attention than the two previous perspectives, equity theory also considers risk, more specifically on the subjective assessment of risk (i.e., risk perception). Broadly speaking, risk perception concerns subjective assessments of the riskiness of an alternative. Under equity theory, equity and expectancy models regard subjectivity as a critical factor in determining how employee behaviors such as effort and turnover depend on the perceived fairness of the pay system. Holtgrave and Weber (1993), in particular, postulate a model of perceived risk that is a linear function of five dimensions: probability of loss, probability of gain or benefit, probability of status quo, expected value of loss, and expected value of gain or benefit. Although some evidence supports his model (Keller, Sarin, and Weber, 1986; Yates and Stone, 1992), other evidence finds that two dimensions, probability and magnitude of loss, explain most of the variance in estimates of risk

(Slovic, Fischhoff, and Lichtenstein, 1985, 1986). Yet perceptions of pay risk are largely ignored in both the conceptual and empirical compensation literature, leaving this topic as an interesting avenue for future research.

Compensation and Risk Research

Risk-return research demonstrates that organizational decisions, risk, and performance are strongly related. This stream of research suggests that CEO pay design varies according to the degree of risk facing a firm and that this association between firm risk and CEO pay is stronger for firm-specific (unsystematic) risk than for market-driven (systematic) risk. It also supports the view that the appropriateness of CEO pay strategies depends on their fit with the unique conditions facing each firm (Gray and Cannella, 1997).

Extending this line of research, Miller and colleagues (2002) compare the effects of firm risk on pay design across different levels and types of risk. In particular, through the use of agency logic it is argued that reliance on performance-contingent pay at both high and low levels of firm risk engenders agency costs for shareholders. Thus, at moderate levels of firm risk, linking pay to performance is most likely to be advantageous to share-holders. In addition, as opposed to Gray and Cannella's findings (1997), they predict that total pay will be greatest when firm risk is moderate, and show that a nonmonotonic (concave association) relation between firm risk and compensation risk sharing is more likely to occur for firm-specific performance risk than for market-driven risk. This work suggests that at low levels of firm risk it may be less meaningful to provide increased incentives, since CEO efforts to influence firm outcomes may be inefficient, which is consistent with Eisenhardt (1989) and Miller and Leiblein (1996). In addition, the stronger findings associated with unsystematic risk (vis-à-vis systematic risk) further support the notion that risk sharing is less desirable when performance outcomes are driven by exogenous noncontrollable factors, such as business cycle effects.

The general conclusion drawn from this stream of research is that organizations transfer pay risk to their CEOs whenever this transfer appears to have the potential to improve performance outcomes—that is, when there is moderate, unsystematic firm risk. When outcomes are largely beyond the control of the CEOs (when unsystematic firm risk is high or low or when exogenous market forces prevail), risk sharing is likely to be dysfunctional, as the observed performance results cannot be unambiguously attributed to CEO decisions. A common result stresses that idiosyncratic firm risk appears to have a stronger influence than exogenous market risk on compensation design (e.g., Bloom and Milkovich, 1998; Gray and Cannella, 1997), although Miller and colleagues (2002) also found that the unsystematic risk effect on performance-contingent pay is concave rather than linear. This observation raises questions about how executives and principals view different forms of risk when negotiating the design of executive compensation.

As commented earlier, challenging the risk-as-variance view, scholars in management and psychology noted that decision makers are in general more sensitive to potential loss than to uncertainty when considering the riskiness of a decision (Duncan, 1972; Slovic et al. 1980, 1985, 1986). That is, decision makers are more concerned with the probability of loss than they are with the entire dispersion of losses and gains. Defining agent risk bearing as perceived loss of wealth provides an alternative view about what is meant by wealth in the context of compensation design to the traditional approach that suggests all income as fungible.

Some scholars criticize the variance measure on conceptual grounds for including positive payoffs (gains), which may not represent the decision maker's concerns about risk. For instance, Yates and Stone (1992) argue that operationalizing risk as total variance leads to a positive bias in the actual representation of risk. This bias occurs because only alternatives that are expected to yield positive outcomes and actually do so are included in the measure. At the extreme, this would mean that managers would have only positive scenarios to choose from. In such cases, the potential for net loss is neither expected nor realized, regardless of the choice made. If there is only a potential for gains but no pay penalty contingent on lower values of the performance indicator, pay may not be seen as risky by decision makers.

This line of research suggests that compensation risk measures and risk bearing should focus on the potential losses of wealth rather than on compensation variability. While measures such as variable pay over total compensation (pay mix) are largely used, they may be capturing a form of uncertainty that is of less concern to executives than measures focusing on potential of wealth, which may be of greater relevance for managers. If traditional measures of compensation risk and risk bearing are faulted, an in-depth revision of conclusions and implications of prior research is urgently needed.

In this setting, there is no single dimension (such as R&D investment) that can adequately capture overall risk propensity since CEOs have a variety of alternatives from which to choose (e.g., acquiring other firms, entering new markets, developing new products). Furthermore, their choice of a strategic option may not be independent of other choices. This is because increased use of one strategic risk may be offset by reductions in other strategic risks (Wiseman and Catanach, 1997). Alternatively, this stream supports the idea that avoiding a risky strategic alternative may not be due to risk aversion, but to limits in managerial discretion regarding that alternative (e.g., Hambrick and Finkelstein, 1987; Larraza-Kintana et al. 2007). In other words, using a specific strategic alternative ignores differences in market power or industry conditions that could influence actual (and thus perceived) risk to the firm from any given strategic action. That is to say, risk is likely to be idiosyncratic for each firm, making universally applied indicators of strategic risk misleading.

Broad firm-level measures of risk (such as variance in returns or in stock analysts' forecasts) are also problematic since these measures not only capture the effects of strategic adjustments but also the effects of exogenous industry factors (Palmer and Wiseman, 1999). Thus, firm-level measures of income uncertainty provide weak proxies of strategic choices involving risk. To avoid these problems Larraza-Kintana and colleagues (2007) developed and validated a measure of strategic risk that extends a measure developed by Khandwalla (1977), which was later used by Singh (1986). Thus, their approach tries to avoid limiting the choice of strategic actions to one or two options, which may not be appropriate for all respondents, focusing on the use of specific strategic alternatives rather than on distal outcomes of these actions such as income uncertainty, and, unlike Khandwalla or Singh, allows respondents to determine the riskiness of each strategic action to their business (rather than imposing a universal standard of risk). This latter point is critical in the model setting in order to capture preferences for risk. The only way to correctly interpret whether an action is risk seeking or risk avoiding is to determine whether the actor perceived the action as risk increasing or risk decreasing.

Regarding different measures of downside risk of pay, no single dimension provides a good proxy for capturing the firm's strategic risk profile. For instance, Tosi and Gomez-Mejia (1989); Hall and Liebman (1998); Perry and Zenner (2000, 2001); and Coles, Suay, and Woodbury (2000) have assessed the degree to which different forms of compensation are at risk of loss: annual base pay; raises and adjustments to base pay; annual cash bonuses; long-term cash compensation (cash awards based on long-term performance—more than one year); and long-term noncash compensation (stock-based awards based on long-term performance—more than one year). Larraza-Kintana and colleagues (2007) measured perceived employment risk by asking CEOs the extent to which each type of pay has faced a change of loss since the introduction of a specific strategic decision.

Similarly, some other scholars have tried to operationalize strategic actions in order to construct composite indexes for each firm to represent CEO risk taking: R&D; entry into a new product market; manufacturing or process innovation; product innovation of an existing product; capital investment in property, plant, or equipment; downsizing through layoffs; increasing long-term debt; acquisition of a business in an unrelated industry; and increasing promotion and advertising.

Some studies have also challenged the alleged risk properties of governance mechanisms. For instance, Sanders (2001) argued that stock ownership differs in risk from stock options. Specifically, when stock price varies, managers who own stock experience wealth changes in direct proportion, both positively and negatively. However, executives with stock options benefit when the stock price rises but experience no reduction in real wealth if the stock price declines. Managers may respond to these asymmetric risks in diametrically opposite ways. Drawing on behavior decision theory, Sanders showed that stock ownership leads to conservative decisions, while stock option pay promotes risk seeking.

In a subsequent analysis, Sanders and Hambrick (2007) tried to unpack the concept of managerial risk taking among three elements: the size of the outlay or bet involved in taking a particular risk, the variance of the potential outcomes, and the likelihood of extreme loss. As opposed to prior research, which has tended either to equate one of these elements with overall risk taking or to speak broadly about risk taking, this new framework is employed in analyzing the effects of CEO stock options on strategic behavior and company performance. In particular, CEO stock options engender high levels of investment outlays and bring about extreme corporate performance (big gains and big losses), suggesting that stock options prompt CEOs to make high-variance bets, not simply larger bets.

In the context of firms undertaking initial public offerings (IPOs), Certo and colleagues (2003) attempt to extend behavioral decision theory by suggesting that different forms of CEO compensation may interact to influence CEO risk taking. In particular, they suggest that although investors view CEO stock options positively, investors view CEO stock options *more* positively when CEOs own more equity. In other words, they suggest that the risk-taking incentives provided by CEO stock options will be more valuable to IPO investors when CEO risk taking is encumbered by high-equity holdings.

In a different setting, Larraza-Kintana and colleagues (2007) stress the idea that capturing the decision maker's assessment of risk is critical to distinguishing between intentional and unintentional risk taking, and distinguishes this measure from proxies that focus on a single action that may or may not be perceived as risky. Thus, employment risk and variability in compensation each correspond to greater risk taking, while downside risk and the intrinsic value of stock options correspond to less risk taking. Likewise, these results have implications on the importance CEOs attach to relatively stable forms of pay, and on the distinction between the potential for loss of pay and uncertainty about the amount of future pay.

Finally, in a context of high-technology firms, Makri and colleagues (2006) propose that firms can simultaneously foster incentive alignment and manage risk aversion by rewarding executives using multiple performance criteria, which include both financial results and behavioral indicators of the quality of innovation efforts. Specifically, they find strong support for the hypothesis that the greater the technological intensity of a firm, the more CEO bonuses are tied to financial results, and the more CEO total incentives are linked to evidence of influential innovations as well as the firm's ability to use scientific knowledge effectively. They report empirical evidence showing that high-technology firms that use more holistic outcome-based and behavior-based performance criteria to reward executives exhibit better market performance than those who do not.

Other Applications of BAM: The Case of Family Business

While not directly addressing compensation issues, the work by Gomez-Mejia and colleagues (2007) is a relevant application of the BAM model in a specific context. Authors hypothesized that for family firms the primary reference point is the loss of socio-emotional wealth (SEW), which they defined as the stock of affect-related value a family derives from its ownership position in a particular firm. According to these authors, SEW is a broad construct encompassing a variety of nonfinancial aspects of the business that meet the family's emotional needs. This SEW endowment includes the unrestricted exercise of personal authority vested in family members (Schulze, Lubatkin, and Dino, 2003a,b); fulfillment of psychological needs for belonging; identification and intimacy (Kepner, 1983; Westhead, Cowling, and Howorth, 2001); the perpetuation of family emblems and values (Handler, 1990); maintaining the legacy of the founder and preservation of family dynasty (Casson, 1999); utility derived from placing trusted relatives in key positions (Athanassiou et al. 2002); enhancing the family's social capital (Arregle et al. 2007); being part of a tight social group or clan (Littunen, 2003); and the opportunity to be altruistic to family members (Schulze et al. 2003b), among others.

Applying BAM's logic, Gomez-Mejia and colleagues (2007) propose that family firms are likely to frame relinquishing SEW as a crucial loss. In their words " . . . preserving the family's SEW, which is inextricably tied to the organization, represents a key goal in and of itself. In turn, achieving this goal requires continued family control of the firm. Hence, independent of financial considerations, family-owned firms are more likely to perpetuate owners' direct control over the firm's affairs" (p.110). Thus, they are more likely to accept threats to the firm's financial well-being (i.e., more concentrated business risk) in order to prevent that loss. That is, when faced with a context that shows loss of SEW, family firms may be willing to become vulnerable to the possibility of financial losses. Thus, contrary to the conventional agency-based view, Gomez-Mejia and colleagues (2007) suggest that family firms are loss averse with respect to SEW and hence are willing to incur significant business risk if necessary in order to preserve that wealth. This creates an apparent paradox, in that organizational failure implies the loss of all SEW, yet this is a gamble that these family firms are often willing to take. Additional supporting evidence on this paradox may be found in Gomez-Mejia et al. (2010).

The possibility that family firms could be both risk willing and risk averse hinges on distinguishing between two types or risk: performance hazard risk and venturing risk. The first type of risk, performance hazard, concerns the potential for negative consequences associated with a decision choice (March and Shapira, 1987; Hoskisson et al. 1990; Shapira, 1995), which can be manifested in two ways. One is the probability of organizational failure or threats to survival. The second is the possibility of below-target performance, where the target for comparison may be the firm's past performance or the performance of other firms in the industry (Cyert and March, 1963). According to the authors, family firms may be willing to incur a greater performance hazard, as evidenced by a greater probability of failure and below-target performance, if this is what it takes to protect their socioemotional wealth.

This second type of risk, venturing, involves the search for alternative routines and opportunities when the firm is unhappy with the status quo, namely, when its performance falls below target (Bromiley, 1991). The search for new approaches, including new products or technologies, may raise organizational performance, but it also increases the chance of unexpected outcomes, causing variance in performance (Wiseman and Bromiley, 1996). According to the authors, family firms may be less likely to make business decisions that increase performance variability even when they face disappointing (below-target) performance. Because their probability of failure is higher, they should be less willing to take on projects with high outcome variance that might further increase the firm's probability of failure. While family firms may avoid venturing risks, they may be willing to incur the risk of greater performance hazard in order to preserve their socioemotional wealth.

Gomez-Mejia and colleagues (2007) found support for their BAM-based predictions after examining the decisions of 1,237 family-owned olive oil mills in southern Spain during a 54-year time span. They showed that family mills were less likely to join co-ops (which greatly reduces financial risks and increases the possibility of long-term survival) because doing so resulted in a loss of SEW. While this and a follow-up study by Gomez-Mejia and colleagues (2010) were not conceptually or empirically concerned with incentive system issues, their logic would apply in that the incentive system in family-owned firms would discourage executives from pursuing diversification strategies that might result in the loss of SEW.

Summary

Risk is perhaps one of the most important elements of compensation research. Despite this, we still know very little about the main impact of different forms of pay on agent's risk bearing and taking. Therefore, there are many lines for future research in the area of risk and compensation. One such approach relates to the distinction between subjective and objective risk assessment. For instance, it is not at all clear that simply because more variable pay is added to a compensation design, agents perceive greater risk to their future wealth. While there is some research that suggests that important differences between subjective and objective measures may arise from a variety of judgmental biases (such as overconfidence, framing effects, and escalation of commitment), very little research has investigated how these differences impact the treatment and perception of compensation.

Also, further understanding of the distinction between the roles that variable pay may play for executives is needed, particularly in the context of the current global financial crisis. In most (if not all) of failed companies in the 2008–2010 financial crisis, the majority of executive compensation packages were provided in the form of a variable, performance-based annual incentive that is delivered in both cash and equity awards. According to the last proxy statement presented by Lehman Brothers, its CEO received more than $34 million as his annual compensation and 85 percent of it was in the form of stock options (yet by that time the average shareholder had lost almost all shareholder value).[1] This is customary in the banking industry. Large financial services firms such as Bank of America, The Bear Stearns Companies, Citigroup, The Goldman Sachs Group, JPMorgan Chase and Co., Merrill Lynch and Co., Morgan Stanley, Wachovia, and Wells Fargo and Co. among other firms in the investment banking sector adopt similar compensation practices. In many cases, this is not only with the argument that it will reduce information asymmetry problems but out of a desire to be on the forefront of or to join other firms that practice clearer corporate disclosure (Westphal and Zajac, 2001).

As commented in this chapter, one potential problem of stock options and similar instruments is that executives rewarded with stock options benefit when the stock price rises, but experience no reduction in real wealth if the stock price declines. Managers may respond to these instruments with excessive risk-taking actions since they would not see their wealth damaged if stock prices drop. That is, managers could have potentially high though highly uncertain earnings, with no downside risk on their wealth. Moreover, executives need only short time improvements in share value to exercise their options. In fact, executives are not required to hold the stocks for more than one day (Pfeffer, 2007). Raising a company's stock price for a single day clearly is not a real advance for the business. Rather, this stimulates balance sheet misrepresentation, tax evasion, and other corporate malfeasances (see Chapter 8 for social issues in compensation research).

Another opportunity for research is to increase understanding of the combined effect that different compensation practices can have on risk. Take for instance the extended practice of exit packages often called golden parachutes. A golden parachute is a clause in an executive's employment contract specifying that he or she will receive certain benefits (usually money and/or stocks) in the event that the employment relationship is terminated (due to acquisition, bankruptcy, or simply termination of the contract). The argument compensation experts normally use to justify golden parachutes is that they protect managers from risks out of their control. But these exit packages may reach exorbitant amounts of money. Take for instance the former CEO of Hewlett-Packard, Carly Fiorina, who received $21 million in severance pay when she was fired as CEO in 2005. She received an additional $21 million when Hewlett-Packard's board bought out her company stock options and pension benefits. During October 2009, another case provoked public criticism, this time in Europe. The board of directors of the Spain's second-biggest bank, BBVA, decided to grant a 52-million-euro pension paid out to the outgoing CEO Jose Ignacio Goirigolzarri. Having such excessive exit packages in place may have an undesired effect because, simply put, they reward failure (for a review of other similar cases see Bebchuk and Fried, 2006). What incentive does a manager have to perform well in the company if he or she gets compensated in the case of failure? Does this provide an incentive to managers to lead the company to the extreme if the future doesn't look rosy? On a related matter, these practices certainly spark frustration in other employees, damage morale and teamwork, and increase the sense of unfairness as they are unlikely to have a golden parachute to fall back on. That is why the recent approved bailout plan states that "institutions that sell assets to Treasury . . . must meet executive compensation standards that will prohibit golden parachute payments . . . Golden parachutes will be completely prohibited for covered executives in the case." Despite the wealth of research and studies in executive pay, both incentives and golden parachutes have been mostly analyzed in isolation and we know very little about the combined effect of different incentive practices. They may be pushing in opposite directions and golden parachutes seem to be winning the fight. Indeed, current practices may be encouraging irresponsible behavior with lethal effect, not only for these companies and employees but for society in general. Just consider that, according to the top budget analyst in the U.S. Congress, Americans' retirement plans lost as much as $2 trillion from June 2007 to September 2008.

Other international institutions have also offered new initiatives in response to the financial crisis. For instance, the European Commission has adopted a recommendation on remuneration in the financial services sector, suggesting that member states should ensure that financial institutions have remuneration policies for risk-taking staff that are consistent with and promote sound and effective risk management. Also, the Group of Twenty Finance Ministers and Central Bank Governors—known as the G-20—agreed to adopt compensation guidelines for banks and other financial companies that are designed to rein in risks These guidelines are intended to discourage bonus guarantees extending more than one year, encourage companies to defer bonuses for senior executives and other key employees, and permit pay to be clawed back if losses occur later. Yet, recommendations are not always precise, opting instead for more general (and sometimes abstract) guidelines.

As noted by Washburn et al. (2010), "all risks are not born equal." Excessive risks can be even more dangerous than avoiding risk. While there is general agreement that in business one has to take risk to get returns, the nature of risks may not lead to a straightforward conclusion. Thus, setting pay strategies that encourage managers to simply take risks without any further consideration may be lethal for the long-term survival of companies. Moreover, current risk management tools do not fully capture the intrinsic traits of risk and uncertainty. They have been proven to be inadequate and need to be revised—or even eliminated—in order to avoid subsequent chaos, particularly considering the interlocking nature of modern finance.

Many compensation designs look "unbeatable" on paper but have unintended—sometimes deleterious—consequences in practice. Compensation design is not an exact science and there is a lot of trial and error in this discipline. Unfortunately, the dominant theory has fallen short in providing satisfactory answers on how to align interests between shareholders, managers, and society as a whole. Thus, both practitioners and academics must join forces and rethink current compensation practices.

Note

1. When Richard Fuld, chief executive of Lehman Brothers, recently testified in Congress, the chairman of the committee held up a chart suggesting that Fuld's personal remuneration totaled $480 million over eight years—including payouts of $91 million in 2001 and $89 million in 2005.

8 CORPORATE SOCIAL PERFORMANCE

An Alternative Criteria for the Design of Executive Compensation Programs

As noted in prior chapters, CEO compensation has been the subject of intense public debate and remains a very controversial issue. Boards and executives have been criticized about the level of executive compensation, which has risen dramatically as compared to the pay of the average worker and to the actual growth of companies. Other aspects of CEO employment contracts that outrage the public are the use of exorbitant perks, golden parachutes for ousted executives, large sign-on packages for their replacements, and very weak to nonexistent pay-for-performance relations. All of these have created the impression that there is something deeply wrong, perhaps even "immoral" (in the words of President Obama) in these corporate practices.

A troubling fact is that corporate malfeasance not only affects investors and pension holders—recent corporate crises have resulted in the loss of many trillions of dollars (Parloff, 2009; Loomis, 2009a)—but also has had important social costs. This brings to the forefront the relevance of corporations to society and their role within it and the influence of executive compensation schemes on corporate behavior. Governance scholars, compensation advisers, and other business experts suggest that CEO employment contracts should incorporate nonfinancial social performance ratings as part of the CEO evaluation and reward process (e.g., Coombs and Gilley, 2005).

Despite the wealth of research on executive compensation, the link between corporate social performance (CSP) and executive pay remains limited at best (with few notable exceptions e.g., Berrone and Gomez-Mejia, 2009; Coombs and Gilley, 2005). This may be simply because the relationship between the two is not believed to exist or is theoretically uninteresting. Or perhaps most likely this dearth of research reflects a strong bias in accounting, economics, and finance to see "shareholders' welfare" as the ultimate criteria.

Theoretically, this novel approach may produce several benefits, such as the promotion of actions that are good for both the firm and society, enhanced organizational legitimacy and reputation, the enrichment of managerial responsibilities, the infusion of moral values at the top, the safeguard of executives from uncontrollable business risks, and a more humanistic leadership style (Berrone and Gomez-Mejia, 2009). In this chapter, we address this issue by discussing challenges that emerge when attempting to include social criteria in executive appraisal and incentive alignment systems, and how some of these difficulties might be overcome.

Social Criteria as Part of Executive Pay

The relationship between financial performance and managerial pay has pervaded the field of executive compensation since its inception. A very plausible justification for this is that the majority of executive compensation research has relied on neoclassical tradition in economics.[1] As seen in Chapters 4, 5, and 6, agency theory (Fama, 1980; Jensen and Meckling, 1976) has been the dominant framework used to analyze executive pay issues.

Despite assumptions that agency theory fits neatly into the actual structure of Anglo-American firms, characterized by widely disperse ownership and the resulting separation of ownership and control (Berle and Means, 1932), in practice this view often leads to "perverse" or unintended consequences (Deyá-Tortella et al. 2005). For instance, scholars such as Kochan (2002, p. 139) have argued that the real root cause of corporate malfeasance is "the overemphasis . . . corporations have been forced to give in recent years to maximizing shareholder value without regard for the effects of their actions on other stakeholders." Even scholars such as Sundaram and Inkpen (2004, p. 358), who feverishly defended shareholder value maximization as the preferred objective for corporations, recognized that "the excessive use (and inadequate policing) of such compensation schemes helped fuel the corporate crisis of 2001 and 2002, and must be reined in." More recently, the debate has regained momentum.

As noted earlier, current trends call for a shift away from the traditional "hard-core" economic perspective, which focuses on accounting and market-based measures of performance and sees social engagement as a diversion of business resources from their proper use (Friedman, 1970). The movement is toward a stakeholder perspective in which the firm has multiple constituencies encompassing a variety of interest groups (such as employees, customers, communities, government officials, and environment groups) (e.g., Berman et al. 1999; Berrone et al. 2009; Chan, 2008; Cox, 2005; Donalson and Preston, 1995; Donoher, Reed, and Storrud-Barnes, 2007; Festing, Eiding, and Roger, 2007; Freeman and McVea, 2001). That is, compensation packages of top managers should contain criteria that account for the interests of important stakeholders, not simply those who own company shares.

Murphy (2000) provided evidence for the dominance of financial performance criteria in executive compensation plans. But these plans very rarely contain other criteria that would account for the interests of varied stakeholders, not just the firm's shareholders, such as environmental performance, employee relations, diversity, and other social issues to which the link to financial performance is not straightforward. For example, Berrone and Gomez-Mejia (2006), who analyzed more than 450 companies from polluting industries over seven years, found that only 5 percent of these companies had an explicit environmental pay policy for their executives.

Corporate Social Performance as an Alternative Approach

The traditional neoclassical perspective and its shareholder maximization point of view were first challenged by Dodd (1932), who viewed the firm as an entity separate from its shareholders. As such, the firm has civic responsibilities and should act on behalf of all constituencies, even if it means a decrease in shareholder value. More recently, R. Edward Freeman's book *Strategic Management: A Stakeholder Approach* (1984), set the basis for what is now known as *stakeholder theory*. Freeman's main thesis is that the manager is responsible for coordinating the constellation of competitive and cooperative interests of various constituencies or stakeholders of the firm. In this context, a stakeholder is broadly defined as "any group or individual who can affect or is affected by the achievement of the organization's objectives" (1984, p. 46).

The stakeholder approach is tied closely to the concept of social responsibility and entails the notion of CSP. Firms that attend the needs of consumers, employees, nongovernmental organizations, government, and other societal groups are considered to perform in a socially responsible fashion, which reflects a broader orientation of the firm (Evan and Freeman, 1988; Jones and Wicks, 1999; Wicks, Gilbert and Freeman, 1994). CSP then evaluates how well the company performs in its efforts to develop practices to deal with and create relationships with its numerous stakeholders. That is, CSP is seen as a source of competitive advantage because when the firm meets the needs of a wide variety of stakeholders it enhances its corporate reputation, improves trusting and cooperative relationships, provides access to superior resources, lowers liability exposure, and enhances social legitimacy, which ultimately is expected to contribute to the bottom line (Hillman and Keim, 2001; Waddock and Graves, 1997).

A significant amount of research has been devoted to understanding whether or not CSP serves as a means to the end of corporate financial performance (CFP), with inconclusive results. Although the CSP–CFP relationship is still open for debate, a recent review and meta-analysis seems to support this positive relationship (Margolis and Walsh, 2003; Orlizky, Schmidt, and Rynes, 2003). This last evidence has motivated some scholars to consider CSP as criteria in executive pay schemes.

The first authors to analyze this issue were Stanwick and Stanwick (2001), who studied the relationship between environmental reputation—a dimension of CSP measured with the Fortune environmental reputation index—and CEO salaries for 188 U.S. companies in 1991. The authors argued that because there is a mismatch between stakeholders who benefit from environmental reputation (the community at large), and shareholders who evaluate CEOs based on financial performance and establish the CEOs' compensation, a negative relationship between environmental reputation and CEO salary was hypothesized. Results confirmed their expectations. Authors concluded that "CEOs are encouraged not to have a high environmental reputation." (2001, p. 180).

Similarly, Coombs and Gilley (2005) tested the effects of a different dimension of CSP in regard to CEOs' salaries, bonus, stock options, and total compensation. The authors used stakeholder agency theory (Hill and Jones, 1992) to argue that CEOs should be compensated for effective management of both shareholders' and nonshareholders' needs. Authors tested their prediction using the Kinder, Lydenberg, Domini (KLD), and Company index, which contains data on five dimensions of CSP: community performance, diversity performance, employee performance, environment performance, and product performance. The authors concluded that in general boards of directors negatively value proactive social initiatives and consequently CEOs "pay the price" for socially correct behaviors.

Using a combined measure derived from KLD data, Deckop, Merriman, and Gupta (2006) found that short-term CEO focus (measured as the ratio of annual bonuses and total pay) had a negative impact on CSP. However, the authors also found that long-term CEO focus actually improved CSP. The latter finding is consistent with those by Berrone and Gomez-Mejia (2009), who found that long-term pay had a positive impact on subsequent environmental performance, suggesting that long-term pay provides incentives to managers to engage in socially responsible strategies. Furthermore, Berrone and Gomez-Mejia analyzed whether or not CEOs in polluting industries receive higher total pay for good environmental performance. The authors combined institutional and agency theories to explain the link between executive pay and environmental performance in polluting industries. They argued that firms that operate in environmentally sensitive sectors[2] but have good environmental performance, enjoy enhanced social legitimacy and organizational survival capabilities, and reward their CEOs accordingly.

Table 8.1 summarizes scholarly work on the topic. Unfortunately, the evidence provided by these studies is far from being conclusive and much more research is still needed to fully comprehend the relationship between incentives and social goals beyond financial performance. In the next section, we attempt to provide some guidelines in this direction.

Issues in Rewarding Social Responsibility at the Top

After reviewing a large number of studies, Gomez-Mejia and Balkin (1992) noted that maximizing a sole set of criteria is one of the biggest dangers in poorly designed incentive programs, as those affected are tempted to engage in criterion manipulation. That is, pay schemes that only reward financial performance may deter managers from engaging in corporate social initiatives, since the link between social actions and financial performance is not straightforward and could actually hinder more immediate results (Berrone and Gomez-Mejia, 2006). Stakeholder theory suggests, however, that over-emphasis on financial performance and ignoring stakeholders' expectations can seriously damage the normal functioning of firms. For example, when a company acquires a particular economically useful input that is harmful to the environment, it risks the support of customers, regulators, local citizens, public interest groups, or other firm stakeholders for the firm's products or services. This implies the adoption of a stakeholder approach, which focuses in the firm's long-term survival by balancing interests of multiple stakeholders. As a consequence, criteria that capture these interests should be included in executive compensation schemes.

Social Criteria and Firm Value

From a normative perspective, including CSP as a criterion in executive compensation would stimulate managers to deploy efforts and resources toward social initiatives, and this in turn should increase the firm's value through greater institutional legitimacy (Clarkson, 1995; McGuire, Dow,

Table 8.1

Studies on the Relation Between Social Performance and Executive Compensation

Authors	Journal	Dependent Variable (DV)	Source (DV)	Independent Variable (IV)	Source (IV)	Level of analysis	Theoretical framework	Expected association	Association found	Longitudinal study
Stanwick and Stanwick, 2001	*Business Strategy and the Environment*	Total compensation and salary	*Forbes* magazine	Environmental reputation	*Fortune* magazine	CEO	Stakeholder mismatch	Negative	As expected	No
McGuire, Dow, and Argheyd, 2003	*Journal of Business Ethics*	Strengths and weaknesses in corporate social responsibility	KLD Index	Salaries, annual bonus and long-term	Compustat	CEO	Stakeholder theory	Positive for salary, bonus and long-term for weakness and contrary for strengths	Salary and long-term have a positive impact on weaknesses Neutral otherwise	No
King and Lenox, 2004	*Strategic Management Journal*	Adoption of environmental strategies	EPA-TRI	Compensation explicitly linked to the implementation of environmental activities	Survey	Environmental managers	Absorptive capacity theory	Not explicit (positive combined with information provision)	Positive, but marginal	Yes
Coombs and Gilley, 2005	*Strategic Management Journal*	Total compensation, salary, annual bonus and long-term	Compustat	Stakeholder management	KLD Index	CEO	Stakeholder-agency	Positive	Neutral and/or negative	Yes

Mahoney and Thorne, 2005	Journal of Business Ethics	Strengths and weaknesses in corporate social responsibility	Canadian Social Investment Database	Pay mix: stock option grants/total; compensation	Blue Book of Canadian Business	CEO	Agency theory	Positive for strengths and negative for weakness	As expected except for the CSR people dimension	Yes
Russo and Harrison, 2005	Academy of Management Journal	Environmental performance	EPA-TRI	Salary explicitly linked to environmental performance	Survey	Plant and environmental managers	Congruence theory	Positive	Positive for the plant managers	No
Deckop, Merriman, and Gupta, 2006	Journal of Management	Corporate social performance	KLD Index	Focus on short-term and long-term (pay mix)	Compustat	CEO	Agency and CSR	Negative for short-term and positive for long-term	As expected	No
Berrone and Gomez-Mejia, 2009	Academy of Management Journal	Total CEO compensation	Compustat	Environmental performance-pollution prevention and end-of-pipe	EPA-TRI	CEO	Institutional and agency theories	Positive	As expected	Yes

and Argheyd, 2003; Weiner, 1964). There seems to be a common agreement in this camp that social actions improve corporate image and reputation, create intangible assets, and positively influence long-term organizational survival. For instance, legitimate companies have better exchange conditions with partners and better access to resources (DiMaggio and Powell, 1983), which can be allocated to further improve social performance.

Moreover, limiting the negative impact of corporate action on society also isolates the firm from stakeholder scrutiny and reduces the likelihood of social (e.g., negative press and boycotts by social activists) or legal sanctions (Berrone, Surroca, and Tribo, 2007; Oliver, 1991). At the same time, socially responsible firms can attract and retain better partners, customers, and employees than poor performers (Buysee and Verbeke, 2003; Henriques and Sadorsky, 1999; Sharma and Henriques, 2005; Turban and Greening, 1997). In sum, firms are likely to recognize the value of conformity to social expectations as the resultant legitimacy would reduce the probability of organizational failure (Scott, 1995; Singh, Tucker, and House, 1984) and may enhance firm performance (King and Lenox, 2002; Klassen and McLaughlin, 1996).

Yet there are at least three concerns that cast doubt on these arguments and should be taken into consideration when analyzing CSP as a component of pay. First, it is not clear whether social initiatives have a positive impact on the firm's economic performance. While some studies have shown a positive association between social performance and financial results, many scholars have professed a negative association. In a recent review of research papers regarding the association between social initiatives and firm performance, Margolis and Walsh (2003) found that less than half of the reviewed studies exhibited a positive relationship and the majority showed a neutral or negative link. This review, together with other extant research, suggests that the link between environmental performance and financial results is ambiguous at best. That is, while socially irresponsible businesses can be punished by society (consumers, employees, local communities, nongovernmental organizations) in their image, reputation, and legitimacy for not fulfilling their public responsibilities, it is unclear how a good social performance can cause their market share to increase.

The second aspect that casts doubts on the benefit of rewarding managers when they undertake social initiatives (which presumably considers the need of a broader array of constituencies) is that *all* stakeholders are assumed to favor responsible actions and thus are treated indiscriminately. But the truth is that while some constituencies may have a general preference for social initiatives, one cannot assume that such policies do not conflict with the interests of other stakeholders and that they are oblivious to trade-offs. This "stakeholder mismatch" problem is particularly severe when the stakeholders who benefit from such actions are not the same stakeholders who evaluate the organization and managers' performance (Wood and Jones, 1995).

A third aspect to consider is that social initiatives are mainly driven by intrinsic motivation. Indeed, many people and firms invest their time and money in improving the environment and supporting charities without economic returns. It could be that some people are altruistic, that is, they seek to improve the welfare of others without receiving any personal benefit. However, another intrinsic motivation is "impure altruism" that is, people (or firms) may intend to improve their image from carrying out social works. In a recent work, Chatterjee and Hambrick (2007) creatively measured managerial narcissism (for instance, by measuring the prominence of the CEO's photograph in annual reports) and showed that narcissistic CEOs favor bold actions that attract attention. A related intrinsic motivation is concern for fairness. Regardless of the reasons for altruism, self-image, or fairness, it can be safely assumed that in many cases underlying motivations for social initiatives are intrinsic. Theoretical and empirical evidence from psychology and economics suggests that such extrinsic incentives can crowd out the intrinsic motivations that underlie voluntary contributions.

Social Criteria and Executive Risk Bearing

Social criteria are rarely included in executive compensation contracts in an explicit fashion (Berrone and Gomez-Mejia, 2006). This fact is a source of uncertainty for managers, since managers do not know whether they will be compensated for good CSP. This is a clear disincentive to engage in socially responsible activities. However, when criteria are explicit, they are expected to promote the desired behaviors. Indeed, Russo and Harrison (2005) showed that environmental performance is enhanced when there is an explicit tie between environmental performance and plant managers' pay.

Results from social endeavor are often ambiguous and, as a consequence, if managers are not compensated for the increased risk associated with social investments, they will presumably allocate capital into less uncertain alternatives.

In addition, a problem with social criteria is that they may be difficult to quantify (Deckop et al. 2006; Russo and Harrison, 2005). Therefore, criteria that are measurable and available across time are needed to secure steady social actions. Otherwise, only isolated and sporadic social initiatives will be undertaken. By including explicit and quantifiable CSP measures in the contract, (1) managerial uncertainty is reduced as firms advise managers as to how their performance will be assessed and (2) permanent stakeholder orientation is guaranteed.

Financial indicators are well developed, but social performance measures are still a field open to exploration. Even with a precise index of social performance, these measures may also be open to manipulation. King and Lenox (2000) found that, absent close government monitoring, there is much potential for managerial opportunism with regard to how chemical-producing firms report emissions. As a consequence, control policies and information systems are needed (Berrone and Gomez-Mejia, 2009), which in turn would increase the cost of effectively rewarding social performance.

Social Criteria and Geographic Level of Analysis

We found no research that explicitly addresses the issue of how incentive schemes may actually have undesired effects on global social actions. For instance, low environmental impact in one specific country does not necessarily indicate superior environmental performance by a firm. That is, managers might behave opportunistically and conduct social initiatives in those countries where such initiatives are deemed important, while performing poorly in countries where social issues are neglected. Companies can relocate their dirty operations to less-developed countries that have poor environmental standards or do not keep such records (also known as pollution havens) and avoid locations that demand careful monitoring of all emissions (Christmann, 2004).

However, according to stakeholder theory, a stakeholder is anyone who is affected by the organization's actions, regardless of country of origin (Freeman, 1984). As a consequence, the systematic advantages of locating activities abroad to face weaker standards are dubious. Indeed, Dowell, Hart, and Yeung (2000) argued that different interest groups and nongovernmental organizations expose dirty firms by stimulating consumer awareness and pressuring local governments to discipline poor environmental performers, even if the pollution occurs in overseas locations. This suggests that while some fines and penalties could be eluded by locating polluting activities in countries with lax environmental regulations, legitimacy losses are unavoidable. Similarly, Kostova and Zaheer (1999) showed that that legitimacy of subsidiaries abroad influences the legitimacy of the whole organization. Therefore, we believe that firms that include global CSP criteria in executive compensation schemes will generate greater sustainable value for all stakeholders, including those that do not include these criteria.

Social Criteria and External Context

It is often said that stakeholders, and particularly consumers, want companies to promote the public good through socially responsible behaviors, such as providing healthier and safer products and retirement and health care benefits for its employees. However, stakeholders' expectations vary by industry and geography.

Each company operates within a particular context comprised of distinct stakeholders, who establish idiosyncratic rules, belief systems, and practices that they deem to be appropriate. Given that CSP is a multidimensional construct (Carroll, 1979), it is reasonable to assume that different dimensions of CSP will have different weight and importance based on the context in which the firm operates. This idea is captured in the work by Berrone and Gomez-Mejia (2006), who analyzed environmental performance as a determinant of CEO total pay *within* polluting industries. Unfortunately, previous studies have ignored contextual and institutional factors that may influence the relationship between CSP and executive pay.

Thus, we suggest that the importance of different dimensions of corporate social responsibility is contingent on contextual and institutional factors, and that firms that design their executive compensation packages accounting for these contingencies will outperform firms that do not consider them.

Social Criteria and the Internal Context

Responses to social pressure should also be consistent with internal aspects of the firm. In this context, traditional corporate governance literature has long stressed boards of directors and their composition as one of the primary mechanisms to monitor managerial actions (Fama and Jensen, 1983b; Jensen and Meckling, 1976). It is generally assumed that board members represent shareholders' interest against the potential self-serving behavior of the management team (Finkelstein and Hambrick, 1996; Jensen, 1993). We argue that the presence of stakeholders (nonshareholders) in corporate boards is a direct means through which firms can (1) assess the value of socially responsible initiatives; (2) monitor managerial social actions; and (3) safeguard different stakeholder interests. Because of these, the inclusion of CSP criteria in executive compensation will be more likely as well as more efficient given the supervision function of board members. Thus, we believe that stakeholder (nonshareholder) representation on boards of directors and in their committees will increase the use of CSP measures in executive compensation and its efficacy in promoting sustainable value for all stakeholders, including shareholders.

Summary

In contrast to neoclassical theory, we presented arguments of stakeholder theory that entertains the notion of the firm as a network of relationships with multiple constituencies, not only shareholders. As such, executive effectiveness should be assessed, rewarded, and stimulated from the global perspective of multiple constituencies.

Our position is by no means that firms should ignore financial concerns or that shareholders are less important than other stakeholders. We are, however, somewhat skeptical of the argument that the sole social function of the firm is to maximize profits. In any case, we believe that if social goals are included in addition to financial objectives, enhanced outcomes can be obtained for multiple stakeholders worldwide and the firm as a whole. In sum, the two approaches do not conflict unless posed in the extreme (Berrone et al. 2009). Firms do not succeed financially by neglecting the expectations of employees, customers, suppliers, creditors, and local communities; nor are they able to satisfy stakeholder needs by failing to meet shareholders' expectations. From a human resource management perspective, it is important to recognize that socially legitimate firms can attract and retain better partners, customers, and employees than can poor performers (Buysee and Verbeke, 2003; Henriques and Sadorsky, 1999; Sharma and Henriques, 2005; Turban and Greening, 1997), and thus have less employee turnover and fewer unproductive associations.

In this context, it seems rather obvious that companies should reward their top managers for good social performance. However, there are many issues that need to be considered for a successful outcome. Aspects such the financial uncertainty surrounding social issues, conflicting interests of stakeholders, the opportunistic use of social criteria, the lack of proper measures, the need for monitoring systems, and the relevance of context are just a few potential shortcomings that pay designers may face when including social criteria in executive compensation packages. Figure 8.1 offers a roadmap for designers interested in including social performance measures in their pay packages.

All of these issues should be taken into account since poorly designed executive compensation packages can reward decisions that are not in the long-term interests of a company, its stakeholders, and society as a whole. Furthermore, HR programs for all employees must be designed in a manner consistent with socially driven incentive programs at the top of the organizational pyramid.

Unfortunately, available studies do not provide definitive evidence on

Figure 8.1   **Toolkit for Linking Social Performance and Pay**

- Be aware of the link between social and economic performances.
- Comprehend the context in which the firm operates and identify those aspects that are highly valued within it.
- Define who and what really counts.
- Define how social initiatives will be measured.
- Have proper information systems and monitoring mechanisms in place.
- Understand how social initiatives affect the different stakeholders of the firm and account for potential trade-offs.
- Have a balance between intrinsic motivation and extrinsic incentives.
- Be sure to communicate your social commitments, actions, and achievements.
- Be consistent between disclosure and actions.

whether firms reward or punish socially responsible strategies and what combination of incentives promotes corporate social behaviors. Neither have they suggested the proper combination between short- and long-term forms of pay to adequately stimulate social strategies.

A careful design and implementation of incentive systems is necessary to maintain and support intrinsic motivation while also providing robust extrinsic rewards. In other words, one should not underestimate the intrinsic value of social initiatives. Rather, we need to recognize the complexity of rewarding social performance at the top. It is only through careful consideration of the costs and risks associated with this practice that firms will be able to draw the desired benefits.

Finally, it is important to note that corporate responses to social claims should not be exclusively assessed in terms of their instrumental value, since financial performance is not the final arbiter of issues that implicate moral values and ethical concerns. As such, a firm's socially responsible efforts should reflect a business's mission, values, and identity orientation.

Notes

1. As discussed in Chapters 1 and 3, in the basic agency setting, it is assumed that principals (shareholders), whose primary (and unique) objective is the maximization of the firm's value, delegate tasks to an effort- and risk-averse, rational, and self-centered agent (manager). Principals design compensation contracts to ameliorate a moral hazard problem (i.e., manager opportunism).

2. These are firms that manufacture or process more than 25,000 pounds and/or use at least 10,000 pounds of substances from a list of chemicals deemed hazardous by the U.S. Environmental Protection Agency (EPA). These firms must report their emissions to the EPA's Toxics Release Inventory program.

9 MEASURING PERFORMANCE AT DIFFERENT LEVELS OF THE ORGANIZATION

Linking compensation elements to performance at different organizational levels and units of analysis presents a number of challenges. This chapter focuses on the major theoretical and empirical considerations pertaining to the measurement of corporate, divisional, team, and individual performance. Actual pay-for-performance programs at these various levels are discussed in Chapter 10.

The Measurement of Performance: Preliminary Thoughts

More than half a century ago, Ridgway (1956) argued that in those days there was a

> strong tendency to state numerically as many as possible of the variables with which management must deal. [...] Performance measures are tools, and are undoubtedly useful. But research indicates that indiscriminate use and undue confidence and reliance in them result from insufficient knowledge of the full effects and consequences. Judicious use of a tool requires awareness of possible side effects and reactions. Otherwise, indiscriminate use may result in side effects and reactions outweighing the benefits. This was the case when penicillin was first hailed as a wonder drug. The cure is sometimes worse that the disease. (p. 240)

Today the tendency to rely on performance measures for decision-making and compensation purposes is nearly ubiquitous. Still, its true value is largely unknown. New evidence (e.g., Ordoñez et al. 2009) and recent corporate scandals (e.g., Lehman Brothers) may suggest that Ridgway was right: performance measures should be used with care as their unintended consequences may seriously outweigh their benefits.

There are a number of aspects associated with performance measures that should be understood by the organizations using them. The aim of this chapter is to present those aspects and review the literature around them. This chapter sets out the theoretical background of performance measurement and potential issues that arose when organizations adopt various performance measures. The specifications that performance measures must meet in order to be appropriate for their use in incentive systems are reviewed along with the choices that organizations must make when defining performance measures. The authors present their conclusions and point out potential areas for further research.

Why Organizations Measure Performance

From a theoretical point of view, five classic organizational theories have provided reasons for measuring performance (Micheli et al. 2004): agency theory, the resource-based view of the firm, stakeholder theory, resource-dependence theory, and institutional theory. Some of these theories have been previously introduced (see Chapter 4) so we only highlight here the aspects that are relevant to performance measurement research.

The measurement of performance is a central point in agency-based studies (Jensen and Meckling, 1976; Eisenhardt, 1989). As seen in previous chapters, agency theory suggests that in order to reduce the agency costs (i.e., moral hazard and adverse selection) principals have two options: they may purchase information about the agents' actions, investing in information systems (i.e., performance measures); or they may design a compensation contract that makes agents contingent upon the performance measures included in the information system (Baiman 1982, 1990; Ellig, 2008; Gibbons and Murphy, 1990; Hannan, Krishnan, and Newman, 2008; Lambert et al. 1993; Barkema and Gomez-Mejia, 1998). Agency theory predicts that if the principals' information system accurately reports agents' actions, and if the compensation contract motivates agents to focus on achieving principals' goals, then adverse selection and moral hazard will be reduced (Baiman, 1982; Eisenhardt, 1989). This means that principals' expected goals would more likely be achieved.

The resource-based view of the firm (Barney, 1991; Barney, Wright, and Ketchen, 2001) has also encouraged organizations to identify and measure the nature of their resources in order to improve the firm's competitive advantage (Widener, 2006). Resource-based theory looks at firms in terms of their resources and not their products (Wernerfelt, 1984). The underlying premise of this theory is that greater competitive advantage and performance can be obtained if a firm is able to hold rare and valuable resources that are not held by other companies. The demand for a rare resource outstrips the supply and a valuable resource is one that contributes to a firm's efficiency and effectiveness (Priem and Butler, 2001). Based on this theory, organizations that periodically measure, record, and monitor their tangible and intangible resources for strategic purposes are likely to outperform their competitors (Gray, 2005).

Under the lens of stakeholder theory (Freeman, 1984), organizations are interested in measuring their performance in order to effectively manage the expectations of their various stakeholders (Jones, 1995; Laplume, Sonpar, and Litz, 2008). Each stakeholder (e.g., owner, customer, employee, supplier, government) has its own performance requirements. For example, shareholders want to maximize the firm's financial value and customers want quality products at competitive prices. For this reason, it is important for organizations to measure and monitor performance drivers that are relevant to each of their stakeholders.

From a resource-dependence perspective organizational success is defined as the maximization of power (Pfeffer, 1981). One of the main assumptions of this theory is that organizations work toward two related objectives:

1. they want to acquire control over resources as this control reduces their dependence on other organizations;
2. they want control over resources that maximize the dependence of other organizations upon them (Pfeffer and Salancik, 1978).

With these objectives in mind, performance measurement becomes a strategic tool that can be used to obtain resources and gain power. In fact, Covaleski, Dirsmith, and Samuel (1996) noticed how performance measurement (in particular, budgeting systems) played a very important role during periods of organizational decline. Organizations tend to use performance measures not only to allocate resources internally, but also to influence the generation of new resources.

Finally, institutional theory (DiMaggio and Powell, 1983) looks into how structures, practices, norms, and routines are created, diffused, adopted, and abandoned in organizations (Scott, 2004). From this point of view, organizations must conform to the rules and beliefs that exist in the environment in order to survive. Therefore, organizations operating in analogous environments and facing similar pressures (e.g., same industry) tend to go through a process of homogenization, becoming isomorphic—i.e., with similar structures or processes (DiMaggio and Powell, 1983; Meyer and Rowan, 1977).

For example, some of the pressures of institutional environments have been found to exert fundamental influences on the adoption of performance measurement practices (e.g., Brignall and Modell, 2000). Thus, according to this theory, organizations measure performance because they are forced to do so due to the pressures of the environment.

Based on the above theories it can be argued that organizations measure performance for the following reasons: (1) They want to motivate and control their employees (i.e., align the interests of stakeholders and managers). Organizations measuring performance for this particular purpose tend to link it to compensation mechanisms. (2) They want to inform their decision-making processes and provide information to their stakeholders. (3) They want to conform to the rules and beliefs of their environment in order to be legitimized. Each of these purposes influences the type and nature of the performance measures that organizations adopt.

Performance Measurement Issues

There are fundamental issues that occur when the measurement of performance is undertaken in an organizational context. The issues raised in the discussion that follows are based on the findings of performance measurement and compensation research.

The Imperfection of Performance Measures

Perfect measures of performance will never be found, as performance cannot be known perfectly until after an action has run its course (Jensen and Meckling, 1990a). Thus, performance measures will always be imperfect representations of true performance. For instance, when a managerial pay-for-performance system is designed, one of the key questions to ask is how managerial performance will be measured. The assumption behind this question is that managerial performance can indeed be measured. However, designers of pay-for-performance systems soon realize that not all the aspects associated with managerial performance are measurable. Managerial performance has multiple dimensions, some of which are not directly observable or measurable, either quantitatively or qualitatively (Feltham and Xie, 1994). The dilemma occurs when performance measures are perceived to represent true performance. As Power (2004) suggests, means tend to become ends. Critical information that cannot be readily quantified is marginalized and becomes invisible, and proxy measures of performance end up representing performance itself. When this occurs the effects can be devastating.

For example, Chwastiak (2006) found that the U.S. government's reliance on measurement and rewards with regard to the military during the war in Vietnam was catastrophic. She shows that the measurement system used at the time provided U.S. leaders with an economically rational discourse that equated truth. U.S. leaders interpreted the information obtained from the measurement system as the reality of war. U.S. leaders used performance information for both motivational and decision-making purposes. Soldiers' rewards were based on performance measures such as "body count" and reliance on performance measures encouraged dysfunctional behavior by some soldiers. Performance data was manipulated and at the same time used for decision making—it is no wonder the war did not change in response to the U.S. leaders' strategic actions. As a result, soldiers started to rebel and this rebellion frequently contributed to the breakdown of the U.S. command in Vietnam.

The Uncontestable Nature of Performance Measures

Once performance measures have been accepted, they cannot be contested. The introduction of new performance measures is always painful and finds serious resistance from employees regardless of their potential value as drivers of performance. Human beings have a natural need for clarity and structure in their environment (Katz and Kahn, 1978). Performance measures reduce role ambiguity and provide clarity and a sense of control over the unknown (Hopwood, 1973; Burney, Henle, and Widener, 2009). These particular attributes of performance measures are very appealing for managers who are desperate to reduce the complexity and uncertainty of their work. Thus, once performance measures have been accepted and used for some time, they become entrenched in the culture and daily activities of the organization (particularly if they are linked to some form of pay). Managers get used to them and resist the introduction of new measures, regardless of their validity, in order to preserve the status quo. As a result, the performance measures and compensation systems used by an organization are not likely to adapt to new situations (e.g., a shift in business strategy, a change in economic circumstances).

The Conflicting Roles of Performance Measures

As reviewed in previous sections, organizations use performance measures for different purposes. According to early agency-based research, firm owners are better off adopting the same performance measures for both informational and motivational purposes (Eisenhardt, 1989). The use of performance measures as an informational mechanism helps managers understand the results of their actions. It encourages them to incorporate the information provided by the measures in their decision-making processes with the aim of improving performance (i.e., meeting owners' objectives). The use of performance measures for motivational or control purposes (e.g., in performance contingent pay plans or in performance evaluation schemes) encourages managers to focus on those aspects of performance that are aligned with the owner's objectives. However, it also creates an environment in which managers are more tempted to distort and corrupt performance information as they have a desire to look good in front of their superiors (Austin, 1996; Campbell, 1979). Thus, the use of the same performance measures for both informational and motivational purposes might become dysfunctional, as the validity of the information delivered by the measurement system is compromised by the unintended reactions of those being measured (i.e., little can be learned from information that has been previously manipulated) (Franco-Santos, 2008). In fact, recent agency-based research has shown that unless the available performance measures are sufficiently precise, owners will obtain greater economic benefits when using performance measures for informational purposes only—that is without linking them to pay (Hannan, Rankin, and Towry, 2006).

The Cost of Performance Measures

The measurement of performance is not free. It has a cost that is not always easy to calculate. This cost includes the overhead necessary to develop and maintain measurement mechanisms as well as the potential for less-than-constructive responses to measurement (Austin, 1996). As found by Gray (2005), the cost of measuring performance is highly dependent on the role of performance measures in the organization. Measuring for motivational and control purposes is more costly than using performance measures strictly for informational purposes. When the overhead necessary to create and maintain these measures becomes more costly, some trade-offs are necessary. Cheaper measures are often adopted despite their lower informative value, which in turn generates additional costs as a result of the less functional (or even dysfunctional) decisions made by employees.

The Diminished Variance of Performance Measures

The usefulness of performance measures decays over time due to a loss of variability (Meyer and Gupta, 1994). In other words, the diminished variance of performance measures reduces their ability to differentiate "good" from "bad" performance over time, and this in turn reduces validity (Franco-Santos, 2008). For instance, earnings per share (EPS) was a performance measure commonly used in executive incentive systems in the early 1970s. This measure soon became irrelevant as it was no longer effective in driving the expected behavior. Executives found a way of getting the expected EPS results. High levels of EPS were achieved but this measure no longer differentiated companies that performed well from those that did not. Although the measure was appropriate when first used, it became distorted over time (Meyer and Gupta, 1994).

Meyer and Gupta (1994) suggest that the usefulness of performance measures decays over time for four reasons: positive learning, perverse learning, selection, and suppression. *Positive learning* refers to the fact that, over time, people learn how to improve their performance of whatever is being measured. *Perverse learning,* or gaming, refers to the idea that people learn how to meet the specific requirements of a performance measure without improving performance. *Selection* refers to the fact that organizations learn over time, either positively or perversely, how their employees perform and decide to replace low performers with high performers. Finally, *suppression* refers to the indication that performance measures are suppressed when performance differences cannot be diminished by either improvement, the appearance of improvement, or selection.

The Correlation of Performance Measures

In the last few decades organizations have started to use multiple measures to assess the multidimensional nature of performance. When multiple measures of performance are used, correlations among the measures might exist. If two performance measures are correlated, researchers such as Meyer and Gupta (1994) argue that only one of them should be used for incentive purposes, as unintended consequences may happen otherwise. For example, a firm with an incentive plan based on the increase of profits, market share, and customer satisfaction may find that the actions required to increase market share may indeed decrease profits in the same year. These two measures are likely to be negatively correlated in the short term and positively correlated in the long term. If the incentive system is designed by taking annual results into consideration, managers will be unlikely to meet their expected performance goals. This phenomenon will generate dissatisfaction among managers, as the problem is inbuilt in the measurement system. Consequently, managers may be tempted to misrepresent their performance information in order to obtain their annual bonus.

The Unintended Consequences of Performance Measures

When organizations use performance measures to influence behavior and in particular to determine pay, there is a set of unintended consequences that are likely to occur. The gravity of these unintended consequences is contingent upon the context in which the measures are used. In some contexts, the unintended consequences of measuring performance may outweigh their beneficial effects (Ordoñez et al. 2009). Research has shown that the following unintended consequences are the most common when performance measures are used mainly for motivational and control purposes:[1] tunnel vision, short-termism, measure fixation, misinterpretation, misrepresentation, gaming, and ossification (Fisher and Downes, 2008; Smith, 1995).

Tunnel Vision

Using an analytical model based on agency theory, Holmstrom and Milgrom (1991) found that the use of performance measures for incentive purposes focuses managerial effort on those aspects of performance that are measured at the expense of those that are not. Based on this evidence they argue that overreliance on a pay-for-performance scheme is imperfect and costly for the firm (Holmstrom and Milgrom, 1994). In their view, the use of performance measures to determine pay is just one way of influencing agents' behavior. There are other mechanisms such as the design of jobs, asset ownership, promotions, implicit incentives, or simple verbal encouragement. All of these motivational instruments are not equally important, but they all should be integrated in a "coherent incentive system" in order to generate potential benefits for the firm (Holmstrom and Milgrom, 1994).

Short-termism

Ideally, managers should take actions that will have positive effects on the long-term value of the firm (Hayes and Abernathy, 1980). Managers should also take actions that generate short-term results in order to ensure the firm's survival. Therefore, firms should be able to balance both long- and short-term focus (Marginson and McAulay, 2008). A problem arises when managerial actions favor short-term results at the expense of long-term value. This problem is known as managerial myopia or short-termism[2] (Laverty, 1996; Merchant, 1990). There are several studies that show how the use of accounting-based performance measures in incentive systems causes short-termism as managers focus on the delivery of short-term financial results to the detriment of longer-term objectives (e.g., Chow, Kato and Merchant, 1996; Merchant, 1990; Van der Stede, 2000).

In order to reduce the short-termism effect of financial performance measures, researchers have proposed the use of multicriteria performance measures, that is, financial and nonfinancial—in incentive contracts (e.g., Feltham and Xie, 1994). As described earlier, nonfinancial indicators focus managers on actions that are likely to have long-term effects (e.g., customer loyalty) (Lambert, 2001). However, the idea that the use of diverse performance measures solves the issues associated with the use of financial performance measures is still unclear. Recent research has found that the use of financial and nonfinancial performance measures for motivational and control purposes can have additional side effects such as "shifting," in which managers focus their attention on nonfinancial performance at the expense of the financial performance (Smith, 2002), or increased subjectivity and perceptions of unfairness (Ittner, Larcker, and Meyer, 2003).

Measure Fixation

The consequence of *measure fixation* is highly cited in public sector research (Smith, 1995). This refers to the emphasis that managers place on the success of the measures rather than on the underlying objective. Some authors refer to this dysfunctional behavior as, "hitting the target and missing the point" (Hood, 2006). According to Smith (1995), this particular issue can be addressed in the design stage, when performance measures are being created.

Misrepresentation and Gaming

According to Power (2004) "performance measurement systems are fatal remedies as they create incentives that undermine the very activity being measured, and make social agents focus on measures as targets to be managed and gamed" (p. 774). In fact, researchers have found that the use of performance measures and targets in incentive systems generates *misrepresentation*— manipulation of information so that reported performance differs from actual performance—or even *gaming*—conscious manipulation of behavior in order to achieve the expected performance (Elayan, Li, Meyer, 2008; Guidry, Leone, and Rock, 1999; Jensen, 2003; Healy, 1985a,b; Holthausen, Larcker, and Sloan, 1995; Schweitzer, Ordoñez, and Douma, 2004). Misrepresentation leads to distortions in reported performance, whereas gaming refers to the manipulation of actual behavior (Smith, 1995). Managers may be tempted to misrepresent or engage in gaming behavior because they find extrinsic and intrinsic benefits in doing so. An example of extrinsic benefits is the pay-ment received when performance targets are met. An example of intrinsic benefits is the increase in self-esteem associated with supervisor's approval when a target is achieved (Leary et al. 2003).

There are a number of contingencies that have been found to affect the level of misrepresentation and gaming, such as the level of information asymmetry. According to Dye (1988) and Trueman and Titman (1988), information asymmetry is a key determinant of earnings manipulation. In line with this research, Richardson (2000) finds that a positive and systematic relationship exists between information asymmetry and the level of earnings manipulation. More recently, Elayan, Li, and Meyer (2008) have shown that firms having greater levels of information asymmetry are more likely to com-mit accounting irregularities. However, Hannan, Rankin, and Towry (2006) provide evidence suggesting that the impact of information asymmetry on managerial honesty cannot be predicted unambiguously, as two offsetting effects jointly determine the overall impact. The decrease in information asymmetry by means of higher performance measures precision limits the amount of misrepresentation that managers can engage in while appearing honest. At the same time, this limitation will motivate more managers to opt for the benefits of misrepresentation rather than the benefits of appearing honest. Overall, it is unclear which of these two effects is dominant.

Another contingency that influences the misrepresentation of data and gaming is managerial discretion, i.e., top management's latitude of action (Hambrick and Finkelstein, 1995). For instance, Salamon and Smith (1979) find that manager-controlled firms tend to over-report their earnings. Blair and Kaserman (1983) also find that companies in which managers have more power than shareholders are more likely to take part in actions that may violate antitrust laws. Merchant's (1990) work shows that environmental uncertainty is a contingency that increases the likelihood of distorted data and gaming behaviors. In his study he finds that managers operating in relatively unstable environments are significantly more likely to react to measurement pres-sures by pulling profits from the subsequent year into the current year than managers operating in relatively stable environments. There is also evidence showing that when performance measures are used to determine pay, mis-representation and gaming are likely to occur (Bar-Gill and Bebchuck, 2003; Goldman and Slezak, 2006). Furthermore, firms that have greater incentive opportunities (i.e., size of incentive pay) have been shown to be more likely to commit accounting irregularities (Elayan et al. 2008).

It has been argued that when performance measures are used for motiva-tional purposes, misrepresentation and gaming might be inevitable (Ordoñez et al. 2009). Some researchers assert that stronger controls should be used in order to minimize these dysfunctional behaviors. Other researchers argue that some degree of misrepresentation and gaming must be tolerated as a necessary part of an efficient contract (e.g., Crocker and Slemrod, 2007). However, to what extent should firms tolerate these toxic behaviors? When do they become intolerable or completely unethical? Recent corporate scandals in the banking industry have shown how far humans can go in order to achieve their personal objectives. Excluding some exceptions (e.g., Fisher and Downes, 2008), few studies to date have tried to identify mechanisms that could reduce or even avoid these types of behaviors. Due to the importance of this issue, further research in this area is highly encouraged.

Misinterpretation

Once performance information is produced, regardless of its technical validity, managers have to interpret it. Human beings have cognitive limitations due to which misinterpretation of measurement information may occur. When data is misinterpreted, the wrong decisions might be made with detrimental effects for both the managers and the firm. For instance, a number of studies have investigated how the information extracted from scorecard incentive schemes—those based on financial and nonfinancial performance measures—is likely to be misinterpreted. Lipe and Salterio (2000, 2002) find evidence showing that the information provided by scorecard systems affects managerial judgment. Wong-On-Wing and colleagues (2007) and Malina, Norreklit, and Selto (2007) more recently found that top managers have the tendency to overlook the validity of the causal links that exist between the input and output measures of a balanced scorecard, and ignore the underlying strategically linked causal business models.

Ossification

Some researchers have found that performance measures can inhibit innovation and lead to ossification (Smith, 1995). Ossification has been defined as "organizational paralysis brought about by an excessively rigid system of performance evaluation" (p. 299). Once accepted, performance measures are rarely contested (Power, 2004). This phenomenon reduces flexibility and the ability of the organization to adjust to new threats or opportunities. Smith (1995) suggests that ossification might be minimized by "ensuring that managers are rewarded for behavior that anticipates new challenges, even if the activity does not yield improvements in existing PIs [performance indicators]." In addition, a periodic formal review of the performance measures scheme might also alleviate this problem (e.g., Kennerley and Neely, 2002; Smith, 1995). To date, limited empirical studies have been conducted in this area, which suggests a potential new avenue for further research.

Some authors stress the idea that the unintended consequences of performance measures can be softened if the design process is carefully considered (Neely, Gregory, and Platts, 1995; Smith, 1995). In the performance measurement and compensation literature a number of specifications of performance measures can be found. When performance measures meet these specifications, their effectiveness is likely to increase.

Specifications of Performance Measures

Accounting and operations researchers have been especially concerned with the identification of characteristics that enable measures to be more appropriate for motivating organizational, team, and individual performance. Based on research obtained from these two bodies of literature the following specifications are highlighted: [3]

1. Congruence
2. Controllability
3. Timeliness
4. Accuracy
5. Understandability
6. Cost-effectiveness
7. Fairness

Congruence

Merchant (2006) argues that congruence is the most important specification a performance measure must meet. In his words,

> a measure should go up when good actions are taken and, hence, the organization's objectives are most likely to be served, and go down when bad actions are taken. If a measure does not reflect progress to the desired ends, or if it does so incompletely, then motivating managers to work to improve the measure will be unproductive, no matter how well the measure satisfies the other measurement criteria." (pp. 894–895)

For example, Kerr (1995) shows several examples of performance measures that were not congruent with the organizational objectives and in turn generated tension and organizational conflicts. Chwastiak (2006) reports that the performance measures used by the U.S. government during the Vietnam War were not congruent with the expected end result (to win the war). This inconsistency was one of the causes of misconduct from U.S. soldiers.

Controllability

According to this specification, performance measures used for motivational purposes should only address those aspects of performance that managers can control (Antle and Demski, 1988; Demski, 1994). When managers are evaluated on things they cannot control, they perceive their evaluation as being unfair and become dissatisfied, which in turn affects their motivation and their tendency to misrepresent their performance data (Giraud and Mendoza, 2008). The level of controllability that a measure has is context-specific (Merchant, 2006). It depends on the authority given to the individual whose performance is being measured. For instance, productivity might be highly controllable by an operations director but largely uncontrollable by his or her secretary. It also depends on the situation being faced. As an example, revenues or market share might be controllable at one point in time and uncontrollable at another due to competitive pressures or economic situations.

Timeliness

Timeliness refers to "the lag between the managers' actions and the measurement/feedback of results (and provision of incentives)" (Merchant, 2006, p. 896). The timeliness of a performance measure depends on the timeframe in which the measure is used. For example, when used in an annual incentive scheme, customer satisfaction is a timely measure only if the manager's actions affect the results of the customer satisfaction measure within the year being assessed. If the time lag between managerial actions and customer satisfaction results is longer than a year, the customer satisfaction measure will not be timely.

Accuracy

Another specification of "good" performance measures is accuracy. This term encapsulates three key concepts: precision, validity, and reliability. Precision refers to the "lack of noise" or variation in a performance measure (Banker and Datar, 1989). Validity refers to the extent to which a performance measure captures what it is intended to measure. Reliability refers to the ability of a measure to be consistent. Without being accurate a performance measure loses its value, as it may cause individuals to misinterpret performance (Merchant, 2006). Research has also found that if a measure is noisy, managers will pay less attention to it (Holmstrom and Milgrom, 1991). Financial performance is likely to be measured with high precision. Other dimensions of performance, such as creativity, leadership, or employee morale, cannot be measured very precisely, which questions their appropriateness as motivational devices (Hannan, Rankin, and Towry, 2006).

Understandability

According to Merchant (2006) there are two important aspects of understandability. On one hand, managers must understand what the measure represents (i.e., how is it calculated and what it means). On the other hand, managers must understand what kinds of actions they must take in order to influence the measure results, which relates back to the controllability specification. When creating new measures of performance, manager's knowledge about the measures should not be taken for granted (Manoochehri, 1999). For instance, Banker, Chang, and Pizzini (2004) show how managers' knowledge about the level of strategic alignment of their performance measures affects their judgment in performance evaluations reviews.

Cost Effectiveness

As discussed earlier, performance measures have a cost to the organization using them (Austin, 1996; Gray, 2005). The cost can be monetary, such as the cost associated with developing a new customer satisfaction survey. The cost can also be nonmonetary, for example, the dysfunctional behaviors that a particular performance measure may generate. Therefore, a specific performance measure should only be used if the benefits of using it outweigh its costs.

Fairness

Finally, performance measures should not benefit a particular group or individual within the organization. Performance measures must be perceived as fair in order to encourage the right behaviors and drive the expected performance (Burney, Henle, and Widener, 2009). Perceptions of fairness or equity remain in the eyes of the beholder. This is why it is so important that managers perceive their performance measures to be fair. From this perspective, for example, the use of nonfinancial performance measures for motivational purposes might be considered inappropriate as research has found that such measures generate feelings of unfairness (e.g., Ittner, Larcker, and Meyer, 2003).

The Choice of Performance Measures

Each firm faces a number of choices when measuring performance. The degree of success associated with each choice depends on three factors. The first factor is to how well the options selected enable the organization to capture its true value as well as that of its teams and individuals. The second factor is how well the options selected drive the expected behavior. The third factor is the extent to which the options selected are in line with the contingencies of the organization (e.g., its strategy, culture, level of risk, etc.).

Financial versus Nonfinancial

The first step in the process of measuring performance is to identify the type of performance information that is critical for the achievement of the organization's objectives. In this instance, managers are likely to have two choices. They can focus their performance measures on financial information alone or they can focus their performance measures on a combination of financial and nonfinancial information. Financial information refers to:

1. a piece of information expressed as a monetary unit;
2. a ratio resulting from mathematical manipulations of information expressed in monetary units; or
3. a piece of information resulting from a ratio that includes a piece of information expressed in a monetary unit and a nonmonetary unit (Morrisette, 1996, p. 12).

Nonfinancial information refers to

1. qualitative information;
2. information expressed in nonmonetary units; or
3. information resulting from mathematical manipulations or ratios of pieces of information expressed in nonmonetary units (Franco-Santos, 2007; Morissette, 1996).[4]

Table 9.1 presents some examples of financial and nonfinancial performance measures and summarizes their potential[5] benefits and drawbacks.

Financial performance measures in general and accounting-based performance measures in particular have historically been the most widely used measures of performance. However, in the last decades they have received great criticism including the following: They promote a backward-looking approach, and over-emphasize short-term returns that discourage long-term investments (Banks and Wheelwright, 1979; Hayes and Abernathy, 1980; Indjejikian, 1999); they are unable to include all the relevant dimensions of firm performance, since they are mainly concerned with outcomes (Hopwood, 1973); they are unable to provide the most efficient means for motivating agents to act in the manner desired by the principal (Feltham and Xie, 1994); and they are not completely informative about agents' actions (Hemmer, 1996). As a result of these criticisms, researchers have suggested that financial measures should be complemented by nonfinancial measures.

Nonfinancial measures focus on the long term as they contain forward-looking information about performance that is absent in financial performance measures (Datar et al. 2001; Feltham and Xie, 1994; Hemmer, 1996; Holmstrom, 1979; Lambert, 2001). They are concerned with outcomes as well as processes, which makes them more informative (Ittner, Larcker, and Rajan, 1997; Ittner and Larcker, 2003). They are useful at predicting future financial performance (Banker, Potter, Srinivasan, 2000; Behn and Riley, 1999; Ittner and Larcker, 1998b; Nagar and Rajan, 2005). Some scholars argue that nonfinancial measures are better than financial measures at capturing the value of intangible assets (Amir and Lev, 1996; Ittner and Larcker, 1998a) and the drivers of value creation (Kaplan and Norton, 1992, 1996). Nevertheless, the use of a diverse set of performance measures is not free of criticism.

Despite the encouraging research that supports the use of nonfinancial information for performance measurement and compensation purposes, researchers have also highlighted potential drawbacks associated with their use. Ittner and Larcker (2003) argue that many organizations fail to identify, analyze, and act on the appropriate nonfinancial measures and, instead, "self-serving managers are able to choose—and manipulate—[nonfinancial] measures solely for the purpose of making themselves look good and earn nice bonuses" (2003, p. 89). They even add that "nonfinancial measures seem to have become a shabby substitute for financial performance" (2003, p. 95).

There is empirical evidence suggesting that the use of measurement diver-

Table 9.1

Financial Performance Measures: Examples, Benefits, and Drawbacks

	Examples	Benefits	Drawbacks
Financial Dimension			
Accounting Measures (they rely upon financial information reported in income statements, balance sheet, and statements of cash flow)	Profitability Measures (e.g., net income, operating income, earnings before taxes); growth measures (e.g., sales growth); leverage; liquidity; cash flow; efficiency (e.g., asset turnover, net profit per employee, sales per employee)	• Managers tend to perceive that changes in these measures explain a high proportion of the changes in firm value • They are objective and subject to external audits • They are cost-effective as they have to be developed for meeting accounting standards • They can be tailored to match the responsibilities of managers at different levels of the organization • They can be measured on a timely basis • They are understandable as firms are likely to spend time and money on training their managers than on how to understand them (not necessarily how to achieve them) • They can be used by public and private organizations	• Accounting measures are based on past performance. They do not take into consideration potential future performance • They encourage short-term focus • These measures are highly influenced by external conditions (e.g., economic downturns) • The results of these measures are highly dependable on the type of financial data selected to compute the measures; in this sense, they can be deliberately manipulated by management • There is a proportion of the firm's value that cannot be explained by accounting measures

Economic Value-added Measures (adjusted accounting measure)	Residual income, cash flow return on investment, EVA®	The correlation between changes in these measures and changes in market value is supposed to be higher than the correlation between changes in accounting measures and changes in market value	• They focus on past performance • They do not fully represent the real economic performance of the firm • In particular, EVA® suffers from accuracy problems and is subject to manipulation • They are difficult to understand • They are likely to be expensive

Financial Dimension

Market Measures (they assess the market value of the firm)	Return to shareholders and market value added	• They are believed to provide direct indications of the amount of value that has been created or destroyed • They are timely (for publicly traded firms) • They are accurate • They are objective • It is difficult for managers at lower levels of the organization to directly manipulate them • They are cost-effective	• Market measures are only available for publicly traded companies • They are highly affected by external factors and only top managers can have some indirect influence over them (through the provision or retention of information to markets) • Market values are not always reflective of realized performance; these measures are highly influenced by future expectations • Market valuations are imperfect; they do not represent the true value of the organization. Managers at top levels understand them well; however, at lower levels of the organization this is not the case

(continued)

Table 9.1 *(continued)*

Nonfinancial Dimensions

	Examples	Benefits	Drawbacks
Operation Measures (based on aspects of performance associated with the internal operations of the organization)	Quality of products; quality of services; number of new products; lead times; operational efficiency	• They contain forward-looking information • They can be use by public and private organizations • Together with financial measures they can explain a high proportion of the changes in firm value • These measures provide richer information to managers about the results of their actions	• Some of these measures might be costly to develop and maintain (e.g., employee morale surveys) • Since these measures are more controllable and do not go through an audit process they can be subject to manipulation • They add complexity to the incentive system • Conceptually they are more difficult to understand than financial measures (i.e., their meaning might be interpreted in different ways by different people) • Their timeliness is difficult to assess • They tend to be less accurate than financial measures • Managers tend to perceive them as less objective than financial measures
Customer Measures (based on customer interactions with the organization)	Customer retention; customer satisfaction; marketing effectiveness; brand recognition; customer responsiveness	• The degree of controllability of these measures tends to be high • They are able to capture the intangible assets of the firm	
People Measures (based on aspects of performance associated with the organization human capital)	Job satisfaction; employees' skills; employees' morale; headcount; turnover; absenteeism		

Source: The information contained in this table is based on the work of Indjejikian (1999), Merchant (2006), and Carton and Hofer (2006).

sity increases systems complexity, which in turn affects managers' cognitive abilities to differentiate good from bad performance (Banker, Chang, and Pizzini, 2004; Gosh and Lusch, 2000; Lipe and Salterio, 2000, 2002; Van der Stede et al. 2006). Measurement diversity also seems to complicate the process of assigning relative weights to the different dimensions of performance (Ittner and Larcker, 1998a; Krishnan, Luft, and Shields, 2005; Moers, 2005) and may generate internal conflicts due to the pursuit of incongruent goals (e.g., increase innovation and reduce cost) (Baker, 1992; Holmstrom and Milgrom, 1991; Jensen, 2001; Lillis, 2002; Van der Stede et al. 2006; Wong-On-Wing et al. 2007). Furthermore, a set of studies have shown that the use of diverse measurement may only be advisable for organizations operating in specific contexts.

For instance, the studies conducted by Govindarajan and Gupta (1985) and by Gupta (1987) found that greater reliance on nonfinancial information for rewarding the business unit's management team contributes to better performance in the "build" phase (increase market share), but hampers it in the "harvest" phase (maximization of short-term earnings and cash flow). The work of Said, HassabElnaby, and Wier (2003) found that firms employing a combination of financial and nonfinancial measures of performance have significantly superior current and future performance. However, they also found that the association between multicriteria measures and firm performance is contingent on the firm's operational and competitive characteristics. More recently, Franco-Santos (2007) found that when the effects of diverse measurement on performance are studied in isolation (without taking into consideration any contextual factors), these effects are likely to be detrimental to a firm. However, under specific circumstances—such as organizations in high- or low-business-risk environments or with clan or adhocracy cultural values—the use of measurement diversity is likely to be beneficial.

Objective versus Subjective Weights

Organizations using multiple performance measures for incentive purposes have to determine a method for assigning relative weights to their different measures. They can choose to follow an objective method or a subjective one. The objective method will imply the development of a formula-based plan that incorporates the specific weights each measure has been assigned. The subjective method can take the form of "flexibility in weighting quantitative performance measures when computing a manager's bonus, the use of qualitative performance evaluations, and/or the discretion to adjust bonus awards based on factors other than the measures specified in the bonus contract" (Ittner, Larcker, and Meyer, 2003, p. 726). The potential superiority of one method over the other is still unclear.

Some agency-based researchers have found that greater subjectivity can improve incentive contracting. Greater subjectivity allows organizations to incorporate additional performance information that might otherwise be ignored. It may also help to minimize the dysfunctional behaviors created by the imperfect nature of the performance measures used in the incentive scheme (e.g., Baker, Gibbons, and Murphy, 1994). Other researchers have found that greater subjectivity in assessing performance measures can be detrimental to the organization as they may introduce favoritisms and bias, which can in turn damage motivation and performance (e.g., Ittner, Larcker, and Meyer, 2003; Prendergast and Topel, 1993).

If a contingency approach is taken, the choice between subjective and objective methods becomes easier to tackle. For example, Gibbs and colleagues (2004) find that the use of subjective methods in incentive systems is positively related to:

1. the extent of long-term investments in intangibles;
2. the extent of organizational interdependencies;
3. the extent to which the achievability of the formula bonus target is both difficult and leads to significant consequences if not met; and
4. the presence of an operating loss (p. 409).

They also find that "the effects of subjective bonuses on pay satisfaction, productivity, and profitability are larger the greater the manager's tenure, consistent with the idea that subjectivity improves incentive contracting when there is greater trust between the subordinate and supervisor" (p. 409).

Internal versus External

Organizations also have to decide upon whether the performance information they are going to be using for incentive purposes is going to be internal or external. Internal information is directly related to the internal functioning of the organization and its effects. Examples of these performance metrics are costs, quality, and productivity. This information is characterized by being more controllable (Indjejikian, 1999; Moers, 2005). Conversely, external information reflects the situation of the market and the external environment—it is less controllable. Examples of this type of measures are market share, customer loyalty, and customer satisfaction. Traditionally, organizations focused on internal information. Currently, most organizations need to adopt both internal and external performance measures in order to cope with their competitive environments (Ittner and Larcker, 2003).

Process versus Outcomes

A further choice that organizations need to make relates to the focus of the performance information they are going to adopt. A question organizations must answer is whether they want to focus on processes, outcomes, or both. Financial performance measures tend to reflect only outcomes (Hopwood, 1973). Nonfinancial performance measures can reflect both outcomes and processes. Outcome information is based on past performance and it cannot always be used to predict future performance. Process information is forward-looking so it can help organizations to project future performance.

Absolute versus Relative

Finally, organizations need to choose whether to measure their performance in absolute or relative terms. A particular measure is of little value by itself. It must be compared against some reference value to be meaningful. An organization may choose to compare measured results against an absolute standard. For example, a firm may want to measure labor cost and compared the results against a particular standard based on historical labor cost performance. An organization may also choose to compare its measured results against those of other organizations. For example, a firm may want to measure its return on assets compared to the average return on assets achieved by a previously selected peer group of companies.

Summary

This chapter has explored the reasons behind performance measurement, the issues associated with the measurement of performance, the specifications that appropriate performance measures must meet, and the set of choices organizations must make when identifying and creating their measures of performance. In sum, this work suggests that the measurement of performance is a complex task, which requires careful consideration and attention to the environmental contingencies that influence it. Chapter 10 focuses on the different methods in which organizational, team, and individual performance can be linked to pay. It highlights the benefits and drawbacks of each method together with their potential impact on performance and behavior.

Notes

1. It must be noted that some researchers have also found that the mere use of measures influences behavior regardless of their relationship to pay (e.g., Hopwood, 1973).

2. In the literature, the terms *managerial myopia* and *short-termism* tend to be used interchangeably. However, it is important to mention that some researchers adopt the term managerial myopia to relate to the cognitive limitations managers have in relation to the temporal dimension of their decisions—managers have difficulty assessing the long-term consequences of their actions (e.g., Marginson and McAulay, 2008).

3. This list of specifications has been extracted mainly from the work of Merchant (2006) and Franco-Santos (2008). This list has been designed to assess the quality of performance measures that may be used for motivational or compensation purposes. Previous research has highlighted two additional specifications: Informativeness, which indicates that a measure should be used for motivational purposes only if it provides information to the agent about the dimensions of managerial action that the owner wishes to motivate (Holmstrom, 1979); and sensitivity, which refers to the degree to which the result of a performance measure changes with the agent's actions (Banker and Datar, 1989). These specifications have not been directly reported in this list as they are thought to be embodied in some of the specifications presented. For instance, informativeness encapsulates notions of congruence, controllability, and accuracy (Merchant, 2006). Sensitivity is embodied in the congruence specification.

4. Based on this definition of *nonfinancial measures* it can be understood why Morissette (1996) classifies market share as financial information, contrary to other authors who suggest that this measure is nonfinancial. According to Morissette, market share tends to be measured as organizational total sales divided by total market sales, both of which are monetary metrics.

5. As suggested in previous sections, performance measures are contextual so their beneficial or detrimental effects depend on the context in which they are used and on the characteristics of the person, team, or organization that uses them.

10 MANAGING PAY-FOR-PERFORMANCE SYSTEMS

This chapter further examines the initial ideas of performance-contingent pay policies introduced in Chapter 2. It highlights the main controversies and critically reviews the theoretical background, operations, drawbacks, and key contextual factors that are likely to influence the adoption and success of performance-contingent plans.

Why Performance-Contingent Pay May Be Counterproductive

As noted in earlier chapters, much has been said about the motivational properties of money, and advocates on both sides of the issue are not difficult to find. However, the notion that rewards should be distributed in proportion to contribution may be considered a received doctrine in organizational life (Barrett, 1972; Copeland and Monnet, 2009; Volpp et al. 2009). This refers to concepts and assumptions that are so deeply held that they are not questioned. Dobbins, Cardy, and Carson (1991, p. 256) noted that "If the assumptions are correct, then received doctrines are valuable in that they allow research to proceed, and clear prescriptions for managerial behavior to be formed. The danger, of course, is that the assumptions are not correct, leading to the dual problem of misleading research and misguided management."

In light of this, one should ask the following questions: What are the key assumptions underlying the "pay according to contribution" doctrine? Are these assumptions well founded? In answer to the first question, there are four ingrained premises in most performance-contingent pay systems:

- Individuals and groups differ significantly in their contribution to the organization, not just in terms of what they do but also how well they do it.

- A substantial amount of variance in organizational performance can ultimately be attributed to the performance of individuals and groups within the firm.
- Performance is a construct that can be accurately measured.
- In order to motivate its human resources and to achieve distributive justice, a firm must be able and willing to remunerate employees differentially according to their relative performance.

There is a vast amount of evidence in support of the first assumption (e.g., Lawler, 1989, 1990; Cardy and Dobbins, 1993; Cascio, 1992; Gomez-Mejia, Balkin, and Cardy, 2010; Mondello and Maxey, 2009). Evidence is limited for the second premise, yet it is generally supported (see Chapter 3). The third assumption can be questioned (see Chapter 9). The fourth assumption is highly controversial among academics and practitioners (e.g., Ukko, Karhu, and Pekkola, 2009; Aime, Meyer, and Humphrey, 2009; McDonald and Roland, 2009; Merriman, 2009). The main points of contention are discussed next.

Single-Mindedness

Performance-contingent pay can be such a powerful motivator that it may induce individuals to develop a very narrow focus to accomplish whatever will trigger the reward and neglect other important components or dimensions of the job. In other words, the closer pay is linked to particular performance indicators, the more employees will focus their attention on those reward-producing outcomes (see Chapter 9). Likewise, superiors are tempted to use the convenience of objective performance indicators to justify pay decisions, avoiding "judgment calls" and the unpleasant task of explaining these to subordinates. In a sense, this gets them "off the hook" even if the available objective criteria may be seriously deficient. For instance, Gomez-Mejia and Balkin (1992) and more recently Langbein (2008) found that most department chairpersons and college deans rely exclusively on student ratings to evaluate teaching performance of faculty. Yet, over three-fourths of faculty surveyed agreed that this measure is more a reflection of popularity rather than knowledge gained, classroom performance, or course rigor.

Thus, one of the ironies with the use of pay as an incentive mechanism is that the greater the strength of the outcome–reward connection and the magnitude of the reward, the more design flaws become apparent and the greater the potential harm to the firm (McDonald and Roland, 2009). As shown in Chapter 9, because it is nearly impossible to capture all important elements of a job on any number of performance measures (particularly in the professional and managerial ranks), there is always the danger that those intangible yet crucial aspects of work will suffer. A few examples will illustrate this point.

Several airlines in the late 1980s began to experience deteriorating customer relations and a large number of "no-shows" after their sales representatives were paid based on the number of bookings. In a midwestern state, paying snowplow operators on a per-mile basis resulted in many roads packed with snow and ice, because it was easier to cover more miles (and, therefore, get paid more) by disengaging the snow-removal equipment. In some academic departments, faculty avoid service on university committees "like the plague" because it is made clear that rewards (in terms of pay, promotion, and tenure) will be based strictly on publications in leading journals. As noted in Chapters 7, 8, and 9, top executives are frequently accused of maximizing short-term gains (reflected in such indicators as EPS or ROI) to trigger larger annual bonuses at the expense of long-term performance. And the Wall Street debacle at the start of the twenty-first century has largely been blamed on bonus systems that offered incentives linked to revenue maximization (not only for top executives but also traders, heads of business units, directors of local bank branches, and such) with little in the way of subsequent accountability for bad decisions (Parloff, 2009; Loomis, 2009b).

Control

In most situations, employees do not control all the factors responsible for performance outcomes. Unless tasks are very simple (e.g., picking watermelons during a normal harvest season), a larger portion of performance variance is attributed to external events or contextual factors that individuals cannot directly affect. For instance, probably less than one-fourth of the variance in firm performance can be directly attributed to executive decisions (as noted in Chapter 6). This problem is just as significant at lower levels in the organization.

A vast amount of research (e.g., Deming, 2000; Gabor, 1991; Grey and Kipnis, 1976; Ilgen and Feldman, 1983; Landy and Farr, 1983; Liden and Mitchell, 1983; Merriman, 2009; Scholtes, 1987; Yammarino, Dubinsky, and Hartley, 1987) confirms that the performance of individuals can be greatly affected by the performance of other employees in a work group. For instance, Scholtes (1987, p. 6) notes that employee performance is dependent on "capricious factors well beyond their ability to influence . . . using performance appraisal of any kind as a basis for reward of any kind is a flat-out catastrophic mistake." This suggests that the more pay is linked to performance of individuals whose work tasks are inextricably tied to those of others, the more "contaminated" the performance judgments—and, by implication, the more tenuous the performance-reward connection.

Measurement

Assessing performance is one of the most difficult and intractable problems management faces, particularly when the objective is to use these judgments to dispense rewards (see Chapter 9). In fact, a huge and ever-growing literature in areas such as psychology (e.g., Bernardin and Pence, 1980; Cardy and Dobbins, 1986, 1993; Denisi, Robbins, and Summers, 1997; Dugan, 1989; Goffin et al. 2009; Grey and Kipnis, 1976; Hoffman, Natham, and Holden, 1991; Lord, 1985; Murphy and Cleveland, 1991; Pfeffer, 1997; Soo, Sims, and Motowidlo, 1986; Sturman, Cherami, and Cashen, 2005; Tsui and Ohlot, 1988) and economics (e.g., Baker, Gibbons, and Murphy, 1994; Indjejikian, 1999; Jensen, 2003; Kachelmeier, Reichert, and Williamson, 2008; McNamee, Ternent, Gbanjou, and Newlands, 2009; Prendergast and Topel, 1993; Lambert, 1993; Raith, 2008; Salamon and Smith, 1979) is exclusively devoted to these measurement issues.

Unfortunately, results are conflicting and the primary conclusion one can draw from all this work is that performance measurement is a very treacherous endeavor, with no generally accepted system. Robert Lord (1989, p. 66), a well-known authority in performance appraisal, noted that "accurate behavioral measurement is integral to the practice of applied psychology but it has proven to be an elusive objective." McBriarty (1988, p. 421) adds that "Few areas of personnel management have received more attention than performance appraisal, and few have remained as shrouded in controversy and contradiction. After ingesting even a small portion of the literature on the subject, one typically ends up with an acute case of mental indigestion." Looking at the measurement of organizational performance March and Sutton (1997, p. 705) state that, "Scholarly virtue is more a struggle than an achievement, and seeking knowledge about historically ambiguous phenomena such as organizational performance is more a form of discipline self-flagellation than a pursuit of happiness."

There are too many performance-measurement problems to enumerate here. Chapter 9 highlighted the set of issues associated with the specific metrics used to measure performance. Issues associated with the evaluation of those metrics by superiors or peers are as follows:

- Rating errors, such as leniency, halo, and central tendency (e.g., Gomez-Mejia, 1988a, 1990a; Gomez-Mejia, Balkin, and Cardy, 2010; Palmer and Loveland, 2008)
- Affective predispositions on the part of the evaluator, biasing performance judgments (e.g., Tsui and Barry, 1986; Zajonc, 1980)
- Hedonic tendencies in the evaluation, referring to a natural inclination of superiors to avoid conflict and unpleasant encounters with subordinates by failing to report actual performance differences among them (Soo, Sims, and Motowidlo, 1986)
- Information framing, whereby prior experiences and expectations distort judgments of actual performance (Landy and Farr, 1983; McNamee et al. 2009)
- Ambiguous attributions of causality (Aime et al. 2009; Feldman, 1981; Mitchell and Liden, 1982; Wexley and Youtz, 1985)
- Lack of adequate performance indicators (Meyer and Gupta, 1994; Ukko et al. 2009)
- Low correlations between subjective and objective assessments of performance (Alexander and Wilkins, 1982; Caranikas-Walker et al. 2008)
- For political purposes, manipulation of performance data in an intentional and systematic manner (Cennamo et al. 2009; Longnecker, Sims, and Gioca, 1987; Smith, 1995)
- Failure to take into account systemwide, contextual influences on performance (Chen and Huang, 2009; Dobbins, Cardy, and Carson, 1991; Jansen, Merchant, and Van der Slede, 2009; Gomez-Mejia and Balkin, 1980a, b; Gomez-Mejia, Hopp, and Sommerstad, 1978; Gomez-Mejia and Page, 1983).

Although they tend to be more severe the more "micro" one gets, difficulties in measuring performance are present at all levels of analysis. At the most micro (i.e., employee) level, the problems noted here are magnified because of the complexity of trying to untangle individual contributions from the work group and reliance on immediate supervisors whose judgments are often subject to bias. At the next level of aggregation (i.e., teams) interdependencies across work units present unique difficulties in ascertaining the specific contributions of any given team. At the SBU level, one faces the problem of factoring out resource interdependencies across various units and their relationship to corporate headquarters. Finally, at the most macro, or corporate, level, numerous problems are faced in assessing performance using accounting conventions, abnormal stock return methodology, and imprecise measures, such as customer satisfaction or employee morale (see Chapters 6–9).

Inflexibility

An issue discussed in Chapters 4 and 5 has added significance to performance-contingent systems. It is difficult to change payoff formulas once they have been installed and employees get used to them. Resistance to change in performance-contingent pay systems results from multiple forces, including fear of the unknown, perceived threats to one's interests, skepticism that changes will produce more favorable outcomes, failure anxiety, and existence of powerful coalitions (perhaps even including a labor union) with a vested interest in preserving the status quo.

Cognitive models provide a conceptual explanation as to why pay-for-performance systems become entrenched (Reger, 1991; Power, 2004). First, employees develop cognitive maps of the organization, and a crucial element of this map is the mechanisms used for reward allocation. These mechanisms create a fabric of beliefs about means-to-ends relationships (read behavior-reward connections) that are learned based on past experience. Redrawing these learned, mental representations is difficult, and any attempts to do so may cause intense opposition.

The natural tendency is to do things as they were done in the past, and resistance to change may become a serious threat to strategic thinking in compensation. A particular performance-contingent system may have outlived its strategic value, may have become obsolete, or may even be counterproductive, given new conditions that face a firm. However, inertia and customary forces may keep it in place. For instance, heavy emphasis on sales volume as a performance criterion for executives and sales personnel may make sense for a small, growing organization trying to expand its market share. However, that same emphasis may foster mergers and acquisitions for larger firms, past the point where further growth occurs, at the expense of efficiency, and may lead to a reduction in shareholder's wealth (see Chapter 6).

Governance and Credibility

Perhaps because of the measurement problems discussed earlier, a large proportion of employees do not see performance-contingent pay systems as fair and truly rewarding for contributions (e.g., Wade, O'Reilly, and Pollock, 2006). This proportion can be as high as 75 percent of those working under pay-for-performance plans (Kanter, 1987). Acceptability by those affected is a crucial aspect of success for these programs if they are going to be seen as legitimate (Gomez-Mejia, Page, and Tornow, 1982). While the credibility gap tends to be more acute for individual-based plans, it can also be present with other programs. For instance, if it is much easier for one unit to receive incentive payments than another, intense conflict and resentment are likely to ensue that may lead to disruptions in internal workflows (see Coombs and Gomez-Mejia, 1991). It is not uncommon for such plans to penalize units that have traditionally been better performers because it is more difficult for those units to show the same degree of improvement as their counterparts, which started out at a lower performance threshold.

The Whole Does Not Equal the Sum of the Parts: The Problem of Local Rationality

While linking pay to productivity may be conducive to greater individual and unit performance, it does not necessarily follow that the performance of the entire organization will improve. This is because organizational performance does not result from the simple additive function of the performance of its individual members and units (Meyer and Gupta, 1994). Rather, it derives from a complex, synergistic interrelation of all its component parts. Thus, performance-contingent pay plans may, in fact, improve the performance of a firm's constituent parts yet have dysfunctional consequences for the entire organization.

The reason for this paradox is that each unit is bound by its own local rationality. Thus, linking rewards to the achievement of each unit's objective (and individuals within it) may exacerbate a natural tendency toward parochialism and a disregard for superordinate goals and organizational interdependence. This is an important issue at all organizational levels, but the lower the unit of performance analysis, the more significant the problem of local rationality becomes.

For individuals, there is the danger of becoming so focused on "What is in it for me?" and personal goals that cooperation with others may suffer. One often finds this situation in academic departments. The emphasis on research to distribute rewards (i.e., pay, promotion, tenure) fosters a disdain of committee activities that are an integral part of university governance. It may also neglect students who, ultimately, are primary customers of these institutions.

At the team level, each group may become so cohesive and enthusiastic about its own sphere that it gives rise to dysfunctional rivalries and intergroup battles over real or imaginary conflict of interest issues. One of the authors was able to observe this process in a large organization whose personnel department was evaluated (and rewarded) according to the number of affirmative action hires. This created much conflict with line managers who felt that the personnel department was encroaching on their hiring discretion and who argued that they were being penalized for the amount of time required to train new recruits. Another example is that of the classical conflict between marketing groups (rewards based on sales) and manufacturing (rewards based on production schedules and cost control) (see, for example, St. John and Rue, 1991). At the business unit level, linking of rewards to SBU performance may produce a situation in which flow of resources and knowledge is impeded because each unit is eagerly trying to accomplish its own agenda.

In short, an inherent danger with performance-contingent pay systems is that they may act as a centrifugal force in organizations and pull each segment away from the common good. While aggregate incentive systems are less susceptible to this problem (because performance is assessed at a higher unit of analysis, such as plant or corporate level), they are at a disadvantage because the line of sight between behavior and reward is very weak.

Line of Sight

At the opposite end of the local rationality problem, rewards become more powerful in energizing behavior the lower the unit of analysis used to measure performance. This is because employees can see how their efforts translate into reward-producing outcomes. Thus, one faces the proverbial horns of the dilemma in trying to emphasize behavior-contingent rewards (which magnify the problem of local rationality) vis-à-vis aggregate performance-contingent programs (which block the line of sight between individual contributions and rewards).

Tradeoffs Between Employee Performance and Satisfaction

Another irony of performance-contingent pay systems is that "they may lead to greater productivity but lower satisfaction" (Schwab, 1974, 197). In his classical work, White (1949) noted that incentive systems frequently disrupt the social fabric in organizations and lead to employee unhappiness. They also produce unwelcome tension in the workforce. Recent research has shown that highly self-efficacious individuals are more likely to perceive a stronger link between pay and performance, but they are also more likely to perceive pay inequity and low pay satisfaction (Kim, Mone, and Kim, 2008; Lemieux, MacLeod, and Parent, 2007). This finding is interesting in that it questions previous beliefs that high achievers are more satisfied when their reward system is contingent on performance (e.g., Rynes, Gerhart, and Parks, 2005).

Translating Performance Expectations from Stakeholder Groups

In classical and neoclassical economic theories, the goal of the firm is to maximize profits. More recent conceptualizations portray top managers as catalysts responsible for translating the often conflicting demands of stakeholder groups into organizational goals and the implementation of complex mechanisms to handle these multiple demands.

When the task environment is less ambiguous and the demands of stakeholder groups are well-defined, relatively stable, and compatible, performance-contingent plans are easier to design and install. For instance, in a closely held corporation whose owners are interested in fast growth, the manager's task is simplified by linking rewards to activities that promote further growth. But if a firm faces stakeholders whose demands are vague, inconsistent over time, and perhaps incompatible with each other, administrators will have a difficult time translating those demands into performance objectives to be used as basis for reward distribution.

Such is the case, for instance, in public sector jurisdictions, universities, and many large corporations that are the target of multiple pressure groups who exert substantial influence. These often operate at crosscurrents. For example, a Fortune 500 firm must often balance the demands of shareholders pressing for more dividends, community leaders interested in preserving jobs, environmental groups advocating ecological concerns, and so on. Universities are often confronted with a classical conflict of satisfying the academic community's interest in research and the need of local citizens who demand better quality instruction in the form of extensive student-faculty interaction and smaller classes.

Reactance

According to agency theory (as discussed in Chapter 4), incentive systems play an integral control function in organizations, particularly when direct supervision (monitoring) is difficult. This feature of incentive systems, however, may be associated with employees' resentment for losing control over their lives. In other words, employees may feel that the incentive system takes away their freedom of action.

Brehn and Cole (1966) refer to this perceived threat to personal autonomy as reactance, which provokes anger at the organization. One consequence may be an increase in dissatisfaction leading to turnover and concerted actions among employees. A more subtle consequence is that employees may be socialized to do whatever it takes to obtain the reward and no more. This may be dysfunctional in that (as noted earlier) important yet intangible aspects of work may not be accomplished, and expectations about the reward system may become too rigid to change.

Reduction of Intrinsic Drives

Financial incentives may become so potent that an individual's intrinsic drives are dominated by extrinsic demands. Expanding upon earlier theories by Likert (1961), White (1959), De Charms (1968), Argyris (1957), McGregor (1960), Maslow (1970), and other organizational humanists, Deci (1975) argues that, first, the most effective form of motivation is that which individuals derive from the job itself and the satisfaction felt for doing a job well, and, second, performance-contingent pay is done at the expense of that natural drive to self-actualize. In Deci's own words:

> When behavior is intrinsically motivated, the perceived locus of causality is said to be internal. This simply means that people perceive the cause of a certain behavior to be their own intrinsic need. When they perceive the cause of the behavior to be intrinsic, they will engage in the activity for intrinsic rewards. However, when they receive extrinsic rewards, their perceived focus of causality becomes external and they do the behaviors only if they believe that the extrinsic rewards will be forthcoming (1975, p. 140).

This type of indictment against the use of pay to direct human behavior has been around in one form or another since the beginning of recorded history (e.g., Plato's Republic). Yet it continues to have a profound effect on organizational development, organizational behavior, and human resource management. While this position has more currency among academics, it also has its adherents among practitioners and consultants. Its policy implication is: Performance-contingent pay may be pushed to the point where individuals lose all interest in exploration, innovation, search for challenges, and enjoyment of work activities outside those prescribed by the incentive system.

Navigating Treacherous "Pay-for-Performance" Waters

The problems discussed here indicate that performance-contingent pay policies may be treacherous, and that the deliberate use of pay as a mechanism to channel individual and group behaviors can inadvertently produce the opposite results of what was intended. The central thesis of this chapter is that performance-contingent pay policies are an indispensable management tool for enhancing organizational performance. However, three important conditions must be met for the success of those policies: a loose relationship between pay and performance, nurturing the belief that performance makes a difference, and the customization of performance-contingent pay systems.

Pay and Performance Must Be Loosely Coupled

There are very few situations in which a tight fit between performance and rewards is justified. The tighter the coupling, the more likely the problems discussed here will be magnified. As performance yardsticks are explicitly identified—and these are used to distribute rewards—single-mindedness and local rationality are reinforced; measurement difficulties are compounded (because unrealistic precision may be required); inflexibility is institutionalized; equity issues mushroom due to logistical problems in developing formulas fair to diverse groups; and individuals are encouraged to avoid activities with intangible benefits but excluded from the performance contract.

Therefore, attempts to use performance-contingent pay in a purely mechanistic fashion are almost certainly doomed to failure. Unfortunately, particularly at the aggregate level, administrators may feel pressured to come up with formula-based approaches. Management must resist the temptation to succumb to those pressures, which at times appear to be the most rational thing to do, yet eventually lead to problems after expectations are cemented and programs are difficult to change. As will be seen later, this is one of the main maladies affecting gain-sharing and profit-sharing plans.

It Is Necessary to Nurture the Belief That Performance Makes a Difference

While survey after survey shows that few employees believe pay and performance are closely linked, almost everyone thinks they should be (Hills et al. 1987; Rynes, Gerhart, and Parks, 2005). Any attempt to systematically institutionalize a non-performance-based pay system for fear of the problems discussed earlier will be almost certain to produce even lower performance levels. In other words, support for the null hypothesis that performance-contingent pay policies seldom work as intended does not imply support for the alternate hypothesis that performance should not be an integral part of pay decisions. Thus, in spite of theoretical and operational problems with performance-contingent pay systems, they may be the lesser evil.

Linking pay to other criteria (e.g., seniority, test scores) removes its normative, symbolic effect on individuals, creating a low-achievement organizational culture that dampens overall productivity and encourages the best performers to move elsewhere. As an analogy, evidence of inequality is not difficult to find in American society. Yet, if the "all men are created equal" myth were not deeply held as a fundamental value, social and racial inequalities would almost certainly be greater. Likewise, many surveys have suggested that marital infidelity is rampant (up to 75 percent by some accounts), but if marital commitment was to be widely viewed as an anachronism, family life is likely to suffer even more. As a third example, even though a small proportion of major crimes are solved, dismantling the criminal justice system is almost certain to increase the crime rate because all potential deterrence is eliminated. The above examples make the point that, as in society at large, there may be a wide gulf between actual values held and observed practices within a firm. However, the normative force of those values can still maintain the system within more acceptable parameters than would otherwise be the case. Thus, the fact that a strong performance-reward norm exists in a firm is likely to enhance performance, if for no other reason than the fact that performance would be lower in the absence of such norms.

Unfortunately, very limited empirical research has been conducted to date on the myth-forming function of performance-contingent pay in organizations. Most investigators focus on technical issues, such as how performance should be measured (most notably individual appraisals) and procedures for linking those measures to rewards. They ignore its normative aspects.

Performance-Contingent Pay Systems Must Be Customized to Each Firm's Unique Situation

Following one of the major conceptual thrusts of this book, the design and mix of performance-based pay programs should vary according to contingency factors internal and external to the firm. As will be seen shortly, there is an extensive menu of pay-for-performance systems, and each of them is more likely to be successful in some conditions than others. For instance, a tighter coupling between pay and specific behavioral outcomes (e.g., piece-rate system) is more likely to produce favorable results in more mechanistic organizations whose technology is relatively unchanging and mature defender-type firms in relatively stable environments. The opposite would be true in organic-type firms with a prospector strategy, because performance criteria and factors impacting that performance are more volatile in nature. In other words, a tight bond between performance outcomes and rewards is difficult to justify in most cases. However, in a relative sense, a closer fit between the two makes more sense at the mechanistic, defender end of the spectrum.

In summary, the relative contributions of a performance-contingent pay system to firm performance are likely to increase as the plan features are molded to internal and external idiosyncrasies facing the organization. A common practice in many companies is to have a set of different performance-contingent plans and to design each of them as a unique and separate program (Abernathy, 1999). Such programs can be classified into three major types, according to their level of performance analysis: individual plans, team-based programs, and organization-wide programs. The theoretical justification for each of these operational systems, potential drawbacks, and conditions under which they are most likely to contribute to firm performance is discussed next.

Rewarding Individual Performance

Programs that reward individual performance are designed to provide monetary rewards to individual employees and require identification of their personal contributions. The theoretical bases for these programs are well developed in the psychological literature, and most compensation texts devote a substantial amount of attention to them.

Theoretical Framework

The following is a brief description of the three major theories underlying individual-based plans. These are equity, expectancy, and goal theory.

Equity Theory

As noted in Chapter 1, equity theory has played a predominant role in traditional compensation theory and practice. To review, its basic tenet is that an individual's motivation is affected by how he or she perceives the ratio of inputs (i.e., work performance) to outcomes (i.e., rewards) relative to referent others. Consequently, from a motivational perspective, the organization must provide rewards that are proportionate to individual inputs. Because work performance is the most important contribution to the organization, it then follows that pay should be distributed accordingly. If inequities are perceived, then one would predict that high performers will either leave the organization (because of dissatisfaction brought about from "cognitive dissonance") or reduce their performance level to make it congruent with the outcomes received (see Adams, 1965).

Expectancy Theory

Expectancy theory is rooted in the "law of effect" (Thorndike, 1910), which states that behaviors that are rewarded will be repeated. Also, Tolman (1932) and Lewin (1938) argue that individuals develop cognitive anticipations about the outcomes associated with various activities and assign a subjective (negative or positive) value to those consequences. An individual's motivation to engage in a particular act results from some combination of these sets of variables. All other things equal, the higher the expectancy for a particular outcome by engaging in certain behaviors and the more valuable the outcome is to the individual, the more likely the employee will be motivated to act accordingly.

More recent interpretations of expectancy theory were articulated in the 1960s and early 1970s in the writings of Vroom (1964), Porter and Lawler (1968), Lawler (1971), Mitchell and Biglan (1971), and Dachler and Mobley (1973). Its specific application to pay-for-performance systems is as follows: If we are to assume that money is an important reward (i.e., it has high "valence") for most people, then in conditions under which there is a high performance-outcome contingency, one would expect individual behaviors conducive to better performance. In the words of Schwab and Dyer (1973):

> With respect to compensation systems, expectancy theory hypothesizes that the effectiveness of such systems in motivating employee performance is simultaneously dependent upon the valence of pay, the instrumentality of performance for the attainment of pay, and expectancies about the relationship between effort and performance.

Thus, from a practical perspective, this means that in order to motivate employees to increase their level of effort or change their behavior in a desired direction (e.g., pay more attention to detail), it is necessary to link pay to those consequences (Lawler, 1971). By repeated association, as predicted by the law of effect (Thorndike, 1910), employees will learn to pair desired behaviors with valued rewards, and this anticipation (expectancy) will evoke more of this behavior in the future.

Goal Theory

The central postulate of goal theory is quite simple, and good managers have probably followed it since the beginning of time: Financial incentives will not have much of an effect on performance unless individuals have a clear sense of what is expected of them (Locke and Latham, 1990; Locke, 1968, 2004; Locke, Bryan, and Kendall, 1968; Tolman, 1932). In other words, an individual's behavior is goal-directed, and people's devotion to certain activities depends on the degree to which achievement of goals resulting from those activities produces desired outcomes. Therefore, an individual's performance is expected to improve if clear standards and objectives are established and pay is made contingent on these being met.

Operational Plans

The two primary performance-contingent pay programs at the individual level consist of merit pay (see Cook, 1999; Gerhart and Milkovich, 1993; Heneman, 1990) and bonuses (see Wallace, 1990, 1991). Despite all the bad publicity over the years (e.g., Kohn, 1993; Pearce, 1987; Pfeffer and Sutton, 2006; Pfeffer, 1998), the use of both merit and bonus pay is almost universal (Gomez-Mejia and Sanchez-Marin, 2006). Merit pay consists of an adjustment to base salary, as a percentage increase, typically done on an annual review cycle. Once dispensed, it becomes an annuity because it remains as part of the employee's salary, regardless of future performance, for the rest of his or her tenure with the firm. Bonus programs (sometimes called short-term incentive plans or lump-sum bonuses), on the other hand, provide a financial incentive on a "one-at-a-time" basis and do not raise the employee's base pay in perpetuity.

For either merit pay or bonuses, the decision criteria may include a form of goal-setting plan (such as management by objectives or a balanced score-card), supervisory appraisals, or achievement of certain milestones (most often used for bonuses, such as devising a new method to cut down on production costs).

It should be noted in passing that the most extreme form of performance-contingent individual-based pay program is the traditional piece-rate incentive system, whereby employees are paid per unit of output. However, this approach has been steadily falling into disfavor since the early 1950s, and relatively few firms in the manufacturing sector rely on it for hourly workers. Besides the difficulty of establishing production standards, particularly when technology is rapidly changing, Sherman and Bohlander (1992, 351) blame the demise of piecework on the fact that:

> Employees, especially those belonging to unions, have held negative attitudes toward piecework plans. Some union leaders have feared that management will use piecework or similar systems to try to speed up production, getting

more work from employees for the same amount of money. Another fear is that the system may induce employees to compete against one another, thereby taking jobs away from workers who are shown to be less productive. There is also the belief that the system will cause some employees to lose their jobs as productivity increases or cause craft standards of workmanship to suffer.

Drawbacks

While each of the operational programs to reward individual performance has pros and cons (see Lawler, 1989, 1990; Milkovich and Newman, 2005), many of the pitfalls in performance-contingent plans reviewed earlier are exacerbated when an individual's pay and behavior are explicitly linked (see Chapter 9). These individual plans promote a narrow focus among employees. It is difficult to untangle an individual's contribution from that of the work group, and measurement difficulties in performance appraisal are rather intractable. There is also a lack of consensus about methodology, and equity issues become paramount as more sophistication is required of the system in making fine distinctions across individuals. In addition, there are some potential problems that are more unique to individual-based plans. These include:

Credibility Gap. Survey after survey indicates that a large number of employees (as high as 80 percent, according to Hills et al. 1987) do not see a connection between individual rewards and actual performance. This perception may be well grounded in reality. Many nonperformance factors enter into these decisions (see Mount, 1987; Schwab and Olson, 1988; Albanesi and Olivetti, 2009), such as position in the salary range, time since last increase, pay relationships within the unit or between units, and supervisor-subordinate pay relationships.

Erratic Patterns over Time. Relative pay raises for individuals occupying the same position are often uncorrelated from one year to the next (Haire, Ghiselli, and Gordon, 1967; Pearce, Stevenson, and Perry, 1985). This means one of two things: Either employee performance is very unstable, which is hard to fathom, or that raises are not attributed to performance but reflect other variable criteria.

Budgetary Determinants. Budgetary restrictions often determine how much and the extent to which pay raises will be distributed, and these restrictions may not be synchronized with achievements during the review period.

Hierarchical Orientation. Because individual-based pay-for-performance systems engender dependence on supervisors, "they accept, indeed, build on and preserve the status and category distinctions already defined by the organization" (Kanter, 1987, p. 14).

Easy-to-achieve Goals. Whenever management by objectives or, as is the more recent trend, scorecard-type systems are utilized, most people achieve their objectives. Thus, it is difficult to compare actual value of contributions across different individuals (McConkie, 1979). The explicit tying of money to goal achievement is likely to make this problem more severe because there is an incentive to "play it safe" and choose more modest goals than may otherwise be the case.

Social Disruption. Many managers believe that below-average raises are demoralizing to the individual, aggravate interpersonal relationships, and discourage better performance (Hughes, 1986).

Balancing Self-interest and Common Goals. Some organizations may attempt to counterbalance the negative "zero sum" effects of merit pay by including factors such as teamwork and cooperation in performance appraisal systems that are the bases for merit pay decisions. While it is plausible for individual-based pay increases to reward cooperative behaviors, this may be difficult to implement. It is a nearly universal practice to allocate a raise budget partitioned among a small group of employees (Lawler, 1989). Since individuals must share a fixed amount of money that has been allocated for raises or bonuses, "this clearly sets up a competition among them for the larger raises. This can be a serious problem if the organization needs them to cooperate in order to be effective" (Lawler, 1989, p. 217).

Conditions Favoring Individual-Based Performance-Contingent Plans

While the potential drawbacks of individual-based plans reviewed here may be serious, the authors do not mean to imply that firms should abandon these programs. Rewards based on individual contributions can be highly motivating. However, they should only be emphasized when conditions exist that minimize the pitfalls discussed earlier. Individual-based performance-contingent pay policies are most likely to be successful under the following circumstances:

- When the nature of the task allows for the isolation of contributions made by specific employees. While there are very few cases in which unambiguous performance attributions can be made, it is easier to do so in some jobs than in others (Paola and Scoppa, 2009; Griffith and Neely, 2009). For example, it is much easier to assess the quality and quantity of the work of data entry operators than it would be for scientists or engineers in R&D labs.

- When a greater the degree of autonomy is enjoyed by incumbents. The more independent the work being performed, the more meaningful are measures of individual contributions. At one extreme, for example, field sales representatives operate in almost total isolation from each other. Thus, individual performance (typically measured in terms of sales volume) can be assessed on a one-to-one basis. At the other extreme, brainstorming or "focus groups" in advertising are composed of individuals whose tasks (i.e., to generate ideas for marketing products) are very intertwined (because ideas are freely bounced around within such groups). Therefore, trying to ascertain the value of individual contributions within the group may be quite difficult and probably indefensible.

- When close cooperation is not required for successful performance, or when competition is desired. While one is hard-pressed to think of a work situation in which no cooperation is needed, a wide range does exist across various jobs. For instance, the degree of cooperation required for successful performance as a professor is much lower than, for example, a pilot in an air force squadron.

- When the organizational culture emphasizes individual achievement. Organizations vary widely in terms of status differentials, structure, and norms of behavior. For instance, the emphasis on group cohesiveness and a paternalistic attitude in many Japanese firms is well documented, and this is reflected in the reward system (where pay for individual performance is generally a foreign concept; see Gomez-Mejia and Welbourne, 1991). Using the congruency argument (see Chapter 3), it seems reasonable to expect that an individual-based performance-contingent program would operate more smoothly and is more likely to contribute to a firm's performance if it is part of a culture that emphasizes personal achievement.

Rewarding Team Performance

Team-based performance-contingent pay plans reward the relative contribution to the firm by groups of employees who have common goals and objectives, work closely with each other, and are dependent on each other for the team's outcome.

Theoretical Framework

Two separate theoretical streams are used to justify these programs.

Psychometric Theory

A large volume of work dealing with rating properties of supervisory appraisals suggests that while performance is commonly specified in individual terms, actual performance can be more accurately assessed by examining the performance of larger units within the firm (Landy and Farr, 1983; Yammarino, Dubinsky, and Hartley, 1987; Welbourne and Gomez-Mejia, 2008). Ilgen and Feldman (1983), Dobbins, Cardy, and Carson (1991), and others have convincingly argued that making comparative judgments is such an innate human predisposition that it is virtually impossible for a supervisor to evaluate an employee's performance without being influenced by the performance of other employees in the group. Likewise, Liden and Mitchell (1983) report that the degree of interdependence within most work groups is so high that it is difficult to filter individual contributions. More disturbingly, these investigators found that as interdependence increases, supervisors rate poor performers higher and good performers lower. Thus, from a measurement perspective, this literature suggests that in most work situations performance can be measured more accurately or reliably at the group level.

Theories of Social Cohesiveness

Research based on social cohesiveness has its roots in social psychology. Because most tasks are conducted by groups of complementary workers with diverse skills and backgrounds, teamwork and cooperation are necessary conditions to high performance outcomes in various organizational subunits. Whenever the goals of separate employees are bound together so that an individual can attain his or her goals if, and only if, other participants can attain their goals, a cooperative social situation exists (Deutsch, 1949). Therefore, a reward system will enhance performance only if it produces a situation in which there is a positive correlation among the goal attainment of group members. Thus, each participant seeks an outcome that is beneficial to all those with whom he or she is cooperatively linked.

In related theoretical work derived from learning theory, Kelly and Thibault (1969) define a cooperative structure as one in which the individual's rewards are directly proportional to the quality of the work group. For Kelly and Thibault, reward contingencies motivate group members to behave as a team or as individuals competing with each other. By utilizing rewards that reinforce cooperation among team members, the performance of a given group (and, implicitly, firm performance by aggregating across various groups) will increase. On the other hand, by focusing on individual outcomes, rather than group results, a reward system may undermine the social foundations needed to succeed in a cooperative setting.

Operational Plans

Team incentives are mainly based on performance metrics assessed at team level. In this type of schemes all team members receive a reward pegged to group outcomes (either financial or nonfinancial, as Chapter 9 suggests). These outcomes may be assessed objectively (e.g., based on cost savings, number of products manufactured, meeting agreed-upon deadlines, rejects, completion of a new product design, obtaining a successful patent, etc.) or subjectively (e.g., based on the collective assessment of a panel of executives) (see Chapter 9). The goals, measurement criteria, and payment amount can be determined in advance and communicated to group members, or management may retain the flexibility to make those decisions on an ad hoc basis. Payments can be made in cash, corporate stocks, or through noncash items such as trips, vacation time, or luxury items (Welbourne and Gomez-Mejia, 2008). Cooperation with other teams might also be an important criterion for payment. Being able to work effectively in problem-solving assignments might also be used. Typically, groups chosen as the unit of analysis to distribute rewards are self-contained and have relatively impermeable boundaries between them. That is, intragroup interdependencies are much greater than intergroup interdependencies.

Drawbacks

While team-based incentives do have some advantages over individual-based performance-contingent plans (primarily in terms of fewer measurement problems and the fostering of cooperative behaviors), they also have their pitfalls.

Free-Riding Effect

A substantial body of literature is concerned with the so-called free-riding effect (see review by Albanese and VanFleet, 1985). This refers to the benefits from the group effort accruing to individuals who provide low work inputs to the team yet receive the same rewards as other group members. If no controls are available, free riders are likely to have a negative influence on group productivity. It can also generate intragroup conflict, requiring supervisors to devote much energy to handling interpersonal conflicts.

Reduction in Performance Variance

Social pressures may inhibit the performance of top producers (i.e., rate busters) and/or induce them to leave. On the other hand, these same group pressures may spur the average or marginal performer to become more productive, which compensates the organization for the loss of a few superstars. Also, because the entire team is better off, the productivity of its best performers is increased, and group dynamics may actually encourage those individuals to maximize their potential. It is not always predictable which of these scenarios will actually materialize. It depends on the nature of the group, the quality of employee-management relations, and historical factors. For instance, workers are more inclined to limit output in firms with a history of "speedups" (increasing standards required to obtain reward) and layoffs (Gordon, Edwards, and Reich, 1982). "Group think" may be such that fear of terminations as a result of greater output and falling demand would induce cohesive teams to damp productivity.

Incompatible Cultural Values

Although the concept of team-based incentives is growing in popularity in places such as the United States or the United Kingdom, they are still foreign to the larger cultural milieu in which most employees have been raised. Hofstede (1980) reports that, based on a sample of 16,000 workers worldwide, the United States ranks number one in individualism. This means that an employee's ability to demonstrate personal deservingness to others is important, as evidenced by the accumulation of rewards such as salary, company car, job title, number of subordinates, and other perquisites found in traditional compensation systems. As team concepts are employed, one must ask how the mentality of individualism, which is typical of the American worker, affects the success of these plans (Gomez-Mejia and Welbourne, 1991; Welbourne and Gomez-Mejia, 2008).

Diluted Contributions

Somewhat related to the previous point and the free-rider effect, individual contributions may be "lost" in a team setting, particularly in larger groups. This may put the supervisor in the difficult position of trying to "fish out" who is not carrying his or her weight. Supervisors may be reluctantly thrown in this situation by pressures from different members (or factions) within the group.

Intragroup Allocations

Group rewards may be provided equally to all team members, or an attempt may be made to distribute the gains differentially based on individual input. If the latter approach is to be chosen, the firm must develop a mechanism to identify individual contributions to team goals. In order to avoid the pitfalls associated with measuring individual performance (as discussed earlier in the chapter), team members may rate each other's performance and the group's consensus can be relied on to distribute rewards. This peer-rating procedure, however, introduces the added political problem of distinguishing between true performance and a popularity contest. In either case, any attempts to identify individual contributors will infuse an element of competition into the team concept, and it could easily evolve into simply just one more method of distributing merit pay or individual incentives.

Organizational Interdependence

Identifying groups whose work is relatively orthogonal from each other is not always easy (Merriman, 2009). A poor job of carving out the various groups to be used as the unit of performance analysis may result in a number of serious problems. First and foremost, if the boundaries separating the chosen groups are permeable, then one is back to the difficult problem of distinguishing who contributed what. Second, one may inadvertently create a situation in which groups that should be cooperating with each other (e.g., marketing and production teams) begin to compete instead, which results in a deterioration of overall performance (e.g., sales commitments outstripping a firm's capacity to meet demands on schedule). Third, expanding the size of the group for performance measurement purposes (to minimize intergroup rivalries or to account for interdependencies) may produce a situation in which the line of sight between individual contributions and the aggregate performance measure may become completely blurred.

Contingencies Favoring Group-Based Incentives

While it may not be possible to avoid the pitfalls discussed here, the effectiveness of group-based incentives is likely to be greater under the following conditions:

- When it would be arbitrary and difficult to identify individual contributors given the nature of the tasks at hand. Such would be the case, for example, among teams of scientists and engineers working on common projects where isolation of individual contributions is likely to produce unrealistic distinctions among employees (Gomez-Mejia and Balkin, 1989). This explains in part why in the hard sciences, published papers by faculty (which are used as the primary criteria for reward distribution in most research universities) often have a large number of coauthors (frequently with 10 or more names on a paper).
- When the organizational structure is conducive to group-based incentives. For firms operating under classical structures based on the concept of unitary authority, individual-based performance-contingent schemes make the most sense. For firms that discourage hierarchical relationships and promote matrix networks, a group-based, performance-contingent system is appropriate. Unless employees see multiple managers in a matrix organization as having equal control over rewards, there will be a natural tendency for them to heed the desires of one manager to the neglect of the other, particularly in conflict situations. How individuals (particularly professionals) perceive the distribution of influence between managers on financial rewards may invalidate the matrix organization, despite any paper claims to the contrary (Katz and Allen, 1985). In other words, if those involved view a particular manager as having more power over chances for salary increases, the employee's behaviors and priorities are more likely to be influenced and directed solely by the side with most control, thereby undermining the matrix network.
- When the nature of the technology and workflows in the organization allow for the identification of distinct groups that are relatively independent of one another. For example, self-contained work crews in a paper mill can be identified much more readily than would be the case of independent teams in a large-batch manufacturing operation. As the technology and workflows become more intertwined, a higher level of aggregation may be necessary to distribute rewards (such as profit sharing and gain sharing, to be discussed shortly).
- Whenever one wishes to capitalize on the cooperative structure of work, assuming that such an arrangement will make a greater contribution to firm performance. In other words, when making individual rewards directly proportional to the performance of the work group will increase the productivity of the entire group. Such would be the case again in an

R&D operation. Where the work itself is highly independent, however, team-based rewards are almost certainly doomed to failure. For instance, the authors are familiar with a university where the merit adjustments of faculty are prorated based on the productivity of each department (using a formula that incorporates publication counts, teaching ratings, and grants generated by the entire department). The highest-rated department may receive a merit allocation three to four times greater than that of the lowest-rated department. This system resulted in a lot of complaints from individual faculty (particularly the high producers in low-scoring departments) because they felt that the amount of research and number of grants of each faculty member was due primarily to the contributions of this individual and not to cooperative efforts of all faculty members in each department.

- Whenever there is a need to align the interests of multiple individuals to a common goal. For instance, scientists and engineers have their own research agendas and professional objectives. These are not necessarily consistent with those of the firm or perhaps even those of other colleagues working on similar projects. Team-based incentives may be set up to induce employees to adopt group goals for themselves by making rewards contingent on the achievement of such goals. Austin and Bobko (1985) argue that group goals serve a socializing role in that team members have a natural tendency to personalize group goals over time. A large body of research suggests that goal setting tends to enhance task performance (Locke et al., 1981; Locke, 2004) While most studies have focused on personal goal setting and individual performance, there is limited evidence available to support the notion that group goal setting improves team performance (a) if goals are accepted by group members; and (b) attainable, yet challenging goals are established (Forward and Zander, 1971; Gowen, 1985).
- Whenever flexibility is desired. Team-based incentives offer great flexibility in timing the reward close to actual task accomplishment, or in making rewards contingent on specific targets or goals. Both timing and reward contingencies are important determinants of the reinforcement value of financial incentives (Nadler, Hackman, and Lawler, 1979; Opsahl and Dunnette, 1966). For instance, a group bonus for engineers can be timed to occur immediately after a new product leaves R&D and goes into production in accordance with the planned timetable. Merit pay policies generally do not offer this timing flexibility because of the budgetary review cycle. This flexibility would be most valuable to organic and prospector-type firms and may actually clash with the

control and normative structure of mechanistic and defender type firms (see Chapter 3).

- Whenever the organization desires to foster entrepreneurship. Because of their greater flexibility, as noted above, team-based incentive programs may be designed to engender an entrepreneurial spirit at the group level within the firm. The kinds of risks that an employee group faces on the magnitude of the financial incentive can be made to resemble the risks that entrepreneurs face. In this manner, by creating an entrepreneurial environment, team-based incentive systems would force each group to share the risks of success or failure with the firm and its owners. Further, employees as part of a team may be more willing to bear risks (and potential failure) than they would as individuals. Since these incentives are not a part of base salary, the organization has greater flexibility and can be more generous with the magnitude of the reward without having to fear inability to pay in future pay periods. However, these features (as discussed in Chapter 3) are more attuned to the basic nature of organic and prospector-type firms and would be foreign to more mechanistic or defender-type firms.

- Whenever potential free-riding problems are less likely to occur because the task at hand is difficult or unique and the employees are professionals who are intrinsically motivated. Individuals working on complex tasks and who have invested a lot of time to attain a given occupational status are more likely to be internally driven and be proud of their work. They are not likely to shirk off responsibility at the expense of the group (Gomez-Mejia and Mussio, 1975; Harkins and Petty, 1982). Social-control mechanisms can help ensure that free-riding problems are minimized when recruitment is highly selective (Harmon, 1965); individuals undergo intensive training (Ben-David, 1971); there are strong professional norms and extensive socialization (Gomez-Mejia, 1983; Gomez-Mejia, Trevino, and Mixon, 2009; Hagstrom, 1965, 1968, 1971, 1974); and individuals derive satisfaction from completing creative work (Guston, 1973).

Rewarding Organizational Performance

This section examines the pay policies that are most typically used for linking pay to either corporate or business unit level performance. There are at least three types of organization-based performance-contingent pay policies. Firms may adopt (1) an efficiency-based plan, commonly known as gain-sharing plan, (2) a profit-sharing plan, or (3) a multicriteria performance-based plan.

Efficiency-Based Pay Policies

Efficiency-based aggregate performance-contingent pay policies, most commonly associated with gain-sharing plans, yield lump-sum awards based on unitwide results, typically at the SBU level (Gomez-Mejia, Welbourne, and Wiseman, 2000). Unlike firm performance-based plans, the key indicator used to distribute awards consists of labor cost (or materials cost) savings, instead of profits. The theoretical underpinnings behind most of these plans are articulated in a variety of academic writings under the umbrella of participative management theory.

Theoretical Framework

Intellectual justification for these programs can be traced to the work of McGregor (1960), who, along with authors such as Kurt Lewis, Frederick Herzberg, and Chris Argyris, posited a distinction between traditional autocratic approaches to management, referred to as "Theory X," from more humanistic (and presumably superior) approaches, referred to as "Theory Y." In the latter theory employees are viewed as part of a team, intrinsically motivated, willing to learn, and eager to use their intellectual capacity. In fact, McGregor was an intimate collaborator of Joseph Scanlon, founder of the well-known gain-sharing program that carries his name. The basic philosophy is that intergroup competition within a firm should be avoided so that the entire organization functions as a unified entity, that workers have the ability and willingness to contribute good ideas, and that any gains resulting from worker inputs should be shared.

Closely related to Theory Y, the so-called participative management movement also provided intellectual impetus to employee involvement programs that emphasize egalitarian, democratic ideals at work. From this perspective, gain sharing is not viewed as simply another incentive plan or as a management tool to improve the efficiency of operations, but as the right way to treat people. According to Kanter (1987, 15), "[Gainsharing] is seen as returning to the employee much of the control and income enhancement opportunities that began to decline with the advent of scientific management and modern managerialism."

In their classical book *The Social Psychology of Organizations,* Katz and Kahn (1978) refer to the Scanlon plan as the "boldest attempt" at democratic governance of the industrial sector in the United States. Scanlon's successor as "plan installer," and his close friend in industry and at Massachusetts Institute of Technology, Frederick Lesieur, remarked that "even though the measurement [to distribute rewards] is important, it is not nearly as important as the participation part of the Scanlon plan. If you don't get participation, I don't care what measurement you have or how good it is, it just won't move" (1959, p. 41).

Most gain-sharing programs, particularly the Scanlon Plan, are based on the following premises, which are derived from Theory Y and participative management notions:

- Maximum contribution to organization performance through worker participation can best be achieved by focusing on the SBU as the unit of analysis for efficiency measures and linking rewards to those aggregate measures.
- Because active participation will lead to better utilization of employees' talents, efficiency of operations will improve by creating a complex system of committees and steering groups, involving most employees in generating ideas, deciding which ones to carry out, and actually implementing those suggestions.
- Distributive justice will contribute to further increments in productivity by divvying up accrued gains attributed to employee inputs between labor (workers) and capital (firm owners or stockholders). Management will also benefit if the executive pay program rewards them for increased efficiency of operations.
- Democratic processes are followed through secret ballots used for plan adoption, committee selection, and procedural issues (e.g., when and how payoff formula may be changed).
- Intensive training, education, and socialization of the workforce increase their level of knowledge and commitment to the employee-involvement programs.

Operational Programs

It is difficult to estimate the number of employees covered by gain-sharing plans but it is likely to be smaller than the number of employees covered by profit sharing, and much smaller than the number of employees working under individual-based performance-contingent pay plans. The most common types of gain-sharing programs are Scanlon, Rucker, and Improshare—in that order. Because of the complexity of each of these plans, only their key features are highlighted here. Readers interested in more detail may wish to refer to several excellent hands-on descriptions of these plans (see Doyle, 1983; Fuehrer, 1991; Geare, 1976; Mericle and Kim, 2004; Miller and Schuster, 1987; Milkovich and Newman, 2009; Moore and Ross, 1990; Roomkin, 1990; Ross and Ross, 1999).

Scanlon Plan

The Scanlon Plan is the most elaborate in terms of employee involvement. It has a dual committee structure designed to provide a system of checks and balances.

First, a production committee (composed of three to five rank-and-file employees elected by their peers and an approximately equal number of supervisors) is responsible for generating ideas, gathering suggestions from employees, and evaluating them within a stipulated cost range. The production committee can implement these ideas without additional approval, provided they do not involve changes in other parts of the business.

The screening committee (composed of employees, union leaders, and top management) is chartered with the following four tasks:

- To evaluate and approve suggestions that involve several parts of the business and/or exceed the maximum allowable discretionary limit of the production committee.
- To provide an appeal forum for suggestions rejected by the production committee.
- To conduct formal and informal studies of current and anticipated business problems and specific concerns for the firm, such as an increase in the amount of returned merchandise.
- To review and update the formulas used to calculate bonuses.

The Scanlon Plan uses a ratio of total sales to payroll expenses to determine bonuses for employees. Using a base ratio, actual versus predicted costs are calculated at the end of the bonus period. If the expected (predicted) costs are lower than the observed costs during this period, this differential is shared between workers (bonus pool) and the firm. Part of the bonus pool is distributed to employees and a portion is held in reserve in a "rainy day" fund. Typically, any gains using this ratio are distributed so that employees receive 75 percent and management receives 25 percent.

Rucker Plan

As in the Scanlon Plan, a belief in participative management is an essential ingredient to Rucker Plan programs, developed by Allen Rucker in the

1950s. Rucker Plans are based on the following notions: employees want to be actively involved in their work, workers have something valuable to say, employee suggestions are instrumental to cost savings and improved corporate performance, and any resulting gains should be shared between labor and management.

Operationally, Rucker Plans have a simpler committee structure than Scanlon Plans. Some have two separate committees (production and screening), while others have only the screening committee. Production committees are not generally involved in problem solving and are used primarily for education/communication purposes. The screening committee (typically composed of hourly workers, union leaders, and top managers) is less involved with immediate production or quality issues but is interested in long-term normative concerns and operation of the bonus program.

While the committee structure and process under the Rucker Plan are simpler than those of the Scanlon Plan, the actual bonus formula is far more complex. It encompasses not only labor costs, but also other expenses that are part of the production process. Productivity improvements at the end of the bonus period are determined by calculating changes in the ratio of value added by the manufacturer (i.e., sales volume minus materials and supplies) to payroll expenses.

Improshare Plan

Both Scanlon and Rucker Plans view participative management systems as an integral part of their success and insist that active employee involvement is necessary during implementation. The Improshare Plan, while not opposed to participation, views it as an outcome of the aggregate bonus plan (see Fein, 1999). A formal system of employee participation is not consistently used in these programs, although labor management committees are often responsible for reviewing and adjusting bonus calculations as necessary. The bonus formulas focus on the direct labor contributions in time units, relative to an established standard for total labor time. A bonus is accrued when the standard is improved.

Bonuses are normally provided monthly and are calculated using the ratio of base-value earned hours (estimated using engineering time standard plus absorption of indirect hours) to total hours worked.

Drawbacks

Efficiency-based programs, like individual- and team-based performance-contingent plans, have their own unique pitfalls. Most of these problems are side effects of their very strength—namely, the aggregate nature of the efficiency measure, the emphasis on productivity changes, and the intense level of participation. These pitfalls include the following.

Weak Line of Sight

The dilution of individual performance problems discussed earlier under team-based rewards is brought one step further here. Because of the long distance between individual contributions and the aggregate efficiency measure, it remains to be shown that they induce those covered under the plan to do their best to improve the quality of the organization's services or products. By implication, the free-rider problem is also more severe because the more people are involved, the less likely group cohesiveness will be able to bring poor performers back into the fold.

Straightjacket Formulas

The calculus used to distribute rewards may have a number of problems, most of them traced to low flexibility. First, the firm may find it locked into rigid sharing formulas, and employees may develop expectations that these are "forever plans" (Welbourne and Gomez-Mejia, 1988). This may neutralize their strategic value or even become a liability as management has less room to maneuver. The greater the rate of technological change and volatility in product mix, the more severe this problem becomes. Second, reliable and meaningful efficiency measures may be difficult to develop and administer, particularly for firms operating in unstable, unpredictable environments. Productivity standards may be arbitrary and fickle, and the labor cost calculations may be complex and controversial.

Third, as discussed in the executive compensation chapters, one faces the peril of linking rewards to "bottom line," single efficiency measures. Such an approach raises the possibility that other important elements not explicitly incorporated into the formula may be ignored (e.g., need to consolidate different production processes to achieve a better economy of scale across several SBUs) or that employees involved may be tempted to engage in excessive risk taking "to see what works" (Gomez-Mejia, Welbourne, and Wiseman, 2000).

Finally, employees and many top managers are prone to believe that productivity and efficiency are necessary antecedents of financial performance. While this is generally true, the correlation between these two sets of measures is far from perfect. Gain sharing may result in a more efficient use of labor, materials, energy, and capital because these are to a large extent controllable. However, profitability measures, particularly in the short run, are affected by many uncontrollable variables that are totally unrelated to efficiency of operations such as market shifts, product life cycles, government policies, and so on. It is not unusual to find situations where a firm's efficiency increases, yet profitability decreases. For instance, employee-owned People Express Airlines was run very efficiently but still went out of business. Even though profitability may have been higher than it would have been had the firm been operating less efficiently, it is difficult for employees—and many managers—to understand and accept situations where their efforts seem to produce no measurable financial results.

Exclusivity

Discriminatory practices in gain-sharing programs, whereby only some types of employees are allowed to participate and receive benefits from it, may engender hard feelings from those individuals who are excluded. Typically, only hourly workers, mostly in manufacturing, are included in these plans.

Regression to Mean Effect

Inadvertently, gain-sharing programs may be designed to favor business units that are poor performers because the lower the starting base, the easier it is to improve on it. Statistically, a regression to the mean effect is likely to occur when repeated measures are used in a pre–post facto mode because low performers tend to move up closer to the mean, and high performers tend to slide down in the opposite direction. In practical terms this means that "gainsharing programs may penalize the previously more efficient organizational components where opportunities for dramatic labor cost savings are much less than those in less efficient organizational components" (Sullivan, 1988, p. 23).

Flooring Effect

Labor cost-saving opportunities available throughout the organization may be limited. It is possible that a saturation point is soon reached where additional improvements in efficiency may be almost nil, and this can be demoralizing. The labor hours required by a complex committee structure may not generate enough efficiency benefits to justify the costs involved.

Power Dilution

Top management may be sold on gain sharing as a productivity enhancing plan but may soon become threatened by it. Management may resent the loss of control involved in handing out discretionary power to multiple committees yet may be reluctant to overhaul the system for fear of reprisals and open conflict. The end result may be a lack of strong commitment from upper management, and this almost always spells failure for any human resource program (Gomez-Mejia, 1990a).

Contingencies Favoring Efficiency-Based Aggregate Pay Plans

The literature on gain sharing is fairly extensive. However, most of it consists of case studies that were specifically written by advocates to justify implementation of such programs. Most of this material was published many years ago (e.g., Alberth, 1960; Beardsley, 1962), although a number of review papers (e.g., Bullock and Lawler, 1984; Welbourne and Gomez-Mejia, 1988, 1995; Gomez-Mejia, Welbourne, and Wiseman, 2000) and some new evidence (e.g., Arthur and Kim, 2005; Kwon et al. 2008) have appeared in recent decades

In addition to the strong advocacy role of much of this literature (which puts in question the scientific value of reported findings), Welbourne and Gomez-Mejia (1988) warn us of other potential problems. First, most conclusions rely on testimonials, rather than on rigorous empirical analysis or controlled research designs. Second, reported studies are predominantly those that are successful, so factors impacting gain-sharing outcomes (both positive and negative) are not well documented. Third, most studies are based on questionnaires distributed to employees after a plan has been in effect for a while. A response bias may exist if those who were dissatisfied had left the company. Fourth, subtle pressures of stewards, managers, or even other fellow workers may affect how people respond to interviews concerning the gain-sharing plan. It is doubtful, for example, that management will open the doors to strangers to interview workers and publish information unless it feels the firm will not be embarrassed. Companies typically censor what they consider as "proprietary information" before such studies are allowed to appear in print. Finally, with a few exceptions (e.g., White, 1979), most studies suffer from an unclear focus of evaluation because consistent definitions of gain sharing (which is often used interchangeably with profit sharing or even as a form of team-based incentives) are missing. This results in a lack of comparability across studies.

Keeping the above caveats in mind, a review of the literature by Welbourne and Gomez-Mejia (1988) identified a number of factors that mediate the relative effectiveness of gain-sharing programs.

Firm Size

The range in terms of number of employees for firms reported to have gain-sharing programs is quite large, from 50 to 10,000, with a mode of approximately 500. While somewhat disputed (see Helfgott, 1962; Lesieur and Puckett, 1968), firm size is likely to make a difference in the success of gain sharing. The reason for this lies in the line of sight argument discussed earlier. Unless employees believe their participation can have an impact on company performance, resulting in a greater bonus, the psychological and monetary incentives of gain sharing are lost. However, the operational definition of "how large is too large" still remains open.

Technological Intensity

While empirical work addressing this issue is minimal, technology is likely to mediate the effect of gain sharing. As technology becomes more extensive, the potential for employee participation is reduced (Helfgott, 1962). In addition, technological constraints limit how much room there is for productivity to expand. Substantial opportunities for improvement should be available so that employees perceive that they can make a difference on productivity and this, in turn, will affect their pay.

Baseline

While success stories for gain sharing have been reported among both struggling and financially healthy firms, the baseline at the start of the program must still be taken into account. Firms or SBUs operating less efficiently are more likely to post gains, while those operating more efficiently are less likely to show improvements. Thus, careful attention needs to be paid not to penalize those units that are doing well (so that marginal improvements are more difficult) and penalize those that are below average (so that marginal improvements are easier to accomplish). This suggests that for firms that are operating at the top of their efficiency capacity, gain sharing will produce negligible benefits in terms of productivity and may tend to demoralize the workforce.

Compatible Managerial Beliefs

In Chapter 5, the importance of meshing the dominant logic of top management groups and compensation strategies was discussed. This is extremely crucial in the case of gain sharing because of the radical participative management philosophy involved, potential loss of management control, and the complex committee structures that are an integral part of most of these programs.

Several case studies have found that the expectations, attitudes, and value system of top managers, particularly CEOs, are important correlates of plan success (see review by Bullock and Lawler, 1984). If the dominant coalition does not believe in shared decision making, is reluctant to give up discretionary power, expresses doubts about the return to time invested in committee meetings, and is unwilling to spend a considerable amount of time in jointly designing, implementing, and communicating the bonus formulas, gain sharing is almost certainly doomed to failure. In other words, if management does not have strong faith in the employee involvement concept, gain sharing will not work; and the essential element of teamwork and communication will not be nurtured by the plan. Unfortunately, based on our experience, a surprisingly large number of firms are willing to adopt such a plan in response to consultants' recommendations and, to "keep up with the Joneses," imitate what other firms are doing, even if not fully aware of its implications. In such cases, either the program has a high probability of failure or the company faces the risk of losing members of the management team.

Corporate Culture

Related to the previous point, the fact that each organization has its own unique set of values is well documented (Kerr and Slocum, 2005). As discussed in Chapter 3, the more a firm's compensation strategies are attuned to its culture, the more likely these will contribute to firm performance. This is of paramount importance for gain sharing because of its intrusive nature in organizational life. Unless complemented by a strong individual-based performance-contingent plan, the firm will take considerable risks when implementing a participative reward system if individualism and competition are important values of the organization's culture. It may be that, in fact, gain sharing is introduced in an attempt to reorient the existing value structure, to make it less competitive and more cooperative. However, when combining it with individual incentives may be wise to allow for a gradual transition and, thus, decrease resistance.

Interdependencies

Unless resource flows across various units are explicitly taken into account in designing the program, gain sharing may precipitate the opposite of what was intended—that is, intense dysfunctional conflict. The authors know of some firms, for example, in which higher production in manufacturing units attributed to gain sharing led to a costly buildup of inventory.

As another example, it is not uncommon for firms to cover sales personnel under a separate commission plan. In these situations, it is important for the commission plan to induce the sales force to work hand in hand with plant and indirect personnel to achieve optimal performance under gain sharing. For instance, if the sales work is primarily paid on salary and nurturing customer relations is the main objective of the sales compensation program, this policy may operate at cross-purposes with the pressure to dispose of additional output generated by units covered under gain sharing.

SBU Strategies

Firms pursuing a prospector or growth strategy need to proceed cautiously when introducing gain-sharing programs because bonuses are based on increases above base productivity measures. A stable history will help ensure a fair bonus distribution and make the calculation of the bonus better understood by employees. Unstable or scanty data based on historical records can make it difficult to establish reliable future performance standards. If the firm is constantly changing the bonus calculations, confidence in the system is likely to suffer. By the same token, prospectors and growth firms need a greater degree of flexibility, and gain sharing tends to work against this. In general, gain sharing is less likely to contribute to firm performance for SBUs that follow a prospector or growth strategy.

In addition to the internal factors noted above, Welbourne and Gomez-Mejia (1988) identified three external factors that mediate the relative effectiveness of gain-sharing programs and their contribution to firm performance.

Product Market

Other things equal, gain sharing is more appropriate if management has confidence in business forecasts indicating that improvements in per capita productivity and total output can be absorbed by the market. Otherwise, the end result may be unwanted inventory expansion, which almost inevitably leads to layoffs, a situation that is seldom conducive to improved labor-management cooperation.

Labor Market

An important issue is the extent to which the applicant pool from which the firm hires workers is agreeable to gain sharing or predisposed against these types of programs. For instance, if the company operates in the so-called secondary labor market—characterized by jobs with low pay, limited job security, poor working conditions, few opportunities for advancement, layoffs, and temporary employment; (see Doeringer and Piore, 1971)—gain sharing is less likely to be effective. If high unemployment is being experienced in the region, employees are less likely to leave the firm because they are more resistant to change and more likely to give their present employer a chance. As the number of job opportunities expands, workers and even managers who are not comfortable with gain-sharing programs are more likely to leave the firm. It is not clear, however, whether the "good" or the "bad" employees are the ones to leave in this situation.

Environmental Turbulence

Firms operating in highly unstable environments are less likely to effectively implement gain-sharing programs. This may be for no other reason than that the relationship between firm profitability and efficiency deteriorates as external factors beyond management control affect their performance.

Profit-Based Pay Policies

Profit-based performance-contingent plans, most commonly known as profit sharing, pay employees based on the profitability of the entire firm or unit, regardless of how efficiently it is being run (Bayo-Moriones and Larraza-Kintana, 2009). More specifically, these programs differ from efficiency-based plans in a number of ways:

- Factors such as depreciation procedures, bad debt expense, and economic conditions (none of which are under the employee's control) contribute to reported profit (and, therefore, affect the amount of profit sharing received). Yet they may have little to do with any productivity improvements or changes in employee behaviors. No attempt is made under profit sharing to reward workers for specific activities that increase productivity.
- Explicit formulas are used to allocate gains in profit levels to employees and the firm. Yet no worker participation is required. In other words, no ideological assumption is made that the success of the program derives

from management's commitment to a democratic leadership style. In fact, profit sharing has its roots in paternalistic, top-down, "welfare capitalism" type of programs that originated in the nineteenth and early twentieth centuries as attempts to limit unionization (Florkowski, 1987).

- Unlike gain sharing, profit-sharing payments accrue on an annual or quarterly basis. Perhaps most importantly, all of the profit allocations under the plan are typically deferred into a retirement fund. Less frequently, profit-sharing payments may be allocated as a lump-sum annual or quarterly bonus. Thus, unlike gain sharing, there are fewer attempts to "personalize" the linkage between rewards and performance, and profit allocations may be viewed more as a mechanism of defraying benefits than as a true incentive program.

- Profit sharing is almost always corporate wide, so that the level of aggregation is much larger than in the case of gain sharing. Further, some SBUs may contribute a disproportionate share of the corporate-wide profits, which can add to the blurring of the line of sight between contributions and rewards.

Theoretical Framework

There are several theoretical rationales in support of profit-sharing programs. Most of these are economic in nature, rather than behavioral.

Shock Absorber Theory

The shock absorber theory, a macroeconomic perspective most notably associated with the work of Weitzman (1984), holds that profit sharing is an important element in monetary and fiscal policies to control inflation. At the same time, profit sharing mitigates their negative effect on employment level. Profit-sharing systems offer strong resistance to demand and cost shocks in the short run because of their built-in flexibility over the business cycle. Thus, from a public policy standpoint, profit sharing promotes full employment because plan contributions are automatically adjusted in downturns, reducing the marginal cost of labor and thereby allowing firms to retain a larger workforce during a recession.

Cash Flow Theory

The arguments in the cash flow theory are very similar to those advanced by life cycle theory discussed in earlier chapters. The central point is this: The greater the proportion of fixed costs in the compensation system, the less strategic flexibility the firm has to direct scarce cash into capital intensive projects such as R&D. This is a particularly crucial issue for firms at the growth stage, those that adopt a prospector strategy, and firms for which labor costs are a high proportion of total costs (see Gomez-Mejia and Balkin, 1989). Reliance on variable compensation allows the firm to channel scarce resources where and when they are most needed. It also ties workers to the firm by increasing their opportunity costs (in terms of foregone benefits) if they were to go elsewhere. Finally, profit sharing allows the firm to take greater risks and deal with short-term setbacks without having to resort to massive layoffs in order to cope with environmental jolts.

In addition to the strategic flexibility afforded the firm and greater employment security for its workers, the funding formula for profit sharing provides a protective security blanket for the aged, because in most plans cash is deposited into a deferred income account that cannot be accessed until retirement. By the late 1980s, it became the most common method of providing retirement income in the United States (Florkowski, 1987).

Distributive Justice

In several encyclicals during the past two centuries, popes have advanced the notion that the sharing of wealth between workers and the owners of capital is necessary to achieve a fair and just distribution of income within the constraints of private property. Union leaders have also been strong proponents of profit sharing, provided that the union actively participates in the design, implementation, and monitoring of these plans (Brandes, 1970). Enlightened managers have instituted profit-sharing plans for at least a century, under the belief that they promote a sense of partnership between capital and labor and a common purpose (Bureau of National Affairs Special Report, 1988; Cheadle, 1989). Moderate socialists, in response to more radical Marxist ideology, have long advocated the use of profit sharing as a way of returning "surplus value" in the capitalist mode of production back to the workers (e.g., Braverman, 1974; Pfeffer, 1979).

The common thread in the above perspectives, despite their disparate origins, is that:

- Profit sharing is the right and moral thing to do.
- Both workers who contribute labor and owners who risk capital are entitled to partake in the fruits of their combined efforts to make the enterprise succeed.
- Profit sharing fosters an equality of exchange (vis-à-vis stratification) in economic relations so that one segment of the population (workers) does not produce value for the exclusive benefit of another segment (firm owners).

Operational Programs

There are two major types of profit-sharing plans. The first kind consists of "in-cash" or "current" (as opposed to deferred) profit sharing. These programs provide employees with a lump-sum award based on the firm's profitability during a stipulated period of time, usually on an annual or quarterly basis. In-cash plans are quite old. For instance, Procter & Gamble introduced a cash profit-sharing program in 1887. In the late 1980s, it was estimated that cash profit-sharing plans had payouts averaging 9.2 percent of wages (Bureau of National Affairs Special Report, 1988). S.C. Johnson & Son has had a cash plan for almost 80 years. The formula is predicated on the employee's base salary, seniority, and level within the company. The payout averages about six week's pay per year (Bureau of National Affairs Special Report, 1988). Occasionally, however, cash compensation in the form of profit sharing is much greater. For instance, Andersen Corporation, a window manufacturer in Bayport, Minnesota, offered its 3,700 employees an annual check in 1987 amounting to 84 percent of annual salary, averaging a whopping $28,620 per employee (Bureau of National Affairs Special Report, 1988).

The second, and by far most common plan, is the tax-deferred, profit-sharing trust. Approximately 80 percent of all plans use this method, whereby the firm will pay benefits based on the value of each participant's fund upon his or her retirement (Florkowski, 1987). In these "defined contribution plans," the fund's growth is directly tied to profit levels, and proceeds are not taxable until employees begin to draw benefits upon retirement or disability. Most of the firms in the remaining 20 percent use a mixed approach, with a portion of profits distributed to employees during the calendar year in which they were earned and the remaining portion set aside in a tax-deferred account. The percent of profits distributed across all types of plans varies between 14 and 33 percent (Bureau of National Affairs Special Report, 1988).

The obvious advantage of tax-deferred plans is that employees do not have to pay federal and state taxes (which could exceed 40 percent of marginal earnings) on the payout. Their main disadvantage is that the payoff is so far into the future that most of its reinforcement value is lost.

Drawbacks

Profit sharing is the most aggregate of all performance-contingent pay plans with little, if any, pretension of using it as a motivational tool at the individual level. Research conducted to date, mostly in the form of case studies, speaks eloquently in favor of profit sharing (Best, 1961; Coords, 1980; Lush, 1975; McNutt, 1991; Coyle-Shapiro et al. 2002). These studies report that profit-sharing firms generally perform better, grow faster, and enjoy higher productivity, job satisfaction, and lower turnover among employees. As in the case of gain sharing, however, it is difficult to ascertain the cause-and-effect relationship in these descriptive studies and whether firms whose plan fell below expectations were excluded because management did not have a success story to tell. The main concerns with profit sharing are noncontingent reinforcement, the inability to redirect funds, limited strategic flexibility, lack of control, and mortgaging the future.

Noncontingent Reinforcement

While noncontingent reinforcement is perhaps an unfair criticism of profit-sharing plans because they are not primarily designed as motivational tools, expectancy theory would predict that their behavioral effect is minimal, given that the connection between individual goal accomplishment, firm performance, and rewards is negligible at best. In other words, the distance between individual behavior and firm outcomes is so remote that few employees will be energized by it. Many consultants (and probably most employees) view profit sharing as another fringe benefit just like health insurance or a pension plan. It may be an important retention tool (because accumulated benefits are tied to seniority), but it does not discriminate between functional and dysfunctional turnover.

Inability to Redirect Funds

As the percent of profits from a firm is channeled into profit-sharing plans, less flexibility is left to use such resources for other types of performance-contingent plans that may be more closely attuned to individual and group performance. It may, in fact, become so high (30 percent is not uncommon) that, in effect, the firm utilizes large resources for across-the-board payments (magnifying the free-rider effect discussed earlier), leaving very little room to bankroll other performance-contingent pay plans.

Limited Strategic Flexibility

Because it is so broad in nature, profit sharing does not offer the maneuverability to target the reward system to attain specific strategic objectives.

For instance, a firm may wish to emphasize a particular product line to take advantage of a promising market niche, and this may require devoting more compensation dollars to attract and retain top-level talent in that area. However, profit sharing will not help the firm accomplish this.

Lack of Control

Lack of control is somewhat akin to the line of sight issue discussed earlier. As noted in Chapters 4, 5, and 6, while estimates vary, most researchers agree that top executives exercise rather limited influence on firm performance. While moving down in the organization, factors outside an employee's sphere of control play an even larger role on firm performance.

Mortgaging the Future

Unlike most other performance-contingent pay plans, profit-sharing money is "painless" in the short run because it is yet to be earned. Therefore, management may be tempted to be generous with this benefit and leave the problem for future management generations to handle. This assumes greater significance in organized firms because unions like to be involved in the program's design, implementation, and operation (Kochan and Dyer, 1976; Schuster, 1983, 1984a, b, 1985). According to Cheadle (1989, p. 388), "many present-day union leaders [are] weary of management-initiated profit-sharing plans." This attitude is based in large measure in the previous history of so-called welfare capitalism, whereby employers relied heavily on profit sharing to check unionization (Brandes, 1970).

Thus, union pressures on the one hand and management's propensity to give in on the other may result in profit-sharing plans that are detrimental to stockholders and that may have long-term negative consequences for workers as less capital is available to finance future growth. Profit sharing may also act as an additional constraint on strategic flexibility because management may be reluctant to make changes in the allocation formulas for fear of provoking a negative union response.

Contingencies Favoring Corporate-Wide Performance-Based Pay Plans

Existing research, while rather limited, along with the theoretical frameworks discussed earlier in this section, suggest that the following factors are likely to affect the outcomes of profit-sharing programs.

Firm Size

Larger firms are more likely to rely on profit-sharing plans, regardless of actual profitability (Cheadle, 1989). Milkovich and Newman (2005, p. 351) add that "until there is more evidence that Scanlon/Rucker plans can be adapted successfully to large organizations, profit sharing plans seem to represent the major alternative for organizations of any size."

Corporate Diversification

Following the logic outlined in Chapters 2 through 5, one would expect profit sharing to be more appropriate when there is extensive interdependence and resource flows across business units because the corporation as a whole is the most obvious level of analysis to assess performance. This means, in terms of extent of diversification, profit sharing should be most suitable for single-product, dominant-product, and related-product firms, in that order, and less appropriate for unrelated-product firms. In terms of diversification patterns, one would expect that profit sharing should be most suitable for vertical, constrained, and linked businesses, in that order, and least appropriate for multibusiness and conglomerate firms.

SBU Strategy

As noted earlier, while profit sharing may be utilized by firms at different life cycle stages, one would expect its contribution to firm performance to be greatest for start-up and growth firms and for companies that follow a prospector strategy. The reason for this is that profit sharing is a variable, rather than a fixed, cost of production. Thus, cash flows would be enhanced by increasing the proportion of pay that is tied to profitability (and, therefore, subject to oscillations, depending on how well the firm is doing). This enables the firm to channel resources into growth areas.

The tax-deferred feature of most profit-sharing plans to finance employees' pensions makes them particularly attractive as a cash flow tool. For instance, the workforce's income and standard of living will not be visibly affected in the near future if profitability drops. This means that the firm enjoys the advantages of adjustable, total compensation without negatively impacting the part of pay (cash) that most employees see as important to their everyday life. Furthermore, the longer the time horizon, the less likely annual ups and downs in the firm's profits will affect the workers' retirement income because it will be calculated over multiple years.

Competitive Strategy Weapon in Local Markets

Of all factors, it appears that regional differences are the main predictors of profit-sharing plan adoption. According to Cheadle's (1989, p. 395) findings, "The explanation [for profit-sharing adoption] with the most consistent support is the customary hypothesis; the idea that the dominant saving plan in an industry/region is determined more by past practice than the inherent superiority of one plan over the other." This suggests that firm location may play a role in whether profit sharing should be implemented. Where profit sharing is customary (as is the case in most of the western United States), the firm may have little choice but to offer such a plan as an integral part of its recruitment and retention strategies or be at a disadvantage in the labor market.

Firms Facing Unstable Demand

Firms operating in turbulent markets with highly elastic products may find that profit sharing can contribute to firm performance by serving as a shock absorber during periods of decline. Because profit sharing operates in a region of "positive excess demand for labor," variable costs can be reduced during downturns without resorting to layoffs. In terms of training expenses, recruitment efforts, and morale problems in addition to the hardships employees and their families suffer during unemployment, layoffs have many associated costs for firms.

Profit Sharing Bundled with Other Plans

From a behavioral perspective, profit sharing is most likely to contribute to firm performance if it is combined with other individual and aggregate incentive plans. The reason for this should be obvious: Namely, profit sharing is not really designed to serve as a motivational or incentive-alignment tool. It should be treated as the top layer in the firm's reward structure. If other programs concurrently exist where the line of sight between behavior and outcomes is stronger, then profit sharing may serve a useful role by creating a sense of common goals, partnership, and mission.

Experiential Compensation Pattern

An experiential compensation strategy (see Chapter 3) should reinforce the cooperation and innovation that profit sharing is intended to promote. An algorithmic compensation strategy, on the other hand, would serve to neutralize the limited behavioral impact one would expect from profit sharing. This is because the algorithmic pay pattern rewards the individual for learning narrowly defined domains and work methods, socializes employees to assume responsibilities for specialized work segments, fosters dependence on supervisors, and engenders centralized organizational networks. In short, profit sharing is less likely to promote greater organizational commitment as the firm's global compensation strategies become more algorithmic in nature.

Multicriteria-Based Pay Policies

This performance-contingent pay program differs from previous organizationwide programs in that it links pay to multiple dimensions of performance both financial and nonfinancial (see Chapter 9). The two other organizationwide programs rely on just one dimension of performance. In the case of gain sharing the focus is on productivity. In the case of profit sharing the focus is on profitability.

Theoretical Background

Agency theory is the main theory underpinning the notion of using multiple performance criteria in organization-wide performance-contingent pay policies (e.g., Ittner, Larcker, and Meyer, 2003). Agency theory has been already reviewed in previous chapters. Here, only the key aspects that predict the use of multicriteria indicators of performance for contractual purposes are emphasized.

Agency-based research has traditionally been concerned with the use of financial measures of performance in incentive pay. In the 1990s, analytical research conducted by Feltham and Xie (1994) suggested that financial measures alone may not provide the most efficient means to motivate agents to act in the manner desired by the principal. Other authors, such as Hemmer (1996), found that due to the imperfection of financial measures, they should be complemented in incentive contracts with nonfinancial performance measures, which are more informative. Conversely, the work by Holmstrom and Milgrom (1991) does not fully support the positive effects of using multicriteria performance measures to determine pay. They suggest that the use of financial and nonfinancial metrics may direct agents' efforts to tasks that are easily measured at the expense of tasks that are harder to measure. These findings suggest that the true benefits of having multicriteria measures of performance are still unclear.

Despite this inconclusive result of research on the potential impact of multicriteria performance-based pay programs, a great number of organizations are currently adopting them. Their beliefs about these programs tend to be as follows.

- Performance-contingent pay policies that rely on financial information tend to generate dysfunctional behaviors, such as short-termism, gaming, or earnings manipulation (e.g., Jensen, 2003; Rappaport, 1999) (see Chapter 9).
- Performance-contingent pay policies that include multicriteria performance measures help managers to balance their efforts (i.e., rather than just focus on the economic side of the organization, also focus on its customers, employees, suppliers, etc.) (e.g., Indjejikian, 1999).
- Pay programs dependent on multicriteria performance measures can help organizations achieve the diverse requirements of stakeholders (e.g., Ittner, Larcker and Meyer, 2003).
- Future firm performance is positively associated with the use of nonfinancial performance measures in addition to financial performance measures used in executive compensation (e.g., Banker, Potter, and Srinivasan, 2000).

Operational Programs

There are at least two ways in which multicriteria performance measures have been used to determine pay (Franco-Santos, 2007). On the one hand, organizations use multicriteria performance measures with a specific framework that (1) categorizes the measures (e.g., financial measures, customer measures, environmental measures); and (2) helps managers understand the relationships among them (e.g., through road maps also known as success maps or strategy maps). An example of such a framework is Kaplan and Norton's (1992, 2006) Balance Scorecard. On the other hand, organizations use multicriteria performance measures in incentives without any clear framework structuring them. These organizations tend to refer to their performance measures as key performance indicators. Both of these programs tend to use specific performance targets (goals) and weights associated with each measure. Some organizations aggregate all the measurement results in a composite measure, while others evaluate them individually.

Drawbacks

Research in this area is relatively new and only a handful of studies has dealt with the potential drawbacks that these types of incentives may generate.

The following points summarize the key issues associated with this method of pay.

Added Subjectivity

Ittner, Larcker, and Meyer (2003), in a study conducted in the financial sector, found that

> the subjectivity in the scorecard [incentive] plan allowed superiors to reduce the "balance" in bonus awards by placing most of the weight on financial measures, to incorporate factors other than the scorecard measures in performance evaluations, to change evaluation criteria from quarter to quarter, to ignore measures that were predictive of future financial performance, and to weight measures that were not predictive of desired results. These outcomes led many branch managers to complain about favoritism in bonus awards and uncertainty in the criteria being used to determine rewards, and caused corporate executive and human resource managers to question the scorecard's use for compensation purposes. (p. 725)

Judgment Bias

A number of studies have examined the impact of multicriteria performance-contingent pay plans on individual performance evaluations (i.e., appraisals). For instance, Lipe and Salterio (2000) show that when evaluators review the results of multicriteria measurements from different departments; they are likely to focus their attention on the common measures (typically financial) at the expense of the unique measures (normally non-financial). Banker, Chang, and Pizzini (2004) extend Lipe and Salterio's work by finding that when strategically linked measures are introduced in incentive plans evaluators are likely to focus more on those measures than on common measures.

Manipulation of Data, Administrative Costs, and Undeserved Benefits

As suggested in Chapter 9, nonfinancial data is not audited. Therefore, managers may find this information easier to manipulate, and even more so when rewards are attached to them (Ittner and Larcker, 2003). Also, due to the complexity of these systems the cost of operating them is likely to increase. Since multiple measures are used to determine performance and pay, the likelihood of some measures being achieved increases (Chatterji and Levine, 2006). Managers that were performing poorly under a profit-based pay program may have a greater chance to perform well on something under a multicriteria performance-contingent program.

Contingencies Favoring Multicriteria Performance-Contingent Pay Policies

As mentioned earlier, in this area research to date is limited. Nevertheless, the following contextual factors have been found to influence the impact of multicriteria performance-contingent pay programs.

Firm Size

Larger firms are more likely to adopt this type of program. First, because they tend to have large reward functions that can deal with the additional administrative cost (in time and other resources) that this type of program generates, and second, as a result of institutional pressures (see Chapter 9).

Industry

Some industries are forced to adopt a multicriteria approach to measure their performance. For example, utilities have to use balanced measurement systems in order to conform to governmental requirements (e.g., corporate social responsibility reports as well as accounting reports). These requirements may encourage them to rely on multicriteria performance-contingent pay policies.

Corporate Culture

Some corporate cultures highly emphasize the intangible aspects of performance (e.g., citizenship behaviors). In this particular culture, multicriteria performance-based pay plans are more likely to be adopted.

Environmental Uncertainty

When organizations operate in highly uncertain environments, their financial performance is likely to be "noisy." Thus organizations operating in this kind of environment are more likely to rely on multicriteria performance-contingent pay programs. These types of programs may be better at capturing the actual performance of the organization.

Business Strategy

As noted earlier, the type of business strategy a firm adopts is likely to influence its decisions about pay. For example, Ittner, Larcker, and Rajan (1997) argue that firms using a cost-leadership strategy will be likely to rely on financial information alone. These firms will more certainly adopt an organization-wide performance-based program that relies solely on financial performance measures. Firms following an innovation strategy that requires long-term orientation and special emphasis on intangible assets will be likely to design a performance-based pay program that is subject to both financial and nonfinancial performance information.

Summary

In short, multiple-reward policies at different levels of aggregation may be used to enhance individual, group, and firm performance. The relative effectiveness of these policies depends on how they are designed and implemented, their intended objectives, and the extent to which they are appropriate for the nature of the task at hand, organizational structure and culture, firm strategy, and the external environment.

REFERENCES

Abernathy, W.B. (1999). Evaluating organization scorecards and incentive-pay systems. *Employment Relations Today*, 25(4), 83–96.

Aboody, D., and Kasznik. R. (2000). CEO stock option awards and the timing of corporate voluntary disclosers. *Journal of Accounting and Economics*, 29(1), 73–100.

Abosch, K.S. (2008). Rationalizing variable pay plans. In L.A. Berger and D.R. Berger (Eds.), *The Compensation Handbook: A State-of-the-art Guide to Compensation Strategy and Design*, 5th ed. New York: McGraw-Hill, 227–240.

Abowd, J.M., and Bognanno, M. (1995). International differences in executive and managerial compensation. In R.B. Freeman, and L. F. Katz (Eds.), *Differences and Changes in Wage Structures*. Chicago: University of Chicago Press, 67–105.

Adam, E. (1983). Towards a typology of production and operations management systems. *Academy of Management Review*, 8, 365–375.

Adams, J.L. (1991). Nonmonetary awards. In L.A. Berger and D.R. Berger (Eds.), *The Compensation Handbook: A State-of-the-art Guide to Compensation Strategy and Design*, 5th ed. New York: McGraw-Hill.

Adams, J.S. (1965). Inequity in social exchange. In L. Berkowitz (Ed.), *Advances in Experimental Social Psychology*, 2. New York: Academic Press, 267–297.

Adams, R., Almeida, H., and Ferreira, D. (2009). Understanding the relationship between founder-CEOs and firm performance. *Journal of Empirical Finance*, 16(1), 136–150.

Adizes, I. (1979). Organizational passages: Diagnosing and treating life cycle problems in organizations. *Organizational Dynamics*, 8(1), 3–24.

Agarwal, N.C. (1981). Determinants of executive compensation. *Industrial Relations*, 20, 36–46.

Aggarwal, R.K., and Samwick, A.A. (2003). Performance incentives within firms: The effect of managerial responsibility. *Journal of Finance*, 58(4), 1613–1649.

Ahimud, Y., and Lev, B. (1981). Risk reduction as a management motive for conglomerate mergers. *Bell Journal of Economics*, 12, 605–617.

Aime, F., Meyer, C.J., and Humphrey, S.E. (2009). Legitimacy of team rewards: Analyzing legitimacy as a condition for the effectiveness of team incentive designs. *Journal of Business Research*, 20, 50–75.

Albanese, R., and VanFleet, D.D. (1985). Rational behavior in groups: The free riding tendency. *Academy of Management Review*, 10(2), 244–255.

Albanesi, S., and Olivetti, C. (2009). Home production, market production, and the gender gap: Incentives and expectations. *Review of Economic Dynamics*, 12(1), 80–107.

Alberth, E.R. (1960). The Scanlon plan applied to an oil refinery: Pros and cons. Unpublished Master's thesis. Massachusetts Institute of Technology.

Alexander, E.R., and Wilkins, R.D. (1982). Performance rating validity: The relationship of objective and subjective measures of performance. *Group and Organization Studies,* 7(4), 485–496.

Allen, M.P. (1981). Power and privilege in the large corporation: Corporate control and managerial compensation. *American Journal of Sociology,* 86(5), 1112–1123.

Almazan, A., Hartzell, J.C., and Starks, L.T. (2005). Active institutional shareholders and cost of monitoring: Evidence from executive compensation. *Financial Management,* 34(4) (Winter), 5–34.

Amir, E., and Lev, B. (1996). Value-relevance of nonfinancial information: The wireless communications industry. *Journal of Accounting and Economics,* 22(1–3), 3–30.

Amuso, L.E., and Knopping, D. (2008). Incentive compensation program design. In L.A. Berger and D.R. Berger (Eds.), *The Compensation Handbook: A State-of-the-art Guide to Compensation Strategy and Design,* 5th ed. New York: McGraw-Hill, 205–214.

Anderson, C.R., and Zeithaml, C.P. (1984). Stage of the product life cycle, business strategy, and business performance. *Academy of Management Journal,* 27(1), 5–24.

Anderson, R.C., Boylan, R.T., and Reeb, D.M. (2007). Paying the CEO: A model of managerial integrity premiums. Unpublished manuscript. Washington, DC: American University.

Anderson, R.C., and Reeb, D.M. (2003). Founding-family ownership and firm performance: Evidence from the S&P 500. *Journal of Finance,* 58(3), 1301–1328.

Andrews, D.R. (1971). *The Concept of Corporate Strategy.* Homewood, IL: Dow-Jones Irwin.

Antle, R., and Demski, J.S. (1988). The controllability principle in responsibility accounting. *The Accounting Review,* 63(4), 700–718.

Antle, R, and Smith, A. (1985). Measuring executive compensation: Methods and an application. *Journal of Accounting Research,* 23(2), 296–325.

———. (1986). An empirical investigation of the relative performance evaluation of corporate executives. *Journal of Accounting Research,* 24(1), 1–39.

Aoki, M. (1984). *The Cooperative Game Theory of the Firm.* Oxford, UK: Clarendon Press.

Argyris, C. (1957). *Personality and Organization.* New York: Harper.

Arnould, R.J. (1985). Agency costs in banking firms: An analysis of expense preference behavior. *Journal of Economics and Business,* 37(1), 103–112.

Arregle, J.L., Hitt, M.A., Sirmon, D.G., and Very, P. (2007). The development of organizational social capital: Attributes of family firms. *Journal of Management Studies,* 44(1), 73–95.

Arthur, J.B., and Kim, D.O. (2005). Gainsharing and knowledge sharing: The effects of labour-management co-operation. *International Journal of Human Resource Management,* 16(9), 1564–1582.

Asch, P., and Quandt, R. (1988). Betting bias in exotic bets. *Economics Letters,* 28, 215–219.

Associated Press. (2008). CEOs pay higher in '07 despite cloudy economy [video file]. June 15. http://www.clipsyndicate.com/video/play/622335/ceos_pay_higher_in_07_despite_cloudy_economy.

Athanassiou, N., Crittenden, W.F., Kelley, L.M., and Marquez, P. (2002). Founder centrality effects on the Mexican family firm's top management group: Firm culture, strategic vision and goals, and firm performance. *Journal of World Business,* 37(2), 139–150.

Austin, J.T., and Bobko, P. (1985). Goal setting theory: Unexplored areas and future research needs. *Journal of Occupational Psychology,* 58(44), 289–308.

Austin, R.D. (1996). *Measuring and Managing Performance in Organizations.* New York: Dorset House Publishing.

Baiman, S. (1982). Agency research in managerial accounting: A survey. *Journal of Accounting Literature,* 2, 154–213.

———. (1990). Agency research in managerial accounting: a second look. *Accounting, Organizations, and Society,* 15, 341–371.

Bajaj, V., and Creswell, J. (2008). A lender failed: Did its auditor? *The New York Times,* April 13, B-1.

Baker, G.P. (1992). Incentive contracts and performance-measurement. *Journal of Political Economy,* 100(3), 598–614.

Baker, G.P., Gibbons, R., and Murphy, K.J. (1994). Subjective performance measures in optimal incentive contracts. *The Quarterly Journal of Economics,* 109(4), 1125.

Balkin, D.B. (2008). Explaining high US CEO pay in a global context: An institutional perspective. In L.R. Gomez-Mejia and S. Werner (Eds.), *Global Compensation: Foundations and Perspectives.* London: Routledge, 192–202.

Balkin, D.B., and Gomez-Mejia, L.R. (1984). Determinants of R&D compensation strategy in high tech industry. *Personnel Psychology,* 37, 635–650.

———. (1985). Compensation practices in high tech industries. *Personnel Administrator,* 30(6), 111–123.

———. (1986). A contingency theory of compensation. In S. Rynes and G.T. Milkovich (Eds.), *Current Issues in Human Resource Management.* Plano, TX: Business Publications.

———. (Eds.). (1987a). *New Perspectives on Compensation.* Englewood Cliffs, NJ: Prentice Hall.

———. (1987b). Toward a contingency theory of compensation strategy. *Strategic Management Journal,* 8(2), 169–182.

———. (1988). Entrepreneurial compensation. In R.S. Shuler, S.A. Youngblood, and V.L. Huber (Eds.), *Readings in Personnel and Human Resource Management.* St. Paul, MN: West Publishing.

———. (1990). Matching compensation and organizational strategies. *Strategic Management Journal,* 11, 153–169.

Balkin, D.B., Markman, G.D., and Gomez-Mejia, L.R. (2000). Is CEO pay in high technology firms related to innovation? *Academy of Management Journal,* 43(6), 1118–1129.

Banker, R.D., Chang, H.S., and Pizzini, M.J. (2004). The balanced scorecard: Judgmental effects of performance measures linked to strategy. *Accounting Review,* 79(1), 1–23.

Banker, R.D., and Datar, S.M. (1989). Sensitivity, precision, and linear aggregation of signals for performance evaluation. *Journal of Accounting Research,* 27(1), 21–39.

Banker, R.D., Lee, S.Y., Potter, G., and Srinivasan, D. (2001). An empirical analysis of continuing improvements following the implementation of a performance-based compensation plan. *Journal of Accounting and Economics,* 30(3), 315–350.

Banker, R.D., Potter, G., and Srinivasan, D. (2000). An empirical investigation of an incentive plan that includes non-financial performance measures. *Accounting Review,* 75(1), 65–92.

Banks, R.L., and Wheelwright, S.C. (1979). Operations versus strategy: Trading tomorrow for today. *Harvard Business Review,* May–June, 112–120.

Barboza, D. (2009). Contradictions in China. *New York Times,* January 2, B-1.

Bar-Gill, O., and Bebchuk, L. (2003). Misreporting corporate performance. Working paper. Cambridge, MA: Harvard Law School.

Barkema, H.G., and Gomez-Mejia, L.R. (1998). Managerial compensation and firm performance: A general research framework. *Academy of Management Journal,* 41(2), 135–145.

Barney, J. (1991). Special theory forum: The resource-based model of the firm: Origins, implications, and prospects. *Journal of Management,* 17(1), 97–98.

Barney, J., Wright, M., and Ketchen, D.J. Jr. (2001). The resource-based view of the firm: Ten years after 1991. *Journal of Management,* 27(6), 625–641.

Barrett, G.V. (1972). Research models of the future for industrial and organizational psychology. *Personnel Psychology,* 25, 1–18.

Baumol, W.J. (1959). Business behavior, value, and growth. New York: Macmillan.

Bayo-Moriones, A., and Larraza-Kintana, M. (2009). Profit sharing plans and affective commitment: Does context matter? *Human Resource Management,* 48(2), 207–226.

Baysinger, B., and Hoskisson, R.E. (1990). The composition of the board of directors and strategic control: Effects of corporate strategy. *Academy of Management Review,* 15, 72–87.

Baysinger, B., Kosnik, R.D., and Turk, T.A. (1991). Effects of board and ownership structure on corporate R&D strategy. *Academy of Management Journal,* 34, 205–214.

Beardsley, D.W. (1962). A look at the Scanlon plan. Unpublished Master's thesis. Massachusetts Institute of Technology.

Beatty, R.P., and Zajac, E.J. (1994). Managerial incentives, monitoring, and risk bearing: A study of executive compensation, ownership, and board structure in initial public offerings. *Administrative Science Quarterly,* 39, 313–335.

Bebchuk, L.A., and Fried, J.M. (2006). Pay without performance: Overview of the issues. *Academy of Management Perspectives,* 20(1), 5–24.

Becerra, M. (2009). *Theory of the Firm for Strategic Management.* Cambridge, UK: Cambridge University Press.

Becker, B. (2006). Wealth and executive compensation. *Journal of Finance,* 61(1), 379–397.

Becker, G.S. (1964). *Human Capital.* New York: National Bureau of Economic Research.

———. (1975). *Human Capital,* 2d ed. New York: National Bureau of Economic Research.

Behn, B., and Riley, R. (1999). Using nonfinancial information to predict financial performance: The case of the U.S. airline industry. *Journal of Accounting, Auditing and Finance,* 14, 29–56.

Belcher, D.W., and Atchison, T.J. (1987). *Compensation Administration.* Englewood Cliffs, NJ: Prentice Hall.

Bell, M.J. (1982). The entrepreneur, the market and venture capital. In R.W. Smilor (Ed.), *Small Business and the Entrepreneurial Spirit*. Austin, TX: University of Texas at Austin, Institute for Constructive Capitalism.

Belliveau, M.A., O'Really, C.A., and Wade, J.B. (1996). Social capital at the top: Effects of social similarity and status on CEO compensation. *Academy of Management Journal*, 39(6), 1568–1593.

Ben-David, J. (1971). *The Scientist's Role in Society*. Englewood Cliffs, NJ: Prentice Hall, Inc.

Berg, N.A. (1969). What's different about conglomerate management? *Harvard Business Review*, 47(6), 112–120.

———. (1973). Corporate role in diversified companies. In B. Taylor and K. Macmillen (Eds.), *Business Policy Teaching and Research*. New York: Halstead Press.

Berger, D.R. (2008). Demographics. The tempest driving compensation. In L.A. Berger and D.R. Berger (Eds.), *The Compensation Handbook: A State-of-the-art Guide to Compensation Strategy and Design*, 5th ed. New York: McGraw-Hill, 49–63.

Berger, L.A. (1991). Trends and issues for the 1990s: Creating a viable framework for compensation design. In M.L. Rock and L.A. Berger (Eds.), *The Compensation Handbook: A State-of-the-art Guide to Compensation Strategy and Design*. New York: McGraw-Hill.

———. (2008a). Employee pay: A riddle wrapped up in a mystery inside enigma. In L.A. Berger and D.R. Berger (Eds.), *The Compensation Handbook: A State-of-the-art Guide to Compensation Strategy and Design*, 5th ed. New York: McGraw-Hill, 3–11.

———. (2008b). Talent management, organization transformation, and compensation. In L.R. Gomez-Mejia and S. Werner (Eds.), *Global Compensation: Foundations and Perspectives*. London, UK: Routledge, 571–584.

Berger, L.A., and Berger, D.R. (Eds.) (2008). *The Compensation Handbook: A State-of-the-art Guide to Compensation Strategy and Design*. New York: McGraw-Hill.

Berger, P.G., and Ofek, E. (1996). Bustup takeovers of value destroying diversified firms. *Journal of Finance*, 51(4), 1175–1200.

Bergman, N., and Jenter, D.C. (2005). Employee sentiment and stock option compensation. Working Paper no. 4504–04, Sloan School of Management, Massachusetts Institute of Technology, Cambridge, Massachusetts.

Bergstresser, D., and Philippon, T. (2006). CEO incentives and earnings management. *Journal of Financial Economics*, 80(3), 511–529.

Berle, A. (1931). Corporate powers as powers in trust. *Harvard Law Review*, 44(7), 1049–1074.

Berle, A., and Means, G.C. (1932). *The Modern Corporation and Private Property*. New York: Macmillan.

Berman, S.L., Wicks, A.C., Kotha, S., and Jones, T.M. (1999). Does stakeholder orientation matter? The relationship between stakeholder management models and firm financial performance. *Academy of Management Journal*, 42(5), 488–506.

Bernardin, H.J., and Pence, E.C. (1980). Rater training: Creating new response sets and decreasing accuracy. *Journal of Applied Psychology*, 65(1), 60–66.

Bernstein, P. (1996). *Against the Gods: The Remarkable Story of Risk*. New York: Wiley.

Berrone, P., Cruz, C., Gomez-Mejia, L.R., and Larraza-Kintana, M. (2010, in press). Governance and environmental performance in family-controlled public corporations, *Administrative Science Quarterly*.

Berrone, P., and Gomez-Mejia, L.R. (2006). Do firms compensate their CEOs for good environmental performance? Paper presented at the Academy of Management, Atlanta, GA.

———. (2008). Beyond financial performance: Is there something missing in executive compensation schemes? In L.R. Gomez-Mejia and S. Werner (Eds.), *Global Compensation: Foundations and Perspectives*. London: Routledge, 205–215.

———. (2009). Environmental performance and executive compensation: An integrated agency-institutional perspective. *Academy of Management Journal*, 52(1), 124–141.

Berrone, P., and Otten, J. (2008). A global perspective on executive compensation. In L.R. Gomez-Mejia and S. Werner (Eds.), *Global Compensation: Foundations and Perspectives*. London: Routledge, 113–122.

Berrone, P., Surroca, J., and Tribo, J. (2007). Corporate ethical identity as a determinant of firm performance: A test of the mediating role of stakeholder satisfaction. *Journal of Business Ethics*, 76(1), 35–53.

Best, R. (1961). Profit sharing and motivation for productivity. In a symposium on profit sharing and productivity motivation. Madison, WI: Center for Productivity Motivation.

Bettis, J.C., Bizjak, J.M., and Lemmon, M.L. (2005). Exercise behavior, valuation, and the incentive effects of employee stock options. *Journal of Financial Economics*, 76(2), 445–470.

Bettis, R.A., and Hall, W.K. (1983). The business portfolio approach—where it falls down in practice. *Long Range Planning*, 12(2), 95–104.

Bhagat, S. (1983). The effect of pre-emptive right amendments on shareholder wealth. *Journal of Financial Economics*, 12(3), 289–310.

Bickford, C.C. (1981). Long-term incentives for management, part 6: Performance attainment plans. *Compensation Review*, 12(3), 14–29.

Biddle, G.C. (1980). Accounting methods and management decisions: The case of inventory costing and inventory policy. *Journal of Accounting Research*, 18 (Suppl.), 235–280.

Biddle, G.C., and Lindahl, F.W. (1982). Stock price reactions to LIFO adoptions: The association between excess returns and LIFO tax savings. *Journal of Accounting Research*, 20(Autumn), 551–558.

Bigley, G.A., and Wiersema, M.F. (2002). New CEOs and corporate strategic refocusing: How experience as heir apparent influences the use of power. *Administrative Science Quarterly*, 47(4), 707–727.

Black, F., and Scholes, M. (1973). The pricing of options and corporate liabilities. *Journal of Political Economy*, 81(3), 637–654.

Blair, R., and Kaserman, L. (1983). Ownership and control in modern organizations: Antitrust implications. *Journal of Business Research*, 11(3), 333–344.

Blau, P.M. (1970). A formal theory of differentiation in organizations. *American Sociological Review*, 35(2), 201–218.

Bliss, R.T., and Rosen, R.J. (2001). CEO compensation and bank mergers. *Journal of Financial Economics,* 61(1), 107–138.

Bloom, M. (1999). The performance effects of pay dispersion on individuals and organizations. *Academy of Management Journal,* 42(1), 25–40.

Bloom, M., and Milkovich, G.T. (1998). Relationship among risk, incentive pay, and organizational performance. *Academy of Management Journal,* 41(3), 283–297.

Boone, A.L., Casares-Field, L., Karpoff, J.M., and Raheja, C.G. (2007). The determinants of corporate board size and composition: An empirical analysis. *Journal of Financial Economics,* 85(1), 66–101.

Booth, J.E., Park, K.W., and Glomb, T.M. (2009). Employer-supported volunteering benefits: Gift exchange among employers, employees, and volunteer organizations. *Human Resource Management,* 48(2), 227–251.

Borjas, G. (2008). *Labor Economics,* 4th ed. New York: McGraw-Hill.

Boschen, J.F., Duru, A., Gordon, L.A., and Smith, K.J. (2003). Accounting and stock price performance in dynamic CEO compensation arrangements. *The Accounting Review,* 78(1), 143–168.

Boudreaux, K.J. (1973). Managerialism and risk-return performance. *Southern Economic Journal,* 39, 366–373.

Boulder Daily Camera. (1989). Fraud, extravagance brought down many of the nation's S&Ls. January 29, 78–79.

Bowen, R., Noreen, E.W., and Lacey, J.M. (1981). Determinants of the corporate decision to capitalize interest. *Journal of Accounting and Economics,* 3(2), 151–179.

Bowman, E.H. (1982). Risk seeking by troubled firms. *Sloan Management Review,* 23(4), 33–42.

———. (1984). Content analysis of annual reports for corporate strategy and risk. *Interfaces,* 14, 61–72.

Boyd, B.K. (1994). Board control and CEO compensation. *Strategic Management Journal,* 15(5), 335–344.

Boyd, B.K., and Salamin, A. (2001). Strategic reward systems: A contingency model of pay system design. *Strategic Management Journal,* 22(8), 777.

Bradley, M., and Wakeman, M. (1983). The wealth effects of targeted share repurchases. *Journal of Financial Economics,* 11(1–4), 301–328.

Brandes, S. (1970). *American Welfare Capitalism: 1880–1940.* Chicago: University of Chicago Press.

Braverman, H. (1974). *Labor and Monopoly Capital.* New York: Monthly Review Press.

Brehn, J.W., and Cole, A.H. (1966). Effect of a favor which reduces freedom. *Journal of Personality and Social Psychology,* 3(4), 420–426.

Brenner, S., and Schwalbach, J. (2009). Legal institutions, board diligence and top executive pay. *Corporate Governance,* 17(1), 1–12.

Brick, I.E., and Chidamibaran, W.A. (2008). Board monitoring, firm risk, and external regulation. *Journal of Regulatory Economics,* 33(1), 87–116.

Brickley, J.A., Bhagat, S., and Lease, R.C. (1985). The impact of long-range managerial compensation plans for shareholder wealth. *Journal of Accounting and Economics,* 7(1), 115–129.

Brigham, E.F. (1985). *Financial Management: Theory and Practice.* Hinsdale, IL: Dryden Press.

Brignall, S., and Modell, S. (2000). An institutional perspective on performance measurement and management in the "new public sector." *Management Accounting Research,* 11(3), 281–306.

Broderick, R.F. (1986). Pay policy and business strategy: Toward a measure of fit. Unpublished doctoral dissertation. Cornell University.

Bromiley, P. (1991). Testing a causal model of corporate risk taking and performance. *Academy of Management Journal,* 34(1), 37–59.

Bronfenbrenner, M. (1956). Potential monopsony power in labor markets. *Industrial and Labor Relations Review,* 9(4), 577–588.

Brouwer, C. (1984). Measuring the division manager's performance. *Management Accounting,* December, 30–33.

Brown, S.J., and Warner, J.B. (1980). Measuring security price performance. *Journal of Financial Economics,* 8(3), 205–258.

———. (1985). Using daily stock returns: The case of event studies. *Journal of Financial Economics,* 14, 3–31.

Brown, T., and York, D. (2008). Salary surveys. In L.A. Berger and D.R. Berger (Eds.), *The Compensation Handbook: A State-of-the-art Guide to Compensation Strategy and Design,* 5th ed. New York: McGraw-Hill, 95–124.

Buchenroth, P. (2006). Driving performance: Making pay work for the organization. *Compensation and Benefits Review,* May–June, 30–35.

Buck, T., Liu, X., and Skovoroda, R. (2008). Top executive pay and firm performance in China. *Journal of International Business Studies,* 39(5), 833–850.

Bullock, R.J., and Lawler, E.E. (1984). Gainsharing: A few questions and fewer answers. *Human Resource Management,* 23(1), 23–40.

Burack, E.H. (1988). *Creative Human Resource Planning and Applications.* Englewood Cliffs, NJ: Prentice Hall.

Bureau of National Affairs. (1988). Special Report: Changing pay practices: New developments in employee compensation. Washington, DC: The Bureau of National Affairs.

Burgelman, R. (1983). A process model of internal corporate venturing in the diversified major firm. *Administrative Science Quarterly,* 28(2), 223–244.

Burney, L.L., Henle, C.A., and Widener, S.K. (2009). A path model examining the relations among strategic performance measurement system characteristics, organizational justice, and extra- and in-role performance. *Accounting, Organizations and Society,* 34(3–4) (April), 305–321.

Burrows, P. (2009). The SEC's Madoff misery. *Business Week,* February 18, 24–25.

Buysee, K., and Verbeke, A. (2003). Proactive environmental strategies: A stakeholder management perspective. *Strategic Management Journal,* 24(5), 453–470.

Cabrales, A., Calvo-Armengol, A., and Pavoni, N. (2008). Social preferences, skill segregation, and wage dynamics. *Review of Economic Studies,* 75(1), 65–98.

Callaghan, S.R., Saly, J.P., and Subramaniam, C. (2004). The timing of option repricing. *Journal of Finance,* 59(4), 1651–1676.

Campbell, B., and Barron, C. (1982). How extensively are human resource management practices being utilized by the practitioners? *Personnel Administrator,* 27(2), 67–71.

Campbell, D.T. (1979). Assessing the impact of planned social change. *Evaluation Program Planning,* 2(1), 67–90.

Cannella, A.A., Jr., and Holcomb, T.R. (2005). A multi-level analysis of the upper-echelons model. In F. Dansereau and F.J. Yammarino (Eds.), *Multi-level Issues in Strategy and Methods.* Oxford, UK: Elsevier, 197–238.

Caranikas-Walker, F., Goel, S., Gomez-Mejia, L.R., Grabke-Rundell, A. (2008). An empirical investigation of the role of subjective performance assessment versus objective performance indicators as determinants of CEO compensation. *Management Research,* 6(1), 1–25.

Cardy, R.L., and Dobbins, G.A. (1993). *Performance Appraisal.* Cincinnati: South-Western Publishing.

———. (1986). Affect and appraisal accuracy: Liking as an integral dimension in evaluating performance. *Journal of Applied Psychology,* 71(4), 672–678.

Carpenter, M.A. (2000). The price of change: The role of CEO compensation in strategic variation and deviation from industry strategy norms. *Journal of Management,* 26(6), 1179–1198.

Carpenter, M.A., and Sanders, W.G. (2002). Top management team composition: The missing link between CEO pay and firm performance? *Strategic Management Journal,* 23(4), 367–375.

———. (2004). The effect of top management team pay and firm internationalization on MNC performance. *Journal of Management,* 30(4), 509–528.

Carpenter, M.A., Sanders, W.G., and Gregersen, H.B. (2001). Bundling human capital with organizational context: The impact of international assignment experience on multinational firm performance and CEO pay. *Academy of Management Journal,* 44(3), 493–511.

Carroll, A.B. (1979). A three-dimensional conceptual model of corporate performance. *Academy of Management Review,* 4(4), 497–505.

Carroll, S.J. (1987). Business strategies and compensation systems. In D.B. Balkin and L.R. Gomez-Mejia (Eds.), *New Perspectives on Compensation.* Englewood Cliffs, NJ: Prentice Hall.

———. (1988). Handling the need for consistency and the need for contingency in the management of compensation. *Human Resource Planning,* 11(3), 191–196.

Carter, M.E., Ittner, C.D., and Zechman, S.L. (2009). Explicit relative performance evaluation in performance-vested equity grants. *Review of Accounting Studies,* 14(2), 40–65.

Carter, M.E., and Lynch, L.J. (2004). The effect of stock option repricing on employee turnover. *Journal of Accounting and Economics,* 37(1), 91–112.

Carton, R., and Hofer, C. (2006). *Measuring Organizational Performance: Metrics for Entrepreneurship and Strategic Management Research.* Cheltenham, UK: Edward Elgar.

Cartter, A.M. (1959). *Theory of Wages and Employment.* Homewood, IL: Richard D. Irwin.

Cascio, W.F. (1992). *Costing Human Resources.* Boston: PWS-Kent Publishing.

———. (2006). Strategies for responsible restructuring. *Academy of Management Executive,* 19(4), 39–51.

Casson, M. (1999). The economics of family firms. *Scandinavian Economic History Review,* 47(1), 10–23.

Castro, J. (1991). CEOs: No pain, just gain. *Time,* 137(15) (April 15), 40.

Cennamo, C. (2008). Shareholders' value maximization and stakeholders' interest: Is CEO long-term compensation the answer? In L.R. Gomez-Mejia and S. Werner (Eds.), *Global Compensation: Foundations and Perspectives.* London: Routledge, 100–110.

Cennamo, C., Berrone, P., and Gomez-Mejia, L.R. (2009). Does stakeholder management have a dark side? *Journal of Business Ethics*, 89(4), 491–507.

Certo, S.T., Daily, C.M., Cannella, A.A., Jr., and Dalton, D.R. (2003). Giving money to get money: How CEO stock options and CEO equity enhance IPO evaluations. *Academy of Management Journal*, 46(5), 643–653.

Chan, M. (2008). Executive compensation. *Business and Society Review*, 113(1), 129–161.

Chandler, A.D. Jr. (1962). *Strategy and Structure: Chapters in the History of American Industrial Enterprise.* Cambridge, MA: MIT Press.

———. (1977). *The Visible Hand: The Managerial Revolution in American Business.* Cambridge, MA: Belknap Press.

Chatterjee, A., and Hambrick, D.C. (2007). It is all about me: Narcissistic chief executive officers and their effects on company strategy and performance. *Administrative Science Quarterly*, 52, 1–38.

Chatterjee, S., and Lubatkin, M. (1990). Corporate mergers, stockholder diversification, and changes in systematic risk. *Strategic Management Journal*, 11(4), 255–269.

Chatterji, A., and Levine, D. (2006). Breaking down the wall of codes: Evaluating nonfinancial performance measurement. *California Management Review*, 48(2), 29–51.

Chauvin, K.W., and Shenoy, C. (2001). Stock price decreases prior to executive stock option grants. *Journal of Corporate Finance*, 7(1), 53–76.

Cheadle, A. (1989). Explaining patterns of profit sharing activity. *Industrial Relations*, 28(3), 387–401.

Chen, C.J., and Huang, J.W. (2009). Strategic human resource practices and innovation performance: The mediating role of knowledge management capacity. *Journal of Business Research*, 62(1), 104–114.

Cherrington, D.L., Reitz, H.J., and Scott, W.E. (1971). Effects of reward and contingent reinforcement on satisfaction and task performance. *Journal of Applied Psychology*, 55(6), 531–536.

Chevalier, J.M. (1969). The problem of control in large American corporations. *Antitrust Bulletin*, 14, 163–180.

Child, J.M. (1972). Organization structure and strategies: A replication of the Aston studies. *Administrative Science Quarterly*, 17(2), 163–176.

Cho, T.S., and Hambrick, D.C. (2006). Attention as the mediator between top management team characteristics and strategic change. The case of airline deregulation. *Organization Science*, 17(4), 453–469.

Cho, T.S., and Shen, W. (2007). Research and commentaries. Changes in executive compensation following an environmental shift: The role of top management team turnover. *Strategic Management Journal*, 28(7), 747–754.

Chow, C.W., Kato, Y., and Merchant, K.A. (1996). The use of organizational controls and their effects on data manipulation and management myopia: A Japan vs. U.S. comparison. *Accounting, Organizations and Society*, 21(2–3), 175–192.

Christmann, P. (2004). Multinational companies and the natural environment: Determinants of global environmental policy standardization. *Academy of Management Journal*, 47(5), 747–760.

Chwastiak, M. (2006). Rationality, performance measures and representations of reality: Planning, programming and budgeting and the Vietnam war. *Critical Perspectives on Accounting,* 17(1), 29–55.

Ciscel, D.H. (1974). Determinants of executive compensation. *Southern Economic Journal,* 40(4), 613–617.

Ciscel, D.H., and Carroll, T.M. (1980). The determinants of executive salaries: An econometric survey. *Review of Economics and Statistics,* 62(1), 7–13.

Claes, B. (2008). Contracting for success in the era of globalization: Aligning the supply chain manager's compensation contract with the company's supply chain strategy. In L.R. Gomez-Mejia and S. Werner (Eds.), *Global Compensation: Foundations and Perspectives.* London: Routledge, 57–69.

Clarkson, M.B.E. (1995). A stakeholder framework for analyzing and evaluating corporate social performance. *Academy of Management Review,* 20(1), 92–117.

Coffee, J.C., Jr. (1988). Shareholders versus managers: The strain in the corporate web. In J.C. Coffee Jr., L. Lowenstein, and S. Rose-Ackerman (Eds.), *Knights, Raiders, and Targets: The Impact of the Hostile Takeover.* New York: Oxford University Press, 77–134.

Coles, J., Suay, J., and Woodbury, D. (2000). Fund advisor compensation in closed-end funds. *Journal of Finance,* 55(3), 1385–1414.

Coles, J.L., Daniel, N.D., and Naveen, L. (2007). Does one size fit all? *Journal of Financial Economics,* 87(2), 329–350.

Coles, J.L., Hertzel, M., and Swaminathan, K. (2006). Earnings manipulation around employee stock option reissues. *Journal of Accounting and Economics,* 41(1–2), 173–200.

Collela, A., Paetzold, R.L., Zardkoohi, A., and Wesson, M.J. (2007). Exposing pay secrecy. *Academy of Management Review,* 32(1), 55–71.

Combs, J.G., and Skill, M.S. (2003). Managerialist and human capital explanations for key executive pay premiums: A contingency perspective. *Academy of Management Journal,* 46(1), 63–73.

CompFlash.com. (1991). New developments in compensation and benefits. April.

Conyon, M.J., and Murphy, K.J. (2000). The prince and the pauper? CEO pay in the United States and United Kingdom. *Economic Journal,* 110(8), 640–671.

Conyon, M.J., and Peck, S.I. (1998). Board control, remuneration committees, and top management compensation. *Academy of Management Journal,* 41(2), 146–157.

Conyon, M.J., Peck, S.I., and Sadler, G.V. (2001). Corporate tournaments and executive compensation: Evidence from the UK. *Strategic Management Journal,* 22(8), 805–815.

———. (2009). Compensation consultants and executive pay: Evidence from the United States and United Kingdom. *Academy of Management Perspectives,* 23(1), February, 43–55.

Cook, F.W. (1981). The compensation director and the board's compensation committee. *Compensation and Benefits Review,* 13(2), 37–41.

———. (1999). Merit pay and performance appraisal. In L.A. Berger and D.R. Berger (Eds.), *The Compensation Handbook: A State-of-the-art Guide to Compensation Strategy and Design,* 5th ed. New York: McGraw-Hill, 509–527.

Coombs, G., and Gomez-Mejia, L.R. (1991). Cross-functional compensation strategies in high technology firms. *Compensation and Benefits Review,* 23(5), 40–49.

Coombs, G., and Rosse, J.G. (1992). Recruiting and hiring the high technology professional. In L.R. Gomez-Mejia and M.W. Lawless (Eds.), *Human Resource Management Strategy in High Technology*. Greenwich, CT: JAI Press.

Coombs, J.E., and Gilley, K.M. (2005). Stakeholder management as a predictor of CEO compensation: Main effects and interactions with financial performance. *Strategic Management Journal,* 26(9), 827–840.

Cooper, M.R. (1991). The compensation handbook. In M.L. Rock and L.A. Berger (Eds.), *The Compensation Handbook: A State-of-the-Art Guide to Compensation Strategy and Design,* 3d ed. New York: McGraw Hill.

Coords, H.H. (1980). Cost control at Fisher-Price toys. In B.L. Metzger (Ed.), *Increasing Productivity through Profit Sharing*. Evanston, IL: Profit Sharing Research Foundation.

Copeland, A., and Monnet, C. (2009). Welfare effects of incentive schemes. *Review of Economic Studies,* 76(1), 93–113.

Core, J.E., and Guay, W.R. (1991). Stock option plans for non-executive employees. *Journal of Financial Economics,* 61(2), 253–287.

Core, J.E., and Larcker, D.F. (2002). Performance consequences of mandatory increases in executive stock ownership. *Journal of Financial Economics,* 64(3), 317–340.

Coughlan, A.T., and Schmidt, R.M. (1985). Executive compensation management turnover and firm performance: An empirical investigation. *Journal of Accounting and Economics,* 7(1), 43–66.

Covaleski, M.A., Dirsmith, M.W., and Samuel, S. (1996). Managerial accounting research: The contributions of organizational and sociological theories. *Journal of Management Accounting Research,* 8, 1–35.

Cox, A. (2005). The outcomes of variable pay systems: Tales of multiple costs and unforeseen consequences. *International Journal of Human Resource Management,* 8(8), 1475–1497.

Coy, P. (2009). Housing: Don't get excited just yet. *Business Week,* April 13, 27–28.

Coyle-Shapiro, J.A.M., Morrow, P.C., Richardson, R., and Dunn, S.R. (2002). Using profit sharing to enhance employee attitudes: A longitudinal examination of the effects on trust and commitment. *Human Resource Management,* 41(4), 423.

Crocker, K.J., and Slemrod, J. (2007). The economics of earnings manipulation and managerial compensation. *The Rand Journal of Economics,* 38(3), 698.

Cronquist, H., Heyman, F., Nilsson, M., Slalaryd, H., and Vlachos, J. (2009). Do entrenched managers pay their workers more? *Journal of Finance,* 64(1), 309–339.

Cruz, C., Gomez-Mejia, L.R., and Becerra, M. (2010, in press). Perceptions of opportunism and the design of agency contracts: CEO-TMT relationships in family firms. *Academy of Management Journal.*

Crystal, G.S. (1988). The wacky, wacky world of CEO pay. *Fortune,* June 6, 68–78.

———. (1990). The great CEO pay sweepstakes. *Fortune,* June 18, 99–102.

———. (1991). Interview. *Time,* 137(15) (April 15), 40.

Cyert, R.M., and March, J.G. (1963). *A Behavioral Theory of the Firm.* Englewood Cliffs, NJ: Prentice Hall.

Dachler, H.P., and Mobley, W.H. (1973). Construct validation of all instrumentality-expectancy-task goal model of reward motivation: Some theoretical boundary conditions. *Journal of Applied Psychology,* 58(3), 397–418.

Daily, C.M., and Dalton, D.R. (1994). Corporate governance and the bankrupt firm: An empirical assessment. *Strategic Management Journal*, 15(8), 643–654.

Dann, L.Y., and DeAngelo, H. (1983). Corporate financial policy and corporate control. *Journal of Financial Economics*, 20(1–2), 87–127.

Das, G. (2009). The new world order. *New York Times*, January 2, A-21.

Datar, S., Kulp, S.C., and Lambert, R.A. (2001). Balancing performance measures. *Journal of Accounting Research*, 39(1), 75–92.

Datta, S., Iskandar-Datta, M., and Raman, K. (2001). Executive compensation and corporate acquisition decisions. *Journal of Finance*, 56(6), 2299–2336.

Davila, A., and Venkatachalam, M. (2004). The relevance of non-financial performance measures for CEO compensation: Evidence from the airline industry. *Review of Accounting Studies*, 9(4), 443–464.

Day, G.S., and Montgomery, D.B. (1983). Diagnosing the experience curve. *Journal of Marketing*, 47(2), 44–58.

Dearden, J. (1960). Problems in decentralized profit responsibility. *Harvard Business Review*, 38(3), 79–86.

———. (1969). The case against ROI control. *Harvard Business Review*, 47(3), 124–135.

De Charms. R. (1968). *Personal Causation: The Internal Affective Determinants of Behavior*. New York: Academic Press.

Deci, E.L. (1975). Notes on the theory and meta-theory of intrinsic motivation. *Organizational Behavior and Human Performance*, 15(4), 130–145.

Deckop, J.R. (1988). Determinants of chief executive officer compensation. *Industrial and Labor Relations Review*, 41(2), 215–226.

Deckop, J.R., Merriman, K.K., and Gupta, S. (2006). The effects of CEO pay structure on corporate social performance. *Journal of Management*, 32(3), 329–342.

Deming, E. (2000). *Out of the Crisis*. Cambridge, MA: MIT Technology Center for Advanced Engineering Study.

Demsetz, H. (1983). The structure of ownership and the theory of the firm. *Journal of Law and Economics*, 26(2), 375–390.

Demski, J. (1994). *Managerial Uses of Accounting Information*. Boston: Kluwer Publishers.

Denisi, A.S., Robbins, T.L., and Summers, T.P. (1997). Organization, processing, and use of performance information: A cognitive role for appraisal instruments. *Journal of Applied Social Psychology*, 27(21), 1884–1905.

Desai, M., and Dharnapala, D. (2006). Corporate tax avoidance and high-powered incentives. *Journal of Financial Economics*, 79(1), 145–179.

Deutsch, M. (1949). A theory of cooperation and competition. *Human Relations*, 2(2), 129–152.

Devanna, M.A., Fombrum, C., and Tichy, N. (1981). Human resource management: A strategic approach. *Organizational Dynamics*, 9(3), 51–67.

Devaro, J. (2006). Strategic promotion tournaments and worker performance. *Strategic Management Journal*, 27(8), 721–740.

Devers, C.E., Cannella, A.A., Reilly, G.P., and Yoder, M.E. (2007). Executive compensation: A multidisciplinary review of recent developments. *Journal of Management*, 33(6), 1016–1066.

Devers, C.E., McNamara, G., Wiseman, R.M., and Arrfelt, M. (2008). Moving closer to the action: Examining compensation design effects on firm risk. *Organization Science*, 20, 1–19.

Devers, C.E., Wiseman, R., and Holmes, R. (2007). The effects of endowment and loss aversion in managerial stock option valuation. *Academy of Management Journal,* 50(1), 191–208.

Deyá-Tortella, B., Gomez-Mejia, L.R., De Castro, J., and Wiseman, R.M. (2005). Incentive alignment or perverse incentives? A behavioral view of stock options. *Management Research,* 3(2), 109–120.

Dhalla, N.K., and Yuspeh, S. (1976). Forget the product life cycle concept! *Harvard Business Review,* 54(1), 102–112.

DiMaggio, P.J., and Powell, W.W. (1983). The iron cage revisited: Institutional isomorphism and collective rationality in organizational fields. *American Sociological Review,* 48(2), 147–160.

Dobbins, G., Cardy, R., and Carson, K. (1991). Examining fundamental assumptions: A contrast of person and system approaches to human resource management. In K.M. Rowland and G.R. Ferris (Eds.), *Research in Personnel and Human Resources Management.* Greenwich, CT: JAI Press.

Dodd, M.E. (1932). For whom are corporate managers trustees. *Harvard Law Review,* 45(7), 1145–1163.

Doeringer, P.B., and Piore, M.J. (1971). Theories of low-wage workers. In L.G. Reynolds, S.H. Masters, and C.H. Moser (Eds.), *Readings in Labor Economics and Labor Relations.* Englewood Cliffs, NJ: Prentice Hall.

Donalson, T., and Preston, L.E. (1995). The stakeholder theory of the corporation: Concepts, evidence, and implications. *Academy of Management Review,* 20(1), 65–91.

Donoher, W.J., Reed, R., and Storrud-Barnes, S.F. (2007). Incentive alignment, control, and the issue of misleading financial disclosures. *Journal of Management,* 23, 547–569.

Douglas, E.J., and Santarre, R. (1990). Incentive contracts and stockholder monitoring: Substitute sources of executive compliance. *Quarterly Review of Economics and Business,* 30(2), 24–31.

Dow, J., and Raposo, C.C. (2005). CEO compensation, change, and corporate strategy. *Journal of Finance,* 60(6), 2701–2727.

Dowell, G., Hart, S.L., and Yeung, B. (2000). Do corporate global environmental standards create or destroy market value? *Management Science,* 46(8), 1059–1074.

Downs, A. (1967). The life cycle of bureaus. In A. Downs (Ed.), *Inside Bureaucracy.* San Francisco: Little, Brown and Rand.

Doyle, R.J. (1983). *Gainsharing and Productivity: A Guide to Planning, Implementation, and Development.* New York: Amacom.

Dugan, W.K. (1989). Ability and effort attributions: Do they affect how managers communicate performance feedback information? *Academy of Management Journal,* 32(1), 87–114.

Duncan, R.B. (1972). Characteristics of organizational environments and perceived environmental uncertainty. *Administrative Science Quarterly,* 17(3), 313–327.

Dunford, B., Boudreau, J., and Boswell, W. (2005). Out-of-the-money: The impact of underwater stock options on executive job search. *Personnel Psychology,* 59(1), 67–102.

Dunlop, J.T. (1957). The task of contemporary wage theory. In G.W. Taylor and F.C. Pierson (Eds.), *New Concepts in Wage Determination.* New York: McGraw-Hill.

Duru, A., and Reeb, D.M. (2002). Geographic and industrial corporate diversification: The level and structure of executive compensation. *Journal of Accounting, Auditing, and Finance,* 17(1), 1–30.

Dye, R.A. (1988). Earnings management in an overlapping generation's model. *Journal of Accounting Research,* 26(2), 195–235.

Dyer, L., and Theriault, R. (1976). Determinants of pay satisfaction. *Journal of Applied Psychology,* 61(5), 596–604.

Dyl, E.A. (1988). Corporate control and management compensation: Evidence on the agency problem. *Managerial and Decision Economics,* 9(1), 21–25.

———. (1989). Agency, corporate control and accounting methods: The LIFO-FIFO choice. *Managerial and Decision Economics,* 10(3), 141–137.

Eaton, J., and Rosen, H. (1983). Agency, delayed compensation, and the structure of executive remuneration. *The Journal of Finance,* 23(1), 489–1505.

Ehrenberg, R.G., and Bognanno, M.L. (1990). The incentive effects of tournaments revisited: Evidence from the European PGA tour. *Industrial and Labor Relations Review,* 43(3), 74–88.

Ehrenberg, R.G., and Smith, R.S. (1988). *Modern Labor Economics.* Glenview, IL: Scott, Foresman.

Eisenhardt, K. (1989). Agency theory: An assessment and a review. *Academy of Management Review,* 14(1), 57–74.

Elayan, F.A., Li, J., and Meyer, T.O. (2008). Accounting irregularities, management compensation structure and information asymmetry. *Accounting and Finance,* 48(5), 741–760.

Ellig, B.R. (1981). *Executive Compensation: A Total Pay Perspective.* New York: McGraw-Hill.

———. (1982). Compensation element: Market phase determines the mix. *Compensation Review,* 16(3), 39–54.

———. (1984). Incentive plans: Over the long-term. *Compensation Review,* 16(3), 39–54.

———. (2006). The evolution of executive pay in the United States. *Compensation and Benefits Review,* 38(1), 55–61.

———. (2007). Fashioning an employee benefits philosophy statement. *Benefits and Compensation Statement,* 44(10), 44–48.

———. (2008). Executive pay plan financial measurements. *Compensation and Benefits Review,* 40(5), 42–50.

Ellsworth, R.R. (1983). Subordinate financial policy to corporate strategy. *Harvard Business Review,* 61(6), 170–181.

Equilar. (2007). 2007 Equity Trends Report. October. San Mateo, CA: Equilar. http://www.equilar.com/Executive_Compensation_Reports.php.

———. (2008). 2008 Executive Stock Ownership Guidelines Report. October. San Mateo, CA: Equilar. http://www.equilar.com/Executive_Compensation_Reports.php.

Ettlie, J.E. (1983). Subordinate financial policy to corporate strategy. *Harvard Business Review,* 61(6), 170–181.

Evan, W.M., and Freeman, R.E. (1988). A stakeholder theory of the modern corporation: Kantian capitalism. In T. Beauchamp and N. Bowie (Eds.), *Ethical Theory in Business.* Englewood Cliffs, NJ: Prentice Hall, 75–93.

Ezzamel, M., and Watson, R. (1998). Market comparison earnings and the bidding up of executive cash compensation: Evidence from the United Kingdom. *Academy of Management Journal,* 41(2), 221–231.

Faccio, M., Lang, L.H., and Young, L. (2001). Dividends and expropriation. *American Economic Review,* 91(1), 54–78.

Fahlenbrach, R. (2009). Shareholder rights, boards, and CEO compensation. *Review of Finance,* 13(1), 81–113.

Fama, E.F. (1980). Agency problems and the theory of the firm. *Journal of Political Economy,* 88(2), 288–298.

Fama, E.F., and Jensen, M.C. (1983a). Agency problems and residual claims. *Journal of Law and Economics,* 26(2), 327–349.

———. (1983b). Separation of ownership and control. *Journal of Law and Economics,* 26(2), 301–325.

Fay, C.H. (1987). Using the strategic planning process to develop a compensation strategy. *Topics in Total Compensation,* 2(2), 117–129.

———. (1989). External pay relationships. In L.R. Gomez-Mejia (Ed.), *Compensation and Benefits.* Washington, DC: Bureau of National Affairs.

———. (2008). The global convergence of compensation practices. In L.R. Gomez-Mejia and S. Werner (Eds.), *Global Compensation: Foundations and Perspectives.* London: Routledge, 131–139.

Fayol, H. (1949). *General and Industrial Management.* London: Pitnam.

Fein, M. (1999). Improshare: Sharing productivity gains with employees. In L.A. Berger and D.R. Berger (Eds.), *The Compensation Handbook: A State-of-the-art Guide to Compensation Strategy and Design,* 5th ed. New York: McGraw-Hill, 217–226.

Feldman, J.M. (1981). Beyond attribution theory: Cognitive processes in performance appraisal. *Journal of Applied Psychology,* 66(2), 127–148.

Feltham, G.A., and Xie, J. (1994). Performance-measure congruity and diversity in multitask principal-agent relations. *Accounting Review,* 69(3), 429–453.

Fenn, G.W., and Liang, N. (2001). Corporate payout policy and managerial stock incentives. *Journal of Financial Economics,* 60(1), 45–72.

Festing, M., Eiding, J., and Roger, S. (2007). Strategic issues and local constraints in transnational compensation strategies: An analysis of cultural, institutional and political influences. *European Management Journal,* 25(2), 118–131.

Festinger, L. (1954). A theory of social comparison processes. *Human Relations,* 7(2), 117–140.

———. (1957). *A Theory of Cognitive Dissonance.* Evanston, IL: Row, Peterson.

Fiegenbaum, A., and Thomas, H. (1986). Dynamic and risk measurement perspectives on Bowman's risk-return paradox for strategic management: An empirical study. *Strategic Management Journal,* 7(5), 395–407.

———. (1988). Attitudes towards risk and risk return paradox: Prospect Theory explanations. *Academy of Management Journal,* 31(1), 81–106.

Fierman, J. (1990). The people who set the CEO's pay. *Fortune,* March 12, 58–66.

Finkelstein, S., and Boyd, B.K. (1998). How much does the CEO matter? The role of managerial discretion in the setting of CEO compensation. *Academy of Management Journal,* 41(2), 179–199.

Finkelstein, S., and Hambrick, D.C. (1988). Chief executive compensation: A synthesis and reconciliation. *Strategic Management Journal,* 9, 43–58.

————. (1996). Boards of directors and corporate performance. In *Strategic Leadership: Top Executives and Their Effects on Organizations*. St. Paul, MN: West Publishing, 209–260.

Finkelstein, S., Hambrick, D.C., and Cannella, A.A. Jr. (2009). *Strategic Leadership: Theory and Research on Executives, Top Management Teams, and Boards*. New York: Oxford University Press.

Fishburn, P. (1989). Retrospective on the utility theory of von Newmann and Morgenstern. *Journal of Risk and Uncertainty*, 2(2), 127–158.

Fisher, C., and Downes, B. (2008). Performance measurement and metric manipulation in the public sector. *Business Ethics: A European Review*, 17(3), 245–258.

Fitzpatrick, I., and McMullen, T.D. (2008). Benchmarking. In L.A. Berger and D.R. Berger (Eds.), *The Compensation Handbook: A State-of-the-art Guide to Compensation Strategy and Design*, 5th ed. New York: McGraw-Hill, 125–142.

Florkowski, G.W. (1987). The organizational impact of profit sharing. *Academy of Management Review*, 12(4), 622–636.

Fogarty, T., Magman, M.L., Markanian, G., Bohdjahian, S. (2008). Inside agency: The rise and fall of Norlet. *Journal of Business Ethics*, April, 21–34.

Fombrun, C.J. (1983). Strategic management: Integrating the human resource systems into strategic planning. In. R.B. Lamb (Ed.), *Advances in Strategic Management*, 2. Greenwich, CT: JAI Press.

————. (1984a). Corporate culture and competitive strategy. In C.J. Fombrun, N.M. Tichy, and M.A. Devanna (Eds.), *Strategic Human Resource Management*. New York: Wiley.

————. (1984b). The external context of human resource management. In C.J. Fombrun, N.M. Tichy, and M.A. Devanna (Eds.), *Strategic Human Resource Management*. New York: Wiley.

————. (1984c). An interview with Reginald H. Jones and Frank Doyle. In C.J. Fombrun, N.M. Tichy and M.A. Devanna (Eds.), *Strategic Human Resource Management*. New York: Wiley.

————. (1993). Reputational rankings: Institutionalizing social audits of corporate performance. New York: Stern School of Business, New York University.

Fombrun, C.J., and Tichy, N.M. (1984). Strategic planning and human resource management: At rainbow's end. In R.B. Lamb (Ed.), *Competitive Strategic Management*. Englewood Cliffs, NJ: Prentice Hall.

Fombrun, C.J., Tichy, N.M., and Devanna, M.A. (1984). *Strategic Human Resource Management*. New York: Wiley.

Fong, E.A., Misangyi, V.F., and Tosi, H.L. (2010, in press). The effect of CEO pay deviations on CEO withdrawal, firm size, and firm profits. *Strategic Management Journal*.

Forward, J., and Zander, A. (1971). Choice of unattainable goals and affects on performance. *Organization Behavior and Human Performance*, 6(2), 184–199.

Foster, K.E. (1985). An anatomy of company pay practices. *Personnel*, September, 66–72.

Franco-Santos, M. (2007). The performance impact of using measurement diversity in executives' annual incentive system. Cranfield School of Management, Cranfield University. Cranfield, Bedford, UK.

————. (2008). Performance measurement issues, incentive application and globalization. In L.R. Gomez-Mejia and S. Werner (Eds.), *Global Compensation: Foundations and Perspectives*. London: Routledge, 41–52.

Frankforter, S., Berman, S., and Jones, T. (2000). Boards of directors and shark repellents: Assessing the value of an agency theory perspective. *Journal of Management Studies,* 37(3), 321–348.

Frederikson, J.W., Hambrick, D.C., and Baumrin, S. (1988). A model of CEO dismissal. *Academy of Management Review,* 13(2), 255–271.

Freeman, E.R. (1984). *Strategic Management: A Stakeholder Approach.* Englewood Cliffs, N.J: Prentice Hall.

Freeman, E.R., and McVea, J. (2001). A stakeholder approach to strategic management. In M. Hitt and E.R. Freeman and J. Harrison (Eds.), *Handbook of Strategic Management,* 189–207. Oxford, UK: Blackwell Publishing.

Friedman, M. (1970). The social responsibility of business is to increase its profits. *New York Times Magazine,* 13, 32–33.

Frisch, C.J., and Dickinson, A.M. (1990). Work productivity as a function of the percentage of monetary incentives to base pay. *Journal of Organization Behavior Management,* 11(1), 13–28.

Fryxrell, G.E. (1990). Managing the culture of innovation. In L.R. Gomez-Mejia and M.W. Lawless (Eds.), *Organizational Issues in High Technology Management.* Greenwich, CT: JAI Press.

Fuchsberg, G. (1990). Notes from the executive compensation front. *Wall Street Journal Reports,* R5.

Fuehrer, W.F. (1991). Practical approaches to gain-sharing design. In M.L. Rock and L.A. Berger (Eds.), *The Compensation Handbook: A State-of-the-art Guide to Compensation Strategy and Design,* 3d ed. New York: McGraw-Hill.

Gabor, A. (1991). *The Man who Discovered Quality.* New York: Time Books.

Galbraith, J.K. (1976). *The Affluent Society.* Boston: Houghton Mifflin.

Garen, J.E. (1994). Executive compensation and principal-agent theory. *Journal of Political Economy,* 102(6), 1175–1199.

Geare, A.J. (1976). Productivity from Scanlon-type plans. *Academy of Management Review,* 20(1), 99–108.

Geneen, H.S. (1984). Why directors can't protect the shareholders. *Fortune,* September 17, 28–32.

Gerhart, B. (2000). Compensation strategy and organizational performance. In S.L. Rynes and B. Gerhart (Eds.), *Compensation in Organizations.* San Francisco: Jossey-Bass, 151–195.

———. (2008). Compensation and national culture. In L.R. Gomez-Mejia and S. Werner (Eds.), *Global Compensation: Foundations and Perspectives.* London: Routledge, 142–155.

Gerhart, B., and Milkovich, G.T. (1990). Organizational differences in managerial compensation and financial performance. *Academy of Management Journal,* 33(4), 663–691.

———. (1993). Employee compensation: Research and practice. In M.D. Dunnette and L.M. Hough (Eds.), *Handbook of Industrial and Organizational Psychology.* Palo Alto, CA: Consulting Psychologists Press.

Gerhart, B., and Rynes, S.L. (2003). *Compensation: Theory, Evidence, and Strategic Implication.* London: Sage.

Gerstein, M., and Reisman, H. (1983). Strategic selection: Matching executives to business conditions. *Sloan Management Review,* 43, 30–51.

Giancola, F. (2007). New forms of organization don't justify skill-based pay. *Compensation and Benefits Review,* May–June, 56–59.

Gibbons, R., and Murphy, K. (1990). Relative performance evaluation for chief executive officers. *Industrial and Labor Relations Review,* 43(3), 30–51.

Gibbs, M., Merchant, K.A., Van Der Stede, W.A., and Vargus, M.E. (2004). Determinants and effects of subjectivity in incentives. *Accounting Review,* 79(2), 409–436.

Giraud, F.L.P., and Mendoza, C. (2008). Justice as a rationale for the controllability principle: A study of managers' opinions. *Management Accounting Research,* 19(1), 32–44.

Goffin, R.D., Jelley, R.B., Powell, D.M., and Johnson, N.G. (2009). Taking advantage of social comparisons in performance appraisal: The relative percentile method. *Human Resource Management,* 48(2), 251–268.

Goldman, E., and Slezak, S.L. (2006). An equilibrium model of incentive contracts in the presence of information manipulation. *Journal of Financial Economics,* 80(3), 603–626.

Goldstein, M. (2009). Out the door, but still on the hook. *Business Week,* March, 25–26.

Gomez-Mejia, L.R. (1978). Strategies for evaluating test effectiveness in public jurisdictions. In S. Mussio (Ed.), *Personnel Selection and Training for Public Sector.* Chicago: Greater Lakes Assessment Centers.

———. (1983). Sex differences in occupational socialization. *Academy of Management Journal,* 26(3), 492–499.

———. (1984). Effect of occupation on task-related, contextual, and job involvement orientation: A cross-cultural perspective. *Academy of Management Journal,* 27(4), 706–720.

———. (1985). Dimensions and correlates of the personnel audit as an organizational assessment tool. *Personnel Psychology,* 38, 293–308.

———. (1986). Determining the cross-cultural structure of task-related and contextual constructs. *Journal of Psychology,* 120, 5–19.

———. (1988a). Evaluating employee performance: Does the appraisal instrument make a difference? *Strategic Management Journal,* 9(2), 155–170.

———. (1988b). The role of human resources strategy in export performance: A longitudinal study. *Strategic Management Journal,* 9(3), 493–505.

———. (Ed.) (1989). *Compensation and Benefits.* Washington, DC: Bureau of National Affairs.

———. (1990a). Increasing productivity: Performance appraisal and reward systems. *Personnel Review,* 19(2), 21.

———. (1990b). Women's adaptation to male-dominated occupations. *International Journal of Manpower,* 11(4), 11–17.

———. (1992). Diversification, compensation strategy, and firm performance. *Strategic Management Journal,* 13(5), 381–397.

———. (1994). Executive compensation: A reassessment and future research agenda. In G.R. Ferris (Ed.), *Research in Personnel and Human Resources Management,* 12. Stamford, CT: JAI Press.

Gomez-Mejia, L.R., and Balkin, D.B. (1980a). Can internal management training programs narrow the male-female gap in managerial skills? *Personnel Administrator,* 77–90.

———. (1980b). Classifying work-related and personal problems of troubled employees in employee assistance programs. *Personnel Administrator,* 23–29.

———. (1984a). Faculty satisfaction with pay and other job dimensions under union and non-union conditions. *Academy of Management Journal,* 27(3), 591–602.

———. (1984b). Union impacts on secretarial earnings. *Industrial Relations,* 23(1), 97–102.

———. (1985). Managing the high tech venture. *Personnel,* 62(12), 31–37.

———. (1987a). Pay compression in an academic environment: The case of business schools. In D.B. Balkin and L.R. Gomez-Mejia (Eds.), *New Perspectives on Compensation.* Englewood Cliffs, NJ: Prentice Hall.

———. (1987b). The causes and consequences of pay compression in business schools. *Compensation and Benefits Review,* 19(5), 43–55.

———. (1987c). Effect of organizational strategy on pay policy. Paper presented at the National Academy of Management Meetings, New Orleans, LA.

———. (1987d). The determinants of personnel manager perceptions of effective drug testing programs. *Personnel Psychology,* 40(4), 745–763.

———. (1987e). The determinants of managerial satisfaction with the expatriation and repatriation process. *Journal of Management Development,* 6(1), 7–17.

———. (1989). Effectiveness of individual and aggregate compensation strategies. *Industrial Relations,* 28(3), 431–445.

———. (1992). *Compensation, Organizational Strategy, and Firm Performance.* Cincinnati: South-Western Publishing Company.

Gomez-Mejia, L.R., Balkin, D.B., and Cardy, R. (2010). *Managing Human Resources.* New York: Pearson-Prentice Hall.

Gomez-Mejia, L.R., Balkin, D.B., and Milkovich, G.T. (1990). Rethinking your rewards for technical employees. *Organizational Dynamics,* 18(4), 62–75.

Gomez-Mejia, L. R, Balkin, D.B., and Welbourne, T.M. (1990). The influence of venture capitalists on management practices in the high technology industry. *Journal of High Technology Management Research,* 1(1), 107–118.

Gomez-Mejia, L.R., Firfiary, S., and Cruz, C. (2011, in press). Family ownership and human resource management practices. In H. Liao and A. Joshi (Eds.) *Research in Personnel and Human Resource Management,* vol. 30. Bingley, UK: Emerald Publishing Group.

Gomez-Mejia, L.R., Hopp, M.A., and Sommerstad, R. (1978). Implementation and evaluation of flexible work hours: A case study. *Personnel Administrator,* 25(2), 39–51.

Gomez-Mejia, L.R., Larraza-Kintana, M., and Makri, M. (2003). The determinants of executive compensation on family-controlled firms. *Academy of Management Journal,* 46(2), 226–237.

Gomez-Mejia, L.R., Makri, M., and Larraza-Kintana, M. (2010, in press). Diversification decisions in family-controlled firms. *Journal of Management Studies.*

Gomez-Mejia, L., and McCann, J.E. (1989). Factors affecting export success in high technology and traditional firms. *International Journal of Management,* 6, 31–39.

Gomez-Mejia, L.R., and Mussio, S. (1975). Job enrichment in a civil service setting. *Public Personnel Management,* 4(1), 49–54.

Gomez-Mejia, L.R., Nunez-Nickel, M., Gutierrez, I. (2001). The role of family ties in agency contracts. *Academy of Management Journal,* 44(1), 1–15.

Gomez-Mejia, L.R., and Page, R.C. (1983). Integrating employee development and performance appraisal. *Training and Development Journal,* 138–145.

Gomez-Mejia, L.R., Page, R.C., and Tornow, W.W. (1979). Development and implementation of a computerized job evaluation system. *Personnel Administrator,* 24(2), 62–73.

———. (1982). A comparison of the practical utility of traditional, statistical, and hybrid job evaluation approaches. *Academy of Management Journal,* 25(4), 790–809.

————. (1985). Improving the effectiveness of performance appraisal. *Personnel Administrator,* 30(1), 74–84.

————. (1987). Computerized job evaluation systems. In D.B. Balkin and L.R. Gomez-Mejia (Eds.), *New Perspectives on Compensation.* Englewood Cliffs, NJ: Prentice Hall.

Gomez-Mejia, L.R., and Sanchez-Marin, G.S. (2006). Paying for results. Madrid, Spain: Prentice Hall/Financial Times.

Gomez-Mejia, L.R., Takacs-Haynes, Nunez-Nickel, Jacobson, and Moyano-Fuentes (2007). Socioemotional wealth and business risks in family-controlled firms: Evidence from Spanish olive oil mills. *Administrative Science,* 52(1), 106–137.

Gomez-Mejia, L.R., Tosi, H., and Hinkin, T. (1987). Managerial control, performance, and executive compensation. *Academy of Management Journal,* 30(1), 51–70.

Gomez-Mejia, L.R., Trevino, L.J., and Mixon, F.G. (2009). Winning the tournament for named professorships in management. *International Journal of Human Resource Management,* 20(9), 1843–1863.

Gomez-Mejia, L.R., and Welbourne, T.M. (1988). Compensation strategy: An overview and future steps. *Human Resource Planning,* 11(3), 173–189.

————. (1989). Executive compensation. In L.R. Gomez-Mejia (Ed.), *Compensation and Benefits.* Washington, DC: Bureau of National Affairs.

————. (1991). Compensation strategy in a global context. *Human Resource Planning,* 14(1), 29–42.

Gomez-Mejia, L.R., Welbourne, T.M., and Wiseman, R. (2000). The role of risk sharing and risk taking under gainsharing. *Academy of Management Review,* 25(3), 492–589.

Gomez-Mejia, L.R., and Werner, S. (Eds.) (2008). *Global Compensation: Foundations and Perspectives.* London: Routledge.

Gomez-Mejia, L.R., and Wiseman, R.M. (1997). Reframing executive compensation: An assessment and outlook. *Journal of Management,* 23(3), 291–374.

————. (2007). Does agency theory have universal relevance? *Journal of Organizational Behavior,* 28(1), 81–98.

Gomez-Mejia, L.R., Wiseman, R.M., and Johnson, B. (2005). Agency problems in diverse contexts: A global perspective. *Journal of Management Studies,* 42(7), 1507–1520.

Gordon, D.M., Edwards, R., and Reich, M. (1982). *Segmented Work, Divided Workers: The Historical Transformation of Labor in the United States.* London: Cambridge University Press.

Gordon, G.G. (1991). Cultural and psychological implications for compensation. In M.L. Rock and L.A. Berger (Eds.), *The Compensation Handbook: A State-of-the-art Guide to Compensation Strategy and Design,* 3d ed. New York: McGraw-Hill.

Gosh, D., and Lusch, R.F. (2000). Outcome effect, controllability and performance evaluation of managers: Some evidence from multi-outlet businesses. *Accounting, Organizations and Society,* 25(4/5), 411–425.

Gouldner, A.W. (1960). The norm of reciprocity: A preliminary statement. *American Sociological Review,* 25(2), 161–178.

Govindarajan, V., and Gupta, A.K. (1985). Linking control-systems to business unit strategy-impact on performance. *Accounting, Organizations and Society,* 10(1), 51–66.

Gowen, C.R. (1985). Managing work group performance by individual goals and group goals for an interdependent group task. *Journal of Organization,* 2(3), 12–22.

Graen, G. (1969). Instrumentality theory of work motivation: Some experimental results and suggested modifications. [Monograph]. *Journal of Applied Psychology,* 53.

Graham, J.R., Lemmon, M.L., and Wolf, J.G. (2002). Does corporate diversification destroy value? *Journal of Finance,* 57(2), 695–720.

Graham-Brown, M. (2008). Performance metrics and compensation. In L.A. Berger and D.R. Berger (Eds.), *The Compensation Handbook: A State-of-the-art Guide to Compensation Strategy and Design,* 5th ed. New York: McGraw-Hill, 511–521.

Graves, S.B. (1988). Institutional ownership and corporate R&D in the computer industry. *Academy of Management Journal,* 31(2), 417–427.

Graves, S.B., and Waddock, S.A. (1990). Institutional ownership and control: Implications for long-term corporate strategy. *Academy of Management Executive,* 4(1), 75–83.

Gray, B., and Ariss, S.S. (1985). Politics and strategic change across organizational life cycles. *Academy of Management Review,* 10(4), 707–723.

Gray, D. (2005). A multi-method investigation into the costs and into the benefits of measuring intellectual capital assets. Cranfield School of Management, Cranfield University. Cranfield, Bedfordshire, UK.

Gray, S.R., and Cannella, A.A. (1997). The role of risk in executive compensation. *Journal of Management,* 23(4), 517–540.

Greeley, T.P., and Oshsner, R.C. (1986). Putting merit pay back into salary administration. *Topics in Total Compensation,* 1(1), 14–30.

Greiner, L. (1972). Evolution and revolution as organizations grow. *Harvard Business Review,* 50(4), 37–46.

Grey, J., and Kipnis. D. (1976). Untangling the performance appraisal dilemma: The influence of perceived organizational context on valuative processes. *Journal of Applied Psychology,* 61, 329–335.

Griffith, D.E. (2008). Compensation practices in a middle market company. In L.A. Berger and D.R. Berger (Eds.), *The Compensation Handbook: A State-of-the-art Guide to Compensation Strategy and Design,* 5th ed. New York: McGraw-Hill, 197–205.

Griffith, R., and Neely, A. (2009). Performance pay and managerial experience in multitask teams: Evidence from within the firm. *Journal of Labor Economics,* 27(1), 15–36.

Grinstein, Y., and Hribar, P. (2004). CEO compensation and incentives: Evidence from M&A bonuses. *Journal of Financial Economics,* 73(1), 119–143.

Groff, J.E., and Wright, C.J. (1989). The market for corporate control and its implications for accounting policy choice. *Advances in Accounting,* 7, 3–21.

Gross, S.E., and Peterson, S. (2008). Total rewards and the future workforce. In L.A. Berger and D.R. Berger (Eds.), *The Compensation Handbook: A State-of-the-art Guide to Compensation Strategy and Design,* 5th ed. New York: McGraw-Hill, 11–21.

Grossman, S.J., and Hart, O. D. (1983). An analysis of the principal-agent problem. *Econometrica,* 51(1), 7–45.

Grossman, W., and Cannella, A.A. (2006). The impact of strategic persistence on executive compensation. *Journal of Management,* 32(2), 257–278.

Grote, D. (2008). Forced ranking. In L.A. Berger and D.R. Berger (Eds.), *The Compensation Handbook: A State-of-the-art Guide to Compensation Strategy and Design,* 5th ed. New York: McGraw-Hill, 479–492.

Guadalupe, M. (2007). Product market completion, returns to skill, and wage inequity. *Journal of Labor Economics,* 25(3), 439–474.

Guest, P.M. (2009). The impact of mergers and acquisitions on executive pay in the United Kingdom. *Economica,* 76(301), 149–175.

Guidry, F.J., Leone, A., and Rock, S. (1999). Earnings-based bonus plans and earnings management by business-unit managers. *Journal of Accounting and Economics,* 26(1–3), 113–142.

Gupta, A.K. (1987). SBU strategies, corporate-SBU relations, and SBU effectiveness in strategy implementation. *Academy of Management Journal,* 30(3), 477–500.

Gupta, A.K., and Govindarajan, V. (1984). Business unit strategy, managerial characteristics, and business unit effectiveness at strategy implementation. *Academy of Management Journal,* 27(1), 25–41.

Guston, B.H. (1973). Charisma, recognition, and the motivation of scientists. *American Journal of Sociology,* 78, 1119–1134.

Hagerman, R.L., and Zmijewski, M.E. (1979). Some economic determinants of accounting policy choice. *Journal of Accounting and Economics,* 1(2), 141–161.

Hagstrom, W.O. (1965). *The Scientific Community.* New York: Basic Books.

———. (1968). Departmental prestige and scientific productivity. Paper presented at the Annual Meeting of the American Sociological Association.

———. (1971). Inputs, outputs and the prestige of university science departments. *Sociology of Education,* 44(4), 375–397.

———. (1974). Competition in science. *American Sociological Review,* 39(1), 1–18.

Haire, M., Ghiselli, E.E., and Gordon, M.E. (1967). A psychological study of pay. *Journal of Applied Psychology,* 51(4), 636.

Hall, B.J., and Liebman, J.B. (1998). Are CEOs really paid like bureaucrats? *Quarterly Journal of Economics,* 113(3), 653–691.

Hall, B.J., and Murphy, K.J. (2002). Stock options for undiversified executives. *Journal of Accounting and Economics,* 33(1), 3–42.

———. (2003). The trouble with stock options, NBER working paper. http://www-rcf.usc.edu/~kjmurphy/HMTrouble.pdf.

Hambrick, D.C. (1981). Environment, strategies, and power within top management teams. *Administrative Science Quarterly,* 26(2), 253–275.

———. (1982). Environmental scanning and organizational scanning. *Strategic Management Journal,* 3(2), 159–174.

———. (1983). An empirical typology of mature industrial-product environments. *Academy of Management Journal,* 10, 27–41.

———. (1984). Taxonomic approaches to studying strategy: Some conceptual and methodological issues. *Journal of Management,* 10, 27–41.

Hambrick, D.C., Black, S., and Frederickson, J.W. (1992). Executive leadership for the high technology firm. In L.R. Gomez-Mejia and M.W. Lawless (Eds.), *Top Management and Effective Leadership in High Technology.* Greenwich, CT: JAI Press.

Hambrick, D.C., and Finkelstein, S. (1995). The effects of ownership structure on conditions at the top: The case of CEO pay raises. *Strategic Management Journal,* 16(3), 175–193.

———. (1987). Managerial discretion: A bridge between polar views of organizational outcomes. In L.L. Cummings and B.M. Staw (Eds.), *Research in Organizational Behavior,* vol. 9. Greenwich, CT: JAI Press.

Hambrick, D.C., Finkelstein, S., and Mooney, A.C. (2005). Executive job demands: New insight for explaining strategic decisions and leader behaviors. *Academy of Management Review,* 30(3), 472–491.

Hambrick, D.C., and Fukutomi, G.D. (1991). The seasons of a CEO's tenure. *Academy of Management Review,* 16(4), 719–743.

Hambrick, D.C., Macmillan, I.C., and Barbarosa, R. (1983). Business unit strategy and changes in the product R&D budget. *Management Science,* 29(7), 757–769.

Hambrick, D.C., and Mason, P.A. (1984). Upper echelons: The organization as a reflection of its top managers. *Academy of Management Review,* 9(2), 193–206.

Hambrick, D.C., and Snow, C.C. (1989). Strategic reward systems. In C.C. Snow (Ed.), *Strategy, Organization Design, and Human Resources Management.* Greenwich, CT: JAI Press.

Hambrick, D.C., Werder, A.V., and Zajac, E.J. (2008). New directions in corporate governance research. *Organization Science,* 19(3), 381–385.

Hamm, S. (2009). Silicon Valley losing its magic? *Business Week,* March 29, 28–36.

Hammer, W.C. (1975). How to ruin motivation with pay. *Compensation Review,* 7(3), 17–27.

Handler, W.C. (1990). Succession in family firms: A mutual role adjustment between entrepreneur and next-generation family members. *Entrepreneurship: Theory and Practice,* 15(1), 37–51.

Hanlon, M., Rajgopal, S., and Shevlin, T. (2003). Are executive stock options associated with future earnings? *Journal of Accounting and Economics,* 36(1–3), 3–43.

Hannan, M.T., and Freeman, J. (1977). The population ecology of organizations. *American Journal of Sociology,* 82, 929–964.

Hannan, R.L., Krishnan, R., and Newman, A.H. (2008). The effects of disseminating relative performance feedback in tournament and individual performance compensation plans. *Accounting Review,* 83(4), 893–913.

Hannan, R.L., Rankin, F.W., and Towry, K.L. (2006). The effect of information systems on honesty in managerial reporting: A behavioral perspective. *Contemporary Accounting Research,* 23(4), 885–918.

Hansen, G.S., and Hill, C.W. (1991). Are institutional investors myopic? *Strategic Management Journal,* 12, 1–16.

Hansen, G.S., and Wernerfelt, B. (1989). Determinants of firm performance: The relative importance of economic and organizational factors. *Strategic Management Journal,* 10(5), 399–411.

Harkins, S.G., and Petty, R.E. (1982). Effects of task difficulty and task uniqueness on social loafing. *Journal of Personality and Social Psychology,* 63, 1214–1229.

Harmon, L.R. (1965). *High School Ability Patterns: A Backward Look from the Doctorate.* Washington, DC: National Academy of Sciences.

Harris, J.P., and Bromiley, P. (2007). Incentives to cheat: The influence of executive compensation and firm performance on financial misrepresentation. *Organization Science,* 18(3), 350–367.

Harris, M., and Holmstrom, B. (1982). A theory of wage dynamics. *Review of Economic Studies,* 49(3), 315–333.

Haspeslagh, P. (1982). Portfolio planning: Uses and limits. *Harvard Business Review,* 60(1): 58–73.

Hausknecht, J.P., Rodda, J., and Howard, M.J. (2009). Targeted employee retention: Performance-based and job-related differences in reported reasons for staying. *Human Resource Management*, 48(2), 269–288.

Hayes, R.H., and Abernathy, W.J. (1980). Managing our way to economic decline. *Harvard Business Review*, 4, 67–77.

Hayes, T.C. (1990). Big oil fearful of backlash, becoming jittery over large profits. *The New York Times*, story appearing in *The Arizona Republic*, September 16, A1.

Haynes, K. T. 2008. CEO pay variance across countries: The role of informal and formal institutions, Unpublished report, Management Department, Arizona State University: 1–44. Tempe, AZ.

Healy, P.M. (1985a). The effect of bonus schemes on accounting decisions. *Journal of Accounting and Economics*, 7(3), 85–107.

———. (1985b). The effect of accounting procedure changes on executives' remuneration. *Journal of Accounting and Economics*, 9(1), 7–34.

Heath, C., Huddart, S., and Lang, M. (1999). Psychological factors and stock option exercise. *Quarterly Journal of Economics*, 114(2), 601–627.

Helfgott, R. (1962). *Group Wage Incentives: Experience with the Scanlon Plan*. New York: Industrial Relations Counselors.

Hellerman, M., and Kochanski, J. (2008). Merit Pays. In L.A. Berger and D.R. Berger (Eds.), *The Compensation Handbook: A State-of-the-art Guide to Compensation Strategy and Design*, 5th ed. New York: McGraw-Hill, 85–95.

Hemmer, T. (1996). On the design and choice of modern management accounting measures. *Journal of Management Accounting Research*, 8, 87–116.

Henderson, A.D., and Fredrickson, J.W. (2001). Top management team coordination needs and the CEO pay gap: A competitive test of economic and behavioral views. *Academy of Management Journal*, 44(1), 96–117.

Heneman, R.L. (1990). Merit pay research. In G. Ferris and K. Rowland (Eds.), *Research in Personnel and Human Resources Management*. Greenwich, CT: JAI Press.

Henriques, I., and Sadorsky, P. (1999). The relationship between environmental commitment and managerial perceptions of stakeholder importance. *Academy of Management Journal*, 42(1), 87–99.

Herbert, T., and Deresky, H. (1987). Generic strategies: An empirical investigation of topology validity and strategy content. *Strategic Management Journal*, 8, 135–147.

Herman, E.S. (1981). *Corporate Control, Corporate Power*. New York: Cambridge University Press.

Herman, E.S., and Lowenstein, L. (1988). The efficiency effects of hostile takeovers. In J.C. Coffee, L. Lowenstein, and S. Rose-Ackerman (Eds.), *Knights, Raiders, and Targets: The Impact of the Hostile Takeover*. New York: Oxford University Press.

Heron, R.A., and Lie, E. (2007). Does backdating explain the stock price pattern around executive stock option grants? *Journal of Financial Economics*, 83(2), 271–295.

Highhouse, S., and Paese, P. (1996). Contrast effect on strategic-issue framing. *Organizational Behavior and Human Resources Processes*, 65(2), 65–105.

Hijazi, S.T., and Bhatti, K.K. (2007). Determinants of executive compensation and its impact on organizational performance. *Compensation and Benefits Review*, March–April, 58–68.

Hill, C.W. (1988). Internal capital market controls and financial performance in multidivisional firms. *Journal of Industrial Economics*, 37(1), 67–83.

Hill, C.W., and Hansen, G.S. (1989). Institutional holdings and corporate R&D intensity in research intensive industries. Academy of Management Best Papers Proceedings, Washington, DC, 49th Annual Meeting of the Academy of Management, 17–21.

Hill, C.W., Hitt, M., and Hoskisson, R. (1988). Declining United States competitiveness: Reflections on a crisis. *Academy of Management Executive,* 2(1), 51–60.

Hill, C.W., and Hoskisson, R.E. (1987). Strategy and structure in the multiproduct firm. *Academy of Management Review,* 12(2), 331–341.

Hill, C.W., and Jones, T.M. (1992). Stakeholder-agency theory. *Journal of Management Studies,* 29(2), 131–154.

Hill, C.W., and Phan, P. (1991). CEO tenure as a determinant of CEO pay. *Academy of Management Journal,* 34(3), 712–717.

Hillman, A.J., and Keim, G.D. (2001). Shareholder value, stakeholder management, and social issues: What's the bottom line? *Strategic Management Journal,* 22(2), 125–139.

Hills, F.S. (1987). *Compensation Decision Making.* Hinsdale, IL: Dryden Press.

———. (1989). Internal pay relationships. In L. R. Gomez-Mejia (Ed.), *Compensation and Benefits.* Washington, DC: Bureau of National Affairs.

Hills, F.S., Scott, D.K., Markham, S.E., and Vest, M.J. (1987). Merit pay: Just or unjust desserts. *Personnel Administrator,* 32(9), 53–64.

Hirschey, M., and Pappas, J.L. (1981). Regulatory and life cycle influences on managerial incentives. *Southern Economic Journal,* 48(2), 327–334.

Hite, G.L., and Long, M.S. (1982). Taxes and executive stock options. *Journal of Accounting and Economics,* 4, 3–14.

Hitt, M.A., Ireland, R.D., and Hoskisson, R.E. (2009). *Strategic Management.* New York: McGraw-Hill/Irwin.

Hofer, C.W. (1975). Toward a contingency theory of business strategy. *Academy of Management Journal,* 18(4), 784–810.

Hoffman, C.C., Natham, B.R., and Holden, L.M. (1991). A comparison of validation criteria: Objective versus subjective performance measures and self-versus supervisor ratings. *Personnel Psychology,* 44(3), 601–621.

Hofstede, G. (1980). *Culture's Consequences.* Newbury Park, CA: Sage Publications.

Holmstrom, B. (1979). Moral hazard and observability. *Bell Journal of Economics,* 10(1), 74–91.

Holmstrom, B., and Milgrom, P. (1991). Multitask principal-agent analyses: Incentive contracts, asset ownership, and job design. *Journal of Law, Economics and Organization,* 7, 24–52.

———. (1994). The firm as an incentive system. *American Economic Review,* 84(4), 972–991.

Holtgrave, D., and Weber, E. (1993). Dimensions of risk perception for financial and health risk. *Risk Analysis,* 13(5), 553–558.

Holthausen, R., Larcker, D.F., and Sloan, R. (1995). Annual bonus schemes and the manipulation of earnings. *Journal of Accounting and Economics,* 19(1), 29–74.

Holthausen, R.W., and Leftwich, R.W. (1983). The economic consequences of accounting choice: Implications of costly contracting and monitoring. *Journal of Accounting and Economics,* 5(1), 77–117.

Hood, C. (2006). Gaming in Targetworld: The targets approach to managing British public services. *Public Administration Review,* 66(4), 515–521.

Hopwood, A.G. (1973). *An Accounting System and Managerial Behaviour.* London: Saxon House.

Hoskisson, R.E., Hitt, M.A., and Hill, C.W.L. (1990). Managerial incentives and investment in R&D in large multiproduct firms. Unpublished report, Management Department, Texas A and M University.

Howard, L.W., and Dougherty, T.W. (2004). Alternative reward strategies and employee reactions. *Compensation and Benefits Review,* Jan-Feb, 41–51.

Hrebiniak, L.G., and Joyce, W.F. (1985). Organizational adaptation: Strategic choice and environmental determinism. *Administrative Science Quarterly,* 30(3), 336–349.

Hughes, C.L. (1986). The demerit of merit. *Personnel Administrator,* 31(6), 40.

Hunt, H.G. (1986). The separation of corporate ownership and control: Theory, evidence and implications. *Journal of Accounting Literature,* 5, 85–124.

Hybels, R.C., and Barley, S. R. (1990). Coaptation and the legitimation of professional identities: Human resource policies in high technology firms. In L.R. Gomez-Mejia and M.W. Lawless (Eds.), *Organizational Issues in High Technology Management.* Greenwich, CT: JAI Press.

Hyman, J.S. (1991). Long-term incentives. In M.L. Rock and L.A. Berger (Eds.), *The Compensation Handbook: A State-of-the-art Guide to Compensation Strategy and Design,* 3d ed. New York: McGraw Hill.

Hymowitz, C. (2003). How to fix a broken system: A rush of new plans promise to make corporate boards more accountable. Will they work? *Wall Street Journal,* R1–R12.

Ilgen, D.R., and Feldman, J.M. (1983). Performance appraisal: A process focus. In L.L Cummings and B.M. Staw (Eds.), *Research in Organizational Behavior.* Greenwich, CT: JAI Press, 51–96.

Indjejikian, R.J. (1999). Performance evaluation and compensation research: An agency perspective. *Accounting Horizons,* 13(2), 147–157.

Ingster, N.B. (2008). Job analysis, documentation, and job evaluation. In L.A. Berger and D.R. Berger (Eds.), *The Compensation Handbook: A State-of-the-art Guide to Compensation Strategy and Design,* 5th ed. New York: McGraw-Hill, 95–110.

Iskandar, M., Datta, S., and Raman, K. (2001). Executive compensation and corporate acquisition decisions. *Journal of Finance,* 56(6), 2299–2336.

Ittner, C.D., and Larcker, D.F. (1998a). Innovations in performance measurement: trends and research implications. *Journal of Management Accounting Research,* 10, 205–238.

―――――. (1998b). Are nonfinancial measures leading indicators of financial performance? An analysis of customer satisfaction. *Journal of Accounting Research,* 36, 1–35.

―――――. (2003). Coming up short on nonfinancial performance measurement. *Harvard Business Review,* 81(11), 88–95.

Ittner, C.D., Larcker, D.F., and Meyer, M.W. (2003). Subjectivity and the weighting of performance measures: Evidence form a balanced scorecard. *The Accounting Review,* 78(3), 725–758.

Ittner, C.D., Larcker, D.F., and Rajan, M.V. (1997). The choice of performance measures in annual bonus contracts. *The Accounting Review,* 72(2), 231–255.

Jackson, S.B. (2008). The effects of firm's depreciation method choice on managers' capital investment decisions. *The Accounting Review,* 83(2), 351–376.

Jansen, E.P., Merchant, K.A., and Van der Slede, V.A. (2009). National differences in incentive compensation practices: The different roles of financial performance measurement in the United States and the Netherlands. *Accounting, Organizations, and Society,* 34(1), 58–84.

Jaques, E. (1961). *Equitable Payment.* New York: Wiley.

———. (1979). Taking time seriously in evaluating jobs. *Harvard Business Review,* 57(5), 124–132.

Jarrell, G.A., Lehn, K, and Marr, W. (1985). Institutional ownership, tender offers and long-term investments. Washington, DC: Office of Chief Economist, Security and Exchange Commission.

Jeffrey, S.A., and Shaffer, V. (2007). Motivational properties of tangible incentives. *Compensation and Benefits Review,* May–June, 44–49.

Jensen, M.C. (1983). Organization theory and methodology. *Accounting Review,* 56, 109–121.

———. (1993). The modern industrial revolution, exit, and the failure of internal control mechanism. *Journal of Finance,* 98, 225–264.

———. (1998). *Foundations of Organizational Strategy.* Cambridge, MA: Harvard University Press.

———. (2001). Value maximization, stakeholder theory, and the corporate objective function. *Journal of Applied Corporate Finance,* 14(3), 8–21.

———. (2003). Paying people to lie: The truth about the budgeting process. *European Financial Management,* 9(3), 379.

Jensen, M.C., and Meckling, W.H. (1976). Theory of the firm: Managerial behavior, agency costs, and ownership structure. *Journal of Financial Economics,* 3(4), 305–360.

Jensen, M.C., and Murphy, K.J. (1990a). Performance pay and top-management incentives. *Journal of Political Economy,* 98(2), 225–264.

———. (1990b). CEO incentives—It's not how much you pay but how. *Harvard Business Review,* 68(3), 138–149.

Johnson, H.T., and Kaplan, R.S. (1987). *Relevance Lost: The Rise and Fall of Management Accounting.* Boston: Harvard Business School Press.

Jolly, D. (2009). Worldwide, a bad year only got worse. *New York Times,* January 2, B-1.

Jones, T.M. (1995). Instrumental stakeholder theory: A synthesis of ethics and economics. *Academy of Management Review,* 20(2), 404–437.

Jones, T.M., and Wicks, A.C. (1999). Convergent stakeholder theory. *Academy of Management Review,* 24(2), 206–221.

Kachelmeier, S.J., Reichert, B.E., and Williamson, M.G. (2008). Measuring and motivating quantity, creativity, or both. *Journal of Accounting Research,* 46(2), 341–373.

Kahneman, D., and Tversky, A. (1979). Prospect theory: An analysis of decision under risk. *Econometrica,* 47(2), 263–291.

Kanter, R.M. (1987). The attack on pay. *Harvard Business Review,* 65(2), 60–67.

Kaplan, R.S., and Norton, D.P. (1992). The balanced scorecard: Measures that drive performance. *Harvard Business Review,* 70(1), 71–79.

———. (1996). *The Balanced Scorecard: Translating Strategy into Action.* Cambridge, MA: Harvard Business School Press.

————. (2006). *Alignment: Using The Balanced Scorecard to Create Corporate Synergies.* Cambridge, MA: Harvard Business School Press.

Kaplan, S.N. (1994). Top executive rewards and firm performance: A comparison of Japan and the United States. *Journal of Political Economy,* 102(3), 510–546.

Katz, D., and Kahn, R.L. (1978). *The Social Psychology of Organizations.* New York: Wiley.

Katz, R., and Allen, T.J. (1985). Project performance and the locus of influence in the R&D matrix. *Academy of Management Journal,* 28(1), 67–87.

Kay, I.T. (1990). Interview appearing in *Wall Street Journal,* 1.

Kay, I.T., Gelfond, P., and Sherman, J. (1991). Ensuring the success of a new compensation program. In M.L. Rock and L.A. Berger (Eds.), *The Compensation Handbook: A State-of-the-art Guide to Compensation Strategy and Design,* 3d ed. New York: McGraw-Hill.

Kazanjian, R.K. (1988). Relation of dominant problems to stages of growth in technology based new ventures. *Academy of Management Journal,* 31(2), 257–279.

Ke, B., Petroni, K., and Safieddine, A. (1999). Ownership concentration and sensitivity of executive pay to accounting performance measures: Evidence from publicly and privately held insurance companies. *Journal of Accounting and Economics,* 28(2), 185–209.

Keller, L., Sarin, R.K., and Weber, M. (1986). Empirical investigation of some properties of the perceive riskiness of gambles. *Organizational Behavior and Human Resources Processes,* 38, 114–130.

Kelly, H.H., and Thibault, J. (1969). Group problem solving. In G. Lindsey and E. Aronson (Eds.), *Handbook of Social Psychology.* Reading, MA: Addison-Wesley.

Kennerley, M.P., and Neely, A.D. (2002). A framework of the factors affecting the evolution of performance measurement systems. *International Journal of Operations and Production Management,* 22(11), 1222–1245.

Kepner, E. (1983). The family and the firm: A co-evolutionary perspective. *Organizational Dynamics,* 12(1), 57–70.

————. (1982). Assigning managers on the basis of the life cycle. *The Journal of Business Strategy,* 2(4), 58–65.

————. (1985). Diversification strategies and managerial rewards: An empirical study. *Academy of Management Journal,* 28(1), 155–179.

Kerr, J.L., and Bettis, R.A. (1987). Boards of directors, top management compensation and shareholder returns. *Academy of Management Journal,* 30(4), 645–664.

Kerr, J.L., and Kren, L. (1992). The effect of relative decision monitoring on chief executive compensation. *Academy of Management Journal,* 35(2), 370–397.

Kerr, J.L., and Slocum, J.W. (1987). Managing corporate cultures through reward systems. *Academy of Management Executive,* 1(2), 3–15.

————. (1988). Linking reward systems and organizational cultures. In R.S. Shuler, S.A. Youngblood, and V.L. Huber (Eds.), *Readings in Personnel and Human Resource Management.* St. Paul, MN: West Publishing.

————. (2005). Managing corporate culture through reward systems. *Academy of Management Executive,* 19(4), 130–148.

Kerr, S. (1995). On the folly of rewarding A, while hoping for B. *Academy of Management Executive,* 9(1), 7–14.

Khandwalla, P.N. (1977). *The Design of Organizations.* New York: Harcourt Brace Jovanovich.

Kim, S., Mone, M.A., and Kim, S. (2008). Relationships among self-efficacy, pay-for-performance perceptions, and pay satisfaction: A Korean examination. *Human Performance,* 21(2), 158–179.

Kimberly, J.R. (1980). The life cycle analogy and the study of organizations: Introduction. In J.R. Kimberly and R.H. Miles (Eds.), *The Organizational Life Cycle.* San Francisco, CA: Jossey-Bass, 1–14.

King, A.A., and Lenox, M.J. (1994). Prospects for developing absorptive capacity through internal information provision. *Strategic Management Journal,* 25(4), 331–345.

———. (2000). Industry self-regulation without sanctions: The chemical industry's responsible care program. *Academy of Management Journal,* 43(4), 698–716.

———. (2002). Exploring the locus of profitable pollution reduction. *Management Science,* 48(2), 289–299.

Klarsfeld, A., Balkin, D.B., and Roger, A. (2003). Pay policy variability within a French firm: The case of skill-based pay in a process technology context. *Journal of High Technology Management Research,* 14(1), 47–70.

Klassen, R.D., and McLaughlin, C.P. (1996). The impact of environmental management on firm performance. *Management Science,* 42(8), 1199–1214.

Knopf, J.D., Nam, J., and Thornton, J.H. (2002). The volatility and price sensitivities of managerial stock option portfolios and corporate hedging. *Journal of Finance,* 57(2), 801–813.

Kochan, T.A. (2002). Addressing the crisis in confidence in corporations: Root causes, victims, and strategies for reform. *Academy of Management Executive,* 16(3), 139–141.

Kochan, T.A., and Dyer, L. (1976). A model of organizational change in the context of union-management relations. *Journal of Applied Behavioral Science,* 12(1), 59–78.

Kohn, A. (1993). Why incentive plans cannot work. *Harvard Business Review,* 71(5), 54.

Kostiuk, P.F. (1990). Firm size and executive compensation. *Journal of Human Resources,* 25(1), 90–105.

Kostova, T., and Zaheer, S. (1999). Organizational legitimacy under conditions of complexity: The case of the multinational enterprise. *Academy of Management Review,* 24(1), 64–81.

Kraft, K., and Niederprum, A. (1999). Determinants of management compensation with risk-averse agents and dispersed ownership of the firm. *Journal of Economic Behavior and Organization,* 40(1), 17–27.

Krishnan, R., Luft, J.L., and Shields, M.D. (2005). Effects of accounting-method choices on subjective performance-measure weighting decisions: Experimental evidence on precision and error covariance. *Accounting Review,* 80(4), 1163–1192.

Kroll, M., Simmons, S.A., and Wright, P. (1990). Determinants of chief executive officer compensation following major acquisitions. *Journal of Business Research,* 20(4), 349–366.

Kroll, M., Theorathorn, P., and Wright, P. (1993). Diversification through acquisitions: Corporate control as a determinant of post-announcement outcomes. Working Paper, University of Texas-Tyler.

Kuckreja, A. (2005). The Disney Decision of 2005 and the precedent it sets for corporate governance and fiduciary responsibility. Akin Gump, Strauss Hauer and Feld, LLP. http://www.akingump.com/docs/publication/795.pdf.

Kwon, S., Kim, M.S., Kang, S.C., and Kim, M.U. (2008). Employee reactions to gainsharing under seniority pay systems: The mediating effect of distributive, procedural, and interactional justice. *Human Resource Management*, 47(4), 757–775.

Lambert, R.A. (1983). Long-term contracts and moral hazard. *The Bell Journal of Economics*, 14(2), 441–445.

———. (1993). The use of accounting and security price measures of performance in managerial compensation contracts: A discussion. *Journal of Accounting and Economics*, 16(1–3), 101.

———. (2001). Contracting theory and accounting. *Journal of Accounting and Economics*, 32(1–3), 3–87.

Lambert, R.A., Larcker, D.F., and Weigelt, K. (1991). How sensitive are executive compensation to organizational size? *Strategic Management Journal*, 12(5), 395–402.

———. (1993). The structure of organizational incentives. *Administrative Science Quarterly*, 38(3), 438–461.

Landy, F.J., and Farr, J.L. (1983). *The Measurement of Work Performance: Methods, Theory, and Applications*. New York: Academic Press.

Langbein, L. (2008). Management by results: Student evaluation of faculty teaching and the miss-measurement of performance. *Economics of Education Review*, 27(4), 417–428.

Laplume, A. O., Sonpar, K., and Litz, R.A. (2008). Stakeholder theory: reviewing a theory that moves us. *Journal of Management*, 34(6), 1152–1189.

La Porta, R., Lopez-de-Silanes, F., and Shleifer, A. (1999). Corporate ownership around the world. *Journal of Finance*, 54(2), 471–517.

Larcker, D.F. (1983). The association between performance plan adoption and corporate capital investment. *Journal of Accounting and Economics*, 5(3), 3–30.

Larcker, D.F., Richardson, S.A., and Tuna, I. (2007). Corporate governance, accounting outcomes, and organizational performance. *The Accounting Review*, 82(4), 963–1008.

Larner, R.J. (1970). *Management Control and the Large Corporation*. New York: Dunellen.

Larraza-Kintana, M., Wiseman, R.M., Gomez-Mejia, L.R., and Welbourne, T.M. (2007). Disentangling compensation and employment risks using the behavioral agency model of managerial risk taking. *Strategic Management Journal*, 28(10), 1001–1019.

Latham, G.P., and Dossett, D.L. (1978). Designing incentive plans for unionized employees: A comparison of continuous and variable ratio reinforcement schedules. *Personnel Psychology*, 31(1), 47–61.

Lattimore, P.M., Baker, J.R., and Witte, A.D. (1992). The influence of probability on risky choice. *Journal of Economic Behavior and Organization*, 17(3), 377–400.

Laverty, K.J. (1996). Economic "short-termism": The debate, the unresolved issues, and the implications for management practice and research. *Academy of Management Review*, 21(3), 825–860.

Lawler, E.E., III. (1965). Managers' perceptions of their subordinates' pay and of their superiors' pay. *Personnel Psychology*, 18(4), 413–422.

————. (1967). Secrecy about management compensation: Are there hidden costs? *Organizational Behavior and Human Performance,* 2, 182–189.

————. (1971). *Pay and Organizational Effectiveness: A Psychological View.* New York: McGraw-Hill.

————. (1981). *Pay and Organization Development.* Reading, MA: Addison-Wesley.

————. (1984). The strategic design of reward systems. In C. Fombrun, N.M. Tichy, and M.A. Devana (Eds.), *Strategic Human Resource Management.* New York: Wiley.

————. (1986). *High Involvement Management.* San Francisco: Jossey-Bass.

————. (1989). The strategic design of pay-for-performance programs. In L.R. Gomez-Mejia (Ed.), *Compensation and Benefits.* Washington, DC: Bureau of National Affairs.

————. (1990). *Strategic Pay.* San Francisco: Jossey-Bass.

Lawrence, P.R., and Lorsch, J.W. (1977). *Organization Environment.* Homewood, IL: Dow Jones-Irwin.

Lazear, E.D., and Rosen, S. (1981). Rank order tournaments as optimum labor contracts. *Journal of Political Economy,* 89(5), 841–864.

Lazear, E.D., and Shaw, L. (2008). Personnel economics: The economist view of human resources. *Journal of Economic Perspectives,* 21(4), 91–114.

Lazer, R.I., and Wikstrom, W.S. (1977). Appraising managerial performance: current practices and future directions (Conference Board Rep. No. 753). New York: Conference Board.

Leary, M.R., Gallagher, B., Fors, E., Buttermore, N., Baldwin, E., Kennedy, K., and Mills, A. (2003). The invalidity of disclaimers about the effects of social feedback on self-esteem. *Personality and Social Psychology Bulletin,* 29(5), 623–636.

Ledford, G.E. Jr. (1991). The design of skill-based pay plans. In M.L. Rock and L.A. Berger (Eds.), *The Compensation Handbook: A State-of-the-art Guide to Compensation Strategy and Design,* 3d ed. New York: McGraw-Hill.

Leland, H., and Pyle, D. (1977). Informational asymmetries, financial structure, and financial intermediation. *Journal of Finance,* 32(2), 371–387.

Lemieux, T. (2007). The changing nature of wage inequality. *Journal of Population Economics,* 21(1), 21–48.

Lemieux, T., MacLeod, W.B., and Parent, D. (2007). Performance pay and wage inequality. IZA Discussion Paper No. 2850. Bonn, Germany: Institute for the Study of Labor.

Leonard, J.S. (1990). Executive pay and firm performance. *Industrial and Labor Relations Review,* 43(3), 13–29.

Leone, A.J., Wu, J.S., and Zimmerman, J.L. (2006). Asymmetric sensitivity of CEO cash compensation to stock returns. *Journal of Accounting and Economics,* 42(1–2), 167–192.

Leontiades, M. (1980). *Strategies for Diversification and Change.* Boston: Little, Brown.

Lesier, F. (1959). *The Scanlon Plan: A Frontier in Labor-Management Cooperation.* Cambridge, MA: Technology Press of MIT.

Lesieur, F., and Puckett, E. (1968). The Scanlon plan: Post, present, future. Proceedings of the Twenty-first Annual Meeting of the Industrial Relations Research Association.

Letza, S., Kirkbride, J., Xiuping, X., and Smallman, C. (2008). Corporate governance theorizing: Limits, critics, and alternatives. *Managerial Law,* 50(1), 17–32.

Lewellen, W.G. (1968). *Executive Compensation in Large Industrial Corporations.* New York: National Bureau of Economic Research.

————. (1969). Management and ownership in the large firm. *Journal of Finance,* 24(2), 299–332.

————. (1971). *The Ownership Income of Management.* New York: Columbia University Press.

Lewellen, W.G., and Huntsman, B. (1970). Managerial pay and corporate performance. *American Economic Review,* 60(4), 710–720.

Lewin, K. (1938). *The Conceptual Representation and Measurement of Psychological Forces.* Durham, NC: Duke University Press.

Liden, R.C., and Mitchell, T.R. (1983). The effects of group interdependence on supervisor performance evaluations. *Personnel Psychology,* 36(2), 289–299.

Lie, E. (2005). On the timing of CEO stock option awards. *Management Science,* 51(5), 802–812.

Lieberson, S., and O'Connor, J.F. (1972). Leadership and organizational performance: A study of large corporations. *American Sociological Review,* 37(2), 117–130.

Likert, R. (1961). *New Patterns of Management.* New York: McGraw-Hill.

Lillis, A.M. (2002). Managing multiple dimensions of manufacturing performance: An exploratory study. *Accounting, Organizations and Society,* 27(6), 497–529.

Lintner, J. (1965). The valuation of risk assets and the selection of risk investment in stock portfolios and capital budgets. *Review of Economics and Statistics,* 47(1), 13–37.

Lipe, M.G., and Salterio, S.E. (2000). The balanced scorecard: judgmental effects of common and unique performance measures. *The Accounting Review,* 75(3), 283–298.

————. (2002). A note on the judgmental effects of the balanced scorecard's information organization. *Accounting, Organizations and Society,* 27(6), 531–540.

Lippitt, G.L. (1967). Crisis in a developing organization. *Harvard Business Review,* 45(6), 102–112.

Littunen, H. (2003). A comparison of Finnish family and non-family firms. *Family Business Review,* 16(3), 183–198.

Livernash, R.E. (1957). The internal wage structure. In G.E. Taylor and F.C. Pierson, (Eds.), *New Concepts in Wage Determination.* New York: McGraw-Hill.

Locke, E.A. (1968). Toward a theory of task motivation and incentives. *Organizational Behavior and Human Performance,* 3(2), 157–189.

————. (2004). Goal-setting theory and its applications to the world of business. *Academy of Management Executive,* 18(4), 124–125.

Locke, E.A., Bryan, J.F., and Kendall, L.M. (1968). Goals and intentions as mediators of the effects of monetary incentives on behavior. *Journal of Applied Psychology,* 52(2), 104–121.

Locke, E.A., and Latham, G. P. (1990). *A Theory of Goal Setting and Task Performance.* Englewood Cliffs, NJ: Prentice Hall.

Locke, E.A., Shaw, K., Saari, L.M., and Latham, G.P. (1981). Goal setting and task performance 1969–1980. *Psychological Bulletin,* 90(1), 125–152.

Loescher, S.M. (1984). Bureaucratic measurement, shuttling stock shares, and shortened time horizons: Implications for economic growth. *Quarterly Review of Economics and Business,* 24(4), 1–23.

Longnecker, B., and Krueger, J. (2007). The next wave of compensation disclosure. *Compensation and Benefits Review,* January/February, 50–70.

Longenecker, C.O., Sims, H.P. Jr., and Gioca, D.A. (1987). Behind the mask: The politics of employee appraisal. *Academy of Management Executive,* 1(3), 183–193.

Loomis, C.J. (1982). The madness of executive compensation. *Fortune,* July 12, 42–51.

⸻. (2009a). AIG: The company that came to dinner. *Fortune,* January 19, 70–78.

⸻. (2009b). More trouble at AIG. *Fortune,* March 15, 70–75.

Lord, R.G. (1985). Accuracy in behavioral measurement: An alternative definition based on raters' cognitive schema and signal detection theory. *Journal of Applied Psychology,* 70, 66–71.

Lorsch, J.W., and Allen, S.A. (1973). *Managing Diversity and Interdependence.* Boston: Division of Research, Harvard Business School.

Lubatkin, M. (1987). Merger strategies and stockholder value. *Strategic Management Journal,* 8, 39–53.

Lublin, J.S. (2008). Boards flex their pay muscles. *Wall Street Journal,* April 14, R-1.

Lush, D.R. (1975). Sharing responsibility, profit, and ownership. In B.A. Diekman and B.L. Metzger (Eds.), *Profit Sharing: The Industrial Adrenalin.* Evanston, IL: Profit Sharing Research Foundation.

Luthans, F. (1988). Successful vs. effective real managers. *Academy of Management Executive,* 2(2), 127–132.

Magenheim, E.B., and Mueller, D.C. (1988). On measuring the effects of acquisitions on acquiring firm shareholders. In J.C. Coffee, L. Lowenstein, and S. Rose-Ackerman (Eds.), *Knights, Raiders, and Targets: The Impact of the Hostile Takeover.* New York: Oxford University Press.

Mahoney, L.S., and Thorne, L. (2005). Corporate social responsibility and long-term compensation: Evidence from Canada. *Journal of Business Ethics,* 57(3), 241–253.

Mahoney, T.A. (1979). Organizational hierarchy and position worth. *Academy of Management Journal,* 22(4), 726–737.

⸻. (1989). Employment compensation planning and strategy. In L.R. Gomez-Mejia (Ed.), *Compensation and Benefits.* Washington, DC: Bureau of National Affairs.

Makri, M. (2008) Incentives to stimulate innovation in a global context. In L.R. Gomez-Mejia and S. Werner (Eds.), *Global Compensation: Foundations and Perspectives.* London: Routledge, 72–82.

Makri, M., and Gomez-Mejia, L.R. (2007). Executive compensation: Something old, something new. In S. Werner (Ed.), *Managing Human Resources in North America.* London: Routledge, 158–171.

Makri, M., Lane, P.J., and Gomez-Mejia, L.R. (2006). CEO incentives, innovation, and performance in technology-intensive firms: A reconciliation of outcome and behavior-based incentive schemes. *Strategic Management Journal,* 27(11), 1057–1080.

Malatesta, P.H., and Walking, R.A. (1988). Poison pill securities: Stockholder wealth, profitability, and ownership structure. *Journal of Financial Economics,* 20, 347–376.

Malina, M.A., Norreklit, H.S.O., and Selto, F.H. (2007). Relations among measures, climate of control, and performance measurement models. *Contemporary Accounting Research,* 24(3), 7.

Manoochehri, G. (1999). Overcoming obstacles to developing effective performance measures. *Work Study-London,* 48(6), 223–229.

March, J.G., and Shapira, Z. (1987). Managerial perspectives on risk and risk taking. *Management Science,* 33(11), 1404–1418.

———. (1992). Variable risk preference and the focus of attention. *Psychological Review,* 99(1), 172–183.

March, J.G., and Sutton, R.I. (1997). Organizational performance as a dependent variable. *Organization Science,* 8(6), 698–706.

Marginson, D., and McAulay, L. (2008). Exploring the debate on short-termism: A theoretical and empirical analysis. *Strategic Management Journal,* 29(3), 273–292.

Margolis, J.D., and Walsh, J.P. (2003). Misery loves companies: Rethinking social initiatives by business. *Administrative Science Quarterly,* 48(2), 268–304.

Marris, R.L. (1964). *The Economic Theory of Managerial Capitalism.* London: Macmillan.

Martell, K., Carroll, S.J., and Gupta, A.K. (1992). What executive human resource management practices are most effective when innovativeness requirements are high? In L.R. Gomez-Mejia and M.W. Lawless (Eds.), *Top Management and Effective Leadership in High Technology.* Greenwich, CT: JAI Press.

Martocchio, J.J. (2009). *Strategic Compensation: A Human Resource Approach.* Upper Saddle River, NJ: Pearson/Prentice Hall.

Martocchio, J.J., and Pandey, N. (2008). Employee benefits around the world. In L.R. Gomez-Mejia and S. Werner (Eds.), *Global Compensation: Foundations and Perspectives.* London: Routledge, 179–191.

Maslow, A.H. (1970). *Motivation and Personality.* New York: Harper and Row.

Masson, R.T. (1971). Executive motivations, earnings, and consequent equity performance. *Journal of Political Economy,* 79(1), 278–1, 294.

Masters, M.F., Tokesky, G.C., Brown, W.S., Atkin, R., and Schoenfeld, G. (1992). Competitive compensation strategies in high technology firms: A synthetic theoretical perspective. In L.R. Gomez-Mejia and M.W. Lawless (Eds.), *Human Resource Management Strategy in High Technology.* Greenwich, CT: JAI Press.

Mayo, M., Pastor, J., Gomez-Mejia, L.R., and Cruz, C. (2010, in press). Why some firms adopt telecommuting while others don't: A contingency perspective. *Human Resource Management.*

McBriarty, M.A. (1988). Performance appraisal: Some unintended consequences. *Public Personnel Management,* 17(4), 421–440.

McCann, J.E., and Gomez-Mejia, L. (1986). Assessing an international "Issue climate": Policy and methodology implications. *Academy of Management Proceedings,* 5, 316–320.

———. (1989). The institute for domain enterprises: A social issues perspectives. Paper presented at the Academy of Management National Convention, Washington, DC.

———. (1990). Exploring the dimensions of an international social issues climate. *Human Relations,* 43(2), 141–167.

———. (1992). Going "on-line" in the environmental scanning process. *IEEE Transactions on Engineering Management,* 39(4), 394–399.

McCann, J.E., Hinkin, T., and Gomez-Mejia, L.R. (1992). Executive transitions in high technology and traditional firms. In L.R. Gomez-Mejia and M. Lawless (Eds.), *Top Management Teams in High Technology Firms.* Greenwich, CT: JAI Press.

McConkie, M.L. (1979). A clarification of the goal setting and appraisal process in MBO. *Academy of Management Review,* 4(1), 29–40.

McDonald, R., and Roland, M. (2009). Pay for performance in primary care in England and California: Comparison of unintended consequences. *Annals of Family Medicine,* 7(2), 121–127.

McEachern, W.A. (1975). *Managerial Control and Performance.* Lexington, MA: D.C. Heath.

McGregor, D. (1960). *The Human Side of Enterprise.* New York: McGraw-Hill.

McGuire, J., Dow, S., and Argheyd, K. (2003). CEO incentives and corporate social performance. *Journal of Business Ethics,* 45(4), 341–359.

McGuire, J.W., Chiu, J.S.Y., and Elbing, A.O. (1962). Executive income, sales, and profits. *American Economic Review,* 52(4), 753–761.

McGuire, S.A. (2008). A vision for information technology in compensation. In L.A. Berger and D.R. Berger (Eds.), *The Compensation Handbook: A State-of-the-art Guide to Compensation Strategy and Design,* 5th ed. New York: McGraw-Hill, 197–204.

McNamee, P., Ternent, L., Gbanjou, A., and Newlands, D. (2009). A game of two halves? Incentive incompatibility, starting point bias and the bidding game contingent valuation method. *Health Economics,* 35(1), 20–44.

McNatt, B.D., Glassman, M., and McAfee, B.R. (2007). Pay inversion versus pay for performance: Can companies have their cake and eat it too? *Compensation and Benefits Review,* March–April, 27–34.

McNichols, M., and Manegold, J.G. (1983). The effect of the information environment on the relationship between financial disclosure and security price variability. *Journal of Accounting and Economics,* 5(1), 49–74.

McNutt, R.P. (1991). Profit sharing: A case study of the fibers department at E.I. du Pont de Nemours and Company. In M.L. Rock and L.A. Berger (Eds.), *The Compensation Handbook: A State-of-the-art Guide to Compensation Strategy and Design,* 3d ed. New York: McGraw-Hill.

Medoff, J.L., and Abraham, K.G. (1980). Experience, performance, and earnings. *Quarterly Journal of Economics,* 95(4), 703–736.

Meeks, G., and Whittington, G. (1975). Directors' pay, growth, and profitability. *The Journal of Industrial Economics,* 24(1), 1–14.

Merchant, K.A. (1990). The effects of financial controls on data manipulation and management myopia. *Accounting, Organizations and Society,* 15(4), 297–313.

———. (2006). Measuring general managers' performances. *Accounting, Auditing and Accountability Journal,* 19(6), 893–917.

Mericle, K., and Kim, D.O. (2004). *Gainsharing and Goalsharing: Aligning Pay and Strategic Goals.* Westport, CT: Praeger Publishers.

Merriman, K.K. (2009). On the folly of rewarding team performance, while hoping for teamwork. *Compensation and Benefits Review,* 41(1), 61–67.

Meyer, J.P., Becker, T.E., and Vandenberghe, C. (2004). Employee commitment and motivation: A conceptual analysis and integrative model. *Journal of Applied Psychology,* 89(6), 991–1007.

Meyer, M.W., and Gupta, V. (1994). The performance paradox. *Research in Organizational Behavior,* 16, 309–369.

Meyer, P. (1983). Executive compensation must promote long-term commitment. *Personnel Administrator,* 28(5), 37–42.

Meyer, P., and Rowan, B. (1977). Institutional organizations: Formal structure as myth and ceremony. *American Journal of Sociology,* 83(2), 340–363.

Micheli, P., Franco-Santos, M., Marr, B., Bourne, M., and Kennerley, M. (2004). Business performance measurement: An organizational theory perspective. *Performance Measurement and Management: Public and Private, Performance Measurement Association Conference.* Cranfield School of Management, Cranfield, UK.

Miles, R.E., and Snow, C.C. (1978). *Organizational Strategy, Structure and Process.* New York: McGraw-Hill.

———. (1984). Designing strategic human resources systems. *Organizational Dynamics,* 13(1), 36–52.

Milkovich, G.T. (1988). A strategic perspective to compensation management. In K. Rowland and G. Ferris (Eds.), *Research in Personnel and Human Resource Management,* 6, 263–288. Greenwich, CT: JAI Press.

Milkovich, G.T., and Broderick, R.F. (1991) Developing a compensation strategy. In M.L. Rock and L.A. Berger (Eds.), *The Compensation Handbook: A State-of-the-art Guide to Compensation Strategy and Design,* 3d ed. New York: McGraw-Hill.

Milkovich, G.T., Gerhart, B., and Hannon, J. (1991). The effects of research and development intensity on managerial compensation in large organizations. *Journal of High Technology Management Research,* 2(1), 133–150.

Milkovich, G.T., and Newman, J.M. (2005). *Compensation,* 7th ed. New York: McGraw-Hill.

———. (2009). *Compensation,* 8th ed. Homewood, IL: Irwin/McGraw-Hill.

Miller, K., and Chen, W.R. (2004). Variable organizational risk preferences: Tests of the March-Shapira model. *Academy of Management Journal,* 47(1), 105–115.

Miller, K., and Leiblein, M. (1996). Corporate risk-return relations: Returns variability versus downside risk. *Academy of Management Journal,* 39(1), 99–122.

Miller, M.H., and Scholes, M.S. (1982). Executive compensation, taxes and incentives. In W.F. Sharpe and C.M. Cootner (Eds.), *Financial Economics.* Boston: Harvard University Press.

Miller, C.S., and Schuster, M.H. (1987). Gainsharing plans: A comparative analysis. *Organizational Dynamics,* 16(1), 44–67.

Miller, J.S., and Wiseman, R.M. (2001). Perceptions of executive pay: Does pay enhance a leader's aura? *Journal of Organizational Behavior,* 22(6), 703–711.

Miller, J.S., Wiseman, R.M., and Gomez-Mejia, L.R. (2002). The fit between CEO compensation design and firm risk. *Academy of Management Journal,* 45(4), 745–756.

Mincer, J. (1975). *Schooling, Experience and Earnings.* New York: National Bureau of Economic Research.

Mintzberg, H. (1973). A new look at the chief executive's job. *Organizational Dynamics,* 1(3), 20–30.

———. (1980). *The Nature of Managerial Work.* Englewood Cliffs, NJ: Prentice Hall.

———. (1984). Power and organization life cycles. *Academy of Management Review,* 9, 207–224.

———. (1990). The design school: Reconsidering the basic premises of strategic management. *Strategic Management Journal,* 11(3), 171–196.

Mitchell, T.R., and Biglan, A. (1971). Instrumentality theories: Current uses in psychology. *Psychological Bulletin,* 76(6), 432–454.

Mitchell, T.R., and Liden, R.C. (1982). The effects of social context on performance evaluations. *Organizational Behavior and Human Performance,* 29, 241–256.

Mitchell, W. (1989). Whether and when? Probability and timing of incumbents' entry into emerging industrial subfields. *Administrative Science Quarterly,* 34(2), 208–230.

Moers, F. (2005). Discretion and bias in performance evaluation: The impact of diversity and subjectivity. *Accounting, Organizations and Society,* 30(1), 67–80.

Mondello, M., and Maxey, J. (2009). The impact of salary dispersion and performance bonuses in NFL organizations. *Management Decision,* 47(1), 110–123.

Montemayor, E.F. (1996). Congruence between pay policy and compensation strategy in high performing firms. *Journal of Management,* 22(6), 889–908.

———. (2008). Universal and national norms for organizational compensation ethics: Using severance pay as an illustration. In L.R. Gomez-Mejia and S. Werner (Eds.), *Global Compensation: Foundations and Perspectives,* London: Routledge, 29–33.

Montgomery, C.A., and Singh, H. (1984). Diversification strategy and systematic risk. *Strategic Management Journal,* 5, 181–191.

Moody, L. (2008). Salary administration at a prestigious cultural institution: Pennsylvania Academy for Performing Arts. In L.A. Berger and D.R. Berger (Eds.), *The Compensation Handbook: A State-of-the-art Guide to Compensation Strategy and Design,* 5th ed. New York: McGraw-Hill, 191–196.

Moore, G., and Ross, T. (1990). *Gainsharing Plans for Improving Performance.* Washington, DC: Bureau of National Affairs.

Morck, R., Shleifer, A., and Vishny, R.W. (1988). Management ownership and market evaluation. *Journal of Financial Economics,* 20, 293–315.

Morgan, A.G., and Poulsen, A.B. (2001). Linking pay to performance: Compensation proposals in the S&P 500. *Journal of Financial Economics,* 62(3), 489–533.

Morissette, R. (1996). Toward a theory of information choices in organizations: an integrative approach. University of Waterloo. Waterloo, Ontario, Canada.

Morrison, E.E. (1966). *New Machines and Modern Times.* Cambridge, MA: MIT Press.

Morse, D.M., and Richardson, G. (1983). The LIFO/FIFO decision. *Journal of Accounting Research,* 21(Spring), 106–127.

Mount, M. K. (1987). Coordinating salary action and performance appraisal. In D.B. Balkin and L.R. Gomez-Mejia (Eds.), *New Perspectives on Compensation.* Englewood Cliffs, NJ: Prentice Hall, 15–29.

Mowen, M., and Mowen, J. (1986). An empirical examination of the biasing effects of framing on business decisions. *Decision Sciences,* 17(Fall), 596–602.

Murphy, K.J. (1985). Corporate performance and managerial remuneration. *Journal of Accounting and Statistics,* 7(1–3), 11–42.

———. (1986a). Top executives are worth every nickel they get. *Harvard Business Review,* 64(2), 125–132.

———. (1986b). Incentives, learning and compensation: A theoretical and empirical investigation of managerial labor contracts. *Rand Journal of Economics,* 17(1), 59–76.

———. (1999). Executive Compensation. In O. Ashenfelter, and D. Card (Eds.), *Handbook of Labor Economics,* 3. Amsterdam: North Holland, 2485–2563.

———. (2000). Performance standards in incentive contracts. *Journal of Accounting and Economics,* 30(3), 245–278.

Murphy, K.J., and Cleveland, J. (1991). *Performance Appraisal: An Organizational Perspective.* Boston: Allyn and Bacon.

Murray, A.I. (1989). Top management group heterogeneity and firm performance. *Strategic Management Journal,* 10, 125–141.

Murray, B., and Gerhart, B. (2000). Skill-based pay and skill seeking. *Human Resource Management,* 10(3), 271–287.

Murthy, K.R., and Salter, M.S. (1975). Should CEO pay be linked to results? *Harvard Business Review,* 53(3), 66–73.

Nadler, D.A., Hackman, J.R., and Lawler, E.E. (1979). *Managing Organization Behavior.* Boston, MA: Little, Brown.

Nagar, V., Nanda, D., and Wysocki, P. (2003). Discretionary disclosure and stock-based incentives. *Journal of Accounting and Economics,* 34(1–3), 283–309.

Nagar, V., and Rajan, M.V. (2005). Measuring customer relationships: The case of the retail banking industry. *Management Science,* 51(6), 904–919.

Napier, N. K., and Smith, M. (1987). Product diversification, performance criteria and compensation at the corporate manager level. *Strategic Management Journal,* 8(2), 195–201.

Neely, A.D., Gregory, M.J., and Platts, K. (1995). Performance measurement system design: A literature review and research agenda. *International Journal of Operations and Production Management,* 15(4), 80–116.

Neidell, L.A. (1983). Don't forget the product life cycle for strategic planning. *Business,* 33(2), 30–55.

Newman, J., and Floersch, R. (2008). Global wages in industries with low entry barrier occupations: The case of quick service restaurants, call centers and hotels/motels. In L.R. Gomez-Mejia and S. Werner (Eds.), *Global Compensation: Foundations and Perspectives.* London: Routledge, 169–177.

Newman, J.M. (1988). Compensation strategy in declining industries. *Human Resource Planning,* 11(3), 197–206.

Ng, L.W., Eby, L., Sorensen, K.L., and Feldman, D.C. (2005). Predictors of objective and subjective career success. *Personnel Psychology,* 58(2), 367–408.

Niehaus, G.R. (1985). The relationship between accounting method choices and ownership structure. Unpublished manuscript, Accounting Department, Washington University.

Niven, P.R. (2008). The balances scorecard and compensation. In L.A. Berger and D.R. Berger (Eds.), *The Compensation Handbook: A State-of-the-art Guide to Compensation Strategy and Design,* 5th ed. New York: McGraw-Hill, 493–510.

Norburn, D., and Miller, P. (1981). Strategy and executive reward: The mismatch in the strategic process. *Journal of General Management,* 6(4), 17–27.

Nussbaum, B., and Dobrzynski, J.H. (1987). The battle for corporate control. *Business Week,* May 18, 102–109.

O'Connor, J.P., Priem, R.L., Coombs, J.E., and Gilley, K.M. (2006). Do CEO stock options prevent or promote fraudulent financial reporting? *Academy of Management Journal,* 49(3), 483–500.

Oliver, C. (1991). Strategic responses to institutional processes. *Academy of Management Review,* 16(1), 145–179.

O'Neill, H.M., Saunders, C., and McCarthy, A. (1989). Board members' background characteristics and their level of corporate social responsiveness orientation: A multivariate investigation. *Proceedings of the Annual Academy of Management,* 49th Annual Meeting, Washington, DC.

Opsahl, R.L., and Dunnette, M.D. (1966). The role of financial compensation in industrial motivation. *Psychological Bulletin,* 66(2), 94–118.

Ordoñez, L.D., Schweitzer, M.E., Galinsky, A.D., and Bazerman, M.H. (2009). Goals gone wild: The systematic side effects of over-prescribing goal setting. Working paper. Harvard Business School, Boston, MA.

O'Reilly, C.A., Main, B.G., and Crystal, G.S. (1988). CEO compensation as tournament and social comparison: A tale of two theories. *Administrative Science Quarterly,* 33(2), 257–274.

Orlizky, M., Schmidt, F. L., and Rynes, S.L. (2003). Corporate social and financial performance: A meta-analysis. *Organization Studies,* 24(3), 403–441.

Ouchi, W.G. (1977). The relationship between organizational structure and organizational control. *Administrative Science Quarterly,* 22(1), 95–113.

———. (1978). Transmission of control through organizational hierarchy. *Academy of Management Journal,* 21(2), 173–192.

———. (1979). Conceptual framework for the design of organizational control mechanisms. *Management Science,* 25(9), 833–848.

———. (1980). Markets, bureaucracies, and clans. *Administrative Science Quarterly,* 25(1), 129–141.

Ouchi, W.G., and Maguire, M.A. (1975). Organizational control: Two functions. *Administrative Science Quarterly,* 20(4), 559–569.

Palmer, J. (1973). The profit variability effects of managerial enterprise. *Western Economic Journal,* 42, 228–231

Palmer, J.K., and Loveland, J.M. (2008). The influence of group discussion on performance judgments: Rating accuracy, contrast effects, and halo. *Journal of Psychology,* 142(2), 117–130.

Palmer, T., and Wiseman, R. (1999). Decoupling risk taking from income stream uncertainty: A holistic model of risk. *Strategic Management Journal,* 20(11), 1037–1062.

Paola, M.D., and Scoppa, V. (2009). Task assignment, incentives and technological factors. *Managerial and Decision Economics,* 30(1), 43–55.

Parloff, R. (2009). Sending Wall Street to jail. *Fortune,* January 19, 56–70.

Pascal, A.H., and Rapping, L.A. (1972). The economics of racial discrimination in organized baseball. In A.H. Pascal (Ed.), *Racial Discrimination in Economic Life.* Lexington, MA: Lexington Books.

Pearce, J.L. (1987). Why merit pay doesn't work: Implications from organization theory. In D.B. Balkin and L.R. Gomez-Mejia (Eds.), *New Perspectives on Compensation.* Englewood Cliffs, NJ: Prentice Hall.

Pearce, J.L., Stevenson, W.B., and Perry, J.L. (1985). Managerial compensation based on organizational performance: A time series analysis of the effects of merit pay. *Academy of Management Journal,* 28(2), 261–279.

Peck, C.A. (1987). *Top Executive Compensation: 1987.* New York: The Conference Board.

Penley, L., and Gould, S. (1988). Etzioni's model of organizational involvement: A perspective to understanding commitment to organizations. *Journal of Organizational Behavior,* 9, 43–59.

Pennings, J.M. (1991). Executive compensation systems: Pay follows strategy or strategy follows pay? In M.L. Rock and L.A. Berger (Eds.), *The Compensation Handbook: A State-of-the-art Guide to Compensation Strategy and Design,* 3d ed. New York: McGraw-Hill.

Perkins, J.S., and Hendry, C. (2005). Ordering top pay: Interpreting the signals. *Journal of Management Studies,* 42(7), 1443–1468.

Perry, T., and Zenner, M. (2000). CEO Compensation in the 1990s: Shareholder alignment or shareholder expropriation? *Wake Forest Law Review,* 35(1), 123–152.

———. (2001). Pay for performance? Government regulation and the structure of compensation contracts. *Journal of Financial Economics,* 62(3), 453–488.

Pfeffer, J. (1981). *Power in Organizations.* Boston: Pitman.

———. (1997). Pitfalls on the road to measurement: The dangerous liaison of human resources with the ideas of accounting and finance. *Human Resource Management,* 36(3), 357–365.

———. (1998). Six dangerous myths about pay. *Harvard Business Review,* 76(3), 109–120.

———. (2007). *What Were They Thinking? Unconventional Wisdom about Management.* Boston, MA: Harvard Business School Press.

Pfeffer, J., and Salancik, G. (1978). *The External Control of Organizations: A Resource Dependence Perspective.* New York: Harper and Row.

Pfeffer, J., and Sutton, R.I. (2006). *Hard Facts, Dangerous Half-Truths and Total Nonsense: Profiting from Evidence-Based Management.* Boston: Harvard Business School Press.

Pfeffer, R.M. (1979). *Working for Capitalism.* New York: Columbia University Press.

Pitts, R.A. (1974). Incentive compensation and organization design. *Personnel Journal,* 20(5), 338–344.

———. (1976). Diversification strategies and organizational policies of large diversified firms. *Journal of Economics and Business,* 8, 181–188.

Pondy, L. (1978). Leadership is a language game. In M.W. McCall, Jr., and M. Lombardo (Eds.), *Leadership: Where Else Can We Go?* Durham, NC: Duke University Press.

Porter, L.W., and Lawler, E.E. (1968). *Managerial Attitudes and Performance.* Homewood, IL: Irwin-Dorsey.

Porter, M. (1985). *Competitive Advantage.* New York: Free Press.

Posner, M. (1987). Prospects for your perks (Tax reform and fringe benefits). *Changing Times,* 41(4), 77.

Power, M. (2004). Counting, control and calculation: Reflections on measuring and management. *Human Relations,* 57(6), 765–783.

Prendergast, C., and Topel, R. (1993). Discretion and bias in performance evaluation. *European Economic Review,* 37(2–3), 355–365.

Priem, R.L., and Butler, J.E. (2001). Is the resource-based "view" a useful perspective for strategic management research? *Academy of Management Review,* 26(1), 22–40.

Puffer, S.M., and Weintrop, J.B. (1991). Corporate performance and CEO turnover: A comparison of performance indicators. *Administrative Science Quarterly,* 36, 1–20.

Purcell, J., and Hutchinson, S. (2007). Rewarding work: The vital role of front line managers. London: CIPD Change Agenda. Available at CIPD.Co.UK.

Quinn, R.E., and Cameron, K. (1983). Organizational life cycles and shifting criteria of effectiveness: Some preliminary evidence. *Management Science,* 29(1), 33–50.

Raith, M. (2008). Specific knowledge and performance measurement. *The Rand Journal of Economics,* 39(4), 1059.

Rajagopalan, N., and Datta, D. (1996). CEO characteristics: Does industry matter? *Academy of Management Journal,* 39(1), 197–215.

Rajagopalan, N., and Prescott, J.E. (1990). Determinants of top management compensation: Explaining the impact of economic, behavioral, and strategic constructs and the moderating effects of industry. *Journal of Management,* 16(3), 515–538.

Rajan, R., and Wulf, J. (2006). The flattering firm: Evidence from panel data on the changing nature of corporate hierarchies. *Review of Economics and Statistics,* 88(4), 759–773.

Rajgopal, S., and Shevlin, T. (2002). Empirical evidence on the relation between stock option compensation and risk taking. *Journal of Accounting and Economics,* 33(2), 145–171.

Ramanujam, R., and Varadajaran, P. (1989). Research on corporate diversification: A synthesis. *Strategic Management Journal,* 10(6), 523–551.

Rappaport, A. (1978). Executive incentives vs. corporate growth. *Harvard Business Review,* 56(4), 81–88.

———. (1981). Selecting strategies that create shareholder value. *Harvard Business Review,* 60(3), 139–149.

———. (1986). *Creating Shareholder Value.* New York: Free Press.

———. (1999). New thinking on how to link executive pay to performance. *Harvard Business Review,* 91–101.

Ravenscraft, D.J., and Scherer, F.M. (1987). *Mergers, Sell-offs, and Economic Efficiency.* Washington, DC: The Brookings Institution.

Rees, D. (2008). Using compensation to win the talent wars. In L.R. Gomez-Mejia and S. Werner (Eds.), *Global Compensation: Foundations and Perspectives.* London: Routledge, 559–570.

Reger, R.K. (1991). Managerial thought structures and competitive positioning. In A.S. Huff (Ed.), *Mapping Strategic Thought.* Chichester, England: Wiley.

Reingold, J. (1997). Executive pay. *Business Week,* 21, 58–66.

Rich, J.T., and Larson, J.A. (1984). Why some long-term incentives fail. *Compensation Review,* 16(1), 26–37.

Richards, D.A. (2006). High involvement firms: Compensation strategies and underlying values. *Compensation and Benefits Review,* May–June, 36–49.

Richardson, V.J. (2000). Information asymmetry and earnings management: Some evidence. *Review of Quantitative Finance and Accounting,* 15(4), 325–347.

Ridgway, V.F. (1956). Dysfunctional consequences of performance measurements. *Administrative Science Quarterly,* 1(2), 240–247.

Roberts, D.R. (1959). A general theory of executive compensation based on statistically tested propositions. *Quarterly Journal of Economics,* 70(2), 270–294.

Roche, G. (1975). Compensation and the mobile executive. *Harvard Business Review,* 53(6), 53–62.

Ronan, W.W., and Organt, G.J. (1973). Determinants of pay and pay satisfaction. *Personnel Psychology,* 26, 503–520.

Roomkin, M. (1990). *Profit Sharing and Gainsharing.* Newark, NJ: The Scarecrow Press.

Rosen, A.S. (2008). Salary administration. In L.A. Berger and D.R. Berger (Eds.), *The Compensation Handbook: A State-of-the-art Guide to Compensation Strategy and Design*, 5th ed. New York: McGraw-Hill, 63–84.

Ross, T.L., and Ross, R.A. (1999). Gain sharing: Sharing improved performance. In M.L. Rock and L.A. Berger (Eds.), *The Compensation Handbook: A State-of-the-art Guide to Compensation Strategy and Design*, 3d ed. New York: McGraw-Hill.

Rothwell, W.J., and Kazanas, H.C. (1988). *Strategic Human Resources Planning and Management*. Englewood Cliffs, NJ: Prentice Hall.

Rubenfeld, S., and David, J. (2006). Multiple employee incentive plans: Too much of a good thing? *Compensation and Benefits Review*, March–April, 35–40.

Rumelt, R.P. (1974). *Strategy, Structure, and Economic Performance*. Boston: Division of Research, Harvard Business School.

————. (1977). Diversity and profitability. Paper presented at the Academy of Management Western Region Meetings, Sun Valley, Idaho.

Russo, M.V., and Harrison, N. S. (2005). Organizational design and environmental performance: Clues from the electronics industry. *Academy of Management Journal*, 48(4), 582–593.

Rynes, S.L. (1987). Compensation strategies for recruiting. *Topics in Total Compensation*, 2(2), 185–196.

Rynes, S.L., Gerhart, B., and Parks, L. (2005). Personnel psychology: Performance evaluation and pay for performance. *Annual Review of Psychology*, 56, 571–600.

Rynes, S.L., and Milkovich, G.T. (1986). Wage surveys: Dispelling some myths about the market wage. *Personnel Psychology*, 39, 71–90.

Ryngaert, M. (1988). The effect of poison pill securities on shareholder wealth. *Journal of Financial Economics*, 20(1–2), 377–418.

Said, A.A., HassabElnaby, H.R., and Wier, B. (2003). An empirical investigation of the performance consequences of nonfinancial measures. *Journal of Management Accounting Research*, 15, 193–223.

Salamon, G.L., and Smith, E.D. (1979). Corporate control and managerial misrepresentation of firm performance. *Bell Journal of Economics*, 10(1), 319–328.

Salancik, G.R., and Pfeffer, J. (1977). Constraints on administrator discretion: The limited influence of mayors on city budgets. *Urban Affairs Quarterly*, 12(4), 475–498.

————. (1980). Effects of ownership and performance on executive tenure in U.S. corporations. *Academy of Management Journal*, 23(4), 653–664.

Salimaki, A., and Heneman, R.L. (2008). Pay for performance for global employees. In L.R. Gomez-Mejia and S. Werner (Eds.), *Global Compensation: Foundations and Perspectives*. London: Routledge, 158–166.

Salscheider, J. (1981). Devising pay strategies for diversified companies. *Compensation Review*, 8, 15–24.

Salter, M.S. (1973). Tailor incentive compensation to strategy. *Harvard Business Review*, 51(2), 94–102.

Salter, M.S., and Weinhold, W.A. (1981). Choosing compatible acquisitions. *Harvard Business Review*, 59(1), 117–127.

Sanchez-Marin, G. (2008a). The influence of institutional and cultural factors on compensation practices around the world. In L.R. Gomez-Mejia and S. Werner (Eds.), *Global Compensation: Foundations and Perspectives*. London: Routledge, 13–15.

————. (2008b). National differences in compensation: The influence of the institutional and cultural context. In L.R. Gomez-Mejia and S. Werner (Eds.), *Global Compensation: Foundations and Perspectives*. London: Routledge, 18–26.

Sanders, W.G. (2001). Behavioral responses of CEOs to stock ownership and stock option pay. *Academy of Management Journal*, 44(3), 477–492.

Sanders, W.G., and Carpenter, M.A. (1998). Internationalization and firm governance: The roles of CEO compensation, top team composition, and board structure. *Academy of Management Journal*, 41(2), 158–178.

————. (2003). Strategic satisficing? A behavioral-agency theory perspective on stock repurchase program announcements. *Academy of Management Journal*, 46(2), 160–178.

Sanders, W.G., and Hambrick, D.C. (2007). Swinging for the fences: The effects of CEO stock options on company risk taking and performance. *Academy of Management Journal*, 50(5), 1055–1078.

Santalo, J., and Becerra, M. (2008). Competition from specialized firms and the diversification-performance linkage. *Journal of Finance*, 63(2), 851–883.

Saura-Diaz, M.D., and Gomez-Mejia, L.R. (1997). The effectiveness of organization-wide compensation strategies in technology intensive firms. *Journal of High Technology Management Research*, 8(2), 301–315.

Schmidt, D.R., and Fowler, K.L. (1990). Post-acquisition financial performance and executive compensation. *Strategic Management Journal*, 11, 559–570.

Scholtes, P.R. (1987). *An Elaboration on Deming's Teachings on Performance Appraisal*. Madison, WI: Joiner Associates.

Scholtner, A. (2008). Fixed-price tournaments versus first-price auctions in innovative contests. *Economic Theory*, 35(1), 57–71.

Schrand, C., and Unal, H. (1998). Hedging and coordinated risk management: Evidence from thrift conversions. *Journal of Finance*, 53(3), 979–1013.

Schuler, R.S. (1987). Personnel and human resource management choices and organizational strategy. *Human Resource Planning*, 10(1), 1–17.

Schulze, W.S., Lubatkin, M.H., and Dino, R.N. (2003a). Exploring the agency consequences of ownership dispersion among the directors of private family firms. In Joseph H. Astrachan, Torsten M. Pieper, and Peter Jaskiewicz (Eds.), *Family Business*. Cheltenham, UK: Edward Elgar Publishing.

————. (2003b). Toward a theory of agency and altruism in family firms. *Journal of Business Venturing*, 18(4), 450–473.

Schuster, M. (1983). The impact of union-management cooperation on productivity and employment. *Industrial and Labor Relations Review*, 36(3), 415–430.

————. (1984a). Cooperation and change in union settings: Problems and opportunities. *Human Resource Management*, 23(2), 145–160.

————. (1984b). *Union-management Cooperation*. Kalamazoo, MI: Upjohn Institute for Employment Research.

————. (1985). Models of cooperation and change in union settings. *Industrial Relations*, 24(3), 382–394.

Schwab, D.P. (1974). Conflicting impacts of pay on employee motivation and satisfaction. *Personnel Journal*, 53(3), 190–206.

Schwab, D.P., and Dyer, L.D. (1973). The motivational impact of a compensation system on employee performance. *Organizational Behavior and Human Performance*, 9(2), 215–225.

Schwab, D.P., and Olson, C.A. (1988). Pay-performance relationships as a function of pay-for-performance policies and practices. *Proceedings of the Academy of Management.*

Schweitzer, M.E., Ordoñez, L. and Douma, B. (2004), Goal setting as a motivator of unethical behaviour, *Academy of Management Journal,* 47(3), 422–432.

Schweyer, A. (2008). Three trends shaping the future of compensation and human resources. In L.A. Berger and D.R. Berger (Eds.), *The Compensation Handbook, A State-of-the-art Guide to Compensation Strategy and Design,* 5th ed. New York: McGraw-Hill, 31–48.

Scott, W.R. (1995). *Institutions and Organizations.* Thousand Oaks, CA: Sage.

———. (2004). Institutional theory. In G. Ritzer (Ed.), *Handbook of Social Problems: A Comparative, International Perspective.* Thousand Oaks, CA: Sage, 408–414.

Sears, D. (1984). Make employee pay a strategic issue. *Financial Executive,* October, 40–43.

Segev, E. (1989). Systematic competitive analysis and synthesis of two business level strategic typologies. *Strategic Management Journal,* 10(5), 487–509.

Seidman, W.L., and Skancke, S.L. (1989). *Competitiveness: The Executive's Guide to Success.* New York: M.E. Sharpe.

Sexton, D. (1990). Propensity for change: A prerequisite for growth in high technology firms. In L.R. Gomez-Mejia and M.W. Lawless (Eds.), *Organizational Issues in High Technology Management.* Greenwich, CT: JAI Press.

Shapira, Z. (1995). *Risk Taking: A Management Perspective.* New York: Russell Sage Foundation.

Sharma, S., and Henriques, I. (2005). Stakeholder influences on sustainability practices in the Canadian forest products industry. *Strategic Management Journal,* 26(2), 159–180.

Sharpe, W.F. (1964). Capital asset prices: A theory of market equilibrium under conditions of risk. *Journal of Finance,* 19(3), 425–442.

Shavell, S. (1979). Risk sharing and incentives in the principal and agent relationship. *Bell Journal of Economics,* 10(1), 55–73.

Shaw, J.D., Gupta, N., and Delery, J.E. (2002). Pay dispersion and workforce performance: Moderating effects of incentives and interdependence. *Strategic Management Journal,* 23(6), 491–512.

Shelton, T. (2008). Global compensation strategies: Managing and administering split pay for an expatriate workforce. *Compensation and Benefits Review,* January–February, 56–60.

Shen, W., and Canella, A. (2002). Revisiting the performance consequences of CEO succession: The impacts of successor type, postsuccession senior executive turnover, and departing CEO tenure. *Academy of Management Journal,* 45(4), 717–733.

Sherman, A.W., and Bohlander, G.W. (1992). *Managing Human Resources.* Cincinnati, Ohio: South-Western Publishing.

Shleifer, A., and Vishny, R.W. (1988). Managerial entrenchment. Unpublished manuscript, University of Chicago, Chicago, IL.

———. (1997). A survey of corporate finance. *Journal of Finance,* 52(2), 737–783.

Shortell, S.M., and Zajac, E. (1990). Perceptual and archival measures of Miles and

Snow's strategic types: A comprehensive assessment of reliability and validity. *Academy of Management Journal,* 33(4), 817–832.

Siegel, P.A., and Hambrick, D.C. (2005). Pay disparities within top management groups: Evidence of harmful effects on performance of high-technology firms. *Organization Science,* 16(3), 259–274.

Simon, H.A. (1957). The compensation of executives. *Sociometry,* March 20, 32–35.

———. (1959). Theories of decision making in economics and behavioral science. *American Economic Review,* 49(3), 253–283.

Singh, J.V. (1986). Performance, slack, and risk taking in organizational information processing. *Academy of Management Journal,* 29(3), 562–585.

Singh, J.V., Tucker, D.J., and House, R.J. (1984). Organizational legitimacy and the liability of newness. *Administrative Science Quarterly,* 31(2), 171–193.

Sitkin, S.B., and Pablo, A.L. (1992). Reconceptualizing the determinants of risk behavior. *Academy of Management Review,* 17(1), (9–39).

Slovic, P., Fischhoff, B., and Lichtenstein, S. (1980). Facts versus fears: Understanding perceived risk. In D. Kahneman, P. Slovic, and A. Tversky (Eds.), *Judgment under Uncertainty: Heuristics and Biases.* Cambridge, UK: Cambridge University Press, 463–489.

———. (1985). Characterizing perceived risk. In R. Kates, C. Hohenemser, and J. Kasperson (Eds.), *Perilous Progress: Managing the Hazards of Technology.* Boulder, CO: Westview Press, 91–125.

———. (1986). The psycometric study of risk perception. In V.T. Covello, J. Menkes, and J. Mumpower (Eds.), *Risk Evolution and Management.* New York: Plenum, 544–574.

Smidts, A. (1997). The relationship between risk attitude and strength of preference: A test of intrinsic risk attitude. *Management Science,* 43(3), 357–370.

Smith, A. (1937). *The Wealth of Nations, 1776.* Ed. Edwin Cannan. New York: Modern Library.

Smith, G.W., and Walts, R.L. (1982). Incentive and tax effects of U.S. compensation plans. *Australian Journal of Management,* 7(2), 139–157.

Smith, J.E., Carson, K.P., and Alexander, R.A. (1984). Leadership: It can make a difference. *Academy of Management Journal,* 27(4), 765–776.

Smith, M.J. (2002). Gaming non-financial performance measures. *Journal of Management Accounting Research,* 14, 119–133.

Smith, P.B., and Schwartz, S.H. (2002). Cultural values, sources of guidance, and their relevance to managerial behavior. *Journal of Cross-Cultural Psychology,* 33(2), 188–208.

Smith, P.C. (1995). On the unintended consequences of publishing performance data in the public sector. *International Journal of Public Administration,* 18(2–3), 277–310.

Smith, R., Lucchetti, A., and Craig, S. (2008). Securities tackle pay issue. *Wall Street Journal,* 252(104), C1–C4.

Smyth, D.J., Boyes, W.J., and Peseau, D.E. (1975). *Size, Growth, Profits, and Executive Compensation in the Large Corporation.* New York: Holmes and Meier.

Snow, C.C., and Hrebiniak, L.G. (1980). Strategy, distinctive competence, and organizational performance. *Administrative Science Quarterly,* 25(2), 317–366.

Soo Park, O., Sims, H.P., and Motowidlo, S.J. (1986). Affect in organizations: How feelings and emotions influence managerial judgment. In H.P. Sims and R. Gioia (Eds.), *The Thinking Organization.* San Francisco, CA: Jossey-Bass.

Stanwick, P.A., and Stanwick, S.D. (2001). CEO compensation: Does it pay to be green? *Business Strategy and the Environment,* 10(3), 176–182.

Stata, R., and Maidique, M. (1980). Bonus system for balanced energy. *Harvard Business Review,* 58(6), 156–163.

John, St., C.H., and St., and Rue, L.W. (1991). Coordinating mechanisms: Consensus between marketing and manufacturing groups, and marketplace performance. *Strategic Management Journal,* 12(7), 549–557.

Steers, R., and Ungson, G.R. (1987). Strategic issues in executive compensation decisions. In D.B. Balkin and L.R. Gomez-Mejia (Eds.), *New Perspectives on Compensation.* Englewood Cliffs, NJ: Prentice Hall.

Stevenson, F. (1984). An empirical test of the FIFO/LIFO change. Unpublished PhD dissertation, University of Oregon.

Stonich, P.J. (1981). Using rewards in implementing strategy. *Strategic Management Journal,* 2(4), 345–352.

Sturman, M.C., Cheramie, R.A., and Cashen, L.H. (2005). The impact of job complexity and performance measurement on the temporal consistency, stability, and test-retest reliability of employee job performance ratings. *Journal of Applied Psychology,* 90(2), 269–283.

Sturman, M.C., Walsh, K., and Cheramie, R.A. (2008). The value of human capital specificity versus transferability. *Journal of Management,* 34(2), 290–216.

Sullivan, J.F. (1988). The future of merit pay programs. *Compensation and Benefits Review,* 20(3), 22–30.

Sundaram, A.K., and Inkpen, A.C. (2004). The corporate objective revisited. *Organization Science,* 15(3), 350–363.

Sunder, S. (1973). Relationship between accounting changes and stock prices: Problems of measurement and some empirical evidence. *Journal of Accounting Research,* 11, 1–45.

———. (1975). Stock prices and risk related accounting changes in inventory valuation. *The Accounting Review,* 50, 305–315.

Sven-Olof, C. (2007). Governance strategy: A property right approach turning governance into action. *Journal of Governance and Finance,* 11(3), 215–237.

Sydow, J., Schreyogg, G. & Koch, J. (2009). Organizational path dependence: Opening the black box. *Academy of Management Review,* 34(4), 689–709.

Takacs-Haynes, K. (2008). Executive compensation in an international context: The role of informal and formal institutions. In L.R. Gomez-Mejia and S. Werner (Eds.), *Global Compensation: Foundations and Perspectives.* London: Routledge, 98–98.

Tauber, D., and Levy, D. (2002). *Executive Compensation.* Bureau of National Affairs.

Taussig, F.W., and Barker, W.S. (1925). American corporations and their executives: A statistical inquiry. *Quarterly Journal of Economics,* 3(November), 1–51.

Tehranian, H., and Waegelein, J.F. (1984). Market reaction to short term executive compensation plan adoption. Unpublished manuscript, Boston College, Boston, MA.

Thomas, A., and Ramaswamy, K. (1989). Executive characteristics, strategy, and performance: A contingency model. *Proceedings of the Annual Academy of Management,* 49th Annual Meeting, Washington, DC.

Thomson, J.D. (1967). *Organizations in Action*. New York: McGraw-Hill.

Thorndike, E.L. (1910). *The Fundamentals of Learning*. New York: Teachers College.

Tichy, N.M. (1983). Managing organizational transformations. *Human Resource Management*, 22(1), 45–60.

Tilles, S. (1966). Strategies for allocating funds. *Harvard Business Review*, 44(1), 72–80.

Tolman, E.L. (1932). *Purposive Behavior in Animals*. New York: Century.

Tosi, H.L., and Gomez-Mejia, L.R. (1989). The decoupling of CEO pay and performance: An agency theory perspective. *Administrative Science Quarterly*, 34(2), 169–189.

————. (1992). On boards and stockholder interests: The emerging debate. Unpublished technical report, University of Florida. Management Department, Gainesville, FL.

————. (1994). CEO compensation monitoring and firm performance. *Academy of Management Journal*, 37(4), 1002–1016.

Tosi, H.L., Gomez-Mejia, L.R., Loughry, M.L., Werner, S., Banning, K., Katz, J., Harris, R., and Silva, P. (1999). Ownership distribution and managerial discretion. In G. Ferris (Ed.), *Research in Personnel and Human Resources Management*, 7. Greenwich, CT: JAI Press.

Tosi, H.L., and Greckhamer, T. (2004). Culture and CEO compensation. *Organization Science*, 15(6), 657–670.

Tosi, H.L., Katz, J., and Gomez-Mejia, L.R. (1997). Disaggregating the agency contract: The effects of monitoring, incentive alignment, and term in office on agent decision making. *Academy of Management Journal*, 40(3), 584–602.

Tosi, H.L., Rizzo, J.R., and Carroll, S.J. (1990). *Managing Organizational Behavior*. Marshfield, MA: Pitman Publishing.

Tosi, H.L., and Tosi, L. (1986). What managers need to know about knowledge-based pay. *Organizational Dynamics*, 14(3), 52–64.

Tosi, H.L., Werner, S., Katz, J., and Gomez-Mejia, L.R. (2000). How much does performance matter? A meta-analysis of CEO pay studies. *Journal of Management*, 26(2), 301–339.

Towers Perrin. (2002). *Global Compensation Report*. New York.

Treiman, D.J., and Hartmann, H.I. (Eds.). (1981). *Women, Work, and Wages: Equal Pay for Jobs of Equal Value*. Washington, DC: National Academy Press.

Tremblay, M., and Chenevert, D. (2008). Influence of compensation strategies in Canadian technology-intensive firms on organizational and human resources performance. *Group and Organization Management*, 33(3), 1–34.

Trueman, B., and Titman, S. (1988). An examination for accounting income smoothing. *Journal of Accounting Research*, 26, 127–139.

Tsui, A.S., and Barry, B. (1986). Interpersonal affect and rating errors. *Academy of Management Journal*, 29(3), 586–599.

Tsui, A.S., and Ohlot, T.P. (1988). Multiple assessment of managerial effectiveness: Interrater agreement and consensus in effectiveness models. *Personnel Psychology*, 41, 779–802.

Tuna, C. (2008). Some firms cut costs without resorting to layoffs. *New York Times*, December 15, B-4.

Turban, D.B., and Greening, D.W. (1997). Corporate social performance and organizational attractiveness to prospective employees. *Academy of Management Journal,* 40(3), 658–672.

Tversky, A., and Fox, C. (1995). Weighing risk and uncertainty. *Psychological Review,* 102(2), 269–283.

Tyler, B., and Steensma, H. (1998). The effects of executives' experiences and perceptions on their assessment of potential. *Strategic Management Journal,* 19(10), 939–966.

Ukko, J., Karhu, J., and Pekkola, S. (2009). Employees satisfied with performance measurement and rewards: Is it even possible? *International Journal of Business Excellence,* 2(1), 1–15.

Ulrich, W.L. (1984). HRM culture: History, ritual, and myth. *Human Resource Management,* 23(2), 117–128.

Ungson, G.R., and Steers, R.M. (1984). Motivation and politics in executive compensation. *Academy of Management Review,* 9(2), 313–323.

Van der Stede, W.A. (2000). The relationship between two consequences of budgetary controls: Budgetary slack creation and managerial short-term orientation, *Accounting, Organizations and Society,* 25(6), 609–622.

Van der Stede, W.A., Chow, C.W., and Lin, T.W. (2006). Strategy, choice of performance measures, and performance. *Behavioral Research in Accounting,* 18, 185–205.

Verespej, M.A. (1987). What's wrong with executive compensation? *Industry Week,* 43–45.

Villalonga, B., and Amit, R. (2006). How do family ownership, control, and management affect firm value? *Journal of Financial Economics,* 80(2), 385–417.

Villena, V., Gomez-Mejia, L.R., and Revilla, E. (2009). The decision of the supply chain executive to support or impede supply chain integration: A behavioral approach. *Decision Sciences,* 40(4), 635–665.

Viteles, M.S. (1941). A psychologist looks at job evaluation. *Personnel,* 10–18.

Volpp, K.G., Pauly, M.V., Loewenstein, G., and Bangsberg, D. (2009). An agenda on pay for performance for patients. *Health Affairs,* 28(1), 206–214.

Von Glinow, M.A. (1985). Reward strategies for attracting, evaluating, and retaining professionals. *Human Resource Management,* 24(2), 191–206.

Vroom, V.H. (1964). *Work and Motivation.* New York: Wiley.

Waddock, S.A., and Graves, S.B. (1997). The corporate social performance-financial performance link. *Strategic Management Journal,* 18(4), 303–319.

Wade, J.B., O'Reilly, C.A., and Pollock, T.G. (2006). Overpaid CEOs and underpaid managers: Fairness and executive compensation. *Organization Science,* 17(5), 527–544.

Wade, J.B., Porac, J.F., Pollock, T.G., and Graffin, S.D. (2006). The burden of celebrity: the impact of CEO certification contests on CEO pay and performance. *Academy of Management Journal,* 49(4), 643–660.

Wai-Lee, K., Lev, B., Hian, G., and Yeo, H. (2008). Executive pay dispersion, corporate governance, and firm performance. *Review of Quantitative Finance and Accounting,* 30(3), 315–338.

Wallace, M.J. (1973). Impact of type of control and industrial concentration on size and profitability in determination of executive income. Unpublished doctoral dissertation, University of Minnesota.

———. (1987). Strategic uses of compensation: Key questions managers should ask. *Topics in Total Compensation,* 2(2), 167–185.

————. (1990). *Rewards and Renewal: America's Search for Competitive Advantage through Alternative Pay Strategies.* Scottsdale, AZ: American Compensation Association.

————. (1991). Sustaining success with alternative rewards. In M.L. Rock and L.A. Berger (Eds.), *The Compensation Handbook: A State-of-the-art Guide to Compensation Strategy and Design,* 3d ed. New York: McGraw-Hill.

Wallace, M.J., and Fay, C.H. (1983). *Compensation Theory and Practice.* Boston: Kent Publishing Company.

Wall Street Journal. (2008a). Persistent pay gains: A survey overview. April 4, R-1.

Wall Street Journal. (2008b). Where were the boards? October 14. http://online.wsj.com/article/SB122391155600528747.html.

Walsh, J.P., and Dewar, R.D. (1987). Formalization of the organizational life cycle. *Journal of Management Studies,* 24(3), 216–231.

Walsh, J.P., and Seward, J.K. (1990). On the efficiency of internal and external corporate control mechanisms. *Academy of Management Review,* 15(3), 421–458.

Washburn, N., Makri, M., and Gomez-Mejia, L.R. (2010, in press). Past performance and efficacy motivated risk taking. Richmond, BC: Thunderbird Press.

Weber, C.L., and Rynes, S.L. (1991). Effects of compensation strategy on pay decisions. *Academy of Management Journal,* 34, 86–109.

Weick, K. (1979a). *The Social Psychology of Organizing,* 2d ed. Reading, MA: Addison-Wesley.

————. (1979b). Cognitive processes in organizations. In B. M. Staw (Ed.), *Research in Organizational Behavior,* 1. Greenwich, CT: JAI Press.

Weinberger, T.E. (2007). The pay-for-strategic-value method. *Compensation and Benefits Review,* January–February, 40–54.

Weiner, J.L. (1964). The Berle-Dodd dialogue on the concept of the corporation. *Columbia Law Review,* 64, 1458–1483.

Weiner, N. (1980). Determinants and behavioral consequences of pay satisfaction: A comparison of two models. *Personnel Psychology,* 33, 741–757.

Weiner, N., and Mahoney, T. (1981). A model of corporate performance as a function of environmental, organization, and leadership influences. *Academy of Management Journal,* 24, 453–470.

Weiss, L.A., and Vedran, C. (2008). Bankruptcy resolution and the restoration of priority of claims. American Law and Economics Association Papers, 41, 1–41.

Weitzman, M.L. (1984). *The Share Economy.* Cambridge, MA: Harvard University Press.

Welbourne, T.M., Balkin, D.B., and Gomez-Mejia, L.R. (1995). Gainsharing and mutual monitoring: A combined agency-organizational justice interpretation. *Academy of Management Journal,* 38(3), 818–834.

Welbourne, T.M., and Gomez-Mejia, L.R. (1988). Gainsharing revisited. *Compensation and Benefits Review,* 20(4), 19–28.

————. (1991). Team incentives in the work place. In L. Berger (Ed.), *Handbook of Wage and Salary Administration.* New York: McGraw-Hill.

————. (1995). Gainsharing: A critical review and a future research agenda. *Journal of Management,* 21(3), 559.

————. (2008). New perspectives on team based incentives. In L.A. Berger and D.R. Berger (Eds.), *The Compensation Handbook: A State-of-the-art Guide to Compensation Strategy and Design,* 5th ed. New York: McGraw-Hill, 236–247.

Welch, D. (2009). Autos: A hundred factories too many. *Business Week,* January 10, 42–44.

Werner, S., Tosi, H., and Gomez-Mejia, L.R. (2005). Organizational governance and employee pay: How ownership structure affects the firm's compensation strategy. *Strategic Management Journal,* 26(4), 377–384.

Werner, S., and Ward, S. (2004). Recent compensation research: An eclectic review. *Human Resource Management Review,* 14, 201–227.

Wernerfelt, B. (1984). A resource-based view of the firm. *Strategic Management Journal,* 5(2), 171.

Westhead, P., Cowling, M., and Howorth, C. (2001). The development of family companies: Management and ownership imperatives. *Family Business Review,* 14(4), 369–382.

Westphal, J.D., and Zajac, E.J. (1994). Substance and symbolism in CEOs' long-term incentive plans. *Administrative Science Quarterly,* 39(3), 367–390.

———. (1998). The symbolic management of stockholders: Corporate governance reforms and shareholder reactions. *Administrative Science Quarterly,* 43(1), 127–153.

———. (2001). Decoupling policy from practice: The case of stock repurchase programs. *Administrative Science Quarterly,* 46, 202–228.

Wexley, K.N., and Youtz, M.A. (1985). Rater beliefs about others: Their effects on rating errors and rater accuracy. *Journal of Occupational Psychology,* 58, 265–275.

White, J.K. (1979). The Scanlon plan: Causes and correlates of success. *Academy of Management Journal,* 22(2), 292–312.

White, R.W. (1959). Motivation reconsidered: The concept of competence. *Psychological Review,* 66, 297–333.

White, W.F. (1949). The social structure of the restaurant. *American Journal of Sociology,* 54, 302–310.

Wicks, A.C., Gilbert, D.R. Jr., and Freeman, E.R. (1994). A feminist reinterpretation of the stakeholder concept. *Business Ethics Quarterly,* 4, 475–498.

Widener, S.K. (2006). Human capital, pay structure, and the use of performance measures in bonus compensation. *Management Accounting Research,* 17, 198–221.

Wiersema, M.P., and Page, R.A. (1992). Patterns of organizational development to maintain strategies of innovation. In L.R. Gomez-Mejia and M.W. Lawless (Eds.), *Organizational Issues in High Technology Management.* Greenwich, CT: JAI Press.

Williams, M.J. (1985). Why chief executives pay keeps rising. *Fortune,* April 1, 66–73.

Williamson, O.E. (1975). *Markets and Hierarchies.* New York: Free Press.

———. (1986a). *Economic Organization: Firms, Markets, and Policy Control.* New York: New York University Press.

———. (1986b). *The Economic Institutions of Capitalism.* New York: Free Press.

Wilson, T.B. (2008). Total rewards strategy. In L.A. Berger and D.R. Berger (Eds.), *The Compensation Handbook: A State-of-the-art Guide to Compensation Strategy and Design,* 5th ed. New York: McGraw-Hill, 21–31.

Wilson, T.B., and Malanowski, S. (2008). Performance management best practices. In L.A. Berger and D.R. Berger (Eds.), *The Compensation Handbook: A State-of-the-art Guide to Compensation Strategy and Design,* 5th ed. New York: McGraw-Hill, 447–458.

Winfrey, F.L. (1990). Executive compensation, corporate control and firm performance: An agency theoretic approach. Unpublished doctoral dissertation. University of South Carolina.

Wiseman, R.M., and Bromiley, P. (1996). Toward a model of risk in declining organizations: An empirical examination of risk, performance and decline. *Organization Science,* 7(5), 524–543.

Wiseman, R.M., and Catanach, A. (1997). A longitudinal dissagregation of operational risk under changing regulations: evidence from de savings and loan industry. *Academy of Management Journal,* 40(4), 799–830.

Wiseman, R.M., and Gomez-Mejia, L.R. (1998). A behavioral agency model of managerial risk taking. *Academy of Management Review,* 22(1), 133–153.

Wiseman, R.M., Gomez-Mejia, L.R., and Cuevas, G. (2010, in press). Executive compensation, agency theory, and institutional forces. *Journal of Management Studies.*

Wiseman, R.M., Gomez-Mejia, L.R., and Fugate, M. (2000). Rethinking compensation risk. In S. Rynes and B. Gerhart (Eds.), *Compensation in Organizations.* San Francisco: Jossey-Bass, 311–347.

Wong-On-Wing, B., Guo, L., Li, W., and Yang, D. (2007). Reducing conflict in balanced scorecard evaluations. *Accounting, Organizations and Society,* 32(4/5), 363–377.

Wood, D.J., and Jones, A.W. (1995). Stakeholder mismatching: A theoretical problem in empirical research on corporate social performance. *International Journal of Organizational Analysis,* 3, 229–267.

Wooldridge, B., and Floyd, S.W. (1990). The strategy process, middle management involvement and organizational performance. *Strategic Management Journal,* 11, 231–242.

Wright, P., Kroll, M., and Elenkov, D. (2002). Acquisitions returns, Increase in firm size, and chief executive compensation: The moderating effect of monitoring. *Academy of Management Journal,* 45(3), 599–609.

Wright, P.M., Gardner, T.M., and Moynihan, L.M. (2003). The impact of HR practices on the performance of business units. *Human Resource Management Journal,* 13(3), 21–36.

Yammarino, F.J., Dubinsky, A.J., and Hartley, S.W. (1987). An approach for assessing individual versus group effects in performance evaluations. *Journal of Occupational Psychology,* 60, 157–167.

Yanadon, Y., and Marler, J.H. (2006). Compensation strategy: Does business strategy influence compensation in high technology firms. *Strategic Management Journal,* 27, 559–570.

Yates, J.F., and Stone, E. (1992). The risk construct. In J.F. Yates (Ed.), *Risk Taking Behavior.* New York: Wiley, 1–25.

Yin-Hua, Y., Tsun-Siou, L., Pei-Gi, S. (2008). The agency problem embedded in firm's equity investment. *Journal of Business Ethics,* 79, 151–166.

York, D., and Brown, T. (2008). Salary surveys. In L.A. Berger and D.R. Berger (Eds.), *The Compensation Handbook: A State-of-the-art Guide to Compensation Strategy and Design,* 5th ed. New York: McGraw-Hill, 11–121.

Yuen, E. (1990). Human resource management and high-and-medium technology. *Personnel Review,* 19, 36–47.

Zajac, E.J. (1990). CEO selection, compensation, and firm performance: A theoretical integration and empirical analysis. *Strategic Management Journal,* 11, 217–231.

Zajac, E.J., and Westphal, J.D. (1994). The costs and benefits of managerial incentives and monitoring in large U.S. corporations: When more is not better. *Strategic Management Journal,* 15, 121–142.

Zajonc, R.B. (1980). Feeling and thinking: Preferences need no inferences. *American Psychologist,* 35, 151–175.

Zattoni, A., and Minichilli, A. (2009). The diffusion of equity incentive plans in Italian listed companies: What is the trigger? *Corporate Governance: An International Review,* 17(2), 224–237.

Zhang, X., Bartol, K.M., Smith, K.G., PFarrer, M.D., and Mikhail-Khanin, D. (2008). CEOs on the edge: Earnings manipulation and stock based incentive misalignment. *Academy of Management Journal,* 51, 1–37.

Zhao, Y., and Chen, K.H. (2008). The influence of takeover protection in earnings management. *Journal of Business Finance and Accounting,* 35, 347–375.

Zhou, X. (1999). Executive compensation and managerial incentives: A comparison between Canada and the United States. *Journal of Corporate Finance,* 5(3), 277–301.

Zingheim, P.K. (2007). What are the key pay issues right now? *Compensation and Benefits Review,* May–June, 51–55.

INDEX

A

ABB, 197
Abercrombie & Fitch, *213*
Abernathy, W.J., 106
abnormal returns, 154
academic research
  availability from other fields, 4
  cross-disciplinary, 19
  gaps in, 101
  inferential leaps in, 155
Academy of Management, 18
Academy of Management Review, 50
accounting choices, 143–144
Ackermann, Josef, 202
acquisitive diversifiers, 78, 96
Adams, J.S., 5
administrative procedures
  algorithmic strategies for, *61*
  centralized versus decentralized,
    48–50
  and decision-making, 47
  experiential strategies for, *61*
  framework in corporate-level strategy,
    113
  and integrity of managers, 47
  for pay issues, 8, 47, 50–51
Agarwal, N.C., 135
age and executive pay, 176
agency theory, 128–131
  pay as signaling device, 104
  and performance measures, 253
  shortcomings of, 167–169, 170
agents
  monitoring of, 170–172
  risks borne by, 223

aggregate pay-for-performance systems.
    See performance-contingent
    compensation
AIG, 201
airline industry, 277
algorithmic compensation strategies,
    60–61, 65
  administrative process for, *61, 64, 113*
  aggregate pay-for-performance systems,
    62, 111
  for analyzer category, 92
  authoritarian pay design system, *64*
  and basis for pay, *61, 62–64*
  in business unit strategies, 73
  compensation level, *63*
  corporate performance, *62, 112*
  in corporate-level strategies, 73
  for defender category, 91–92
  design issues, *61*
  and diversification, 75–76
  fixed pay, *63, 113*
  hierarchical strategic pay dimension,
    63, 112
  incentives, *63, 113*
  individual contingent rewards, *62, 111*
  interdependency of corporate units, 95
  and internal growth, 96
  internal pay equity, *62, 63, 112*
  job-based pay, *62, 111*
  long-term orientation, *62, 111*
  market dimension, *63*
  and mature stage of life cycle, 93–95
  mechanistic internal organization, 98
  mistakes, low tolerance for, 98–99
  with narrow market focus, 96–97
  nonmonetary rewards, *64*

ABOUT THE AUTHORS

Luis R. Gomez-Mejia holds the Benton Cocanougher Chair in Business at Texas A&M University. Prior to that he held the Horace Steel Chair in Management at Arizona State University. He has published more than 200 articles and 12 books, many of them focused on compensation and rewards. His research has appeared in leading management journals including *Academy of Management Journal, Academy of Management Review, Administrative Science Quarterly, Strategic Management Journal,* and *Decision Sciences.* He has received numerous awards for his research—"best paper" at the Academy of Management, selection to the "Hall of Fame" and Fellows of the Academy of Management, Honoris Causa at Carlos III University in Madrid, Outstanding Alumni Award from the University of Minnesota, "best researcher" and Regent's Professor from Arizona State University, among others. His research has been cited more than 6,000 times in literature, making him one of the most frequently cited management scholars.

Pascual Berrone is Assistant Professor in Strategic Management at IESE Business School. Dr. Berrone earned a B.S. in Business Administration from the Universidad Catolica de Cordoba (Argentina), holds a Senior degree in Management and International Business from the FUNCER Business School, and completed his PhD in Business Administration and Quantitative Methods degree at Universidad Carlos III de Madrid. Before joining the IESE Business School, he held two visiting scholar appointments at Arizona State University in recent years.

Originally from Argentina, Dr. Berrone has extensive managerial experience throughout Latin America, Europe, and the United States. His professional interests include ongoing programmatic work in three areas: (1) corporate governance, (2) social issues in management, and (3) family firms. His most recent studies uncover the linkages between executive compensation and environmental performance of firms. Dr. Berrone's academic work has been published in international journals such as *Academy of Management Journal,*

International Journal of Human Resource Management, Journal of Business Ethics, Journal of Business Research, and *Corporate Governance: An International Review*. He has been recognized on several occasions for his outstanding research. In 2008, he won the "Best Paper Proceedings Award" at the EURAM conference, and the "Best Doctoral Dissertation Award" granted by the Academy of Management (SIM Division).

Monica Franco-Santos (PhD) is a Senior Research Fellow and the Director of the Business Performance Roundtable (Cranefield School of Management, UK). Her teaching and research interests are in the areas of performance measurement and compensation management. She is a reviewer for several top-ranked academic journals, such as the *Academy of Management Journal* and the *International Journal of Human Resource Management*. Her work is published internationally in both top academic and practitioner journals. Before joining Cranfield University, Dr. Franco-Santos worked as a remuneration consultant for Watson Wyatt and as an internal HR consultant for Endesa (Spain). For information about her courses, recent research projects, and publications, please visit http://www.som.cranfield.ac.uk.